INTRODUCTION TO COMPUTING & PROGRAMMING IN JAVA™

INTRODUCTION TO COMPUTING & PROGRAMMING IN JAVA™

A MULTIMEDIA APPROACH

Mark Guzdial and Barbara Ericson

College of Computing/GVU
Georgia Institute of Technology

PEARSON

Prentice
Hall

Upper Saddle River, New Jersey 07458

Library of Congress Cataloging-in-Publication Data

Guzdial, Mark.
  Introduction to computing and programming in Java : a multimedia approach / Mark
  Guzdial and Barbara Ericson.
      p. cm.
  Includes index.
  ISBN 0-13-149698-0
  1. Java (Computer program language). 2. Multimedia systems. I. Ericson, Barbara. II.
Title.
QA76.73J38G84 2005
005.13′3—dc22   2005051335

Vice President and Editorial Director, ECS: *Marcia J. Horton*
Executive Editor: *Tracy Dunkelberger*
Assistant Editor: *Carole Snyder*
Editorial Assistant: *Christianna Lee*
Executive Managing Editor: *Vince O'Brien*
Managing Editor: *Camille Trentacoste*
Production Editor: *Donna Crilly*
Director of Creative Services: *Paul Belfanti*
Art Director and Cover Manager: *Jonathan Boylan*
Cover Designer: *Jonathan Boylan*
Managing Editor, AV Management and Production: *Patricia Burns*
Managing Editor, Art Project Management: *Abigail Bass*
Art Editor: *Rhonda Aversa*
Director, Image Resource Center: *Melinda Reo*
Manager, Rights and Permissions: *Zina Arabia*
Manager, Visual Research: *Beth Brenzel*
Manager, Cover Visual Research and Permissions: *Karen Sanatar*
Image Permission Coordinator: *Angelique Sharps*
Manufacturing Manager, ESM: *Alexis Heydt-Long*
Manufacturing Buyer: *Lisa McDowell*
Executive Marketing Manager: *Robin O'Brien*

© 2007 Pearson Education, Inc.
Pearson Prentice Hall
Pearson Education, Inc.
Upper Saddle River, New Jersey 07458

Printed in the United States of America
10 9 8 7 6 5 4 3 2 1

ISBN: 0-13-149698-0

Pearson Education Ltd., *London*
Pearson Education Australia Pty. Ltd., *Sydney*
Pearson Education Singapore, Pte. Ltd.
Pearson Education North Asia Ltd., *Hong Kong*
Pearson Education Canada, Inc., *Toronto*
Pearson Educación de Mexico, S.A. de C.V.
Pearson Education—Japan, *Tokyo*
Pearson Education Malaysia, Pte. Ltd.
Pearson Education, Inc., *Upper Saddle River, New Jersey*

Dedicated to our children
Matthew, Katherine, and Jennifer.

Trademark Page

PHOTO CREDITS

Brief Table of Contents

A "GUIDED TOUR"

The media computation approach used in this book starts with what students use computers for: image maninpulation, digital music, Web pages, games and so on… a proven and enjoyable experience for students learning to program!

The book is full color throughout

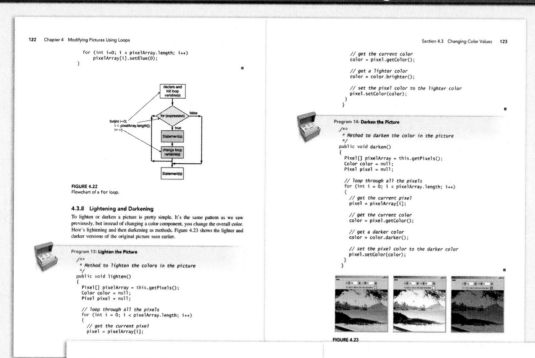

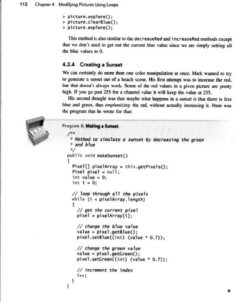

Java code examples are easy to find and read

TYPOGRAPHICAL NOTATIONS

Examples of Java code look like this: x = x + 1;. Longer examples look like this:

```java
public class Greeter
{
  public static void main(String[] args)
  {
    // show the string "Hello World" on the console
    System.out.println("Hello World");
  }
}
```

When showing something that the user types in the interactions pane with DrJava's response, it will have a similar font and style, but the user's typing will appear after a DrJava prompt (>):

```
> 3 + 4
7
```

User interface components of DrJava will be specified using a smallcaps font, like FILE menu item and the COMPILE ALL button.

There are several special kinds of sidebars that you'll find in the book.

Side Bars further support your students' learning experience

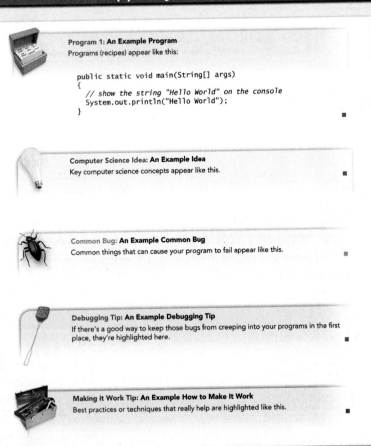

Program 1: An Example Program
Programs (recipes) appear like this:

```java
public static void main(String[] args)
{
  // show the string "Hello World" on the console
  System.out.println("Hello World");
}
```

Computer Science Idea: An Example Idea
Key computer science concepts appear like this.

Common Bug: An Example Common Bug
Common things that can cause your program to fail appear like this.

Debugging Tip: An Example Debugging Tip
If there's a good way to keep those bugs from creeping into your programs in the first place, they're highlighted here.

Making it Work Tip: An Example How to Make It Work
Best practices or techniques that really help are highlighted like this.

APPENDIX A

Quick Reference to Java

A.1 VARIABLES

Variables allow us to associate names with values. In Java you must declare a variable before you use it. To declare a variable you specify a type and a name followed by a semicolon.

```
type name;
```

You can also set the value of the variable when you declare it to the result of an expression.

```
type name = expression;
```

The type can be any of the primitive types (`int`, `boolean`, `byte`, `char`, `double`, `float`, `long`, `short`), a class name, or an interface name. The convention is to start variable names with a lowercase letter and uppercase the first letter of each additional word.

```
> int i;
> double totalBill = 32.43 + 20 * 32.43;
> String name = "Mark Guzdial";
> Picture pictureObj;
> List studentList = null;
```

543

The CD-ROM has media materials and programming source code from the book's exercises and all the necessary software, including Sun Microsystems' Java 2 Platform, standard edition and more!

We are proud to publish this unique and innovative approach. Although it is different from many introductory programming books, the same concepts are covered, but not necessarily in the usual order. As referenced in the preface, research indicates this class-tested approach is proven to improve your students' learning experience and success in CS1!

Contents

7 Drawing   212

PART 3   SOUNDS   251

8   Modifying All Samples in a Sound   252

9   Modifying Samples Using Ranges   293

10   Making Sounds by Combining Pieces   312

PART 4   TEXT, FILES, NETWORKS, DATABASES, AND UNIMEDIA   385

12   Creating and Modifying Text   386

13 Making Text for the Web   442

PART 5   MOVIES   483

14 Encoding, Manipulating, and Creating Movies   484

Preface

This book is intended to introduce computing, including programming, to students with no prior programming experience. One of the lessons from the research on computing education is that one doesn't just "learn to program." One learns to program *something* [4, 17]. How motivating that *something* is can make the difference between learning to program or not [6]. Some people are interested in learning programming just for programming's sake—but that's not most people.

Unfortunately, most introductory programming books are written as if students have a burning desire to learn to program. They emphasize programming concepts and give little thought to making the problems that are being solved interesting and relevant. They introduce new concepts without showing why the students *should* want to know about them.

In this book students will learn about programming by writing programs to manipulate media. Students will create and modify images, such as correcting for "red-eye" and generating negative images. Students will modify sounds, like splicing words into sentences or reversing sounds to make interesting effects. Students will write programs to generate Web pages from data in databases, in the same way that CNN.com and Amazon.com do. They will create animations and movies using special effects like the ones seen on television and in movies.

Students in courses taught at Georgia Tech have found these programs interesting and motivating. Students have even reported turning in their programs and then continuing to work on them to see what else they can make.

This book is about teaching people to program in order to communicate. People want to communicate. We are social creatures, and the desire to communicate is one of our primal motivations. Increasingly, the computer is used as a tool for communication even more than as a tool for calculation. Virtually all published text, images, sounds, music, and movies today are prepared using computing technology. This book focuses on how to manipulate images, sounds, text, and movies as professionals might, but with programs written by the students.

We realize that most people will use professional-grade applications to perform these same manipulations. So why learn to program these manipulations *yourself*? Why not just leave it to the developers of *Photoshop* and *iMovie*? The answer depends on your interests and career choices.

- If you have an interest in becoming a computing professional, then it's worth-while for you to understand how to build programs used in communication. Much of the software in the future will be used for communications, so this is a great domain to start learning useful skills. Most computing classes today are taught in Java, so this book presents the right context for learning programming and in the right language for you.

- If you expect to be a *user* of applications in the future, knowing something of how your tools works can make you a so-called "*Power User.*" Most common applications today are much more powerful than most users realize. Many communications applications are actually themselves programmable with *scripting languages* that enable users to automate tasks in the application. To use all the facilities of an application, it helps to have an understanding of what the application is doing—if you know what a *pixel* is, you can understand better why it's useful to manipulate. To use the scripting facilities of an application, some knowledge of programming is a requirement.

- If you are a creative person who wants complete control of your communications, you want to know how to do without your applications if you need to, in order to implement your vision. Knowing *how* to do manipulate media with your own programs means that you *can* do what you want, if you ever need to. You may want to say something with your media, but you may not know how to make Photoshop or Final Cut Pro do what you want. Knowing how to program means that you have power of expression that is not limited by your application software.

- Finally, you may have no interest in programming your applications, or programming at all. Is it worthwhile for you to learn this stuff? Students who took our media computation classes at Georgia Tech told us *a year later* that the course was relevant *in their daily life* [15]. We live in a technological society, and much of that technology is used to manipulate what we see and hear in our media. If you know something of how that technology works, you have a way of thinking about how to use it, and how it may be used to change your perceptions. Students who are not computer science majors told us a year after finishing the course that they now had a new confidence around computers because they knew something about how they worked [15].

This book is not *just* about programming to manipulate media. Media manipulation programs can be hard to write, or behave in unexpected ways. Questions arise like "Why is this same image filter faster in Photoshop?" and "That was hard to debug—are there ways of writing programs that are *easier* to debug?" Answering questions like these is what computer scientists do. The last chapters at the end of the book are about *computing*, not just programming (Chapters 15 and 16).

The computer is the most amazingly creative device that humans have ever conceived of. It is literally completely made up of mind-stuff. The notion "Don't just dream it, be it" is really possible on a computer. If you can imagine it, you can make it "real" on the computer. Playing with programming can be and *should* be enormous fun.

TO TEACHERS

The *media computation* approach used in this book starts with what students use computers for: image manipulation, digital music, Web pages, games, and so on. We then explain programming and computing in terms of these activities. We want students to visit Amazon (for example) and think, "Here's a catalog Web site—and

I know that this is implemented with a database and a set of programs that format the database entries as Web pages." Starting from a relevant context makes transfer of knowledge and skills more likely, and it also helps with retention.

The majority of the book spends time giving students experiences with a variety of media in contexts that they find motivating. After that, though, they start to develop questions. "Why is it that Photoshop is faster than my program?" and "Movie code is slow—how slow do programs get?" are typical. At that point, we introduce the abstractions and the valuable insights from computer science that answer *their* questions. That's what the last part of this book is about.

Researchers in computing education have been exploring why withdrawal or failure rates in college-level introductory computing courses have been so high. The rate of students withdrawing from college-level introductory computing courses or receiving a D or F grade (commonly called the *WDF rate*) has been reported in the 30–50% range, or even higher. One of the common themes from research into why the WDF rate is so high is that computing courses seem "irrelevant" and unnecessarily focusing on "tedious details" such as efficiency [22, 1].

However, students have found media computation to be relevant as evidenced by survey responses and the reduction in our WDF rate from an average of 28% to 11.5% for the pilot offering of this course. Spring 2004 was the first semester taught by instructors other than Mark Guzdial, and the WDF rate dropped to 9.5% for the 395 students who enrolled. Charles Fowler at Gainesville College in Georgia has been having similar results in his courses there.

The approach in this book is different than in many introductory programming books. We teach the same computing concepts but not necessarily in the usual order. For example, while we create and use objects early, we don't have students defining new classes till fairly late. Research in computing education suggests that learning to program is hard and that students often have trouble with the basics (variables, iteration, and conditionals). We focus on the basics for ten chapters: three introductory, four on pictures, and three on sounds. We introduce new concepts only after setting the stage for why we would need them. For example, we don't introduce iteration until after we change pixel colors one-by-one. We don't introduce procedural decomposition until our methods get too long to easily be debugged.

Our approach isn't the more common approach of introducing one computing topic per chapter. We introduce computing concepts as needed to do a desired media manipulation (like using nested loops to mirror a picture). Some chapters introduce several computing concepts, while others repeat computing concepts in a different medium. We repeat concepts in different media to increase the odds that students will find an explanation and relevance that works for them, or better yet, find *two* or more explanations that work for them. The famous artificial intelligence researcher Marvin Minsky once said that if you understand something in only one way, you don't understand it at all. Repeating a concept in different relevant settings can be a powerful way of developing flexible understandings.

Memory is associative—we remember things based on what else we relate to those things. People can learn concepts and skills on the promise that it will be useful some day, but the concepts and skills will be related only to the promises, not to everyday life. The result has been described as "brittle knowledge" [7]—the kind of knowledge that gets you through the exam but promptly gets forgotten because it doesn't relate to anything but being in that class. If we want students to gain *transferable* knowledge (knowledge that can be applied in new situations), we have to help them to relate the knowledge to more general problems, so that the memories get indexed in ways that associate with those kinds of problems [20]. Thus, we teach with concrete experiences that students can explore and relate to (e.g., iteration for removing red-eye in pictures).

We do know that starting from the abstractions doesn't really work for students. Ann Fleury has shown that novice students just don't buy what we tell them about encapsulation and reuse (e.g., [10]). Students prefer simpler code that they can trace easily, and actually think that code that an expert would hate is *better*. Some of the early methods are written the way that a beginning student would prefer, with values hard-coded rather than passed in as parameters. It takes time and experience for students to realize that there is value in well-designed systems. Without experience to give the abstractions value, it's very difficult for beginning students to learn the abstractions.

Another unusual thing about this book is that we start using arrays in Chapter 4, in our first significant programs. Typically, introductory computing courses push arrays off until later, since they're obviously more complicated than variables with simple values. But a relevant context is very powerful [17]. The matrices of pixels in images occur in the students' everyday life—a magnifying glass on a computer monitor or television makes that clear.

Our goal is to teach programming in a way that students find relevant, motivating, and social. To be relevant we have the students write programs to do things that students currently use computers for: namely, image, sound, and text manipulation. For motivation we assign open-ended creative assignments, such as: Create an image collage with the same image at least four times using three different image manipulations and a mirroring. As for the social aspect, we encourage collaboration on assignments and on-line, public posting of student work. Students learn from each other and try to outdo each other, in a spirit of creative competition.

Ways to Use this Book

This book is based on content that we teach at Georgia Tech. Individual teachers may skip some sections (e.g., the section on additive synthesis, MIDI, and MP3), but all of the content here has been tested with our students.

However, we can imagine using this material in many other ways:

- A short introduction to computing could be taught with just Chapters 2–4. We have taught even single day workshops on media computation using just this material.

- Students with some programming experience could skip or review Chapters 1–2 and begin at Chapter 3. Students with object-oriented experience could start at Chapter 4.

- Chapter 7 is about drawing using existing Java classes. It also introduces the concepts of inheritance and interfaces. The concepts introduced here are also used in Chapter 14 (movies). If you are skipping movies you could skip this chapter as well.

- Chapters 8 through 10 replicate much of the computer science basics from Chapters 4 through 6, but in the context of sounds rather than images. We find the replication useful—some students seem to relate better to the concepts of iteration and conditionals better when working with one medium than the other. Further, it gives us the opportunity to point out that the same *algorithm* can have similar effects in different media (e.g., scaling a picture up or down and shifting a sound higher or lower in pitch is the same algorithm). But it could certainly be skipped to save time. You might want to at least cover class methods and private methods in Chapter 10.

- Chapter 11 explains how to create classes. This is an essential chapter.

- Chapters 12 and 13 manipulate text. They also cover exceptions, reading and writing files, reading from the network, import statements, helper methods, some collection classes, iterators, generics, and working with databases. We recommend covering these chapters.

- Chapter 14 (on movies) introduces no new programming or computing concepts. While motivating, movie processing could be skipped for time.

- We do recommend getting to Chapter 15 on speed. This is the first chapter that is more about computing than programming.

- Chapter 16 is about JavaScript. This gives students exposure to another language that is similar to Java. It also discusses interpreters and compilers. It could be skipped to save time.

JAVA

The programming language used in this book is Java. Java is a high-level object-oriented programming language that runs on most computers and many small electronic devices. It is widely used in industry and in universities.

The development environment used in this book is DrJava. It was created at Rice University. It is free and easy to use. DrJava lets the student focus on learning to program in Java and not on how to use the development environment. An advantage of DrJava is that you can try out Java code in the interactions pane without having to write a "main" method.

You don't have to use this development environment. There are many development environments that are available for use with Java. If you use another development environment, just add the directory that has the Java classes developed for this book to the classpath. See the documentation for your development environment for how to do this. Of course, you can also use more than one development environment. You could use DrJava for the interactions pane as well as another environment.

TYPOGRAPHICAL NOTATIONS

Examples of Java code look like this: x = x + 1;. Longer examples look like this:

```java
public class Greeter
{
  public static void main(String[] args)
  {
    // show the string "Hello World" on the console
    System.out.println("Hello World");
  }
}
```

When showing something that the user types in the interactions pane with DrJava's response, it will have a similar font and style, but the user's typing will appear after a DrJava prompt (>):

```
> 3 + 4
7
```

User interface components of DrJava will be specified using a smallcaps font, like FILE menu item and the COMPILE ALL button.

There are several special kinds of sidebars that you'll find in the book.

Program 1: An Example Program

Programs (recipes) appear like this:

```java
public static void main(String[] args)
{
  // show the string "Hello World" on the console
  System.out.println("Hello World");
}
```

Computer Science Idea: An Example Idea

Key computer science concepts appear like this.

Common Bug: An Example Common Bug

Common things that can cause your program to fail appear like this.

Debugging Tip: An Example Debugging Tip

If there's a good way to keep those bugs from creeping into your programs in the first place, they're highlighted here.

Making it Work Tip: An Example How to Make It Work

Best practices or techniques that really help are highlighted like this.

ACKNOWLEDGMENTS

Our sincere thanks go out to the following:

- Adam Wilson built the MediaTools that are so useful for exploring sounds and images and processing video.
- Matthew, Katherine, and Jennifer Guzdial all contributed pictures for use in this book.
- Thanks for permission to use their snapshots to Georgia Tech students: Jakita N. Owensby, and Tammy C.
- Thank you to the anonymous reviewers and to Brent Laminack for finding problems and for making suggestions to improve the book.
- Thank you to Thomas Bressoud and Matt Kretchmar at Denison University for trying an early version of the book and for their feedback on it.
- Thank you to the high school teachers in Georgia who took summer workshops using versions of this material and taught it to their classes.

About the Authors

Mark Guzdial is a Professor at the College of Computing at Georgia Tech, member of the GVU Center, and Director of the Collaborative Software Laboratory. His Prentice Hall books include *Squeak: Object-Oriented Design with Multimedia Applications; Squeak: Open Personal Computing and Multimedia;* and *Introduction to Computing and Programming in Python: A Multimedia Approach.*

Barbara J. Ericson is a highly-rated instructor for the College of Computing at Georgia Tech. She has taught continuing education and undergraduate courses for Georgia Tech and authored continuing education courses on Java and Object-Oriented Analysis and Design. Her current position is the Director of CS Outreach for the Institute for Computing Education (ICE) which works to improve computing education at the secondary level in Georgia. An ACM member, Ericson has worked at several leading industrial research labs, including General Motors Research Labs and Bell Communications Research.

About the CD-ROM

The CD-ROM that accompanies this book includes everything students need to complete the exercises in the book using either Windows or Macintosh OS X operating systems.

Sample media files: All media materials are provided, including JPG images and WAV sound files, and sources for all required Java media classes.

DrJava–This simple, free Java development environment lets students focus on learning Java and not the development environment. It has an interactions pane which allows students to easily try out Java code. Experienced users may also use another development environment (such as Eclipse or Sun Java Studio Creator) to run and edit the book's programs if desired.

MediaTools and Squeak: MediaTools allows students to work with multimedia files. With MediaTools, users can understand sounds at the sampling level, record new sounds, play back movies, and view pictures at the pixel level. The MediaTools are built on top of the object-oriented programming environment Squeak. When users install MediaTools they will also be installing Squeak.

Java: Created by Sun Microsystems, this is the complete Java 2 Standard Edition environment you need in order to develop and run Java applications. The accompanying CD-ROM contains the Java 2 Standard Edition 1.4 and 5.0 (also known as "1.5") for Windows. Mac users already have Java installed as part of the OS X operating system.

PART 1

INTRODUCTION

1

Introduction to Computer Science and Media Computation

Chapter Learning Objectives

- To explain what computer science is about and what computer scientists are concerned with.
- To explain why we digitize media.
- To explain why it's valuable to study computing.
- To use the concept of an *encoding*.
- To explain what computers understand.

1.1   WHAT IS COMPUTER SCIENCE ABOUT?

Computer science is the study of *process*: how we do things, how we specify what we do, how we specify what the stuff is that you're processing. But that's a pretty dry definition. Let's try a metaphorical one.

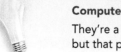

Computer Science Idea: Computer Science is the Study of Recipes (Programs)

They're a special kind of recipe—one that can be executed by a computational device, but that point is only of importance to computer scientists. The important point overall is that a computer science program defines *exactly* what's to be done as shown in the recipe in (Figure 1.1). ∎

If you're a biologist who wants to describe how migration works or how DNA replicates, or if you're a chemist who wants to explain how an equilibrium is reached in a reaction, or if you're a factory manager who wants to define a machine-and-belt layout and even test how it works before physically moving heavy things into position, then being able to write a program that specifies *exactly* what happens, in terms that can be completely defined and understood, is *very* useful. This exactness is part of why computers have radically changed so much of how science is done and understood.

CHICKEN CACCIATORE

3 whole, boned chicken breasts	1 (28 oz) can chopped tomatoes
1 medium onion, chopped	1 (15 oz) can tomato sauce
1 tbsp chopped garlic	1 (6.5 oz) can mushrooms
2 tbsp and later 1/4 c olive oil	1 (6 oz) can tomato paste
1 1/2 c flour	1/2 of (26 oz) jar of spaghetti
1/4 c Lawry's seasoning salt	sauce
1 bell pepper, chopped (optional)	3 tbsp Italian seasoning
any color	1 tsp garlic powder (optional)

Cut up the chicken into pieces about 1 inch square. Saute the onion and garlic until the onion is translucent. Mix the flour and Lawry's salt. You want about 1:4–1:5 ratio of seasoning salt to flour and enough of the whole mixture to coat the chicken. Put the cut up chicken and seasoned flour in a bag, and shake to coat. Add the coated chicken to the onion and garlic. Stir frequently until browned. You'll need to add oil to keep from sticking and burning; I sometimes add up to 1/4 cup of olive oil. Add the tomatoes, sauce, mushrooms, and paste. (And the optional peppers, too.) Stir well. Add the Italian seasoning. I like garlic, so I usually add the garlic powder, too. Stir well. Because of all the flour, the sauce can get too thick. I usually cut it with the spaghetti sauce, up to 1/2 jar. Simmer 20–30 minutes.

FIGURE 1.1
A cooking recipe—the order of the steps is important.

It may sound funny to call *programs* or *algorithms* a recipe, but the analogy goes a long way. Much of what computer scientists study can be defined in terms of recipes:

- Some computer scientists study how recipes are written: Are there better or worse ways of doing something? If you've ever had to separate whites from yolks in eggs, you know that knowing the right way to do it makes a world of difference. Computer science theoreticians worry about the fastest and shortest recipes, and the ones that take up the least amount of space (you can think about it as counter space—the analogy works). *How* a recipe works, completely apart from how it's written, is called the study of *algorithms*. Software engineers worry about how large groups can put together recipes that still work. (The recipe for some programs, like the one that keeps track of Visa/MasterCard records, has literally millions of steps!)

- Other computer scientists study the units used in recipes. Does it matter whether a recipe uses metric or English measurements? The recipe may work in either case, but if you have to read the recipe and you don't know what a pound or a cup is, the recipe is a lot less understandable to you. There are also units that make sense for some tasks and not others, but if you can fit the units to the tasks well, you can explain yourself more easily and get things done faster—and avoid errors. Ever wonder why ships at sea measure their speed in *knots*? Why not use things like meters per second? There are places, like at sea, where more common terms aren't appropriate or don't work as well. The study of computer science units is referred to as *data structures*. Computer scientists who study ways of keeping track of lots of data in lots of different kinds of units are studying *databases*.

- Can recipes be written for anything? Are there some recipes that *can't* be written? Computer scientists actually do know that there are recipes that can't be written. For example, you can't write a recipe that can absolutely tell, for any other recipe, if the other recipe will actually work. How about *intelligence*? Can we write a recipe that, when a computer followed it, the computer would actually be *thinking* (and how would you tell if you got it right)? Computer scientists in *theory*, *intelligent systems*, *artificial intelligence*, and *systems* worry about things like this.

- There are even computer scientists who worry about whether people like what the recipes produce, like the restaurant critics for the newspaper. Some of these are *human–computer interface* specialists who worry about whether people like how the recipes work (those "recipes" that produce an *interface* that people use, like windows, buttons, scrollbars, and other elements of what we think about as a running program).

- Just as some chefs specialize in certain kinds of recipes, like crepes or barbecue, computer scientists also specialize in special kinds of recipes. Computer scientists who work in *graphics* are mostly concerned with recipes that produce pictures, animations, and even movies. Computer scientists who work in *computer music* are mostly concerned with recipes that produce sounds (often melodic ones, but not always).

- Still other computer scientists study the *emergent properties* of recipes. Think about the World Wide Web. It's really a collection of *millions* of recipes (programs) talking to one another. Why would one section of the Web get slower at some point? It's a phenomena that emerges from these millions of programs, certainly not something that was planned. That's something that *networking* computer scientists study. What's really amazing is that these emergent properties (that things just start to happen when you have many, many recipes interacting at once) can also be used to explain non-computational things. For example, how ants forage for food or how termites make mounds can also be described as something that just happens when you have lots of little programs doing something simple and interacting.

The recipe metaphor also works on another level. Everyone knows that some things in a recipe can be changed without changing the result dramatically. You can always increase all the units by a multiplier (say, double) to make more. You can always add more garlic or oregano to the spaghetti sauce. But there are some things that you cannot change in a recipe. If the recipe calls for baking powder, you may not substitute baking soda. If you're supposed to boil the dumplings then saute' them, the reverse order will probably not work well (Figure 1.1).

Similarly, for software recipes (programs), there are usually things you can easily change: The actual names of things (though you should change names consistently), some of the *constants* (numbers that appear as plain old numbers, not as variables), and maybe even some of the data *ranges* (sections of the data) being manipulated. But the order of the commands to the computer, however, almost always has to stay exactly as stated. As we go on, you'll learn what can be changed safely, and what can't.

Computer scientists specify their programs with *programming languages* (Figure 1.2). Different programming languages are used for different purposes. Some of them are wildly popular, like Java and Visual Basic. Others are more obscure, like Squeak and T. Others are designed to make computer science ideas very easy to learn, like Scheme or Python, but the fact that they're easy to learn doesn't always make them very popular nor the best choice for experts building larger or more complicated programs. It's a hard balance in teaching computer science to pick a language that is easy to learn *and* is popular and useful enough that students are motivated to learn it.

Why don't computer scientists just use natural human languages, like English or Spanish? The problem is that natural languages evolved the way that they did to enhance communications between very smart beings, humans. As we'll go into

Python/Jython

```
def hello():
  print "Hello World"
```

Java

```
public class HelloWorld
{
  public static void main(String[] args)
  {
    System.out.println( "Hello World!" );
  }
}
```

C++

```
#include <iostream.h>

main() {
    cout << "Hello World!" << endl;
    return 0;
}
```

Scheme

```
(define helloworld
        (lambda ()
                (display "Hello World")
                (newline)))
```

FIGURE 1.2
Comparing programming languages: A common simple programming task is to print the words "Hello, World!" to the screen.

more in the next section, computers are exceptionally dumb. They need a level of specificity that natural language isn't good at. Further, what we say to one another in natural communication is not exactly what you're saying in a computational recipe (program). When was the last time you told someone how a videogame like Doom or Quake or Super Mario Brothers worked in such minute detail that they could actually replicate the game (say, on paper)? English isn't good for that kind of task.

There are so many different kinds of programming languages because there are so many different kinds of programs to write. Programs written in the programming language *C* tend to be very fast and efficient, but they also tend to be hard to read, hard to write, and require units that are more about computers than about bird migrations or DNA or whatever else you want to write your program about. The programming language *Lisp* (and its related languages like Scheme, T, and Common Lisp) is very flexible and is well suited to exploring how to write programs that have never been written before, but Lisp *looks* so strange compared to languages like C that many people avoid it and there are (natural consequence) few people who know it. If you want to hire a hundred programmers to work on your project, you're going to find it easier to find a hundred programmers who know a popular language than a less popular one—but that doesn't mean that the popular language is the best one for your task!

The programming language that we're using in this book is *Java* (`http://java.sun.com` for more information on Java). Java is a very popular programming language. Delta uses it to handle its web site (`http://www.delta.com`). NASA used it on the Mars Rover "Spirit" (`http://www.sun.com/aboutsun/media/features/mars.html`). It has been used in touchscreen kiosks for Super Bowl fans (`http://java.sun.com/features/1998/01/superbowl.html`).

Java is known for being object-oriented, platform neutral (runs on many computers and electronic devices), robust, and secure. An early drawback to Java was that programs written in Java often had a slower execution time than ones written in C or C++. However, current Java compilers and interpreters have substantially reduced this problem.

Let's make clear some of the terms that we'll be using in this book. A *program* is a description of a process in a particular programming language that achieves some result that is useful to someone. A program could be small (like one that implements a calculator), or could be huge (like the program that your bank uses to track all of its accounts). An *algorithm* (in contrast) is a description of a process apart from any programming language. The same algorithm might be implemented in many different languages in many different ways in many different programs—but it would all be the same *process* if we're talking about the same algorithm.

Computer Science Idea: Programs versus Algorithms

A program is written in a programming language and can be executed by a computer. An algorithm can be written in English and is a description of a process. Many programs can implement an algorithm in many different programming languages.

1.2   WHAT COMPUTERS UNDERSTAND

Programs are written to run on computers. What does a computer know how to do? What can we tell the computer to do in the program? The answer is "Very, very little." Computers are exceedingly stupid. They really only know about numbers.

Actually, even to say that computers *know* numbers is a myth. It might be more appropriate to say that computers are used to *encode* (represent) numbers. Computers are electronic devices that react to voltages on wires. We group these wires into sets (a set of eight of these wires is called a *byte* and one wire is called a *bit*). If a wire has a voltage on it, we say that it encodes a 1. If it has no voltage on it, we say that it encodes a 0. So, from a set of eight wires (a byte), we get a pattern of eight 0's and 1's, e.g., 01001010. Using the *binary* number system, we can interpret this byte as a *decimal number* (Figure 1.3). That's where we come up with the claim that a computer knows about numbers.[1]

Computer Science Idea: Binary Number System

Binary numbers are made up of only 2 digits (0 and 1). We usually work in the decimal number system which has the digits (0 to 9). The value of a decimal number is calculated by multiplying each digit by a power of 10 and summing the result. The powers of 10 start at 0 and increase from right to left. The value of a binary number is calculated by multiplying each digit by a power of 2 and summing the result (Figure 1.3). ■

The computer has a *memory* filled with bytes. Everything that a computer is working with at a given instant is stored in its memory. That means that everything that a computer is working with is *encoded* in its bytes: JPEG pictures, Excel spreadsheets, Word documents, annoying Web pop-up ads, and the latest spam email.

A computer can do lots of things with numbers. It can add them, subtract them, multiply them, divide them, sort them, collect them, duplicate them, filter them (e.g., "make a copy of these numbers, but only the even ones"), and compare them and do things based on the comparison. For example, a computer can be told in a program

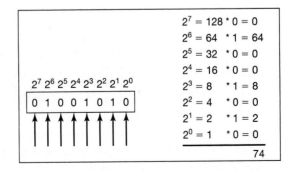

FIGURE 1.3
Eight wires with a pattern of voltages is a byte, which gets interpreted as a pattern of eight 0's and 1's, which gets interpreted as a decimal number.

[1] We'll talk more about this level of the computer in Chapter 15.

"Compare these two numbers. If the first one is less than the second one, jump to step 5 in this program. Otherwise, continue on to the next step."

It sounds like computers are incredible calculators, and that's certainly why they were invented. The first use of computers was during World War II for calculating trajectories of projectiles ("If the wind is coming from the SE at 15 MPH, and you want to hit a target 0.5 miles away at an angle of 30 degrees East of North, then incline your launcher to …"). The computer is an amazing calculator. But what makes it useful for general programs is the concept of *encodings*.

Computer Science Idea: Computers can Layer Encodings

Computers can layer encodings to virtually any level of complexity. Numbers can be interpreted as characters, which can be interpreted in groups as Web pages. But at the bottommost level, the computer *only* "knows" voltages which we interpret as numbers.

If one of these bytes is interpreted as the number 65, it could just be the number 65. Or it could be the letter *A* using a standard encoding of numbers-to-letters called the *American Standard Code for Information Interchange (ASCII)*. If that 65 appears in a collection of other numbers that we're interpreting as text, and that's in a file that ends in ".html" it might be part of something that looks like this <a href=…, which a Web browser will interpret as the definition of a link. Down at the level of the computer, that *A* is just a pattern of voltages. Many layers of programs up, at the level of a Web browser, it defines something that you can click on to get more information.

If the computer understands only numbers (and that's a stretch already), how does it manipulate these encodings? Sure, it knows how to compare numbers, but how does that extend to being able to alphabetize a class list? Typically, each layer of encoding is implemented as a piece or layer of software. There's software that understands how to manipulate characters. The character software knows how to do things like compare names because it has encoded that *a* comes before *b* and so on, and that the numeric comparison of the order of numbers in the encoding of the letters leads to alphabetical comparisons. The character software is used by other software that manipulates text in files. That's the layer that something like Microsoft Word or Notepad or TextEdit would use. Still another piece of software knows how to interpret *HTML* (the language of the Web), and another layer of that software knows how to take HTML and display the right text, fonts, styles, and colors.

We can similarly create layers of encodings in the computer for our specific tasks. We can teach a computer that cells contain mitochondria and DNA, and that DNA has four kinds of nucleotides, and that factories have these kinds of presses and these kinds of stamps. Creating layers of encoding and interpretation so that the computer is working with the right units (recall back to our recipe analogy) for a given problem is the task of *data representation* or defining the right *data structures*.

If this sounds like lots of software, it is. When software is layered like this, it slows the computer down somewhat. But the amazing thing about computers is that they're *amazingly* fast—and getting faster all the time!

Computer Science Idea: Moore's Law

Gordon Moore, one of the founders of Intel (maker of computer processing chips for computers running the Windows operating systems), made the claim that the number of transistors (a key component of computers) would double at the same price every 18 months, effectively meaning that the same amount of money would buy twice as much computing power every 18 months. This law has continued to hold true for decades. ■

Computers today can execute literally *BILLIONS* of program steps per second! They can hold in memory entire encyclopedias of data! They never get tired nor bored. Search a million customers for a particular card holder? No problem! Find the right set of numbers to get the best value out of an equation? Piece of cake!

Process millions of picture elements or sound fragments or movie frames? That's *media computation*.

1.3   MEDIA COMPUTATION: WHY DIGITIZE MEDIA?

Let's consider an encoding that would be appropriate for pictures. Imagine that pictures were made up of little dots. That's not hard to imagine: Look really closely at your monitor or at a TV screen and see that your images are *already* made up of little dots. Each of these dots is a distinct color. You may know from physics that colors can be described as the sum of *red*, *green*, and *blue*. Add the red and green to get yellow. Mix all three together to get white. Turn them all off, and you get a black dot.

What if we encoded each dot in a picture as a collection of three bytes, one each for the amount of red, green, and blue at that dot on the screen? We could collect a bunch of these three-byte-sets to specify all the dots of a given picture. That's a pretty reasonable way of representing pictures, and it's essentially how we're going to do it in Chapter 4.

Manipulating these dots (each referred to as a *pixel* or *picture element*) can take a lot of processing. There can be thousands or even millions of them in a picture. But, the computer doesn't get bored and it's mighty fast.

The encoding that we will be using for sound involves 44,100 two-byte-sets (called a *sample*) for each *second* of time. A three-minute song requires 158,760,000 bytes. Doing any processing on this takes a *lot* of operations. But at a billion operations per second, you can do lots of operations to every one of those bytes in just a few moments.

Creating these kinds of encodings for media requires a change to the media. Look at the real world: It isn't made up of lots of little dots that you can see. Listen to a sound: Do you hear thousands of little bits of sound per second? The fact that you *can't* hear little bits of sound per second is what makes it possible to create these encodings. Our eyes and ears are limited: We can only perceive so much, and only things that are just so small. If you break up an image into small enough dots, your eyes can't tell that it's not a continuous flow of color. If you break up a sound into small enough pieces, your ears can't tell that the sound isn't a continuous flow of auditory energy.

The process of encoding media into little bits is called *digitization*, sometimes referred to as "*going digital*." *Digital* means (according to the *American Heritage Dictionary*) "Of, relating to, or resembling a digit, especially a finger." Making things digital is about turning things from continuous, uncountable, to something that we can count, as if with our fingers.

Digital media, done well, feel the same to our limited human sensory apparatus as the original. Phonograph recordings (ever seen one of those?) capture sound continuously, as an *analog* signal. Photographs capture light as a continuous flow. Some people say that they can hear a difference between phonograph recordings and CD recordings, but to my ear and most measurements, a CD (which *is* digitized sound) sounds just the same—maybe clearer. Digital cameras at high enough resolutions produce photograph-quality pictures.

Why would you want to digitize media? Because it's easier to manipulate, to replicate, to compress, and to transmit. For example, it's hard to manipulate images that are in photographs, but it's very easy when the same images are digitized. This book is about using the increasingly digital world of media and manipulating it—and learning computation in the process.

Moore's Law has made media computation feasible as an introductory topic. Media computation relies on the computer doing lots and lots of operations on lots and lots of bytes. Modern computers can do this easily. Even with slow (but easy to understand) languages, even with inefficient (but easy to read and write) programs, we can learn about computation by manipulating media.

1.4   COMPUTER SCIENCE FOR EVERYONE

But why should *you* learn about computation? Of course, people who want to be computer scientists will need to learn about computation. Why should anyone who doesn't want to be a computer scientist learn about computer science?

Most professionals today do manipulate media: Papers, videos, tape recordings, photographs, drawings. Increasingly, this manipulation is done with a computer. Media are very often in a digitized form today.

We use software to manipulate these media. We use Adobe Photoshop for manipulating our images, and Macromedia SoundEdit to manipulate our sounds, and perhaps Microsoft PowerPoint for assembling our media into slideshows. We use Microsoft Word for manipulating our text, and Netscape Navigator or Microsoft Internet Explorer for browsing media on the Internet.

So why should anyone who does *not* want to be a computer scientist study computer science? Why should you learn to program? Isn't it enough to learn to *use* all this great software? The following two sections provide two answers to these questions.

1.4.1   It's About Communication

Digital media are manipulated with software. *If you can only manipulate media with software that **someone else** made for you, you are limiting your ability to communicate.* What if you want to say something or say it in some way that Adobe, Microsoft,

Apple, and the rest don't support you in saying? If you know how to program, even if it would take you *longer* to do it yourself, you have that freedom.

What about learning those tools in the first place? In my years in computers, I've seen a variety of software come and go as *the* package for drawing, painting, word-processing, video editing, and beyond. You can't learn just a single tool and expect to be able to use that your entire career. If you know *how* the tools work, you have a core understanding that can transfer from tool to tool. You can think about your media work in terms of the *algorithms*, not the *tools*.

Finally, if you're going to prepare media for the Web, for marketing, for print, for broadcast, for any use whatsoever, it's worthwhile for you to have a sense of what's possible, what can be done with media. It's even more important as a consumer of media that you know how the media can be manipulated, to know what's true and what could be just a trick. If you know the basics of media computation, you have an understanding that goes beyond what any individual tool provides.

1.4.2 It's About Process

In 1961, Alan Perlis gave a talk at MIT where he made the argument that computer science, and programming explicitly, should be part of a general, liberal education [13]. Perlis is an important figure in the field of computer science. The highest award that a computer scientist can be honored with is the ACM Turing Award. Perlis was the first recipient of that award. He's also an important figure in software engineering, and he started several of the first computer science departments in the United States.

Perlis's argument can be made in comparison with calculus. Calculus is generally considered part of a liberal education: Not *everyone* takes calculus, but if you want to be well-educated, you will typically take at least a term of calculus. Calculus is the study of *rates*, which is important in many fields. Computer science, as we said before (page 2), is the study of *process*. Process is important to nearly every field, from business to science to medicine to law. Knowing process formally is important to everyone.

PROBLEMS

1.1 What is a program?

1.2 What is an algorithm?

1.3 What is memory used for in a computer?

1.4 What type of computer scientist studies how recipes are written? What type of computer scientist studies how to make a computer think? What type of computer scientist studies the units used in recipes?

1.5 What is Moore's Law? What does it have to do with computers getting faster and cheaper?

1.6 *Every* profession uses computers today. Use a Web browser and a search engine like *Google* to find sites that relate your field of study with computer science or computing or computation. For example, search for "biology computer science" or "management computing."

1.7 Look in the classified section of your newspaper. What kinds of jobs can people get with a degree in computer science? How much money do they make? How many jobs are available?

1.8 Go to http://www.howstuffworks.com and find out how digital cameras work.

1.9 Go to http://www.howstuffworks.com and find out how digital recording and CDs work.

1.10 Go to http://www.howstuffworks.com and find out how remote entry devices work.

1.11 Find an ASCII table on the Web: A table listing every character and its corresponding numeric representation. Write down the sequence of numbers whose ASCII values make up your name.

1.12 Find a *Unicode* table on the Web. What's the difference between ASCII and Unicode? How many bytes does each use to represent a character?

1.13 Consider the representation for pictures described in Section 1.3, where each "dot" (pixel) in the picture is represented by three bytes, for the red, green, and blue components of the color at that dot. How many bytes does it take to represent a 640×480 picture, a common picture size on the Web? How many bytes does it take to represent a $1{,}024 \times 768$ picture, a common screen size? (What do you think is meant now by a "3 megapixel" camera?)

1.14 How many digits are used in the binary number system? How many digits are used in the decimal number system? How would you represent 3, 5, 8, and 13 in the binary number system?

1.15 What is the hexadecimal number system? How many digits are used in the hexadecimal number system? How would you represent 4, 18, 33, and 64 in this number system?

1.16 What is the octal number system? How many digits are used in the octal number system? How would you represent 4, 18, 33, and 64 in this number system?

1.17 How many digits are in one byte? How many different numbers can be represented by one byte? What if you have two bytes? Four bytes?

1.18 How would you represent negative numbers in bytes? Do a search on the Web for "negative numbers" and see what you find.

1.19 How might you represent a *floating point number* in terms of bytes? Do a search on the Web for "floating point" and see what you find.

1.20 Look up Alan Kay and the *Dynabook* on the Web. Who is he, and what does he have to do with media computation?

1.21 Look up Alan Turing on the Web. Who was he, and what does he have to do with our notion of what a computer can do and how encodings work?

1.22 Look up Kurt Goedel on the Web. Who was he, and what amazing things did he do with encodings?

TO DIG DEEPER

James Gleick's book *Chaos* describes more on emergent properties—how small changes can lead to dramatic effects, and the unintended impacts of designs because of difficult-to-foresee interactions.

Mitchel Resnick's book *Turtles, Termites, and Traffic Jams: Explorations in Massively Parallel Microworlds* [23] describes how ants, termites, and even traffic jams and slime molds can be described pretty accurately with hundreds or thousands of very small processes (programs) running and interacting all at once.

Exploring the Digital Domain [3] is a wonderful introductory book to computation with lots of good information about digital media.

2 Introduction to Java

Chapter Learning Objectives

The computer science goals for this chapter are:

- To introduce objects and classes.
- To use DrJava to execute Java statements.
- To use Java math and relational operators.
- To recognize different types (encodings) of data, such as integers, floating point numbers, booleans, characters, and strings.
- To introduce casting.
- To introduce variables and show the difference between primitive and object variables.

2.1 JAVA

The programming language that we're going to be using in this book is called *Java*. It's a language invented by James Gosling (`http://java.sun.com/people/jag/`) at Sun Microsystems.

2.1.1 History of Java

Back in 1990 Sun created Project Green to try and predict the next big thing in computers. The goal of the project was to try and develop something to position Sun ahead of its competitors. They thought that the next big thing would be networked consumer electronics devices like set-top boxes for downloading video on demand. They tried to develop a prototype using C++, but after many problems they decided to develop a new *object-oriented* language which they originally named Oak, after a tree outside James Gosling's office. They created a demonstration but the cable companies weren't really interested and the future of the project was in doubt.

At a brainstorming session they decided to try to reposition the language for use with the Internet. They created a Web browser that had programs (*applets*) embedded in HTML pages to do 3D rotation of a molecule and animation of a sorting algorithm. They showed this at a conference. At that time Web pages didn't respond to user action. They simply displayed text and unchanging graphics. The audience was amazed to see the user rotate a 3D molecule on a Web page.

A patent search found that there was an existing programming language with the copyrighted name Oak, so the team brainstormed new names at a local coffee house and Java was selected. Java was released for free in 1995. Since then it has become one of the fastest adopted technologies of all times. It is now used for more than just Web pages. It is used in many devices from cell phones to Web servers. For more on the history of Java see `http://java.sun.com/features/1998/05/birthday.html`.

2.1.2 Introduction to Objects and Classes

Java is an object-oriented programming language. This means that the focus is on objects (who) as well as procedures (what). Objects are persons, places, or things that do the action in a situation or are acted upon.

An example might help you to understand what focusing on the objects means. When customers enter a restaurant a greeter will welcome them to the restaurant and show them to their table. A waiter will take the order and bring the drinks and food. One or more chefs will cook the food. The waiter will create the bill and give it to the customers. The customers will pay the bill.

How many people does it take to get a customer fed in a restaurant? Well, you need at least a customer, greeter, waiter, and a chef. What other things are doing action or being acted upon? We mentioned order, table, drink, food, and bill. Each of these are objects. The objects in this situation are working together to feed the customer.

What types of objects are they? We have given names to each thing we mentioned: customer, waiter, food, and so on. The names we gave are how we classify these objects. You probably know what we mean by a customer or food. But the computer doesn't know what we mean by these things. The way that we get the computer to understand what we mean is by defining a *class*. A class in Java tells the computer what data we expect objects of that class to have and what they can do. We would expect that food would have a name, a price, and a way to prepare it. We would expect that a customer would know what they can afford to pay and how to pay a bill.

Every object of the same class will have the same skills or operations (things it can do) and data or variables (things it knows about). For example, each object of the order class should know which customer placed that order and what food is in the order. An object of the chef class should know how to prepare the food.

There can be many objects of the same class. A restaurant might have three chefs, ten waiters, two greeters, and 100 food objects on its menu. On a given day and time it might have 100 customers.

Why don't restaurants just have one type of employee? One person could greet the customers, take the orders, cook the food and deliver the food. That might be okay if there is only one customer but what about when there are many customers? You can imagine that one person wouldn't be able to handle so many tasks and food would get burnt, orders would take too long to fill, and customers wouldn't be happy. Restaurants break the tasks into different jobs so that they can be efficient and effective. Object-oriented programs also try to distribute the tasks to be done so that no one object does all the work. This makes it easier to maintain and extend the program. It can also make the program more efficient.

2.2 INTRODUCTION TO DrJAVA

We recommend that you program using a tool called *DrJava*. DrJava is a simple *editor* (tool for entering program text) and interaction space so that you can try things out in DrJava and create new programs (methods) and classes. DrJava is available for free under the DrJava Open Source License, and it is under active development by the JavaPLT group at Rice University.

If you don't wish to use DrJava, you can use this book with another development environment. Simply set the classpath (place to look for classes that you are using in your program) to include the classes used in this book. Check your documentation for your development environment to see how to do this. We recommend using DrJava because it is free, easy to use, has an interactions pane for trying out Java statements, is written in Java so it works on all platforms, and it includes a debugger. Since it is free, you can use it just for the interactions pane, and do your coding in another development environment if you prefer.

To install DrJava, you'll have to do these things:

1. Make sure that you have Java 1.4 or above installed on your computer. If you don't have it, load it from the CD, or you can get it from the Sun site at `http://www.java.sun.com`.

2. You'll need to install DrJava. You can either load it from the CD or get it from `http://drjava.org/`. Be sure to get a version of DrJava that works with the version of Java you are using! See the CD for more information on installing DrJava.

3. Add the Java classes that come with the book to the extra classpaths for DrJava. Start DrJava (see the next section for how to do this), click on EDIT and then PREFERENCES. This will show the Preferences window (Figure 2.1). Click on the ADD button below the EXTRA CLASSPATH textarea and add the path to the directory where the classes that come with the book are, such as: `c:/intro-prog-java/bookClasses`.

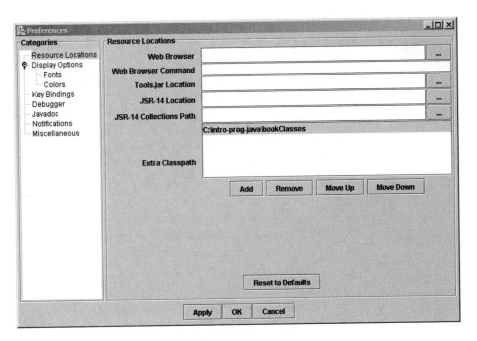

FIGURE 2.1
DrJava Preferences window.

2.2.1   Starting DrJava

How you start DrJava depends on your platform. In Windows, you'll have a DrJava icon that you'll simply double-click. In Linux, you'll probably cd into your DrJava directory and type a command like java -jar drjava-DATE-TIME.jar where DATE-TIME are values for the release of DrJava that you are using. On the Macintosh, you'll probably have to type commands in your *Terminal* application where you cd to the correct directory then type ./DrJava. See the instructions on the CD for what will work for your kind of computer.

Common Bug: DrJava is Slow to Start

DrJava will take a while to load on all platforms. Don't worry—you'll see (Figure 2.2) for a long time. This is called a *splash screen*, which is a small picture that displays while a program is loading. If you see the splash screen (Figure 2.2), DrJava will load.

FIGURE 2.2
DrJava Splash Screen.

Common Bug: Making DrJava Run Faster

As we'll talk more about later, when you're running DrJava, you're actually running Java. Java needs memory. If you're finding that DrJava is running slowly, give it more memory. You can do that by quitting out of other applications that you're running. Your e-mail program, your instant messenger, and your digital music player all take up memory (sometimes lots of it!). Quit out of those and DrJava will run faster.

Once you start DrJava, it will look something like Figure 2.3. There are three main areas in DrJava (the bars between them move so that you can resize the areas):

- The top-left window pane is the *files pane*. It has a list of the open files in DrJava. In Java each class that you create is usually stored in its own file. Java programs often consist of more than one class, thus more than one file. You can click on a file name in the Files pane to view the contents of that file in the top right window pane (definitions pane).

- The top-right part is the *definitions pane*. This is where you write *your* classes: a collection of related data and methods. This area is simply a text editor—think of it as Microsoft Word for your programs. The computer doesn't actually try to interpret the names that you type up in the program area until you compile. You can *compile* all the current files open in the files pane by clicking on the COMPILE ALL button near the top of the DrJava window. Compiling your code changes it into instructions that the computer understands and can execute.

- The bottom part is the *interactions pane*. This is where you can literally *command* the computer to do something. You type your commands at the > prompt, and when you hit return, the computer will interpret your words (i.e., apply the meanings and encodings of the Java programming language) and do what you have told it to do. This interpretation will include whatever you typed and compiled in the definitions pane as well.

There are other features of DrJava visible in Figure 2.3. The OPEN button will let you open a file, it will add the file name to the files pane, and show the code in that file in the definitions pane. The SAVE button will save the file that is currently displayed in the definitions pane. The JAVADOC button creates HTML documentation from the *Javadoc comments* in your files (comments that start with '/**' and end with '*/'.

Making it Work Tip: Get to Know Your Help!

An *important* feature to already start exploring is the HELP. If you click on HELP and then click on HELP again when a menu is displayed you will see a help window. Start exploring it now so that you have a sense for what's there.

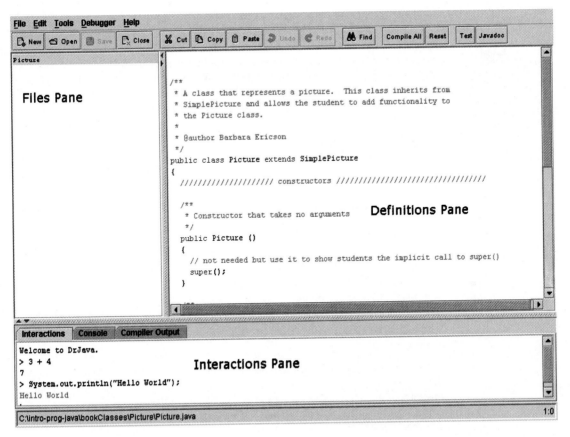

FIGURE 2.3
DrJava (with annotations).

2.3   JAVA BASICS

We're going to start out by simply typing commands in the interactions pane—not defining new names yet, but simply using the names and symbols that Java knows.

2.3.1   Math Operators

Try typing the following in the interactions pane.

```
> 34 + 56
90
> 26 - 3
23
> 3 * 4
12
> 4 / 2
2
```

As you can see Java understands how to recognize numbers, add, subtract, multiply, and divide. You can type a mathematical expression in the interactions pane and then hit the "Enter" key and it will display the result of the expression. Go ahead and try it.

Making it Work Tip: Using Another Development Environment

If you are not using DrJava you will need to type all code that we show in the interactions pane in a `main` method instead. Compile and execute the class with a `main` method. To get the above example to work in another development environment we could have written the following class definition in a file named "Test.java".

```java
public class Test
{
  public static void main(String[] args)
  {
    System.out.println(34 + 56);
    System.out.println(26 - 3);
    System.out.println(3 * 4);
    System.out.println(4/2);
  }
}
```

The next step is to compile the Java source file. This changes it from something people can read and understand into something the computer can read and understand. To compile the source file with the free command line tools from Sun do the following:

```
> javac Test.java
```

When you compile a Java source file the compiler will create a class file, so if you compile the source file "Test.java" the compiler will create the file "Test.class". This file will have the same name as the source file but will have an extension of ".class". After you have compiled the source you can execute the class. To execute it using the free command-line tools from Sun is to use:

```
> java Test
```

We have included this `Test` class in your `bookClasses` directory. You can continue to use the `Test` class and just change the code in the `main` method to try the examples we show in DrJava's interactions pane. We will explain all about classes and `main` methods in Chapter 11.

The ability to try things in the interactions pane without having to create a class and a `main` method is one of the major advantages to using DrJava. Remember that it is **free**, so even if you use another development environment you can download it and use it too, at least for the interactions pane!

2.3.2   Printing the Result of a Statement

In English you end sentences with a period. In Java you typically end a programming statement with a semicolon. However, in the interactions pane you can leave off the semicolon and it will print the result of whatever you have typed (as you saw in the interactions pane). If you do add the semicolon at the end of a Java statement in the interactions pane, it will execute the statement but not automatically print the result in the interactions pane.

Even though you do not *have* to type the semicolon after statements in the interactions pane you *must* type the semicolon at the end of your statements in the definitions pane or the code will not compile.

Since you will need to provide the semicolon at the end of statements in the definitions pane, you should get used to using them in the interactions pane too. But, how do you show the result of a statement in the interactions pane? The phrase `System.out.println()` is an important one to know. The meaning for `System.out.println()` is "Use the `PrintStream` object known as `out` in the `System` class to print out the value of whatever is in the parentheses followed by an end-of-line character." DrJava will print the result of an expression in the interactions pane when you use `System.out.println(expression)`.

You can have nothing in the parentheses which will just move the output to a new line, or it can be a name that the computer knows, or an *expression* (literally, in the algebraic sense). Try typing `System.out.println(34 + 56)` by clicking in the interactions area, typing the command, and hitting return—like this:

```
> System.out.println(34 + 56);
90
> System.out.println(26 - 3);
23
> System.out.println(3 * 4);
12
> System.out.println(4 / 2);
2
> System.out.println(9 % 4);
1
> System.out.println(9 / 5 * -3 + 32);
29
> System.out.println(3 + 2 * 4);
11
> System.out.println((3 + 2) * 4);
20
```

The code `34 + 56` is a numeric expression that Java understands. Obviously, it's composed of two numbers and an operation that Java knows how to do, `'+'` meaning "add." In Java we call math symbols like `'+'` and `'-'` *operators*. The operator `'-'` means subtract. The operator `'*'` means multiply. The operator `'/'` means divide. The operator `'%'` means calculate the remainder of the first number divided by the second one. This is called the *modulus* operator.

Notice that you get a different result from `System.out.println(3 + 2 * 4);` than from `System.out.println((3 + 2) * 4);`. This is because multiplication has higher *precedence* than addition (meaning it is done first by default). You can use parentheses to change the default order of evaluation of an expression or to make the order clear.

Common Bug: Matching Parentheses

When you use parentheses you will need an open parenthesis for each close parenthesis. If you don't have a match you will get an error.

```
> System.out.println(3 + 2) * 4);
Syntax Error: ")"
> System.out.println((3 + 2 * 4);
Syntax Error: ";"
```

2.3.3 Data Types in Math Expressions

Java takes how you specify numbers seriously. If it sees you using integers, it thinks you want an integer result. If it sees you using floating point numbers, it thinks you want a floating point result. Sounds reasonable, no? But how about:

```
> System.out.println(1.0/2.0);
0.5
> System.out.println(1/2);
0
```

The answer to 1/2 is 0? Well, sure! The numbers 1 and 2 are integers. There is no integer equal to 1/2, so the answer must be 0 (the part after the decimal point is thrown away)! Simply by adding ".0" to a number convinces Java that we're talking about floating point numbers (specifically the Java primitive type double), so the result is in floating point form.

We call integer and floating point numbers two different types of *data*. By data we mean the values that we use in computation. The type of the data, which is also called the *data type*, determines how many bits are used to represent the value and how the bits are interpreted by the computer.

2.3.4 Casting

We could also have used *casting* to get the correct result from the division of two integers. Casting is like using a mold to give some material a new shape. It tells the compiler to change a value to a particular type even if it could lead to a loss of data. To cast you put the type that you want the value changed to inside an open and close parenthesis: (type). There are two floating point types in Java: float and double. The type double is larger than the type float and thus more precise. We will use this type for most of the floating point numbers in this book. Notice that we can cast either the 1 or 2 to double and the answer will then be given as a double. We could cast both the 1 and 2 to double and the result would be fine. However, if we cast the result of the integer division to a double it is too late since the result of integer division of 1 by 2 is 0 since the result is an integer.

```
> System.out.println((double) 1 / 2);
0.5
> System.out.println(1 / (double) 2);
0.5
> System.out.println((double) (1/2));
0.0
```

2.3.5 Relational Operators

We can write Java statements that do simple math operations. But if that was all we could do, computers wouldn't be terribly useful. Computers can also decide if something is true or false.

```
> System.out.println(3 > 2);
true
```

```
> System.out.println(2 > 3);
false
> System.out.println('a' < 'b');
true
> System.out.println('j' > 'c');
true
> System.out.println(2 == 2);
true
> System.out.println(2 != 2);
false
> System.out.println(2 >= 2);
true
> System.out.println(2 <= 2);
true
> System.out.println(true == false);
false
```

Using symbols we can check if one value is greater than another '>', less than another '<', equal to another '==', not equal to another '!=', greater or equal to another '>=', and less than or equal to another '<='. You can use these relational operators on many items such as numbers and characters as shown above. A character can be specified between a pair of single quotes ('a').

You might find '==' odd as a way to test for equality. But, in Java '=' is used to assign a value, not check for equality, as you will see in the next section.

Notice that Java understands the concepts true and false. These are *reserved words* in Java, which means that they can't be used as names.

Making it Work Tip: Java Primitive Types

- Integers are numbers without a decimal point in them. Integers are represented by the types: int, byte, short, or long. Example integers are: 3, 5,02,893, and -2,350. In this book we will only use int to represent integers. Each integer takes up 32 bits of memory (4 bytes).

- Floating point numbers are numbers with a decimal point in them. Floating point numbers can be represented by the types: double or float. Example doubles are 3.0, -19.23, and 548.675. In this book we will use mostly use double to represent floating point numbers. Each double in memory takes up 64 bits (8 bytes).

- Characters are individual characters that can be made with one key stroke on your keyboard. Characters are represented by the type: char. Characters are specified inside single quotes, like 'a' or 'A'. Each character in memory takes up 16 bits (2 bytes).

- True and false values are represented by the type boolean. Variables of type boolean can only have true or false as values. While a boolean could be represented by just one bit the size of a boolean is up to the virtual machine. ∎

2.3.6   Strings

Computers can certainly work with numbers and even characters. They can also work with strings. Strings are sequences of characters. Try the following in the interactions pane.

```
> System.out.println("Mark");
Mark
> System.out.println("13 + 5");
13 + 5
```

Java knows how to recognize *strings* (lists of characters) that start and end with " (a double quote). Notice what happens when you enclose a math expression like 13 + 5 in a pair of double quotes. It doesn't print the result of the math expression but the characters inside the pair of double quotes. Whatever is inside a pair of double quotes is not evaluated, the value of it is exactly what was entered.

Now try the following in the interactions pane.

```
> System.out.println("Barbara" + "Ericson");
BarbaraEricson
> System.out.println("Barbara" + " " + "Ericson");
Barbara Ericson
> System.out.println("Barbara " + "Ericson");
Barbara Ericson
```

You can "add" strings together using a + operator as you see in "Barbara" + "Ericson". It simply creates a new string with the characters in the first string followed by the characters in the second string. This is called *appending* or *concatenating* strings. Notice that no space is added automatically. If you want space in your string you will need to put it there using a space between a pair of double quotes as shown above with "Barbara" + " " + "Ericson". Or you can have a space inside a string as shown in "Barbara " + "Ericson".

Now try the following in the interactions pane.

```
> System.out.println("The total is " + (13 + 5));
The total is 18
> System.out.println("The total is " + 13 + 5);
The total is 135
```

You can "add" a string and a number. It will turn the number into a string and then append the two strings. This does what you would expect to show the result of "The total is " + (13 + 15) but you may not expect what happens with "The total is " + 13 + 5.

The computer evaluates statements from left to right so the computer evaluates this as "add" the string "The total is" to the number 13 by turning the number 13 into a string "13". Next it sees the + 5 as adding a number to the string "The total is 13". It turns the second number into a string and results in The total is 135.

The way to get what you would expect is to use parentheses to enclose the math expression. Just like in algebra the parentheses change the order things are evaluated. The (13 + 5) will be evaluated before the append of the string and the resulting number 18.

If you want to put a double quote inside of a string you will need some way to tell the computer that this isn't the ending double quote. In Java the backslash

\ character is used to treat the next character differently. So using \" results in a double quote inside a string. Some other special characters are \n to force a new line and \t to force a tab.

```
> System.out.println("Barb says, \"Hi\".");
Barb says, "Hi."
> System.out.println("This is on one line.\nThis is on the next");
This is on one line.
This is on the next
```

2.4   VARIABLES

We have used Java to do calculations and to append strings, but we have not stored the results. The results would be in memory but we don't know where they are in memory and we can't get back to them. On a calculator we can store the result of one calculation to memory (Figure 2.4). We can then use that stored value in other calculations. On a calculator you also have access to the result of the last calculation.

2.4.1   Declaring Variables

On a computer we can store many calculated values by naming them. We can then access those values by using the variable names. The computer takes care of mapping the name to the memory location (address) that stores the value. We call naming values *declaring a variable*.

When you declare a variable in Java you specify the type for the variable and a name (*type name*). You need to specify a type so that Java knows how many bits to reserve in memory and how to interpret the bits. You can also assign a value to a variable using the '=' operator and provide a value or an expression (*type name = expression*). Don't read '=' as equals but assign the value of the right side to the variable on the left (which makes using '==' for 'is equal to' or 'is equivalent to' make more sense). The bits in the variable will be set to represent the value. We will use the type int for storing integer values (numbers without decimal points) and the type double for storing floating point values (numbers with decimal points).

FIGURE 2.4
A calculator with a number in memory.

2.4.2   Using Variables in Calculations

What if you want to calculate the total bill for a meal including the tip? You would start with the bill value and multiply it by the percentage you want to tip (20%), that would give you the tip amount. You could then add the tip amount to the bill total to get the total amount to leave.

We will use the type double to store the bill amount, tip, and total amount since these can have decimal points. If we also wanted to calculate the cost per person we could divide the total by the number of people. We could use an integer variable to hold the number of people.

```
> int numPeople = 2;
> System.out.println(numPeople);
2
> double bill = 32.45;
> System.out.println(bill);
32.45
> double tip = bill * 0.2;
> System.out.println(tip);
6.490000000000001
> double total = bill + tip;
> System.out.println(total);
38.940000000000005
> double totalPerPerson = total / numPeople;
> System.out.println(totalPerPerson);
19.470000000000002
```

Common Bug: Mistyping

You just saw a whole bunch of Java statements, and some of them are pretty long. What happens if you type one of them wrong? DrJava will complain that it doesn't know what you mean, like this:

```
> double tip = bil * 0.2;
Error: Undefined class 'bil'
```

It's no big deal. Use the up arrow on the keyboard to bring up the last thing you typed into DrJava and then use the left arrow to get to the place with the error and then fix it. You can use the up arrow to get to any of the commands you have typed in the interactions pane since you started DrJava.

So, each person would need to pay $19.47, which they would probably round up to $19.50.

Making it Work Tip: Variable Names

By convention the first word in a variable name is lowercase. So if the variable name is just one word, then the whole thing is lowercase, such as bill. The first letter of each additional word in a variable name should be uppercase, as shown by the variables named numPeople and totalPerPerson. This is a Java convention (usual way something is done), and it will make your programs easier to read.

We don't have to print out the value of the variable after we assign a value to it. We are doing that so that you see that the computer does return a value when you use the name of a variable. What about the extra amount for the final answer? The answer should be just $19.47 per person. If we look back at the printing of the tip amount we see where this first occurred. Floating point numbers do not always give exact results.

2.4.3   Memory Maps of Variables

In Java when you declare variables to be of the type int or double you are asking the computer to set aside space for a variable of that type (32 bits for int and 64 for double) and to remember the address of that space. When you assign a value to a variable using the '=' operator you change the value in that space to represent the new value. The code int numPeople reserves 32 bits of space and associates the name "numPeople" with that reserved space (Figure 2.5). The code = 2 sets the value of that space to the integer value 2. The code double bill reserves 64 bits of space and associates the name "bill" with that space. The = 32.45 changes the values in the reserved space to represent the value 32.45.

When we print out a variable name using System.out.println(bill); the computer looks up the name bill to find the address of that variable in memory and prints the value stored in that space. It knows how many bytes to use and how to interpret the bytes in calculating the value based on the declared type of the variable.

How would you calculate the cost of a shirt that was originally $47.99, but is now 40% off? And, what if you also had a coupon for an additional 20% off the sale price? First you would need to determine the first discount amount by multiplying 40% (0.40) times the original price. Next, calculate the first discount total by subtracting the first discount amount from the original price. Then calculate the second discount amount by multiplying 20% (0.20) times the second discount amount. The second discount total is the first discount total minus the second discount amount. We would

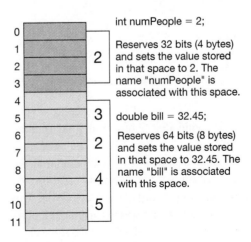

FIGURE 2.5
Declaring primitive variables and memory assignment.

need variables to hold the first discount amount, first discount total, second discount amount, and second discount total. What type should those variables be declared to be? Since they have fractional parts they can be declared as `double`.

```
> double originalPrice = 47.99;
> double firstDiscountAmount = originalPrice * 0.40;
> System.out.println(firstDiscountAmount);
19.196
> double firstDiscountTotal = originalPrice - firstDiscountAmount;
> System.out.println(firstDiscountTotal);
28.794
> double secondDiscountAmount = firstDiscountTotal * 0.20;
> System.out.println(secondDiscountAmount);
5.758800000000001
> double secondDiscountTotal = firstDiscountTotal -
secondDiscountAmount;
> System.out.println(secondDiscountTotal);
23.0352
```

When these statements are executed 64 bits of space is reserved for each variable declared as a double. So how much memory does this calculation take? We have declared five doubles so we have used 5 times 64 bits of space. Each byte has eight bits in it so how many bytes have we used? How much memory does your computer have and how much of it have you used? If your computer has 128 megabytes of memory then that is 128,000,000 bytes of memory and we used 40 bytes then we have only used 0.0000003125% of memory. That isn't very much. We can declare lots of variables and still not use up all of the memory.

Each time we use the variable name above the computer substitutes the value in the memory location associated with that name. What are the values in each of the five declared variables when these statements are finished?

2.4.4 Object Variables

Variables that are declared to be of any of the primitive types: `byte`, `short`, `int`, `long`, `float`, `double`, `boolean` or `char` reserve space and associate the variable name with the starting location of that space. Variables that are declared to be of any other type are object variables. This is because all other types *inherit* from the class `Object`.

You can think of inheritance as saying that one class "is a kind of" another class, like saying that a dog is a kind of mammal (Figure 2.6). If you need a mammal you can use a dog, but if you need a dog another mammal (like a cat) won't do. Because a dog is a kind of mammal we know that it has the same characteristics that a mammal does such as breathing oxygen, bearing live young, having hair, etc. We say that it inherits characteristics from mammal. The `String` class is a child of the `Object` class so it is a kind of object (Figure 2.6). All of the classes that you define will inherit from the `Object` class either directly or indirectly.

When you declare a variable you specify the type and a name *type name*; or *type name = expression*;. What if you want to declare a variable that will refer

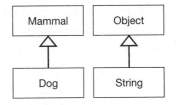

FIGURE 2.6
Showing the parent and child relationship between mammal and dog (left) and `Object` and `String` (right).

to a string? What type can you use? Well it can't be `int` or `double` because those represent numbers. It can't be `char` because that represents a single character.

Java has a class `String` that is used to represent character strings. The `String` class inherits from the `Object` class. So to declare a variable that represents a string of characters use: `String` *name*;.

Object variables reserve space for something which is a *reference* to an object. A reference isn't the address of the object in memory. It is more like a Dewey Decimal System number. Once you know the Dewey Decimal System number for a book, you can find the book on the library shelves. An object reference gives the computer a way to find an object in memory.

Object variables do not reserve space for the object. If the object variable doesn't reference an object yet it has the value `null`.

```
> String test;
> System.out.println(test);
null
> test = "Hi";
> System.out.println(test);
Hi
> test = new String("Bye");
> System.out.println(test);
Bye
```

When the variable `test` was declared as type `String` space was reserved for an object reference and the value of the `test` variable was set to `null` (Figure 2.7). The default value for an object variable is `null` which means it isn't referring to any object yet. The compiler will create a `String` object when it sees characters enclosed in double quotes so the `"Hi"` creates an object of the `String` class and sets the characters in that `String` object to be the characters `"Hi"`. The code `test = "Hi"` changes the value of the space reserved for the object reference from `null` to a reference to the `String` object with the characters `"Hi"`.

What happens to the `String` object with the characters `"Hi"` in it when you changed the variable `test` to refer to the new `String` object with the characters `"Bye"`? Java keeps track of used space and if there are no valid references to the used space it will put it back into available space. This is called *garbage collection*.

The fact that Java automatically handles freeing used memory when it is no longer needed is one of the advantages to Java over languages like C++ which required the

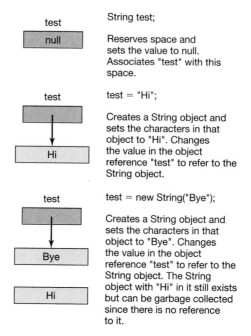

FIGURE 2.7
Declaring object variables and memory assignment.

programmer to free memory when it was no longer needed. Programmers aren't very good at keeping track of when memory is no longer needed, so many programs never free memory when it is no longer needed. This is called a *memory leak*, and it is why some programs use more and more memory while they are running. Sometimes programmers free memory when it is still being used, which can cause major problems, such as incorrect results, and even cause your computer to crash.

Making it Work Tip: Variables versus Literals

Notice that we have changed the value of the variable test in Figure 2.7 several times. We call items like test variables because the values inside of them can change. This is different from literals such as the string literal "Hi" in that the value of that won't change. You can set the value of a variable to a literal but you can't set the value of a literal to a variable.

◼

2.4.5   Reusing Variables

Once we have declared variables we can reuse them by assigning new values to them.

```
> String myName = "Mark";
> System.out.println(myName);
Mark
> myName = "Barb";
> System.out.println(myName);
Barb
```

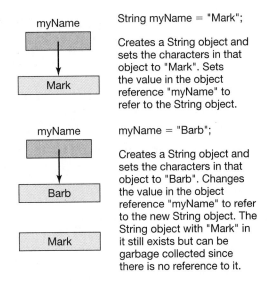

myName

```
String myName = "Mark";
```

Mark

Creates a String object and sets the characters in that object to "Mark". Sets the value in the object reference "myName" to refer to the String object.

myName

```
myName = "Barb";
```

Barb

Mark

Creates a String object and sets the characters in that object to "Barb". Changes the value in the object reference "myName" to refer to the new String object. The String object with "Mark" in it still exists but can be garbage collected since there is no reference to it.

FIGURE 2.8
Shows creation and reuse of an object variable.

This actually means to first set the variable myName to refer to the String object with the characters "Mark" in it. Then it changes the variable myName to refer to another String object with the characters "Barb" in it. The first String object with the characters "Mark" in it still exists and can be garbage collected (reused as available space) (Figure 2.8).

You can't declare the same variable name twice. Declare the name one time (by specifying the type and name) and then you can use it many times.

```
> String myName = "Mark";
> System.out.println(myName);
Mark
> String myName = "Sue";
Error: Redefinition of 'myName'
```

The *binding* between the name and the data only exists (a) until the name gets assigned to something else or (b) you quit DrJava or (c) you reset the interactions pane (by clicking on the RESET button). The relationship between names and data in the interactions pane only exists during a session of DrJava.

Common Bug: Redefinition Error
You can't declare a variable with the same name more than once in the interactions pane. If you do you will get a "Redefinition Error". If you want to "start over" click the RESET button in DrJava to let it know that you want to get rid of all currently defined variables. Or, just remove the types and you won't be redeclaring the variables, just changing their values (reusing them).

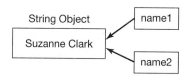

FIGURE 2.9
An object with multiple references to it.

2.4.6 Multiple References to an Object

You can have several variables that reference an object. You can use any of the references to access the object.

```
> String name1 = "Suzanne Clark";
> System.out.println(name1);
Suzanne Clark
> String name2 = name1;
> System.out.println(name2);
Suzanne Clark
```

When the compiler encounters the characters inside the pair of double quotes it creates a `String` object. The code `String name1` creates a variable `name1` that will refer to this string object. Print out `name1` to see what it refers to using `System.out.println(name1);`. Next the code `String name2 = name1;` creates another variable `name2` and sets the value of it to refer to the same string. Printing the new variable `name2` will result in the same string being printed (Figure 2.9).

An object can only be garbage collected when there are no current references to it. To allow the `String` object with the characters `"Suzanne Clark"` in it to be garbage-collected set the variables that refer to it to `null`.

```
> name1 = null;
> System.out.println(name1);
null
> System.out.println(name2);
Suzanne Clark
> name2 = null;
> System.out.println(name2);
null
```

Now all references to the `String` object are set to `null` so the object can be garbage-collected (Figure 2.10).

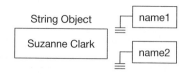

FIGURE 2.10
An object with no references to it.

2.5 CONCEPTS SUMMARY

This chapter introduced many basic concepts: printing the result of a statement (expression), math operators, relational operators, types, casting, and variables.

2.5.1 Statements

Java programs are made of statements. Java statements can end in semicolons ';' just like sentences can end in periods "." in English. When you type statements in the definitions pane (when you define methods) they *must* have some sort of punctuation to show the end of the statement. One way to do this is to use a semicolon ';'.

If you leave off the semicolon in the interactions pane, it will print the result of the statement. If you do end a statement with a semicolon in the interactions pane, and you want to print the result, use `System.out.println(expression);` to print the result of the expression.

```
> int numPeople = 3;
> double bill = 52.49;
> double amountPerPerson = bill / numPeople;
> System.out.println("Each person should pay: " + amountPerPerson);
Each person should pay: 17.496666666666666
```

Math Operators

+	Addition	Used to add numbers together $(3 + 4) = 7$
-	Subtraction	Used to subtract one number from another $(5 - 2) = 3$
*	Multiplication	Used to multiply two numbers together $(2 * 3) = 6$
/	Division	Used to divide one number by another $(18/2) = 9$
%	Modulus (Remainder)	Used to find the remainder of one number divided by another $(19 \% 2) = 1$

2.5.2 Relational Operators

<	Less Than	Used to check if one value is less than another $(2 < 3)$ is true
>	Greater Than	Used to check if one value is greater than another $(3 > 2)$ is true
==	Equals	Used to check if two values are the same $(2 == 2)$ is true
!=	Not Equals	Used to check if two values aren't equal $(2 != 3)$ is true

<=	Less Than or Equal	Used to check if one value is less than or equal to another (2 <= 3) is true
>=	Greater Than or Equal	Used to check if one value is greater than or equal to another (3 >= 2) is true

2.5.3 Types

A type is a description of the "kind of" thing something is. It affects how much space is reserved for a variable and how the bits in that space are interpreted. In this chapter, we talked about several kinds of types (encodings) of data.

Floating point numbers	Java primitive types `double` or `float`, e.g., 5.2, -3.01, 928.3092	Numbers with a decimal point in them.
Integers	Java primitive types `int`, `byte`, `short`, `long`, e.g., -3, 5,239, 0	Numbers without a decimal point—they can't represent fractions.
Characters	Java primitive type `char`, e.g., `'a'`, `'b'`, `'?'`	A character is delimited by a pair of single quotes.
Strings	Java `String` object, e.g., `"Hello!"`	A sequence of characters (including spaces, punctuation, etc.) delimited on either end with a double quote character.
Booleans	Java primitive type `boolean` with only two possible values	The value of a boolean can be the reserved word `true` or the reserved word `false`.

2.5.4 Casting

Java compilers recognize integer (-3) and floating point values (32.43). The result of a mathematical expression depends on the types involved in the expression. Expressions that involve integer values will have integer results. Expressions that have floating point (decimal) values will have floating point results.

   This can lead to unexpected results.

```
> 1 / 2
0
```

   There are two ways to fix this problem. One is to make one of the numbers a floating point number by adding '.0' (it doesn't matter which one) and the other is to use casting to change the type of one of the numbers to a floating point number (the primitive type `float` or `double`).

```
> 1.0 / 2
0.5
> (double) 1 / 2
0.5
```

2.5.5   Variables

Variables are used to store and access values. You create variables by declaring them: `type name`; or `type name = expression`;. Declaring a variable reserves space for the variable and allows the computer to map the variable name to the address of that reserved space.

We introduced two types of variables: primitive and object. Primitive variables are any of the types: `int`, `byte`, `short`, `long`, `float`, `double`, `char`, or `boolean`. Object variables refer to an object of a class. Use the class name as the type when declaring object variables `ClassName name`; or `ClassName name = expression`;.

Primitive variables store a value in the reserved space for that variable. You can change the value using `variableName = value`;. You can access the value using `variableName`.

Object variables store a reference to an object in the reserved space for that variable. Object variables do not just store the address of the object. They store a reference to an object which allows the address of the object to be determined.

If the object variable doesn't refer to any object yet it has the value `null`. You can change what object a variable references using `variableName = objectReference`;. You can access the referenced object using `variableName`.

PROBLEMS

2.1   Some computer science concept questions:

- What is an object?
- What is a class?
- What is a type? Why are types important?
- What is casting? What is it used for?
- What is a variable? When do you need one? What are the differences between object variables and primitive variables?
- What is garbage collection?
- What are relational operators? What are math operators?
- What is a string?

2.2   What objects would you encounter in a bank?

2.3   What objects would you encounter in going to a movie?

2.4   What objects would you encounter in a clothing store?

2.5   What objects are involved in a airplane flight?

2.6   What objects are in your classroom?

2.7   What objects would you encounter when you go to the dentist?

2.8   Use the interactions pane to calculate how long it will take to travel 770 miles at an average speed of 60 miles per hour? How much shorter will it take if you average 70 miles per hour?

2.9 Use the interactions pane to calculate how much money you will make if you work 40 hours at $13.00 and 10 hours at time and a half?

2.10 Test your understanding of Java with the following:

- What does `System.out.println();` do?
- What does the statement `System.out.println(3 + 2);` do?
- What does the statement `System.out.println("The answer is: " + 3 + 2);` do?
- What does the statement `System.out.println("Hi " + " there");` do?

2.11 Test your understanding of Java with the following:

- What does the code `int x = 3; System.out.println("The result is" + x);` do?
- What does the code `String firstName = "Sue"; System.out.println(firstName);` do?
- What does the code `System.out.println(2 < 3);` do?
- What does the code `System.out.println(2 == 3);` do?
- What does the code `System.out.println(3 >= 2);` do?

2.12 What does `int x = 1 / 3; System.out.println(x);` do and why?

2.13 What does `double d = 1 / 2.0; System.out.println(d);` do and why?

2.14 What does `double d1 = 1 / 3; System.out.println(d1);` do and why?

2.15 What does the `double d2 = (double) 1 / 3; System.out.println(d2);` do and why?

2.16 Declare variables for each of the following:

- the number of people in your family
- the cost of a video game
- your name
- answer to, "Are you righthanded?"
- the temperature in your room
- the number of items in a shopping cart

2.17 Declare variables for each of the following:

- your grade point average
- your telephone number
- the number of times you were absent from class
- the number of miles from your home to school
- answer to, "Do you wear glasses?"
- your credit card number

2.18 Which of the following is the correct way to declare a variable that represents a price?

- `declare double price = 0;`
- `int price = 0;`
- `Integer price = 0.0;`
- `double PRICE = 0.0;`
- `double price;`

2.19 Which of the following is the correct way to declare a variable that represents the desired quantity of an item in an order?

- `double numItems;`
- `INT numItems;`
- `int numItems;`
- `DOUBLE numItems;`

2.20 Which of the following is the correct way to declare a variable that represents whether an order has been canceled?

- `BOOLEAN canceled = false;`
- `boolean canceled = false;`
- `boolean CANCELED = false;`
- `boolean canceled = FALSE;`

TO DIG DEEPER

There is a wealth of material for Java on Sun's Java Web site `http://java.sun.com` including tutorials, papers, and APIs. To learn more about DrJava, see the Web site `http://www.drjava.org/`. *Thinking in Java* by Bruce Eckel is a good book for those who have some coding experience and like to understand a language deeply. Beginners might want to start with *Headfirst Java* by Kathy Sierra and Bert Bates. If you are someone who wants lots and lots of examples, see Deitel and Deitel's *Java, How to Program.*

3

Introduction to Programming

Chapter Learning Objectives

The media learning goals for this chapter are:

- To create a World object and Turtle objects and move the turtles to draw shapes.
- To create Picture objects and show them.
- To create Sound objects and play them.

The computer science goals for this chapter are:

- To invoke (execute) class and object methods.
- To create objects using the new keyword.
- To write methods (functions).
- To introduce using parameters to make methods more reusable.
- To introduce method overloading.

3.1   PROGRAMMING IS ABOUT NAMING

Computer Science Idea: Much of Programming is About Naming

A computer can associate names, or *symbols*, with just about anything: With a particular byte; with a collection of bytes making up a numeric variable or a string of letters; with a media element like a file, sound, or picture; or even with more abstract concepts, like a named recipe (a *program* or *method*) or a named encoding (a *type* or *class*). A computer scientist sees a choice of names as high quality in the same way that a philosopher or mathematician might: If the names are elegant, parsimonious, and usable.

Obviously, the computer itself doesn't *care* about names. Names are for the humans. If the computer were just a calculator, then remembering names and the names' association with values would be just a waste of the computer's memory. But for humans, it's *very* powerful. It allows us to work with the computer in a natural way.

A *programming language* is really a set of names that a computer has encodings for, such that those names make the computer do expected actions and interpret our data in expected ways. Some of the programming language's names allow us to define *new* names—which allows us to create our own layers of encoding. We can associate a name with a location in memory, this is called declaring a variable. We can associate a name with a group of Java statements, we call this defining a method (function). In Java you can also assign a name to a group of related variables and methods (functions) when you define a class (type).

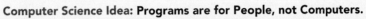

Computer Science Idea: Programs are for People, not Computers.

Remember that names are only meaningful for people, not computers. Computers just use the names to find the values associated with them. A good program is meaningful (understandable and useful) for humans. ∎

A *program* is a set of names and their values, where some of these names have values of instructions to the computer ("*code*"). Our instructions will be in the Java programming language. Combining these two definitions means that the Java programming language gives us a set of useful names that have a meaning to the computer, and our programs are then made up of Java's useful names as a way of specifying what we want the computer to do.

There are good names and bad names. Bad names aren't curse words, or TLA's (Three-Letter Acronyms), but names that aren't understandable or easy to use. A good set of encodings and names allow one to describe methods in a way that's natural, without having to say too much. The variety of different programming languages can be thought of as a collection of sets of namings-and-encodings. Some are better for some tasks than others. Some languages require you to write more to describe the same program (function) than others—but sometimes that "more" leads to a much more (human) readable program that helps others to understand what you're saying.

Philosophers and mathematicians look for very similar senses of quality. They try to describe the world in few words, using an elegant selection of words that cover many situations, while remaining understandable to their fellow philosophers and mathematicians. That's exactly what computer scientists do.

How the units and values (*data*) of a program can be interpreted is often also named. Remember how we said in Section 1.2 (page 7) that everything is stored in groups of eight bits called bytes, and we can interpret those bytes as numbers? In some programming languages, you can say explicitly that some value is a *byte*, and later tell the language to treat it as a number, an *integer* (or sometimes *int*). Similarly, you can tell the computer that these series of bytes is a collection of numbers (an *array of integers*), or a collection of characters (a *String*), or even as a more complex encoding of a single *floating point number* (any number with a decimal point in it).

In Java, we will explicitly tell the computer how to interpret our values. Languages such as Java, C++, and C# are *strongly typed*. Names are strongly associated with certain types or encodings. They require you to say that this name will only be associated with integers, and that one with floating point numbers. In Java, C++, and C# you can also create your own types which is part of what makes object-oriented languages so powerful. We do this in Java by defining classes such as Picture which represents a simple digital picture. An object of the `Picture` class has a width and height and you can get and set the pixels of the `Picture` object. This isn't a class that is part of the Java language, but a class that we have defined using Java to make it easier for students to work with digital pictures.

3.2   FILES AND THEIR NAMES

A programming language isn't the only place where computers associate names and values. Your computer's *operating system* takes care of the files on your disk, and it associates names with those files. Operating systems you may be familiar with include Windows XP, Windows 2000 (Windows ME, NT, . . .), MacOS, and Linux. A *file* is a collection of values (bytes) on your *hard disk* (the part of your computer that stores things after the power gets turned off). If you know the name of a file, you can tell it to the operating system, and it can give you the values associated with that name.

You may be thinking, "I've been using the computer for years, and I've *never* 'given a file name to the operating system.' " Maybe you didn't realize that you were doing it, but when you pick a file from a file choosing dialog in Photoshop, or double-click a file in a *directory* window (or Explorer or Finder), you are asking some software somewhere to give the name you're picking or double-clicking to the operating system, and get the values back. When you write your own programs, though, you'll be explicitly getting file names and asking for the values stored in a file.

Files are *very* important for media computation. Disks can store acres and acres of information on them. Remember our discussion of Moore's Law (page 9)? Disk capacity per dollar is increasing *faster* than computer speed per dollar! Computer disks today can store whole movies, hours (days?) of sounds, and the equivalent of hundreds of film rolls of pictures.

These media are not small. Even in a *compressed* form, screen size pictures can be over a million bytes large, and songs can be three million bytes or more. You need to keep them someplace where they'll last past the computer being turned off and where there's lots of space. This is why they are stored on your hard disk.

In contrast, your computer's memory (RAM) is impermanent (the contents disappear when the power does) and is relatively small. Computer memory is getting larger all the time, but it's still just a fraction of the amount of space on your disk. When you're working with media, you will load the media from the disk into memory, but you wouldn't want it to stay in memory after you're done. It's too big.

Think about your computer's memory as your desk. You would want to keep books that you are currently working with on your desk, but when you are done you will probably move them to a book shelf. You may have many more books on your book shelf than can fit on your desk. A computer can fit much more data on the hard disk than can fit in memory. However, data must be read from disk into memory before you can work with it.

When you bring things into memory, you usually will name the value, so that you can retrieve it and use it later. In that sense, programming is something like *algebra*. To write generalizable equations and functions (those that work for any number or value), you wrote equations and functions with *variables*, like $PV = nRT$ or $e = Mc^2$ or $f(x) = sin(x)$. Those P's, V's, R's, T's, e's, M's, c's, and x's were names for values. When you evaluated $f(30)$, you knew that the x was the name for 30 when computing f. We'll be naming values when we program.

3.3 CLASS AND OBJECT METHODS

Java also understands about *functions*. Remember functions from algebra? They're a "machine or box" into which you put one value, and out comes another. Java calls these *methods*.

However, you can't just call a function or method in Java like you can in some other languages. Every method or function in Java must be defined inside a class. There are two types of methods in Java: *class methods* or *object methods*. Class methods are methods that can be executed using the class name or on an object of the class. Object methods can only be executed on an object of the class. Class methods are used for general methods that don't pertain to a particular object. They are defined using the keyword `static`. Object methods work with a particular object's data (the object the method was called on).

3.3.1 Invoking Class Methods

Class methods can be invoked (executed) by using the class name followed by a period and then the method name: `ClassName.methodName();`. By convention, class names in Java start with an uppercase letter: like `Character`. The Character class is a *wrapper* class for the primitive type `char`. It also provides general character methods.

Making it Work Tip: Wrapper Classes

Wrapper classes are classes that you use to "wrap" around primitive types in order to have objects to work with. Many general purpose classes in Java, such as the collection classes (List and Set), require the values that you add to the collections to be objects. Since primitive types are *not* objects you wouldn't be able to use them in collections (prior to Java version 5.0). However, if you wrap a primitive type with a wrapper object you will be able to use it with classes that require objects. As of Java version 5.0 (also called jdk 1.5) the wrapping of a primitive value is automatically done when it is needed. This is called boxing and unboxing.

One of the class methods for the Character class takes a character as the *input* value (the value that goes into the box) and returns (the value that comes out of the box) the number that is the integer value for that character. Characters in Java are specified between single quotes: 'A'. The name of that method is getNumericValue and you can use System.out.println to display the value that the method getNumericValue returns:

```
> System.out.println(Character.getNumericValue('A'));
10
```

Another class method that's built in to the Math class in Java is named abs—it's the absolute value function. It returns the absolute value of the input numeric value.

```
> System.out.println(Math.abs(1));
1
> System.out.println(Math.abs(-1));
1
```

Debugging Tip: Common Typos

If you type a class name and Java can't figure out what class you are talking about, you will get an undefined class error.

```
> Mat.abs(-3);
Error: Undefined class 'Mat'
```

If you mistype a method (function) name, you will get the following error:

```
> Math.ab(-3);
Error: No 'ab' method in 'java.lang.Math'
```

3.3.2 Executing Object Methods

Object methods are methods that ***must*** be executed on an object using:

objectReference.methodName();

An object reference can be the name of an object variable. You can't invoke object methods using the class name like you can with class methods.

In Java there is a String class, which is how you represent lists of characters (letters), like the letters of a person's name. Objects of the String class are created by the compiler whenever it sees string literals (characters enclosed with double quotes), like "Barbara" or "cat.jpg". The double quotes tell the compiler that this is an object of the String class and not a variable name.

There are many object methods in the String class, such as toLowerCase() and toUpperCase(). These methods actually create and return new String objects (objects of the class String). See the API (application program interface) for the String class for a full listing of the available methods.

```
> String name = "Fred Farmer";
> System.out.println(name);
Fred Farmer
> String lowerName = name.toLowerCase();
> System.out.println(lowerName);
```

```
fred farmer
> String upperName = name.toUpperCase();
> System.out.println(upperName);
FRED FARMER
> System.out.println(name);
Fred Farmer
```

Notice that the value of name didn't change even though we invoked the method toLowerCase on it. All of the String methods that can modify a string don't change the original string but instead return a new string with the action done on that string. We say that strings are *immutable*, meaning that they don't change.

3.4   WORKING WITH TURTLES

Dr. Seymour Papert, at MIT, used robot turtles in the late 1960s to help children think about how to specify a procedure. The turtle had a pen in the middle of it that could be raised and lowered to leave a trail of its movements. As graphical displays became available he used a virtual turtle on a computer screen.

We are going to work with some turtle objects that move around a world. The turtles know how to move forward, turn left, turn right, and turn by some specified angle. The turtles have a pen in the middle of them that leaves a trail to show their movements. The world keeps track of the turtles that are in it.

3.4.1   Defining Classes

How does the computer know what we mean by a world and a turtle? We have to define what a world is, what it knows about, and what it can do. We have to define what a turtle is, what it knows about, and what it can do. We do this by writing class definitions for World and Turtle. In Java each new class is usually defined in a file with the same name as the class and an extension of ".java". Class names start with a capital letter and the first letter of each additional word is capitalized. So we define the class Turtle in the file Turtle.java. We define the class World in the file World.java. The class Turtle inherits from a class called SimpleTurtle (notice that the first letter of each additional word is capitalized). We have defined these classes for you so that you can practice creating and sending messages to objects.

3.4.2   Creating Objects

Object-oriented programs consist of objects. But how do we create those objects? The class knows what each object of that class needs to keep track of and what it should be able to do, so the class creates the objects of that class. You can think of a class as an object factory. The factory can create many objects. A class is also like a cookie cutter. You can make many cookies from one cookie cutter and they will all have the same shape. Or you can think of the class as a blueprint and the objects as the houses that you can create from the blueprint.

To create and initialize an object use new *Class(parameterList)* where the parameter list is a list of items used to initialize the new object. This asks the object that defines the class to reserve space in memory for the data that an object of that class needs to keep track of and also keep a reference to the object that defines the class. The new object's data will be initialized based on the items passed in the parameter list. There can be several ways to initialize a new object and which one you are using depends on the order and types of things in the parameter list.

One way to create an object of the class `World` is to use `new World()`. We don't *have* to pass any parameters to initialize the new world. Objects can have default values.

```
> System.out.println(new World());
A 640 by 480 world with 0 turtles in it.
```

Common Bug: Finding Classes

You should have set your classpath to include the classes from the book in Chapter 2. If you didn't do this you will get an error message (Undefined Class) when you try to create a `World` object. Make sure that the full path to the directory that has the classes from the book is in your classpath. The classpath tells Java where to look for the compiled class definitions. Java needs to load the class definition before it can create an object of a class.

When you type the above in the interactions pane you will see a window appear with the title "World", as shown in Figure 3.1. We have created an object of the `World` class which has a width of 640 and a height of 480. The world doesn't have any turtles in it yet. We would like to add a turtle to this world, but we have a problem. We don't have any way to refer to this `World` object. We didn't declare a variable that refers to that object in memory, so it will just be garbage collected after you close the window. Go ahead and close the window and let's try again, but this time we will declare a variable to let us refer to the `World` object again.

When we declare a variable we are associating a name with the memory location so that we can access it again using it's name. To declare a variable in Java you must give the type of the variable and a name for it:

Type name;

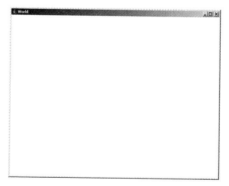

FIGURE 3.1
A window that shows a `World` object.

The *Type* is the name of the class if you are creating a variable that refers to an object. So to create a variable that will refer to a `World` object we need to say the type is `World` and give it a name. The first word in the variable name should be lowercase but the first letter of each additional word should be uppercase. The name should describe what the variable represents. So, let's declare a variable that refers to an object of the class `World` using the name `worldObj`.

```
> World worldObj = new World();
> System.out.println(worldObj);
A 640 by 480 world with 0 turtles in it.
```

This says to create a variable with the name of `worldObj` that will be of type `World` (will refer to an object of the class `World`). It will refer to the object created by the `World` class because of the code: `new World()`. We can use `System.out.println(worldObj)` to ask the new `World` object to print out some information about itself.

To create a turtle object in this world we will again use:

new *Class(parameterList)*

This time we will ask the `Turtle` class to create the object in our `World` by passing a reference to the world to create it in. We will declare a variable so that we can refer to the `Turtle` object again.

```
> Turtle turtle1 = new Turtle(worldObj);
> System.out.println(turtle1);
No name turtle at 320, 240 heading 0.
```

Now a `Turtle` object appears in the middle of the `World` object, as shown in Figure 3.2. This turtle hasn't been assigned a name and has a location of (320,240) and a heading of 0 which is north. The default location for a new turtle is the middle of the `World` object. The default heading is 0 (north).

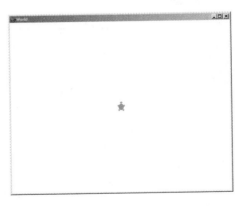

FIGURE 3.2
A window that shows a `Turtle` object in a `World` object.

We can create another `Turtle` object and this time we can say what location we want it to appear at. To do this we need to pass more than one parameter in the parameter list of items used to initialize the new object. To do this separate the values with commas.

```
> Turtle turtle2 = new Turtle(30,50,worldObj);
> System.out.println(turtle2);
No name turtle at 30, 50 heading 0.
```

Notice that the second turtle appears at the specified location (30,50) as shown in Figure 3.3. The top left of the window is location (0,0). The x values increase going to the right and the y values increase going down.

3.4.3   Sending Messages to Objects

We have been talking about executing or invoking methods on classes and objects. A more object-oriented way of saying that is that we send messages to objects to ask them to do things. The full syntax for sending a message is

objectReference.message(parameterList);

The `objectReference` is a reference to an object, `message` is what we want the object to do, and `parameterList` is any additional information that more fully describes what we want the object to do. The '.' and '()' are required even if there is no parameter list.

Turtles know how to go forward, turn left, turn right, turn by a specified angle, change their color, and set their names. So if we want turtle1 to go forward 20 steps we would use `turtle1.forward(20);`. If we want it to turn left we would use `turtle1.turnLeft();`. If we want it to turn right, we would use `turtle1.turnRight();`. If we want it to turn by an angle to the left by 45 degrees, we would use `turtle1.turn(-45);`. To turn turtle1 to the right 45 degrees, use `turtle1.turn(45);`. Negative angles turn to the left, and positive angles turn that amount to the right.

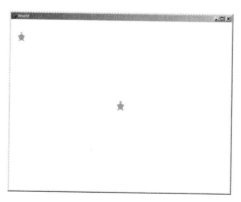

FIGURE 3.3
A window that shows two `Turtle` objects in a `World` object.

We actually don't need to use `System.out.println()`; *every* time we ask the computer to do something. If we want to call a method that doesn't return anything we can just ask the method to be executed by typing the variable name for the object followed by a '.' and then the method name and its input (if any) in parentheses followed by a semicolon.

```
> turtle1.forward(20);
> turtle1.turnLeft();
> turtle1.forward(30);
> turtle1.turnRight();
> turtle1.forward(40);
> turtle1.turn(-45);
> turtle1.forward(30);
> turtle1.turn(90);
> turtle1.forward(20);
```

In Figure 3.4 we see the trail of the first turtle's movements. Notice that all of the messages were sent to the first `Turtle` object that is referenced by the `turtle1` variable. The messages only get sent to that object. Notice that the second `Turtle` object didn't move. It didn't get any messages yet. To send a message to the second `Turtle` object, we use the variable name that refers to that `Turtle` object which is `turtle2`.

```
> turtle2.turnRight();
> turtle2.forward(200);
> turtle2.turnRight();
> turtle2.forward(200);
```

In Figure 3.5 we see the trail of the second turtle's movement. Can you draw a square with a turtle? Can you draw a triangle with a turtle? Can you draw a pentagon with a turtle? How about a circle?

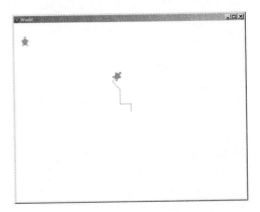

FIGURE 3.4
The result of messages to the first `Turtle` object.

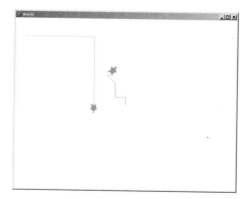

FIGURE 3.5
The result of messages to the second Turtle object.

3.4.4   Objects Control Their State

In object-oriented programming we ask an object to doing something by sending it a message. The object can refuse to do what you ask it to do. Why would an object refuse? An object *should* refuse when you ask it to do something that would cause its data to be wrong. The world that the turtles are in is 640 by 480. Try asking the Turtle object to go forward past the end of the world. What happens? First click the RESET button to reset the interactions pane. When you reset the interactions pane you get rid of any currently declared variables. Then create a new World and Turtle.

```
> World world1 = new World();
> Turtle turtle1 = new Turtle(world1);
> System.out.println(turtle1);
No name turtle at 320, 240 heading 0.
> turtle1.turnRight();
> turtle1.forward(400);
> System.out.println(turtle1);
No name turtle at 639, 240 heading 90.
> System.out.println(world1.getWidth());
640
```

Remember that Turtle objects are first created in the middle of the world (320, 240) facing the top of the world. When the turtle turned right it was facing the right side of the window. If the turtle went forward 400 steps, it would be past the right edge of the window ($320 + 400 = 720$) because the x values increase to the right. Notice that the turtle stops when the middle of it reaches the limit of the window (639) as shown in Figure 3.6. This means your turtle will always have at least part of it in the world.

It may seem strange that turtle1 stopped when it reached 639 but the first pixel is at 0 and the last is 639. If we asked you to count 10 numbers starting at 0, you should end at 9. The number of items is the ending value minus the starting value plus 1. So $639 - 0 + 1$ is 640, which means that a window with a width of 640 that starts with 0 must end at 639.

FIGURE 3.6
The turtle won't leave the world.

3.4.5   Additional Turtle Capabilities

You may not want to see the turtle, but just the trail of its movements. To ask the turtle to stop drawing itself, send it the message hide(). To start drawing the turtle again send it the message show().

On the other hand you may not want to see the trail. Ask the turtle to stop showing the trail by asking it to pick up the pen penUp(). To start showing the trail again send the turtle the message penDown().

You can ask a turtle to move to a particular location by sending it the message moveTo(x,y) where x is the x value that you want to move to and y is the y value that you want to move to.

You can ask a turtle to use a particular name by sending it the message setName(*name*) where name is the new name to use. If you print the variable that refers to a turtle, you will see the name printed. You can also get a turtle's name by sending it the message getName().

We can use these new messages to draw two squares with a turtle. First reset the interactions pane and create a world and a turtle. Name the turtle "Jane". Draw one square with an upper left corner at (50, 50) and a width and height of 30. Draw another square at (200, 200) with a width and height of 30. We can use new Turtle(x,y,world) to create a turtle object that is located at (x,y). Let's turn off seeing the turtle when we draw the second square by sending it the message hide().

```
> World world1 = new World();
> Turtle turtle1 = new Turtle(50,50,world1);
> turtle1.setName("Jane");
> turtle1.turnRight();
> turtle1.forward(30);
> turtle1.turnRight();
> turtle1.forward(30);
> turtle1.turnRight();
> turtle1.forward(30);
> turtle1.turnRight();
```

```
> turtle1.forward(30);
> turtle1.penUp();
> turtle1.moveTo(200,200);
> turtle1.hide();
> turtle1.penDown();
> turtle1.turnRight();
> turtle1.forward(30);
> turtle1.turnRight();
> turtle1.forward(30);
> turtle1.turnRight();
> turtle1.forward(30);
> turtle1.turnRight();
> turtle1.forward(30);
> System.out.println(turtle1);
Jane turtle at 200, 200 heading 0.
```

You can see the result of these commands in Figure 3.7.

FIGURE 3.7
Drawing two squares with a turtle.

Making it Work Tip: Reuse the Previous Line in DrJava

You can use the up arrow on the keyboard to bring up previous lines you have typed in the interactions pane in DrJava. This is easier than typing the same line in again.

3.5   CREATING METHODS

We had to send many messages to our Turtle object just to draw two squares. Do you notice any similarities in how we draw the squares? Each time we draw a square we turn right and go forward by 30 steps for a total of four times. It would be nice to name the list of steps for drawing a square and then just do the list of steps when a turtle is asked to draw a square. We do this by creating a method that knows how to draw a square. Methods are named blocks of commands that are defined inside a class definition. Once we have defined a method and successfully compiled the class definition, the objects of the class will respond to a message with the same name and parameters as the new method. So if we want `Turtle` objects to understand the message `drawSquare()`, we define a method `drawSquare()`.

Computer Science Idea: Messages Map to Methods

When we send an object a message, it must map to a method that objects of that class understand. If objects of the class don't understand the message, you will get an error when you compile. Be sure that the parameter list is correct, because if it isn't you will get an error that says such a method does not exist. Make sure that you compile a new method before you try and use it. ■

You have seen how to declare variables in Java:

`type name;` or `type name = expression;`.

To declare a method in Java use:

`visibility type methodName(parameterList)`

The structure of how you declare a method is referred to as the *syntax* — the words and characters that have to be there for Java to understand what's going on, and the order of those things.

A method declaration has a *visibility* (usually the keyword `public`), the type of the thing being returned from the method, the method name, and the parameter list in parentheses. This is usually followed by a *block* of statements which is an open curly brace followed by a series of statements followed by a close curly brace. The statements in the block will be executed when the method is invoked.

Common Bug: Curly Braces Come in Pairs

Each open curly brace in your Java code must have a matching close curly brace. You should indent code inside of a pair of curly braces. Indentation doesn't matter to the compiler but makes your code easier to read and understand. Be careful not to mix up curly braces and parentheses. ■

To declare a method that will draw a square we can use:

```
public void drawSquare()
{
    // statements to execute when the method is executed
}
```

The visibility in this method declaration is `public`. **Visibility** means who can invoke the method (ask for the method to be executed). The keyword `public` means that this method can be invoked by any code in any class definition. If the keyword `private` is used then the method can only be accessed from inside the class definition. You can think of this as a security feature. If you keep your journal on the Web (a blog), then it is open and anyone can read it. If you keep it hidden in your room then it is private and hopefully only you can read it.

The return type in this method declaration is `void`. The return type is required and is given before the method name. If you leave off a return type you will get a compiler error. If your method returns a value the return type must match the type of the value returned. Remember that types can be any of the primitive types (`char`, `byte`, `int`, `short`, `long`, `float`, `double`, or `boolean`) or a class name. Methods that don't return any value use the Java keyword `void` for the return type in the method declaration.

The method name in this declaration is `drawSquare`. By convention method names start with a lowercase letter and the first letter of each additional word is uppercase: `drawSquare`. Another example method name is `turnRight`.

A method **must** have parentheses following the method name. If any parameters are passed to the method then they will be declared inside the parentheses separated by commas. To declare a parameter, you must give a type and name. The type can be any primitive type or class name. The name can be used by the code in the body of the method to refer to the passed value.

We create a collection of statements by defining a *block*. A block is code between an open curly brace '{'and a close curly brace'}'. The block of commands that follow a method declaration are the ones associated with the name of the method (function) and are the ones that will be executed when the method is invoked.

Most real programs that do useful things require the definition of more than one method (function). Imagine that in the definitions pane you have several method declarations. How do you think Java will figure out that one method has ended and a new one begun? Java needs some way of figuring out where the *method body* ends: Which statements are part of this method and which are part of the next? Java uses curly braces to do this. All statements between the open curly brace and close curly brace are part of the method body.

Debugging Tip: Proper Method Declarations

All method declarations must be **inside** a class definition which means that they are defined inside the open '{' and close '}' curly braces that enclose the body of the class definition. If you put a method declaration after the end of the class definition you will get "Error: 'class' or 'interface' expected". Methods can not be defined inside of other methods. If you accidently do this you will get "Error: illegal start of expression" at the beginning of the inner method declaration. Statements in a method end in a semicolon (this is not optional in the definitions pane). If you forget to put the semicolon at the end of a statement, you will get "Error: ';' expected". All compiler errors will highlight the line of code that caused the error. If you don't see the error on that line of code, check the preceding line. You can double-click on an error in the "Compiler Output" area and it will place the cursor at that line of code and highlight it.

We can now define our first program (method)! Open Turtle.java by clicking on the OPEN button near the top of the window and using the file chooser to pick "Turtle.java". Type the following code into the definitions pane of DrJava before the last closing curly brace '}' (which ends the class definition). When you're done, save the file and click the COMPILE ALL button near the top of the window (Figure 3.8).

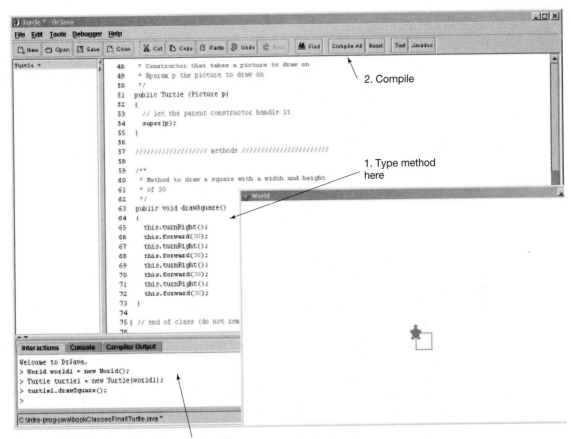

FIGURE 3.8
Defining and executing drawSquare().

Debugging Tip: Compile All

The COMPILE ALL button will compile all open files. If you have an empty file open named (UNTITLED) go ahead and close it. DrJava creates this for you so that you can start writing a new class definition. But we won't do that right away. Select the name of the file in the Files Pane and press the CLOSE button to close a file.
■

Program 2: Draw a Square

```java
public void drawSquare()
{
    this.turnRight();
    this.forward(30);
    this.turnRight();
    this.forward(30);
    this.turnRight();
```

```
    this.forward(30);
    this.turnRight();
    this.forward(30);
}
```

Making it Work Tip: Copying and Pasting

Text can be copied and pasted between the interactions pane and definitions pane. To copy text select it and click COPY (in the EDIT menu), then click in the definitions pane and click on PASTE (also in the EDIT menu). You can also use keyboard shortcuts for copy (Control-c) and paste (Control-v). This means to hold the "Ctrl" key and then press the "c" key to copy and hold the "Ctrl" key and the 'v' key to paste. You can copy entire methods in the definitions pane by selecting the text in the method and then copying and pasting it. You can select a method name in the definitions pane and paste it in the interactions pane to send a message asking for that method to be executed. You can also try things out in the interactions pane and later save them in a method in the definitions pane.

Notice that we changed `turtle1.turnRight();` to `this.turnRight();`. The variable `turtle1` isn't defined inside the method `drawSquare()`. Variables names are known in a *context* (area that they apply). This is also known as the *scope* of a variable. The variables that we define in the interactions pane are only known in the interactions pane, they aren't known inside methods. We need some other way to reference the object that we want to turn. Object methods are *implicitly* passed a reference to the object the method was invoked on. You can refer to that current object using the keyword `this`.

Compiling a Java class definition "Turtle.java" will produce a "Turtle.class" file. Compiling translates the Java source code which is in a format that humans understand into a format that computers understand. One of the advantages to Java is that the ".class" files aren't specific to any particular type of computer. They can be understood by any computer that has a Java run-time environment. So you can create your Java source code on a Window's based computer and run the compiled code on an Apple computer.

Making it Work Tip: Try *Every* Program!

To really understand what's going on, type in, compile, and execute *every* program (method) in the book. *EVERY* one. None are long, and the practice will go a long way toward convincing you that the programs work, developing your programming skill, and helping you understand *why* they work.

This code creates a method with the name `drawSquare` that takes no parameters and whenever the method is executed it will execute the statements inside of the open and close curly braces. It is a `public` method. It doesn't return anything so it uses the keyword `void` to indicate this. This method **must** be called on an object of the Turtle class. The this is a keyword that refers to the object this method was invoked on. Since this method is defined in the Turtle class the keyword this will refer to a Turtle object.

Once the method has successfully compiled you can ask for it to be executed by sending a message to a Turtle object with the same name and parameter list as the method. Click on the INTERACTIONS tab in the interactions pane (near the bottom of the window). This method doesn't take any parameters, so just finish with the open and close parentheses and the semicolon. When you compile the interactions pane will be reset, meaning that all the variables we have defined in the interactions pane will no longer be understood. We will need to create a World and Turtle object again.

```
> World world1 = new World();
> Turtle turtle1 = new Turtle(world1);
> turtle1.drawSquare();
```

When you invoke the method drawSquare() on the Turtle object referenced by the variable turtle1, the Java Virtual Machine has to find the method to execute. Methods are defined inside of a class definition so we defined drawSquare inside of the class Turtle by editing the file Turtle.java. Next we compiled the source file Turtle.java which created a Turtle.class file which contained the code for the Turtle class in byte codes for the Java virtual machine.

The first time you use a class the Java Virtual Machine loads the compiled class definition (the Turtle.class file) and creates an object that contains all the information about the class including the code for the methods. Every object has a reference to the object that defines its class as shown by Figure 3.9. The object that defines a class is an object of a class named Class. You can get the Class object using the method getClass().

```
> System.out.println(world1.getClass());
class World
> System.out.println(turtle1.getClass());
class Turtle
```

The Java Virtual Machine will check for a method with the same name and parameter list in the object that defines the class (an object of the class Class) and if it is found it will execute that method. This means that the statements in the body of the method will be executed starting with the first statement. The object that the method was invoked on is implicitly passed to the method as well and can be referred to using the keyword this.

What if we want to draw a larger or smaller square? We could change each of the this.forward(30); lines to the new width and height and then compile. But, it would be easier to declare a variable in the method that would represent the width of the square and then use that variable name as the amount to go forward by like this: this.forward(width);. Then if we want to change the size of the square we only have to change 1 line. You can declare a variable anywhere in the body of a method but you *must* declare it before you use it. The name will be known and the

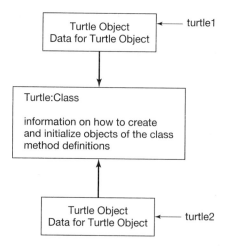

FIGURE 3.9
An object stores data for that object and has a reference to the class that created it.

value substituted for each occurrence of the name in the rest of the method. But the name will only be known inside the method it is declared in.

We can't have two methods with the same name and the same parameter list so we need a new name for this method. We simply named it drawSquare2 to show that it is the second version. We can copy the first method and paste it and rename it and then change it to declare and use the width variable.

Program 3: Draw Square Using a Variable for Width

```
public void drawSquare2()
{
    int width = 30;
    this.turnRight();
    this.forward(width);
    this.turnRight();
    this.forward(width);
    this.turnRight();
    this.forward(width);
    this.turnRight();
    this.forward(width);
}
```

Compile and run this method and check that you get the same results as with drawSquare().

```
> World world = new World();
> Turtle turtle1 = new Turtle(world);
> turtle1.drawSquare2();
```

3.5.1   Methods that Take Input

This is a bit better than the first version and a bit easier to change. But, you still have to recompile after you change the width to draw a larger or smaller square. Wouldn't it be nice if there was a way to tell the method what size you want when you ask for the method to be executed by sending a message that matches the method? Well you can! That is what the parameter list is for.

We can make the width of the square a parameter. Remember that if a method takes a parameter you must list the type and name for the parameter in the parameter list. What type should we use for width? Well, in the second version we used `int` because the turtle only takes whole steps not fractional ones so let's use that. What should we call this method? We could call it `drawSquare3(int width)` but someone may think this means it draws a square with a width of 3. We could call it `drawSquareWithPassedWidth(int width)` but that is rather long and you can tell it takes a passed width by looking at the parameter list. How about if we just call it `drawSquare(int width)`? You may think that isn't allowed since we have a method `drawSquare()`, but that method doesn't take any parameters and our new method does. Java allows you to use the same method name as another method as long as the parameter list is different. This is called *method overloading*.

Program 4: Draw Square with Width as a Parameter
```java
/**
 * Method to draw a square with a width and height
 * of some passed amount.
 * @param width the width and height to use
 */
public void drawSquare(int width)
{
  this.turnRight();
  this.forward(width);
  this.turnRight();
  this.forward(width);
  this.turnRight();
  this.forward(width);
  this.turnRight();
  this.forward(width);
}
```

Type in the new method declaration and compile. Let's try this new method out.

```java
> World world1 = new World();
> Turtle turtle1 = new Turtle(world1);
> turtle1.drawSquare(200);
```

When you execute `turtle1.drawSquare(200);` you are asking the object referred to by the variable named turtle1 to execute a method named `drawSquare` that takes an integer parameter. The method `drawSquare` will use 200 for the parameter

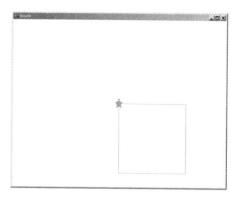

FIGURE 3.10
Showing the result of sending the width as a parameter to drawSquare.

width everywhere it appears in the method drawSquare, with the result shown in Figure 3.10. The parameter name width is known throughout the body of the method. This is very similar to drawSquare2() but has the advantage that we don't need to change the method and recompile to use a different width.

An important reason for using parameters is to make a method more *general*. Consider method drawSquare(int width). That method handles the *general* case of drawing a square. We call that kind of generalization *abstraction*. Abstraction leads to general solutions that work in lots of situations.

Making it Work Tip: Use Names that Make Sense

We called the first method drawSquare() and the second drawSquare2(). Does it matter? Absolutely not! Well, not to the computer, at any rate. The computer doesn't care what names you use—they're entirely for your benefit. Pick names that (a) are meaningful to you (so that you can read and understand your program), (b) are meaningful to others (so that others can read and understand it), and (c) are easy to type. Long names, like,

drawARectangleWithEqualWidthAndHeight

are meaningful, easy-to-read, but are a pain to type.

Does this mean that you can use "orange" as a method name? Yes, you can, but it may be confusing even for you, and especially confusing for others. It helps to use method names that indicate what the method does.

Defining a method that takes input is very easy. It continues to be a matter of *substitution* and *evaluation*. We'll put a type and name inside those parentheses after the method name. The names given inside the parentheses are called the *parameters* or *input variables*.

When you evaluate the method, by specifying its name with *input values* (also called the *arguments*) inside parentheses, such as turtle1.drawSquare(20); or new Turtle(20,30,world1), each parameter variable is set to **a copy** of the argument value. This is called *pass by value*. All arguments in Java are passed by making a copy of their value. Does this mean that we make a copy of the World object when we pass it as a parameter? No, we just make a copy of the object reference which means we make another reference to that World object.

3.6   WORKING WITH MEDIA

What if we want to create and manipulate media like pictures or sounds? Just as we created the World and Turtle classes to define what we mean by these to the computer we have created Picture and Sound classes.

3.6.1   Creating a Picture Object

How would you create a picture? The syntax for creating an object is

new *Class(parameterList)*

Try entering the following in the interactions pane.

```
> System.out.println(new Picture());
Picture, filename null height 100 width 200
```

It looks like we created a Picture object with a height of 100 and a width of 200, but why don't we see it? New objects of the class Picture aren't shown automatically. You have to ask them to show themselves using the message show(). So let's ask the Picture object to show itself. Oops, we forgot to declare a variable to refer to the Picture object, so we don't have any way to access it. Let's try it again and this time declare a variable for it. The syntax for declaring a variable is *type name*; or *type name = expression*;. The type is the name of the class so we will use a type of Picture. What should the name be? Well the name should describe what the object is so let's use picture1.

```
> Picture picture1 = new Picture();
> picture1.show();
```

Now we can see the created picture in Figure 3.11.

FIGURE 3.11
Creating a Picture object using new Picture().

Why doesn't it have anything in it? When you create a `Picture` object using `new Picture()` the default width is 200 and the default height is 100 and the default is that all of the pixels in the picture are white. How can we create a picture from data in a file from a digital camera? We can use `new Picture(String fileName)` which takes an object of the `String` class which is the fully qualified file name of a file to read the picture information from.

What is the *fully qualified file name* of a file? The full or complete name of a file is the path to the file as well as the base file name and extension. How can we get the full file name for a file? One way is to use another class we have created for you. The `FileChooser` class has a class method `pickAFile()` which will display a dialog window that will help you pick a file.

```
> System.out.println(FileChooser.pickAFile());
```

Common Bug: File Chooser doesn't Appear

If you don't see the window with the file chooser in it after typing in the code above, try minimizing your DrJava window. Sometimes the file chooser comes up behind the DrJava window.

You're probably already familiar with how to use a file chooser or file dialog as shown in Figure 3.12:

- Double-click on folders/directories to open them.
- Click on the top right iconic button to see the details about the files such as the types of files they are (if you put the cursor over the button and leave it there it

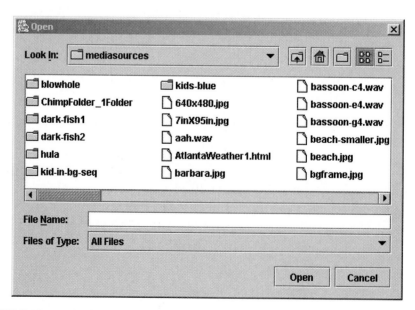

FIGURE 3.12
The File Chooser.

will show "Details"). To create a picture we want to pick a file with a type of "JPEG Image". To create a sound we would pick a file with a type of "Wave Sound".

- Click on the file name to select it and then click OPEN, or double-click, to select a file.

Once you select a file, what gets returned is the *full file name* as a string (a sequence of characters). (If you click CANCEL, pickAFile() returns null which is a predefined value in Java that means that it doesn't refer to a valid object). Try it, type the code below after the > in the interactions pane and select a file by clicking the mouse button when the cursor points to the desired file name, then click on the OPEN button.

```
> System.out.println(FileChooser.pickAFile());
C:\intro-prog-java\mediasources\flower1.jpg
```

What *you* get when you finally select a file will depend on your operating system. On Windows, your file name will probably start with C: and will have backslashes in it (e.g., \). There are really two parts to this file name:

- The character between words (e.g., the \ between "intro-prog-java" and "mediasources") is called the *path separator*. Everything from the beginning of the file name to the last path separator is called the *path* to the file. That describes exactly *where* on the hard disk (in which *directory*) a file exists. A directory is like a drawer of a file cabinet and it can hold many files. A directory can even hold other directories.

- The last part of the file (e.g., "flower1.jpg") is called the *base file name*. When you look at the file in the Finder/Explorer/Directory window (depending on your operating system), that's the part you see. The last three characters (after the period) are called the *file extension*. They identify the encoding of the file. You may not see the extension depending on the settings you have. But, if you show the detail view (top right iconic button on the file chooser) you will see the file types. Look for files of type "JPEG Image".

Files that have an extension of ".jpg" or a type of "JPEG Image" are *JPEG* files. They contain pictures. (To be picky, they contain data that can be *interpreted* to be a *representation* of a picture—but that's close enough to "they contain pictures.") JPEG is a standard *encoding* (a representation) for any kind of image. The other kind of media files that we'll be using frequently are ".wav" files (Figure 3.13). The ".wav" extension means that these are *WAV* files. They contain sounds. WAV is a standard encoding for sounds. There are many other kinds of extensions for files, and there are even many other kinds of media extensions. For example, there are also GIF (".gif") files for images and AIFF (".aif" or ".aiff") files for sounds. We'll stick to JPEG and WAV in this text, just to avoid too much complexity.

3.6.2 Showing a Picture

So now we know how to get a complete file name: path and base name. This *doesn't* mean that we have the file itself loaded into memory. To get the file into memory,

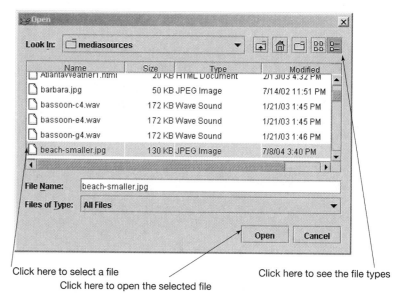

Click here to select a file
Click here to open the selected file
Click here to see the file types

FIGURE 3.13
File chooser with media types identified.

we have to tell Java how to interpret this file. *We* know that JPEG files are pictures, but we have to tell Java explicitly to read the file and make a Picture object from it (an object of the Picture class).

The way we create and initialize new objects in Java is to ask the class to create a new object using new *ClassName(parameterList)*. The class contains the description of the data each object of the class needs to have so it is the thing that knows how to create objects of that class. You can think of a class as a factory for making objects of that class. So, to create a new object of the Picture class from a file name use new Picture(fileName). The fileName is the name of a file as a string. We know how to get a file name using FileChooser.pickAFile().

```
> System.out.println(new Picture(FileChooser.pickAFile()));
Picture, filename
c:\intro-prog-java\mediasources\beach-smaller.jpg height 360 width
480
```

The result from System.out.println suggests that we did in fact make a Picture object, from a given filename and with a given height and width. Success! Oh, you wanted to actually *see* the picture? We'll need another method! The method to show the picture is named show().

You ask a Picture object to show itself using the method show(). It may seem strange to say that a picture knows how to show itself but in object-oriented programming we treat objects as intelligent beings that know how to do the things that we would expect an object to be able to do, or that someone would want to do to it. We typically show pictures, so in object-oriented programming Picture objects know how to show themselves (make themselves visible).

3.6.3 Variable Substitution

We can now pick a file, make a picture, and show it in a couple of different ways.

- We can do it all at once because the result from one method can be used in the next method: `new Picture(FileChooser.pickAFile()).show()`. That's what we see in Figure 3.14. This code will first invoke the `pickAFile()` class method of the class `FileChooser` because it is inside the parentheses. The `pickAFile()` method will return the name of the selected file as a string. Next it will create a new `Picture` object with the selected file name. And finally it will ask the created `Picture` object to show itself.

- The second way is to *name* each of the pieces by declaring variables. To declare a *variable* (a name for data) use `type name;` or `type name=expression;`.

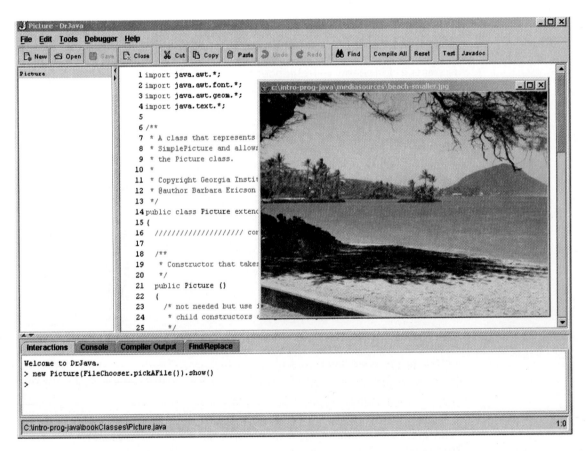

FIGURE 3.14
Picking, making, and showing a picture, using the result of each method in the next method. The picture used is beach-smaller.jpg.

Making it Work Tip: Types in Java

A type in Java can be any of the predefined *primitive* types (char, byte, int, short, long, float, double, or boolean) or the name of a class. Java is not a completely object-oriented language in that the primitive types are not objects.

Why are there so many primitive types? The answer has to do with how many bits you want to use to represent a value. The more bits you use the larger the number that you can store. We will only use int, float, double, and boolean in this book. The type int is for integer numbers and takes up 32 bits. The type float is for floating point numbers and takes up 32 bits. The type double is for floating point numbers and takes up 64 bits. The type boolean is for things that are just true or false so a boolean value could be stored in just 1 bit. However, how much space a boolean takes isn't specified in the Java language specifications (it depends on the Virtual Machine). Java uses primitive types to speed calculations.

A class name used as a type can be either a class defined as part of the Java language like (String, JFrame, or BufferedImage) or a class that you or someone else created (like the Picture class we created).

Try the following in the interactions pane. Pick a file name that ends in ".jpg".

```
> String fileName = FileChooser.pickAFile();
> Picture pictureObj = new Picture(fileName);
> pictureObj.show();
```

As you can see we can name the file that we get from FileChooser.pickAFile() by using (String fileName =). This says that the variable named fileName will be of type String (will refer to an object of the String class) and that the String object that it will refer to will be returned from FileChooser.pickAFile(). In a similar fashion we can create a variable named pictureObj that will refer to an object of the Picture class that we get from creating a new Picture object with the fileName using Picture pictureObj = new Picture(fileName). We can then ask that Picture object to show itself by sending it the show() message using pictureObj.show(). That's what we see in Figure 3.15.

Making it Work Tip: Java Conventions

By convention all class names in Java begin with an uppercase letter, all variable and method names begin with a lowercase letter. This will help you tell the difference between a class name and a variable or method name. So, Picture is a class name since it starts with a uppercase letter and pictureObj is a variable name since it starts with a lowercase letter. If a name has several words in it, the convention is to uppercase the first letter of each additional word like pickAFile(). A convention is the usual way of doing something, which means that the compiler won't care if you don't do it this way, but other programmers will tar and feather you because it will make your programs harder to understand.

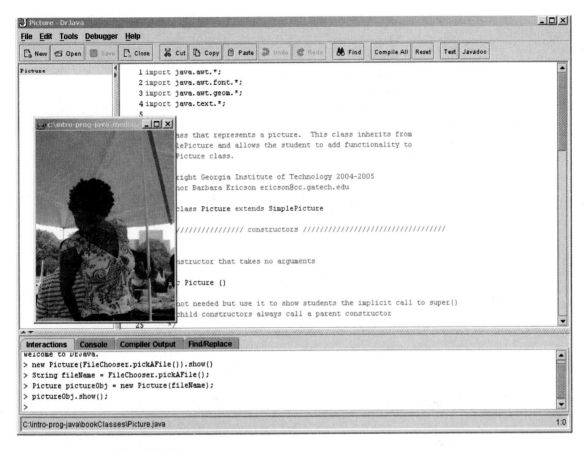

FIGURE 3.15
Picking, making, and showing a picture, when naming the pieces. The picture shown is tammy.jpg. Tammy is computer science graduate student at Georgia Tech.

Debugging Tip: Method Names must be Followed by Parentheses!

In Java all methods have to have parentheses after the method name both when you declare the method and when you invoke it. You can't leave off the parentheses even if the method doesn't take any parameters. So, you must type `pictureObj.show()` not `pictureObj.show`.

If you try `pictureObj.show()`, you'll notice that there is no output from this method. Methods in Java don't *have* to return a value, unlike real mathematical functions. A method may just do something (like display a picture).

3.6.4   Object References

When the type of a variable is `int` or `double` or `boolean` we call that a *primitive* variable. As you have seen when a primitive variable is declared space is reserved to represent that variable's value and the name is used to find the address of that reserved space. If the type is `int` then 32 bits of space (4 bytes) is reserved. If the type is `double` then 64 bits of space (8 bytes) is reserved.

When the type of a variable is the name of a class (like `String`) then this is called an *object variable* or *object reference*. Unlike primitive variables, object variables do not reserve space for the value of the variable. How could they? How much space do you need for an object? How about an object of the class `String`? How about an object of the class `Picture`? The amount of space you need for an object depends on the number and types of fields (data) each object of that class has.

Object variables (references) reserve space for a *reference* to an object of the given class. A reference allows the computer to *determine* the address of the actual object (it isn't just the address of the object). If the object variable is declared but not assigned to an object the reference is set to `null` which means that it doesn't refer to any object yet.

3.6.5 Playing a Sound

We can replicate this entire process with sounds.

- We still use `FileChooser.pickAFile()` to find the file we want and get its file name.

- We use `new Sound(fileName)` to make a `Sound` object using the passed `fileName` as the file to read the sound information from.

- We will use `play()` to play the sound. The method `play()` is an object method (invoked on a `Sound` object). It plays the sound one time. It doesn't return anything.

Here are the same steps we saw previously with pictures:

```
> System.out.println(FileChooser.pickAFile());
C:\intro-prog-java\mediasources\croak.wav
> System.out.println(new Sound(FileChooser.pickAFile()));
Sound file: croak.wav length: 17616
> new Sound(FileChooser.pickAFile()).play();
```

The `FileChooser.pickAFile();` allows you to pick a file with a file chooser and the `System.out.println` that is around this displays the full file name that was picked. The code `System.out.println(new Sound(FileChooser.pickA-File()));` also allows you to pick a file, then it creates a sound object from the full file name, and finally it displays information about the sound object: the file name, and the length of the sound. We'll explain what the length of the sound means in Chapter 8. The code `new Sound(FileChooser.pickAFile()).play();` has you pick a file name, creates the sound object using that file name, and tells that sound object to play.

Please do try this on your own, using WAV files that you have on your own computer, that you make yourself, or that came on your CD. (We talk more about where to get the media and how to create it in future chapters.)

3.6.6   Naming Your Media (and other Values)

The code `new Sound(FileChooser.pickAFile()).play()` looks awfully complicated and long to type. You may be wondering if there are ways to simplify it. We
can actually do it just the way that mathematicians have for centuries: We name the
pieces! The results from methods (functions) can be named, and these names can be
used as the inputs to other methods.

```
> String fileName = FileChooser.pickAFile();
> Sound soundObj = new Sound(fileName);
> soundObj.play();
```

3.6.7   Naming the Result of a Method

We can assign names to the *results* of methods (functions). If we name the result
from `FileChooser.pickAFile()`, each time we print the name, we get the same
result. We don't have to rerun `FileChooser.pickAFile()`. Naming code in order
to re-execute it is what we're doing when we define methods (functions), which
comes up in Section 3.5.

```
> String fileName = FileChooser.pickAFile();
> System.out.println(fileName);
C:\intro-prog-java\mediasources\beach-smaller.jpg
> System.out.println(fileName);
C:\intro-prog-java\mediasources\beach-smaller.jpg
```

Notice that we named the `String` returned from `FileChooser.pickAFile`. We
can use that name many times and each time it will have the same value (until we
change it).

In the below example, we declare variables (assign names) for the file name (a
`String` object) and the `Picture` object.

```
> String myFileName = FileChooser.pickAFile();
> System.out.println(myFileName);
C:\intro-prog-java\mediasources\katie.jpg
> Picture myPicture = new Picture(myFileName);
> System.out.println(myPicture);
Picture, filename C:\intro-prog-java\mediasources\katie.jpg height
360 width 381
```

Notice that the algebraic notions of *substitution* and *evaluation* work here as well.
Executing the code:

```
Picture myPicture = new Picture(myFileName);
```

causes the exact same picture to be created as if we had executed: `Picture
myPicture = new Picture(FileChooser.pickAFile());,`[1] because we set
`myFileName` to be equal to the result of `FileChooser.pickAFile()`. The values get substituted for the names when the expression is evaluated. The code `new`

---

[1]Assuming, of course, that you picked the same file.

Picture(myFileName) is an expression which, at evaluation time, gets expanded into:

```
new Picture ("C:\intro-prog-java\mediasources\katie.jpg")
```

because C:\intro-prog-java\mediasources\katie.jpg is the name of the file that was picked when FileChooser.pickAFile() was evaluated and the returned value was named myFileName.

We can also replace the method method invocations ("function calls") with the *value* returned. FileChooser.pickAFile() returns a *String* object—a bunch of characters enclosed inside of double quotes. We can make the last example work like this, too.

Common Bug: Backslashes and Slashes

You have seen the names of files displayed with backslashes in them, such as C:\intro-prog-java\mediasources\beach.jpg. However, when you create an object of the String class in Java you might not want to use backslashes because they are used to create special characters in strings like tab or newline. You can use slashes '/' instead as a path separator C:/intro-prog-java/mediasources/beach.jpg. Java can still figure out the path name when you use slashes. You *can* still use backslashes in the full path name, but you need to double each one C:\\intro-prog-java\\mediasources\\beach.jpg.

```
> String myFileName =
"C:/intro-prog-java/mediasources/katie.jpg";
> System.out.println(myFileName);
C:/intro-prog-java/mediasources/katie.jpg
> Picture myPicture = new Picture(myFileName);
> System.out.println(myPicture);
Picture, filename C:/intro-prog-java/mediasources/katie.jpg height
360 width 381
```

Or even substitute for the name.

```
> Picture aPicture = new
Picture("C:/intro-prog-java/mediasources/katie.jpg");
> System.out.println(aPicture);
Picture, filename C:/intro-prog-java/mediasources/katie.jpg height
360 width 381
```

Computer Science Idea: We can Substitute Names, Values, and Methods

We can substitute a value, a name assigned to that value (the variable name), and the method returning that value *interchangeably*. The computer cares about the values, not if it comes from a string, a name (a variable), or a method (function) call.

We call statements to the computer that are telling it to do things *commands*. System.out.println(aPicture); is a command. So is String myFileName =

`FileChooser.pickAFile();`, and `aPicture.show(;)`. These are more than expressions: They're telling the computer to *do* something.

3.7   CONCEPTS SUMMARY

This chapter introduced many concepts: invoking object and class methods, creating objects, and how to create new methods.

3.7.1   Invoking Object Methods

You must invoke an `object` method on an object.

`objectReference.methodName(parameterList);`

Here is an example of invoking an object method:

`> turtle1.turnLeft();`

The object that the method is invoked on will be implicitly passed to the method and can be referred to using the keyword `this` inside of the method. Object methods usually work with the data in the current object.

3.7.2   Invoking Class Methods

You can invoke a `class` method using the name of the class.

`ClassName.methodName(parameterList);`

Here is an example of invoking a class method:

```
> System.out.println(Math.abs(-3));
3
```

Class methods are used for general methods like absolute value. Class methods do not have access to object data.

3.7.3   Creating Objects

To create an object, ask the class to create and initialize a new object. This is also called creating an *instance* of a class or *instantiating* an object.

`new ClassName(parameterList)`

Here is an example of creating an object of the class `World`:

`> World worldObj = new World();`

3.7.4   Creating New Methods

To create a method in a class, open the class definition file `ClassName.java`, and put the method before the closing curly brace at the end of the file.

To define a method use:

```
public returnType methodName(parameterList)
{
  // statements in the body of the method
}
```

If the method doesn't return a value, use the keyword "void" as the return type. Each parameter in the parameter list has a type and name. Parameters are separated by commas. Method and parameter names start with a lowercase letter, but the first letter of each additional word is capitalized.

Here is an example method in the Turtle class:

```
/**
 * Method to draw a square with a width and height
 * of 30
 */
public void drawSquare()
{
  this.turnRight();
  this.forward(30);
  this.turnRight();
  this.forward(30);
  this.turnRight();
  this.forward(30);
  this.turnRight();
  this.forward(30);
}
```

OBJECTS AND METHODS SUMMARY

In this chapter we talk about several kinds of encodings of data (or objects).

Pictures	Objects of our Picture class	Pictures are encodings of images, typically coming from a JPEG file.
Sounds	Objects of our Sound class	Sounds are encodings of sounds, typically coming from a WAV file.
Strings	Java String object, e.g., "Hello"	A sequence of characters (including spaces, punctuation, etc.) delimited on either end with a double-quote character.
Turtles	Objects of our Turtle class	Turtles can move forward, turn left, turn right, turn by a specified angle, and leave a trail.
Worlds	Objects of our World class	Worlds can hold objects, such as objects of the Turtle class.

Here are the methods introduced in this chapter:

`Character.getNumericValue` `(Character character)`	Returns the equivalent numeric value in Unicode for the input character.
`FileChooser.pickAFile()`	Lets the user pick a file and returns the complete path name as a string.
`Math.abs(int number)`	Takes a number and returns the absolute value of it.
`show()`	Shows the `Picture` object that it is invoked on. No return value.
`play()`	Plays the sound object (object of the `Sound` class) that it is invoked on. No return value.
`forward(int numberOfSteps)`	Asks the `Turtle` object that it is invoked on to move forward by the passed number of steps. No return value.
`setPenDown(boolean value)`	Asks the `Turtle` object that it is invoked on to set the pen up or down depending on the passed value. If you pass in `false` for value, the pen is lifted and no trail will be drawn when the turtle moves. If you pass in `true`, the pen will be put down and the trail will be drawn.
`hide()`	Asks the `Turtle` object that it is invoked on to stop showing itself. No return value.
`moveTo(int x, int y)`	Asks the `Turtle` object that it is invoked on to move to the specified x and y location. No return value.
`penDown()`	Asks the `Turtle` object that it is invoked on to put down the pen and draw the trail of future movements. No return value.
`penUp()`	Asks the `Turtle` object that it is invoked on to pick up the pen so you don't see the trail of future movements. No return value.
`show()`	Asks the `Turtle` object that it is invoked on to show (draw) itself. No return value.
`turn(int angle)`	Asks the `Turtle` object that it is invoked on to turn by the specified angle. A negative angle will turn that much to the left and a positive angle will turn that much to the right. No return value.
`turnLeft()`	Asks the `Turtle` object that it is invoked on to turn left 90 degrees. No return value.
`turnRight()`	Asks the `Turtle` object that it is invoked on to turn right 90 degrees. No return value.

PROBLEMS

3.1 Some computer science concept questions:

- What is a file?
- What is an operating system?
- What does a compile do?
- What does method visibility mean?
- What is a classpath?
- What is a wrapper class?
- What is a hard disk?
- What is a method?
- What creates new objects?
- What does "pass by value" mean?
- What is a primitive variable?
- What is an object variable?

3.2 Test your understanding of Java with the following:

- What does `pictureObj.show()` do?
- What does `soundObj.play()` do?
- What does `FileChooser.pickAFile()` do?
- What does `turtle1.turnLeft()` do?

3.3 Test your understanding of Java with the following:

- What does `turtle1.forward()` do?
- What does `turtle1.turn(-45)` do?
- What does `turtle1.turn(45)` do?
- What does `turtle1.penUp()` do?
- What does `turtle1.hide()` do?

3.4 How do you create new objects in Java? How do you create a `World` object? How do you create a `Turtle` object?

3.5 Which of the following are class methods and which are object methods? How can you tell which are which?

- `Math.abs(-3);`
- `soundObj.play();`
- `FileChooser.pickAFile();`
- `pictureObj.show();`
- `ColorChooser.pickAColor();`
- `turtle1.turnLeft();`

3.6 What does this do? `System.out.println(new Picture());`

3.7 How many and what kind of variables (primitive or object) are created in the code below?
```
> String fileName = FileChooser.pickAFile();
> Picture p1 = new Picture(fileName);
> p1.show();
```

3.8 How many and what kind of variables (primitive or object) are created in the code below?
```
> World worldObj = new World();
> Turtle turtle1 = new Turtle(worldObj);
> turtle1.forward(30);
> Turtle turtle2 = new Turtle(worldObj);
> turtle2.turnRight();
> turtle2.forward(30);
```

3.9 How many and what kind of variables (primitive or object) are created in the code below?
```
> double cost = 19.20;
> double percentOff = 0.4;
> double salePrice = cost * (1.0 - percentOff);
```

3.10 We evaluated the expression `FileChooser.pickAFile()` when we wanted to invoke the method named `pickAFile()`. But what does this do? Open the `FileChooser` class and find the method declaration.

3.11 Write a method for `Turtle` to draw a rectangle. Pass in the width and height for the rectangle.

3.12 Write a method for `Turtle` to draw a hexagon. Pass in the length of the sides.

3.13 Write a method for `Turtle` to draw a pentagon. Pass in the length of the sides.

3.14 Write a method for `Turtle` to draw an equilateral triangle. Pass in the length of the sides.

3.15 Create a `World` object and a `Turtle` object and use the `Turtle` object to draw a star.

3.16 Create a `World` object and a `Turtle` object and use the `Turtle` object to draw an arrow.

3.17 Create a `World` object and a `Turtle` object and use the `Turtle` object to draw a pyramid.

3.18 Create a `World` object and a `Turtle` object and use the `Turtle` object to draw a flower.

3.19 Create a `World` object and a `Turtle` object and use the `Turtle` object to draw a house.

3.20 Create a `World` object and a `Turtle` object and use the `Turtle` object to draw your first name.

TO DIG DEEPER

The best (deepest, most material, most elegant) computer science textbook is *Structure and Interpretation of Computer Programs* [2], by Abelson, Sussman, and

Sussman. It's a hard book to get through, though. Somewhat easier, but in the same spirit is the new book *How to Design Programs* [9].

Neither of these books is really aimed at students who want to program because it's fun or because they have something small they want to do. They're really aimed at future professional software developers. The best books aimed at the less-hardcore user are by Brian Harvey. His book *Simply Scheme* uses the same programming language as the earlier two, Scheme, but is more approachable. My favorite of this class of books, though, is Brian's three-volume set *Computer Science Logo Style* [18], which combines good computer science with creative and fun projects.

PART 2

PICTURES

4 Modifying Pictures Using Loops

Chapter Learning Objectives

The media learning goals for this chapter are:

- To understand how images are digitized by taking advantage of limits in human vision.
- To identify different models for color, including RGB, the most common one for computers.
- To manipulate color values in pictures, like increasing or decreasing red values.
- To convert a color picture to grayscale, using more than one method.
- To convert a color picture to its negative representation.

The computer science goals for this chapter are:

- To introduce arrays.
- To write object methods.
- To do iteration with while and for loops.
- To introduce comments.
- To understand the *scope* of a variable name.
- To introduce breaking a method into smaller methods.

4.1 HOW PICTURES ARE ENCODED

Pictures (images, graphics) are an important part of any media communication. In this chapter, we discuss how pictures are represented on a computer (mostly as *bitmap* images—each dot or *pixel* is represented separately) and how they can be manipulated.

Pictures are two-dimensional arrays of *pixels* (which is short for picture element). In this section, each of these terms will be described.

For our purposes, a picture is an image stored in a JPEG file. JPEG is an international standard for how to store images with high quality but in little space. JPEG is

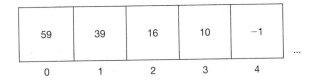

FIGURE 4.1
A depiction of the first five elements in an array.

a *lossy compression* format. That means that it is *compressed*, made smaller, but not with 100% of the quality of the original format. Typically, though, what gets thrown away is stuff that you don't see or don't notice anyway. For most purposes, a JPEG image works fine.

If we want to write programs to manipulate JPEG images we need to understand how they are stored and displayed. To do this we need to understand arrays, matrices, pixels, and color.

An array is a sequence of elements, each with an index number associated with it (Figure 4.1). The first element in an array is at index 0, the second at index 1, the third at index 2, and so on. The last element of the array will always be at the length of the array minus one. An array with five elements will have its last element at index 4.

It may sound strange to say that the first element of an array is at index 0 but the index is based on the distance from the beginning of the array to the element. Since the first item of the array is at the beginning of the array the distance is 0. Why is the index based on the distance? Array values are stored one after the other in memory. This makes it easy to find any element of the array by multiplying the size of each element by the index and adding it to the address of the beginning of the array. If you are looking for the element at index 3 in an array and the size of each element is 4 bytes long and the array starts at memory location 26 then the 3rd element is at $(3 * 4 + 26 = 12 + 26 = 38)$.

Every time you join a line (queue) of people, you are in something like an array. All you usually care about is how far you are from the front of the line. If you are at the front of the line, then that is index 0 (you are next). If you are the second one in line, then you are at index 1 (there is one person in front of you). If you are the third person in line, then you are at index 2 (there are two people in front of you).

Arrays are a great way to store lots of data of the same type. You wouldn't want to create a different variable for every pixel in a picture when there are hundreds of thousands of pixels in a picture. Instead you use an array of pixels. You still need a way to refer to a particular pixel, so we use an index for that. You can access elements of an array in Java using `arrayName[index]`. For example, to access the first element in an array variable named pixels use `pixels[0]`. To access the second element use `pixels[1]`. To access the third element use `pixels[2]`. You can get the number of items in an array using `arrayName.length`. So, to access the last element in the array use `arrayName[arrayName.length - 1]`.

To declare an array in Java you specify the type and then use open and close square brackets followed by a name for the array.

```
> double[] grades;
> System.out.println(grades);
null
```

or you could have specified the square brackets after the variable name:

```
> double grades[];
> System.out.println(grades);
null
```

The above code declares an array of doubles with the name `grades`. Notice though that this just declared an object reference and set it to null. *It didn't create* the array. In Java you can create an array and specify the values for it at the same time:

```
> double[] gradeArray = {80, 90.5, 88, 92, 94.5};
> System.out.println(gradeArray.length);
5
> System.out.println(gradeArray[0]);
80.0
> System.out.println(gradeArray[4]);
94.5
```

Making it Work Tip: Using Dot Notation for Public Fields

Notice that there are no parentheses following `arrayName.length`. This is because length is not a method but a public field (data). Public fields can be accessed using dot notation *objectName.fieldName*. Methods **always** have parenthesis after the method name even if there are no input parameters, such as `FileChooser.pickAFile()`.

A two-dimensional array is a *matrix*. A matrix is a collection of elements arranged in both a horizontal and vertical sequence. For one-dimensional arrays, you would talk about an element at index *i*, that is `array[i]`. For two-dimensional arrays, you can talk about an element at row *r* and column *c*, that is, `matrix[r][c]`. This is called *row-major order*.

Have you ever played the game Battleship™? If you have, then you had to specify both the row and column of your guess (B-3). This means row B and column 3 (Figure 4.2). Have you ever gone to a play? Usually your ticket has a row and seat number. These are both examples of row-major two-dimensional arrays.

Another way to specify a location in a two-dimensional array is *column-major order* which specifies the column first and then the row: `matrix[c][r]`. This is how we normally talk about pictures by using an x for the horizontal location and a y for the vertical location such as `matrix[x][y]`. Picture data is represented as a column-major two-dimensional array.

Java actually creates multidimensional arrays as arrays of arrays. When you have a two-dimensional array, the first index is the location in the outer array, and the second is the location in the inner array. You can think of the outer array as either the rows or the columns. So Java isn't row-major or column-major, but you will create and work with your arrays in either row-major or column-major fashion (Figure 4.3). Just be sure to be consistent.

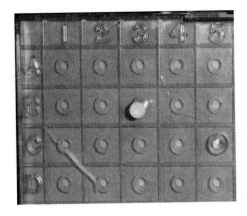

FIGURE 4.2
The top-left corner of a Battleship guess board with a miss at B-3.

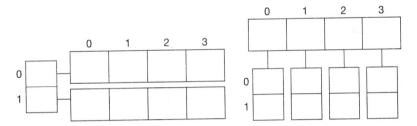

FIGURE 4.3
Picturing a 2D array as row-major or column-major.

	0	1	2	3
0	15	12	13	10
1	9	7	43	23
2	6	13	15	16

FIGURE 4.4
An example matrix (two-dimensional array) of numbers.

In Figure 4.4, you see an example matrix. Using column-major order for the *coordinates* $(0, 0)$ (horizontal, vertical), you'll find the matrix element whose value is 15. The element at $(1, 1)$ is 7, $(2, 1)$ is 43, and $(3, 1)$ is 23. We will often refer to these coordinates as (x, y) (*horizontal, vertical*).

What's stored at each element in the picture is a *pixel*. The word "pixel" is short for "picture element." It's literally a dot, and the overall picture is made up of lots of these dots. Have you ever taken a magnifying glass to view pictures in a newspaper

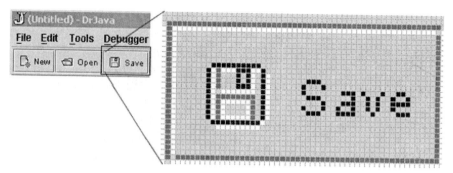

FIGURE 4.5
Upper-left corner of the DrJava window with a portion magnified 600%.

or magazine, or to a television or even your own computer monitor? Figure 4.5 was generated by capturing as an image the top-left part of the DrJava window and then magnifying it 600%. It's made up of many, many dots. When you look at the picture in the magazine or on the television, it doesn't look like it's broken up into millions of discrete spots, but it is.

You can get a similar view of individual pixels using the picture explorer, which is discussed later in this chapter. The picture explorer allows you to zoom a picture up to 500% so that each individual pixel is visible (Figure 4.6).

Our human sensor apparatus can't distinguish (without magnification or other special equipment) the small bits in the whole. Humans have low visual *acuity*—we don't see as much detail as, say, an eagle. We actually have more than one kind of vision system in use in our brain and our eyes. Our system for processing color is different than our system for processing black-and-white (or *luminance*). We actually pick up luminance detail better with the sides of our eyes than the center of our eyes.

FIGURE 4.6
Image shown in the picture explorer: 100% image on left and 500% on right (close-up of the branch over the mountain).

That's an evolutionary advantage because it allows you to pick out the sabertooth tiger sneaking up on you from the side.

The lack of resolution in human vision is what makes it possible to digitize pictures. Animals that perceive greater details than humans (e.g., eagles or cats) may actually see the individual pixels. We break up the picture into smaller elements (pixels), but there are enough of them and they are small enough that the picture doesn't look choppy when viewed from a normal viewing distance. If you *can* see the effects of the digitization (e.g., lines have sharp edges, you see little rectangles in some spots), we call that *pixelization*—the effect when the digitization process becomes obvious.

Picture encoding is actually more complex than sound encoding. A sound is inherently linear—it progresses forward in time. It can be represented using a one-dimensional array. A picture has two dimensions, a width and a height.

4.1.1 Color Representations

Visible light is continuous—visible light is any wavelength between 370 and 730 nanometers (0.00000037 and 0.00000073 meters). But our perception of light is limited by how our color sensors work. Our eyes have sensors that trigger (peak) around 425 nanometers (blue), 550 nanometers (green), and 560 nanometers (red). Our brain determines what color we "see" based on the feedback from these three sensors in our eyes. There are some animals with only two kinds of sensors, like dogs. Those animals still perceive color, but not the same colors nor in the same way as humans do. One of the interesting implications of our limited visual sensory apparatus is that we actually perceive two kinds of orange. There is a *spectral* vision—a particular wavelength that is natural orange. There is also a mixture of red and yellow that hits our color sensors just right so that we perceive it as the same orange.

Based on how we perceive color, as long as we encode what hits our three kinds of color sensors, we're recording our human perception of color. Thus, we can encode each pixel as a triplet of numbers. The first number represents the amount of red in the pixel. The second is the amount of green, and the third is the amount of blue. We can make up any human-visible color by combining red, green, and blue light (Figure 4.7). Combining all three gives us pure white. Turning off all three gives us black. We call this the *RGB color model*.

There are other models for defining and encoding colors besides the RGB color model. There's the *HSV color model* which encodes Hue, Saturation, and Value (sometimes also called the *HSB* color model for Hue, Saturation, and Brightness). The nice thing about the HSV model is that some notions, like making a color "lighter" or "darker" map cleanly to it, e.g., you simply change the saturation (Figure 4.8). Another model is the *CMYK color model*, which encodes Cyan, Magenta, Yellow, and blacK ("B" could be confused with Blue). The CMYK model is what printers use—those are the inks they combine to make colors. However, the four elements means more to encode on a computer, so it's less popular for media computation. RGB is the most popular model on computers.

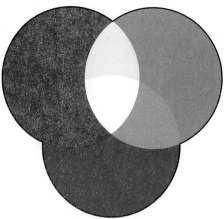

FIGURE 4.7
Merging red, green, and blue to make new colors.

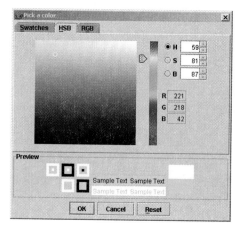

FIGURE 4.8
Picking colors using the HSB color model.

Each color component (sometimes called a *channel*) in a pixel is typically represented with a single byte, eight bits. Eight bits can represent 256 patterns (2^8): 0000000, 00000001, up through 11111111. We typically use these patterns to represent the values 0 to 255. Each pixel, then, uses 24 bits to represent colors. That means that there are 2^{24} possible patterns of 0's and 1's in those 24 bits. That means that the standard encoding for color using the RGB model can represent 16,777,216 colors. We can actually perceive more than 16 million colors, but it turns out that it just doesn't matter. Humans have no technology that comes even close to being able to replicate the whole color space that we can see. We do have devices that can represent 16 million distinct colors, but those 16 million colors don't cover the entire space of color (nor luminance) that we can perceive. So, the 24 bit RGB model is adequate until technology advances.

There are computer models that use more bits per pixel. For example, there are 32 bit models which use the extra 8 bits to represent *transparency*—how much of the color "below" the given image should be blended with this color? These additional 8 bits are sometimes called the *alpha channel*. There are other models that actually use more than 8 bits for the red, green, and blue channels, but they are uncommon.

We actually perceive borders of objects, motion, and depth through a *separate* vision system. We perceive color through one system, and *luminance* (how light/dark things are) through another system. Luminance is not actually the *amount* of light, but our *perception* of the amount of light. We can measure the amount of light (e.g., the number of photons reflected off the color) and show that a red and a blue spot each are reflecting the same amount of light, but we'll perceive the blue as darker. Our sense of luminance is based on comparisons with the surroundings—the optical illusion in Figure 4.9 highlights how we perceive gray levels. The two end quarters are actually the same level of gray, but because the two mid quarters end in a sharp contrast of lightness and darkness, we perceive that one end is darker than the other.

Most tools for allowing users to pick out colors let the users specify the color as RGB components. The Macintosh offers RGB sliders in its basic color picker (Figure 4.10). The color chooser in Java offers a similar set of sliders (Figure 4.11).

FIGURE 4.9
The ends of this figure are the same colors of gray, but the middle two quarters contrast sharply so the left looks darker than the right.

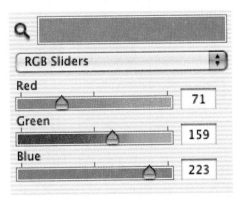

FIGURE 4.10
The Macintosh OS X RGB color picker.

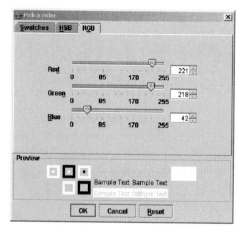

FIGURE 4.11
Picking a color using RGB sliders from Java.

As mentioned a triplet of $(0, 0, 0)$ (red, green, blue components) is black, and $(255, 255, 255)$ is white. $(255, 0, 0)$ is pure red, but $(100, 0, 0)$ is red, too—just darker. $(0, 100, 0)$ is a dark green, and $(0, 0, 100)$ is a dark blue.

When the red component is the same as the green and as the blue, the resultant color is gray. $(50, 50, 50)$ would be a fairly dark gray, and $(150, 150, 150)$ is a lighter gray.

Figure 4.12 is a representation of pixel RGB triplets in a matrix representation. In column-major order the pixel at $(1, 0)$ has color $(30, 30, 255)$ which means that it has a red value of 30, a green value of 30, and a blue value of 255—it's a mostly blue color, but not pure blue. Pixel at $(2, 1)$ has pure green but also more red and blue $((150, 255, 150))$, so it's a fairly light green.

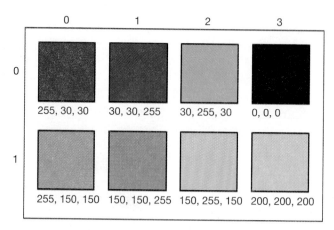

FIGURE 4.12
RGB triplets in a matrix representation.

TABLE 4.1   Number of bytes needed to store pixels at various sizes and formats

	320×240	**640×480**	**1,024×768**
24-bit color	230,400 bytes	921,600 bytes	2,359,296 bytes
32-bit color	307,200 bytes	1,228,800 bytes	3,145,728 bytes

Images on disk and even in computer memory are usually stored in some kind of *compressed* form. The amount of memory needed to represent every pixel of even small images is pretty large (Table 4.1). A fairly small image of 320 pixels wide by 240 pixels high, with 24-bits per pixel, takes up 230,400 bytes—that's roughly 230 *kilobytes* (1,000 bytes) or 1/4 *megabyte* (million bytes). A computer monitor with 1,024 pixels across and 768 pixels vertically with 32-bits per pixel takes up over 3 megabytes just to represent the screen.

Computer Science Idea: Kilobyte (kB) versus Kibibyte (KiB or K or KB)

The term kilobyte has caused problems because it has been interpreted differently by different groups. Computer scientists formerly used it to mean 2 to the 10th power which is 1,024 bytes. Telecommunications engineers used it to mean 1,000 bytes. The International Electrotechnical Commission (IEC) decreed in 1998 to call 1,024 bytes a kibibyte (KiB) and 1,000 bytes a kilobyte. Similarly a mebibyte is defined to be 2 raised to the 20th power, and a megabyte is 1,000,000 bytes (one million bytes). A gibibyte is defined to be 2 raised to the 30th power, and a gigabyte is defined to be 1,000,000,000 (one billion bytes). ■

4.2   MANIPULATING PICTURES

We manipulate a picture in DrJava by making a picture object out of a JPEG file, then changing the pixels in that picture. We change the pixels by changing the color associated with the pixel—by manipulating the red, green, and blue components.

We make a picture using new Picture(*fileName*). We make the picture appear with the method show(). We can also explore a picture with the method explore(). These are both object methods so they must be called on an object of the class that understands the method. This means that show() and explore() must be called on a Picture object (object of the Picture class) using dot notation as in pictureObject.show().

```
> String fileName = FileChooser.pickAFile();
> System.out.println(fileName);
c:\intro-prog-java\mediasources\caterpillar.jpg
> Picture pictureObject = new Picture(fileName);
> pictureObject.show();
> System.out.println(pictureObject);
Picture, filename c:\intro-prog-java\mediasources\caterpillar.jpg
height 150 width 329
```

What new `Picture(fileName)` does is to scoop up all the bytes in the input filename, bring them in to memory, reformat them slightly, and place a sign on them "This is a picture object!" When you execute `Picture pictureObject = new Picture(fileName)`, you are saying "The name `pictureObject` is referring to a `Picture` object created from the contents of the file."

Picture objects know their width and their height. You can query them with the methods `getWidth()` and `getHeight()`.

```
> System.out.println(pictureObject.getWidth());
329
> System.out.println(pictureObject.getHeight());
150
```

We can get any particular pixel from a picture using `getPixel(x,y)` where x and y are the coordinates of the pixel desired. This returns an object of the class `Pixel` which knows the picture it is from and the x and y position of the pixel in that picture. The x coordinate starts at 0 at the top left of the picture and increases horizontally. The y coordinate starts at 0 at the top left of the picture and increases vertically. We can also get a one-dimensional array containing all the pixels in the picture using the method `getPixels()`. This just grabs all the pixels in the first row from left to right followed by all of the pixels in the second row from left to right and so on till it has all of the pixels.

```
> Pixel pixelObject = pictureObject.getPixel(0,0);
> System.out.println(pixelObject);
Pixel red=252 green=254 blue=251
> Pixel[] pixelArray=pictureObject.getPixels();
> System.out.println(pixelArray[0]);
Pixel red=252 green=254 blue=251
```

Pixels know where they came from. You can ask them their *x* and *y* coordinates with `getX()` and `getY()`.

```
> System.out.println(pixelObject.getX());
0
> System.out.println(pixelObject.getY());
0
```

Each pixel object knows how to get the red value `getRed()` and set the red value `setRed(redValue)`. (Green and blue work similarly.)

```
> System.out.println(pixelObject.getRed());
252
> pixelObject.setRed(0);
> System.out.println(pixelObject.getRed());
0
```

You can ask a pixel object for its color with `getColor()`, and you can ask the pixel object to set the color with `setColor(color)`. Color objects (objects of the class `Color` in package java.awt) know their red, green, and blue components. You can also create new `Color` objects with

`new Color(redValue,greenValue,blueValue)`

(the color values must be between 0 and 255). The `Color` class also has several colors predefined that you can use. If you need a color object that represents the color black you can use `Color.black` or `Color.BLACK`, for yellow use `Color.yellow` or `Color.YELLOW`. Other colors that are predefined are: `Color.blue`, `Color.green`, `Color.red`, `Color.gray`, `Color.orange`, `Color.pink`, `Color.cyan`, `Color.magenta`, and `Color.white` (or use all capitals for the color names). Notice that this is accessing fields on the `Color` class, not invoking class methods (no parentheses). Public class variables (fields) can be accessed using *ClassName.fieldName*.

Making it Work Tip: Importing Classes from Packages

`Color` is a Java class in the package java.awt. A package is a group of related classes. Java uses packages to group classes that you need for a particular purpose. To use classes in packages other than java.lang (which contains System and Math), you will need to *import* them. Importing a class or all classes in a package allows you to use the name of a class without fully qualifying it. To fully qualify a name, use the package name followed by a period (dot) and the class name. The *fully qualified name* for the `Color` class is java.awt.Color. You can always use the fully qualified name instead of importing, but people don't usually want to type that much. To import all classes in the package java.awt use `import java.awt.*;`. To import just the Color class from the package java.awt use `import java.awt.Color;`. Importing doesn't make your class larger, it is just used to determine what class you mean. ■

Debugging Tip: Undefined Class Error

If you get the message "Error: Undefined class Color" it means that you didn't import the class `Color`. You must either import classes that are in packages other than java.lang or fully qualify them. ■

```
> import java.awt.Color;
> Color colorObj=pixelObject.getColor();
> System.out.println(colorObj);
java.awt.Color[r=0,g=254,b=251]
> Color newColorObj=new Color(0,100,0);
> System.out.println(newColorObj);
java.awt.Color[r=0,g=100,b=0]
> pixelObject.setColor(newColorObj);
> System.out.println(pixelObject.getColor());
java.awt.Color[r=0,g=100,b=0]
```

If you change the color of a pixel, the picture that the pixel is from does get changed. However, you won't see the change until the picture repaints.

```
> System.out.println(pictureObject.getPixel(0,0));
Pixel red=0 green=100 blue=0
```

Common Bug: **Not Seeing Changes in the Picture**
If you show your picture, and then change the pixels, you might be wondering, "Where are the changes?!?" Picture displays don't automatically update. If you ask the Picture object to repaint using pictureObject.repaint(), the display of the Picture object will update. Asking the picture to show itself again pictureObject.show() will also repaint it.

You can automatically get a darker or lighter color from a Color object with colorObj.darker() or colorObj.brighter(). (Remember that this was easy in HSV, but not so easy in RGB. These methods do it for you.)

```
> Color testColorObj = new Color(168,131,105);
> System.out.println(testColorObj);
java.awt.Color[r=168,g=131,b=105]
> testColorObj = testColorObj.darker();
> System.out.println(testColorObj);
java.awt.Color[r=117,g=91,b=73]
> testColorObj = testColorObj.brighter();
> System.out.println(testColorObj);
java.awt.Color[r=167,g=130,b=104]
```

Notice that even though we darken the color and then brighten it the final color doesn't exactly match the original color. This is due to *rounding errors*. A rounding error is when calculations are done in floating point but the answer is stored in an integer. The floating point result can't fit in the type of the result (integer) and so some of the detail is lost.

You can also get a color using ColorChooser.pickAColor(), which gives you a variety of ways of picking a color. ColorChooser is a class that we have created to make it easy for you to pick colors using the Java class javax.swing.JColorChooser.

```
> import java.awt.Color;
> Color pickedColorObj = ColorChooser.pickAColor();
> System.out.println(pickedColorObj);
java.awt.Color[r=51,g=255,b=102]
```

When you have finished manipulating a picture, you can write it out to a file with write(fileName).

```
> pictureObject.write("newPicture.jpg");
```

Common Bug: **End filenames with .jpg**
Be sure to end your filename with ".jpg" in order to get your operating system to recognize it as a JPEG file.

Common Bug: Saving a File Quickly—and How to Find it Again!
What if you don't know the whole path to a directory of your choosing? You don't have to specify anything more than the base name. The problem is finding the file again! In what directory did it get saved? This is a pretty simple bug to resolve. The default directory (the one you get if you don't specify a path) is wherever DrJava is. ■

We don't have to write new methods to manipulate pictures. We can do it from the command area using the methods (functions) just described. Please reset the interactions pane by clicking the RESET button at the top of DrJava before you do the following.

```
> import java.awt.Color;
> String fName = "C:/intro-prog-java/mediasources/caterpillar.jpg";
> Picture picture = new Picture(fName);
> picture.show();
> picture.getPixel(10,100).setColor(Color.black);
> picture.getPixel(11,100).setColor(Color.black);
> picture.getPixel(12,100).setColor(Color.black);
> picture.getPixel(13,100).setColor(Color.black);
> picture.getPixel(14,100).setColor(Color.black);
> picture.getPixel(15,100).setColor(Color.black);
> picture.getPixel(16,100).setColor(Color.black);
> picture.getPixel(17,100).setColor(Color.black);
> picture.getPixel(18,100).setColor(Color.black);
> picture.getPixel(19,100).setColor(Color.black);
> picture.repaint();
> picture.explore();
```

Making it Work Tip: Reuse the Previous Line in DrJava
You can use the up arrow on the keyboard to bring up previous lines you have typed in the interactions pane in DrJava. You can then use the left arrow key to get to a character to correct or change and then execute it by pressing the 'Enter' key. ■

The result showing a small black line on the left side below the middle of the leaf appears in Figure 4.13. The black line is 100 pixels down, and the pixels 10 through 19 from the left edge have been turned black.

4.2.1   Exploring Pictures

On your CD, you will find the *MediaTools* application with documentation for how to get it started. You can also open a picture explorer in DrJava. Both the MediaTools application and the picture explorer will let you get pixel information from a picture. You can see the picture explorer in Figure 4.14 and the MediaTools application appears in Figure 4.15. Both of these will display the x, y, red, green, and blue values for a pixel. They will also both let you zoom in or out.

The picture explorer can be opened on a Picture object. Picture p = new Picture(FileChooser.pickAFile()); will allow you to define a Picture object

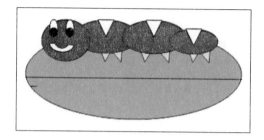

FIGURE 4.13
Directly modifying the pixel colors via commands: Note the small black line on the left under the line across the leaf.

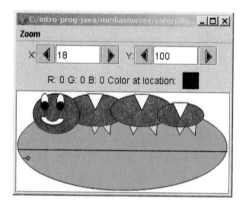

FIGURE 4.14
Exploring the caterpillar with the line.

and name it p. You can open a picture explorer on the picture using p.explore(). The picture explorer will make a **copy** of the current picture and show it. The copy **will not** be affected by any changes you make to the picture.

The picture explorer allows you to zoom at various levels of magnification, by choosing one in the ZOOM menu. As you move your cursor around in the picture, press down with the mouse button. You'll be shown the (x, y) (horizontal, vertical) coordinates of the pixel your mouse cursor is currently over, and the red, green, and blue values at that pixel. You can use the next and previous buttons to change the pixel that you want to examine. You can also type in the x and y values and press 'Enter' to see the pixel information for a particular pixel.

The MediaTools application works from files on the disk. If you want to check out a file before loading it into DrJava, use the MediaTools application. Click on the PICTURE TOOLS box in MediaTools, and the tools will open. Use the OPEN button to bring up a file selection box—you click on directories you want to explore on the left, and images you want on the right, then click OK. When the image appears, you have several different tools available. Move your cursor over the picture and press down with the mouse button.

FIGURE 4.15
Using the MediaTools image exploration tools on barbara.jpg.

- The red, green, and blue values will be displayed for the pixel you're pointing at. This is useful when you want to get a sense of how the colors in your picture map to numeric red, green, and blue values. It's also helpful if you're going to be doing some computation on the pixels and want to check the values.

- The x and y values will be displayed for the pixel you're pointing at. This is useful when you want to figure out regions of the screen, e.g., if you want to process only part of the picture. If you know the range of x and y coordinates where you want to process, you can tune your program to reach just those sections.

- Finally, a magnifier is available to let you see the pixels magnified. (The magnifier can be clicked and dragged around.)

4.3 CHANGING COLOR VALUES

The easiest thing to do with pictures is to change the color values of their pixels by changing the red, green, and blue components. You can get radically different effects by simply tweaking those values. Many of Adobe Photoshop's *filters* do just what we're going to be doing in this section.

The way that we're going to be manipulating colors is by computing a *percentage* of the original color. If we want 50% of the amount of red in the picture, we're going to set the red channel to 0.50 times whatever it is right now. If we want to increase the red by 25%, we're going to set the red to 1.25 times whatever it is right now. Recall that the asterisk (*) is the operator for multiply in Java.

4.3.1   Using a For-Each Loop

We know that we can use the getPixels() method to get an array of Pixel objects from a Picture object. We can use the getRed() method to get the red value from a Pixel object, then we can multiply it by 0.5 to decrease the red value, and then we can use setRed() to set the red value of a Pixel object.

We will need to cast back to integer after we multiply the red value by 0.5. Remember that if the computer sees you using a double value it assumes that the result should be a double. However, pixel color values must be integers. We could write the code to change the first three pixels like this:

```
> String fName = "C:/intro-prog-java/mediasources/caterpillar.jpg";
> Picture pict = new Picture(fName);
> pict.show();
> Pixel[] pixelArray = pict.getPixels();
> Pixel pixelObj = pixelArray[0];
> int red = pixelObj.getRed();
> red = (int) (red * 0.5);
> pixelObj.setRed(red);
> pixelObj = pixelArray[1];
> red = pixelObj.getRed();
> red = (int) (red * 0.5);
> pixelObj.setRed(red);
> pixelObj = pixelArray[2];
> red = pixelObj.getRed();
> red = (int) (red * 0.5);
> pixelObj.setRed(red);
> pict.explore();
```

This only changes the first three pixels. We don't want to write out statements like this to change *all* of the pixels in the array even for a small picture. We need some way to repeat the statements that get the red value, change it, and then set the red value for each pixel in the array. As of Java 5.0 (1.5) we can do that using a for-each *loop*. A loop is a way to repeat a statement or a block of statements. The syntax for a for-each loop is

```
for (Type variableName : array)
```

You can read this as "first declare a variable that will be used in the body of the loop," then "for each element in the array execute the body of the loop." The body of the loop can be either one statement or a series of statements inside of an open curly brace '{' and a close curly brace '}'. The statements in the body of the loop are indented to show that they are part of the loop. A method that will loop through all the pixels in the current picture and set the red value in each to half the original value is:

```
public void decreaseRed()
{
  Pixel[] pixelArray = this.getPixels();
  int value = 0;
```

```
// loop through all the pixels in the array
for (Pixel pixelObj : pixelArray)
{

    // get the red value
    value = pixelObj.getRed();

    // decrease the red value by 50% (1/2)
    value = (int) (value * 0.5);

    // set the red value of the current pixel to the new value
    pixelObj.setRed(value);
}
}
```

If you are using Java 5.0 (1.5) or above add the decreaseRed() method to the Picture.java file before the last closing curly brace '}'. Then click the COMPILE ALL button in DrJava to compile the file. You can try this method out by typing the following in the interactions pane.

```
> String fName = "C:/intro-prog-java/mediasources/caterpillar.jpg";
> Picture pict = new Picture(fName);
> pict.explore();
> pict.decreaseRed();
> pict.explore();
```

You can compare the original picture with the changed picture. Use the picture explorer to check that the amount of red was decreased.

When you execute pict.decreaseRed() the Java runtime checks the Picture class to see if it has a decreaseRed() method. The Picture class does have this method so it will execute that method and implicitly pass in the Picture object the method was invoked on. The keyword this is used to refer to the object the method was invoked on (the one referred to by the variable pict).

The first time through the loop the pixelObj will refer to the first element of the array (the one at index 0). The second time through the loop the pixelObj will refer to the second element of the array (the one at index 1). The last time through the loop the pixelObj will refer to the last element of the array (the one at index (length − 1)).

For-each loops are very useful for looping through each of the elements in an array. If you are still using Java 1.4, you can't use a for-each loop. You can use a while loop instead. Even if you are using Java 5.0 while loops can help you solve problems that for-each loops can't solve.

4.3.2 Using While Loops

A while loop executes a statement (command) or group of statements in a block (inside open and close curly braces). A while loop continues executing until a continuation test is false. When the continuation test is false execution continues with the statement following the while loop.

The syntax for a `while` loop is:

```
while (test)
{
  /** commands to be done go here */
}
```

Let's talk through the pieces here.

- First comes the required Java keyword `while`.
- Next we have a required opening parenthesis
- Next is the continuation test. While this test is true the loop will continue to be executed. When this test is false the loop will finish and the statement following the body of the loop will be executed.
- Next is the required closing parenthesis.
- Usually this is followed by a block of commands to be executed each time the expression following the while keyword is true. The block of commands is enclosed by curly braces. This is called the body of the loop. If there is only one command to be executed you may leave off the curly braces but you should still indent the command to show it is in the body of the `while` loop.

Tell someone to clap their hands 12 times. Did they do it right? How do you know? In order to tell if they did it right, you would have to count each time they clapped, and when they stopped clapping your count would be 12 if they did it right. A loop often needs a counter to count the number of times you want something done and an expression that stops when that count is reached. You wouldn't want to declare the count variable inside the `while` loop because you want it to change each time through the loop. Typically you declare the count variable just before the `while` loop and then increment it just before the end of the block of commands you want to repeat.

Computer Science Idea: Flowcharts

Figure 4.16 shows the flowchart of a `while` loop. A flowchart is a visual representation of the execution of a method or function. It shows the order in which statements are executed and branches or conditional execution. Normal statements are shown in rectangles. Tests are shown in diamonds and have a true branch which is executed when the test is true and a false branch that is executed when the test is false. A flowchart can help you understand what a method is doing.

A typical `while` loop will look like the following code.

```
int count = 0;
while (count < target)
{
  // commands to be done inside loop
  count = count + 1;
}
```

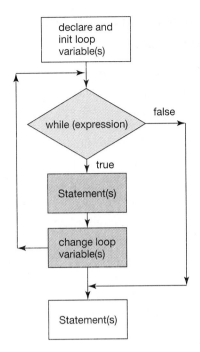

FIGURE 4.16
Flowchart of a `while` loop.

What if you want to write out the same sentence five times. You know how to print out a string using `System.out.println("some string");`. So, put this in the body of the loop. Start the count at 0 and increment it each time after the string is printed. When the count is 5 the string will have been printed five times, so stop the loop.

```
> int count = 0;
> while (count < 5)
{
  System.out.println("This is a test.");
  count = count + 1;
}
This is a test.
This is a test.
This is a test.
This is a test.
This is a test.
```

Debugging Tip: Stopping an Infinite Loop
If you forget to increment the count in the body of the `while` loop, or if you close the body of the `while` loop before the count is incremented you will have an *infinite loop*. An infinite loop is one that will never stop. You can tell that you are in an infinite loop in this case because many more than five copies of "This is a test." will be printed. To stop an infinite loop click on the RESET button near the top of the DrJava window.

What if we want to change the color of all the pixels in a picture? Picture objects understand the method getPixels(), which returns a one-dimensional array of pixel objects. Even though the pixels are really in a two-dimensional array (a matrix), getPixels() puts the pixels in a one-dimensional array to make them easy to process if we just want to process all the pixels. We can get a pixel at a position in the array using pixelArray[index] with the index starting at 0 and changing each time through the loop by one until it is equal to the length of the array of pixels. Instead of calling the variable "count," we will call it "index" since that is what we are using it for. It doesn't matter to the computer, but it makes the code easier for people to understand.

Here is the while loop that simply sets each pixel's color to black in a picture.

```
> import java.awt.Color;
> String fName = "C:/intro-prog-java/mediasources/caterpillar.jpg";
> Picture pict = new Picture(fName);
> pict.show();
> Pixel[] pixelArray = pict.getPixels();
> Pixel pixel = null;
> int index = 0;
> while (index < pixelArray.length)
  {
    pixel = pixelArray[index];
    pixel.setColor(Color.black);
    index++;
  }
> pict.repaint();
```

Let's talk through this code.

- We will be using the Color class so we need to either use the fully qualified name (java.awt.Color) or import the Color class using:

  import java.awt.Color;

- Next we declare a variable with the name fileName to refer to the string object that has a particular file name stored in it:

  C:/intro-prog-java/mediasources/caterpillar.jpg

- The variable pict is created and refers to the new Picture object created from the picture information in the file named by the variable fName.
- We tell the Picture object to show (display) itself using pict.show();
- Next we declare a variable pixelArray that references an array of Pixel objects (Pixel[]). We get the array of Pixel objects by asking the Picture object for them using the getPixels() method.
- We declare an object variable, Pixel pixel, that will refer to a pixel object but initialize it to null to show that it isn't referring to any pixel object yet.
- We declare a primitive variable index and initialize its value to 0.

- Next we have the while loop. First we test if the value of index is less than the length of the array of pixels with while (index < pixelArray.length). While it is, we set the variable pixel to refer to the pixel object at the current value of index in the array of pixel objects. Next we set the color of that pixel to the color black. Finally, we increment the variable index. Eventually the value of the variable index will equal the length of the array of pixels and then execution will continue after the body of the loop. Remember that in an array of five items the valid indexes are 0–4, so when the index is equal to the length of the array you need to stop the loop.

- The statement after the body of the while loop will ask the Picture object pict to repaint so that we can see the color change.

Debugging Tip: Loops and Variable Declarations

Declare any variables that you will need before you start the loop. "While" loops typically need some sort of counter or index declared outside the loop but changed inside the loop. If you forgot to change the counter or index, you will end up with a loop that never stops. This is called an infinite loop. Use the RESET button to stop if your code is in an infinite loop.

■

Now that we see how to get the computer to do thousands of commands without writing thousands of individual lines, let's do something useful with this.

4.3.3   Increasing/Decreasing Red (Green, Blue)

A common desire when working with digital pictures is to shift the *redness* (or greenness or blueness—but most often, redness) of a picture. You might shift it higher to "warm" the picture, or to reduce it to "cool" the picture or deal with overly-red digital cameras.

The method below decreases the amount of red by 50% in the current picture.

Program 5: Decrease the Amount of Red in a Picture by 50%

```
/**
 * Method to decrease the red by half in the
 * current picture
 */
public void decreaseRed()
{
  Pixel[] pixelArray = this.getPixels();
  Pixel pixel = null;
  int value = 0;
  int index = 0;

  // loop through all the pixels
  while(index < pixelArray.length)
  {
    // get the current pixel
    pixel = pixelArray[index];
```

```
    // get the value
    value = pixel.getRed();

    // decrease the red value by 50% (1/2)
    value = (int) (value * 0.5);

    // set the red value of the current pixel to the new value
    pixel.setRed(value);

    // increment the index
    index = index + 1;
  }
}
```

Go ahead and type the above into your DrJava definitions pane before the last curly brace in the Picture.java file. Click COMPILE ALL to get DrJava to compile the new method. Why do we have to compile the file before we can use the new method? Computers don't understand the Java source code directly. We must *compile* it, which translates the class definition from something people can read and understand into something a computer can read and understand.

Common Bug: **Methods with the Same Name**

If you added the method decreaseRed with a for-each loop in it to your Picture.java source code you will get an error when you add this decreaseRed method and compile. You can't have two methods with the same name and parameter list in a class. Just rename the first decreaseRed method to decreaseRedForEach and compile again.

Unlike some other computer languages, Java doesn't compile into *machine code*, which is the language for the machine it is running on. When we compile Java source code we compile it into a language for a *virtual machine*, which is a machine that doesn't necessarily exist.

When we successfully compile a *ClassName*.java file the compiler outputs a *ClassName*.class file which contains the instructions that a Java virtual machine can understand. If our compile is not successful we will get error messages that explain what is wrong. We have to fix the errors and compile again before we can try out our new method.

When we execute a Java class the Java Virtual Machine will read the compiled code and map the instructions for the virtual machine to the machine it is currently executing on. This allows you to compile Java programs on one type of computer and run them on another without having to recompile.

Making it Work Tip: **Comments in Java**

You may notice that there are some interesting characters in the reduceRed method. The '/**' and '//' are comments in Java. Comments are descriptions of what your code is doing. Use comments to make the code easier to read and understand (not only for yourself but also for others). There are actually three kinds of comments in Java. The '//' starts a comment and tells the computer to ignore everything else till the end of the current line. You can use '/*' followed at some point by '*/' for a multi-line comment. The '/**' followed at some point by '*/' creates a JavaDoc comment. JavaDoc is a utility that pulls the JavaDoc comments from your class files and creates hyperlinked documentation from them. All of the Java class files written by Sun have JavaDoc comments in them and that is how the API documentation was created.

This program works on a `Picture` object—the one that we'll use to get the pixels from. To create a `Picture` object, we pass in the filename. After we ask the picture to `decreaseRed()`, we'll want to repaint the picture to see the effect. Therefore, the `decreaseRed` method can be used like this:

```
> String fName = "C:/intro-prog-java/mediasources/caterpillar.jpg";
> Picture picture = new Picture(fName);
> picture.show();
> picture.decreaseRed();
> picture.repaint();
```

Common Bug: Patience: Loops can Take a Long Time

The most common bug with this kind of code is to give up and quit because you don't think the loop is working. It might take a full minute (or two!) for some of the manipulations we'll do—especially if your source image is large.

The original picture and its red-decreased version appear in Figure 4.17. 50% is obviously a *lot* of red to reduce! The picture looks like it was taken through a blue filter.

Computer Science Idea: Changing Memory Doesn't Change the File

If you create another `Picture` object from the same file will you get the original picture or the picture with red decreased? You will get the original picture. The `Picture` object `picture` was created by reading the file data into memory. The change to the `Picture` object was done in memory, but the file wasn't changed. If you want to save your changes write them out to a file using the method *pictObj*`.write(String fileName);` where `pictObj` is the name of the `Picture` object and `fileName` is the full path name of the file. So to save the changed `Picture` object above use `picture.write("c:/caterpillarChanged.jpg");`.

Tracing the program: How did that work?

Computer Science Idea: The Most Important Skill is Tracing

The most important skill that you can develop in programming is the ability to *trace* your program. This is also called *stepping* or *walking through* your program. To trace your program is to walk through it, line-by-line, and figure out what happens. Looking at a program, can you *predict* what it's going to do? You should be able to by thinking through what it does.

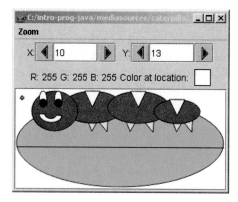 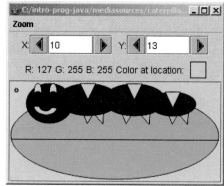

FIGURE 4.17
The original picture (left) and red-decreased version (right).

Let's *trace* the method to decrease red and see how it worked. We want to start tracing at the point where we just called decreaseRed()

```
> String fileN = "C:/intro-prog-java/mediasources/caterpillar.jpg";
> Picture picture = new Picture(fileN);
> picture.show();
> picture.decreaseRed();
```

What happens now? picture.decreaseRed() really means invoking the decreaseRed method which you have just added to the Picture.java file on the Picture object referred to by the variable picture. The picture object is implicitly passed to the decreaseRed method and can be referenced by the keyword this. What does "implicitly passed" mean? It means that even though decreaseRed doesn't have any parameters listed it is passed the Picture object it was invoked on. So, picture.decreaseRed() is like decreaseRed(Picture this). All object methods (methods without the keyword static in them) are implicitly passed the object that they are invoked on and that object can be referred to as this.

The first line we execute in Program 5 (page 97) is Pixel[] pixelArray = this.getPixels(). Let's break this down.

- The Pixel[] pixelArray is a declaration of a variable pixelArray that references an array of Pixel objects. The '=' means that the variable pixelArray will be initialized to the result of the right side expression which is a call to the method this.getPixels() which returns a one-dimensional array of Pixel objects in the current Picture object.

- The this is a keyword that represents the current object. Since the method declaration doesn't have the keyword static in it this is an object method. Object methods are always implicitly passed the current object (the object the method was invoked on). In this case the method decreaseRed() was invoked by picture.decreaseRed(); so the Picture object referenced by the variable picture is the current object. We could leave off the this and get the same result. If you don't reference any object when invoking a method the compiler will assume you mean the current object (referenced by the `this` keyword).

- The `this.getPixels()` invokes the method `getPixels()` on the current object. This method returns a one-dimensional array of `Pixel` objects which are the pixels in the current `Picture` object.

So at the end of the first line we have a variable `pixelArray` that refers to an array of `Pixel` objects. The `Pixel` objects came from the `Picture` object which was referred to as `picture` in the interaction pane and as `this` in the method `decreaseRed()`.

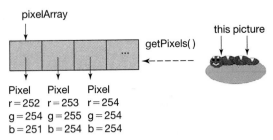

Next is a declaration of a couple of variables that we will need in the for loop. We will need something to represent the current `Pixel` object so we declare a variable `pixel` of type `Pixel` by `Pixel pixel =`. We start it off referring to nothing by using the defined value `null`. We also will need a variable to hold the current red value and we declare that as `int value = 0;`. We initialize the variable `value` to be 0. Finally we declare a variable to be the index into the array and the value that changes in the loop `int index = 0;`. Remember that array elements are indexed starting with 0 and ending at the length of the array minus one.

Variables that you declare inside methods are not automatically initialized for you, so you **should** initialize them when you declare them.

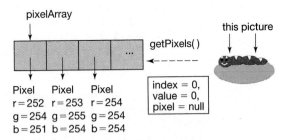

Computer Science Idea: Scope

The names inside a method like `pixel` and `value` are *completely* different than the names in the interactions pane or any other method. We say that they have a different *scope*. The scope of a variable is the area in which the variable is known. The variables that we declare inside of a method are only known from where they are declared until the end of the method. Variables declared in the interactions pane are known in the interactions pane until it is reset or until you exit DrJava.

Next comes the loop while (index < pixelArray.length). This tests whether the value of the variable index is less than the length of the array of pixels referred to by pixelArray. If the test is true, the body of the loop will be executed. The body of the loop is all the code between the open and close curly braces following the test. If the test is false, execution continues after the body of the loop.

In the body of the loop we have pixel = pixelArray[index];. This will set the pixel variable to point to a Pixel object in the array of pixels with an index equal to the current value of index. Since index is initialized to 0 before the loop, the first time through this loop the pixel variable will point to the first Pixel object in the array.

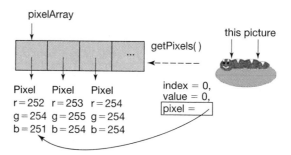

Next in the body of the loop is value = pixel.getRed();. This sets the variable value to the amount of red in the current pixel. Remember that the amount of red can vary from a minimum of 0 to a maximum of 255.

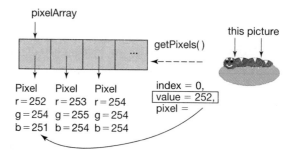

Next in the body of the loop is value = (int) (value * 0.5);. This sets the variable value to the integer amount that you get from multiplying the current contents of value by 0.5. The (int) is a cast to integer so that the compiler doesn't complain about losing precision since we are storing a floating point number in an integer number. Any numbers after the decimal point will be discarded. We do this because colors are represented as integers. The (int) (value * 0.5) is needed because the variable value is declared of type int and yet the calculation of (value * 0.5) contains a floating point number and so will automatically be done in floating point. However, a floating point result (say of 1.5) won't fit into a variable of type int. So, the compiler won't let us do this without telling it that we really want it to by including the (int). This is called *casting* and is required whenever a larger value is being placed into a smaller variable. So if the result of a multiplication has a fractional part, that fractional part will just be thrown away so that the result can fit in an int.

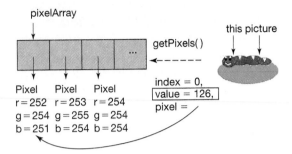

The next step in the body of the loop is `pixel.setRed(value);`. This changes the amount of red in the current pixel to be the same as what is stored in variable `value`. The current pixel is the first one, so we see that the red value has changed from 252 to 126 after this line of code is executed.

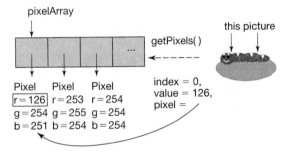

After the statements in the body of the loop are executed the `index = index + 1;` will be executed which will add one to the current value of index. Since index was initialized to 0 this will result in index holding the value 1.

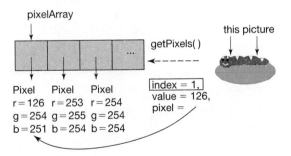

What happens next is very important. The loop starts over again. The continuation test will again check that the value in variable `index` is less than the length of the array of pixels, and since the value of `index` is less than the length of the array, the statements in the body of the loop will be executed again. The variable `pixel` will be set to the pixel object in the array of pixels at index 1. This is the second `Pixel` object in the array `pixelArray`.

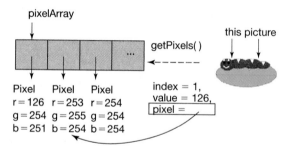

The variable `value` will be set to the red amount in the current pixel referred to by the variable `pixel`, which is 253.

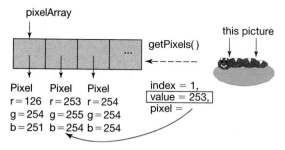

The variable `value` will be set to the result of casting to integer the result of multiplying the amount in value by 0.5. This results in $(253 * 0.5) = 126.5$ and after we drop the digits after the decimal this is 126. We drop the digits after the decimal point because of the cast to the type `int` (integer). We cast to integer because colors are represented as integer values from 0 to 255.

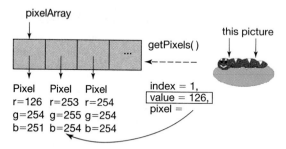

The red value in the current pixel is set to the same amount as what is stored in `value`. So the value of red in the second pixel changes from 253 to 126.

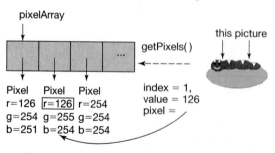

The variable index is set to the result of adding 1 to its current value. This adds 1 to 1, resulting in 2.

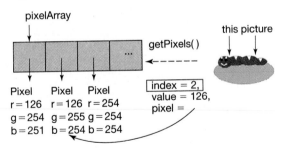

pixelArray

getPixels( )

this picture

Pixel   Pixel   Pixel
r=126 r=126 r=254
g=254 g=255 g=254
b=251 b=254 b=254

index = 2,
value = 126,
pixel =

At the end of the loop body we go back to the continuation test. The test will be evaluated and if the result is true the commands in the loop body will be executed again. If the continuation test evaluates to false execution will continue with the first statement after the body of the loop.

Eventually, we get Figure 4.17 (and at Figure 4.18). We keep going through all the pixels in the sequence and changing all the red values.

Testing the program: Did that really work?

How do we know that that really worked? Sure, *something* happened to the picture, but did we really decrease the red? By 50%?

Making it Work Tip: Don't Just Trust Your Programs!

It's easy to mislead yourself that your programs worked. After all, you told the computer to do a particular thing, you shouldn't be surprised if the computer did what you wanted. But computers are really stupid—they can't figure out what you want. They only do what you actually tell them to do. It's pretty easy to get it *almost* right. Actually check. ∎

We can check it several ways. One way is with the picture explorer. Create two Picture objects: `Picture p = new Picture(FileChooser.pickAFile());` and

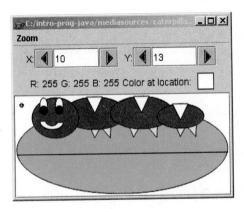
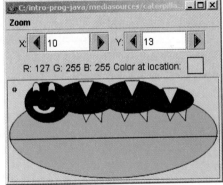

FIGURE 4.18
Using the picture explorer to convince ourselves that the red was decreased.

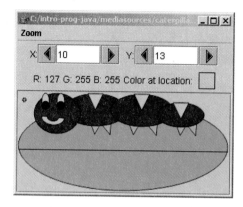 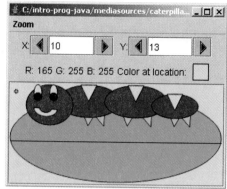

FIGURE 4.19
Overly blue (left) and red increased by 30% (right).

`Picture p2 = new Picture(FileChooser.pickAFile());` and pick the same picture each time. Decrease red in one of them. Then open a picture explorer on each of the `Picture` objects using `p.explore();` and `p2.explore();`.

We can also use the methods that we know in the Interactions pane to check the red values of individual pixels.

```
> String fName = "C:/intro-prog-java/mediasources/caterpillar.jpg";
> Picture pict = new Picture(fName);
> Pixel pixel = pict.getPixel(0,0);
> System.out.println(pixel);
Pixel red=252 green=254 blue=251
> pict.decreaseRed();
> Pixel newPixel = pict.getPixel(0,0);
> System.out.println(newPixel);
Pixel red=126 green=254 blue=251
> System.out.println( 252 * 0.5);
126.0
```

Increasing red

Let's increase the red in the picture now. If multiplying the red component by 0.5 decreased it, multiplying it by something over 1.0 should increase it. I'm going to apply the increase to the exact same picture, to see if we can reduce the blue (Figure 4.19).

Program 6: Increase the Red Component by 30%

```
/**
 * Method to increase the amount of red by 30%
 */
public void increaseRed()
{
  Pixel[] pixelArray = this.getPixels();
  Pixel pixel = null;
```

```
int value = 0;
int index = 0;

// loop through all the pixels
while (index < pixelArray.length)
{
  // get the current pixel
  pixel = pixelArray[index];

  // get the value
  value = pixel.getRed();

  // change the value to 1.3 times what it was
  value = (int) (value * 1.3);

  // set the red value to 1.3 times what it was
  pixel.setRed(value);

  // increment the index
  index++;
}
}
```

This method works much the same way as the method decreaseRed. We set up some variables that we will need such as the array of pixel objects, the current pixel, the current value, and the current index. We loop through all the pixels in the array of pixels and change the red value for each pixel to 1.3 times its original value.

Making it Work Tip: Shortcuts for Increment and Decrement

Adding one or subtracting one from a current value is something that is done frequently in programs. Programmers have to do lots of typing, so they try to reduce the amount of typing they have to do for things they do frequently. Notice the index++; in the increase red program. This has the same result as index = index + 1; and can also be written as ++index;. You can also use index--; or --index; which will have the same result as index = index - 1;. Be careful about using this when you are also assigning the result to a variable. If you do int x = index++; x will be assigned the original value of index and then index will be incremented. If you do int x = ++index; first index will be incremented and then the value assigned to x.

Compile the new method increaseRed and first use decreaseRed and then increaseRed on the same picture. Explore the picture objects to check that increaseRed worked. Remember that the method explore makes a copy of the picture and allows you to check the color values of individual pixels.

```
> String fName = "C:/intro-prog-java/mediasources/caterpillar.jpg";
> Picture picture = new Picture(fName);
> picture.decreaseRed();
> picture.explore();
> picture.increaseRed();
> picture.explore();
```

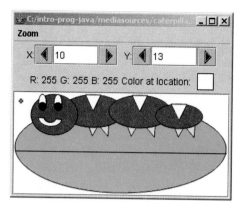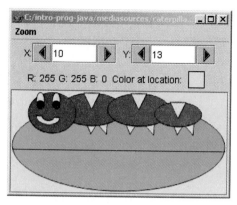

FIGURE 4.20
Original (left) and blue erased (right).

We can even get rid of a color completely. The method below erases the blue component from a picture by setting the blue value to 0 in all pixels (Figure 4.20).

Program 7: Clear the Blue Component from a Picture

```
/**
 * Method to clear the blue from the picture (set
 * the blue to 0 for all pixels)
 */
public void clearBlue()
{
  Pixel[] pixelArray = this.getPixels();
  Pixel pixel = null;
  int index = 0;

  // loop through all the pixels
  while (index < pixelArray.length)
  {
    // get the current pixel
    pixel = pixelArray[index];

    // set the blue on the pixel to 0
    pixel.setBlue(0);

    // increment index
    index++;
  }
}
```

Compile the new method clearBlue and invoke it on a Picture object. Explore the picture object to check that all the blue values are indeed 0.

```
> String fName = "C:/intro-prog-java/mediasources/caterpillar.jpg";
> Picture picture = new Picture(fName);
```

```
> picture.explore();
> picture.clearBlue();
> picture.explore();
```

This method is also similar to the `decreaseRed` and `increaseRed` methods except that we don't need to get out the current blue value since we are simply setting all the blue values to 0.

4.3.4 Creating a Sunset

We can certainly do more than one color manipulation at once. Mark wanted to try to generate a sunset out of a beach scene. His first attempt was to increase the red, but that doesn't always work. Some of the red values in a given picture are pretty high. If you go past 255 for a channel value it will keep the value at 255.

His second thought was that maybe what happens in a sunset is that there is *less* blue and green, thus *emphasizing* the red, without actually increasing it. Here was the program that he wrote for that:

Program 8: Making a Sunset

```java
/**
 * Method to simulate a sunset by decreasing the green
 * and blue
 */
public void makeSunset()
{
  Pixel[] pixelArray = this.getPixels();
  Pixel pixel = null;
  int value = 0;
  int i = 0;

  // loop through all the pixels
  while (i < pixelArray.length)
  {
    // get the current pixel
    pixel = pixelArray[i];

    // change the blue value
    value = pixel.getBlue();
    pixel.setBlue((int) (value * 0.7));

    // change the green value
    value = pixel.getGreen();
    pixel.setGreen((int) (value * 0.7));

    // increment the index
    i++;
  }
}
```

Making it Work Tip: Using Short Variable Names for Loop Counters

Notice that instead of using index as the counter for the loop we are using i. Again, programmers like to reduce the amount of typing, and so the simple variable name i is commonly used to represent the counter or index for a loop.

Compile the new method makeSunset and invoke it on a Picture object. Explore the picture object to check that the blue and green values have been decreased.

```
> String fName = "C:/intro-prog-java/mediasources/beach-smaller.jpg";
> Picture picture = new Picture(fName);
> picture.explore();
> picture.makeSunset();
> picture.explore();
```

What we see happening in Program 8 (page 109) is that we're changing both the blue and green channels—reducing each by 30%. The effect works pretty well, as seen in Figure 4.21.

4.3.5 Making Sense of Methods

You probably have lots of questions about methods at this point. Why did we write these methods this way? How is that we're reusing variable names like pixel in every method? Are there other ways to write these methods? Is there such a thing as a better or worse method?

Since we're always picking a file (or typing in a filename) *then* making a picture, before calling one of our picture manipulation methods, and *then* showing or repainting the picture, it's a natural question why we're not building those in. Why doesn't *every* method have String fileName = FileChooser.pickAFile(); and new Picture(fileName); in it?

FIGURE 4.21
Original beach scene (left) and at (fake) sunset (right).

We actually want to write the methods to make them more *general* and *reusable*. We want our methods to do one and only one thing, so that we can use the method again in a new context where we need that one thing done. An example might make that clearer. Consider the program to make a sunset (Program 8 (page 109)). That works by reducing the green and blue, each by 30%. What if we rewrote that method so that it called two *smaller* methods that just did the two pieces of the manipulation? We'd end up with something like Program 9 (page 111).

Program 9: Making a Sunset as Three Methods

```
/**
 * Method to decrease the green in the picture by 30%
 */
public void decreaseGreen()
{
  Pixel[] pixelArray = this.getPixels();
  Pixel pixel = null;
  int value = 0;
  int i = 0;

  // loop through all the pixels in the array
  while (i < pixelArray.length)
  {
    // get the current pixel
    pixel = pixelArray[i];

    // get the value
    value = pixel.getGreen();

    // set the green value to 70% of what it was
    pixel.setGreen((int) (value * 0.7));

    // increment the index
    i++;
  }
}

/**
 * Method to decrease the blue in the picture by 30%
 */
public void decreaseBlue()
{
  Pixel[] pixelArray = this.getPixels();
  Pixel pixel = null;
  int value = 0;
  int i = 0;

  // loop through all the pixels in the array
  while (i < pixelArray.length)
  {
```

```
    // get the current pixel
    pixel = pixelArray[i];

    // get the value
    value = pixel.getBlue();

    // set the blue value to 70% of what it was
    pixel.setBlue((int) (value * 0.7));
  }
}

/**
 * Method to make a picture look like it was taken at sunset
 * by reducing the blue and green to make it look more red
 */
public void makeSunset2()
{
  decreaseGreen();
  decreaseBlue();
}
```

■

The first thing to note is that this actually does work. makeSunset2() does the same thing here as in the previous method. It's perfectly okay to have one method (makeSunset2() in this case) use other methods in the same class (decreaseBlue() and decreaseGreen()). You use makeSunset2() just as you had before. It's the same algorithm (it tells the computer to do the same thing), but with different methods. The earlier program did everything in one method, and this one does it in three. In fact, you can also use decreaseBlue() and decreaseGreen() by themselves too—make a picture in the Command Area and invoke either method on the Picture object. They work just like decreaseRed().

What's different is that the method makeSunset2() is much simpler to read. That's very important.

Computer Science Idea: Programs are for People

Computers don't care about how a program looks. Programs are written to communicate with *people*. Making programs easy to read and understand means that they are more easily changed and reused, and they more effectively communicate process to other humans.

■

What if we had written decreaseBlue() and decreaseGreen() so that each asked you to pick a file and created the picture before changing the color. We would be asked to pick a file twice—once in each method. Because we wrote these methods to *only* decrease the blue and decrease the green ("one and only one thing") in the implicitly passed Picture object, we can use them in new methods like makeSunset().

There is an issue that the new makeSunset2() will take twice as long to finish as the original makeSunset(), since every pixel gets changed twice. We address that issue in Chapter 15 on speed and complexity. The important issue is still to write the code readably *first*, and worry about efficiency later. However, this could also be handled by a method that changes each color by some passed in amount. This would be a very general and reusable method.

Now, let's say that we asked you to pick a picture and created the picture in makeSunset2() before calling the other methods. The methods decreaseBlue() and decreaseGreen() are completely flexible and reusable again. But the method makeSunset2() is now less flexible and reusable. Is that a big deal? No, not if you only care about having the ability to give a sunset look to a single picked picture. But what if you later want to build a movie with a few hundred frames of Picture objects, to each of which you want to add a sunset look? Do you really want to pick out each of those few hundred frames? Or would you rather write a method to go through each of the frames (which we'll learn how to do in a few chapters) and invoke makeSunset2() on each Picture object. That's why we make methods general and reusable—you never know when you're going to want to use that method again, in a larger context.

Making it Work Tip: Don't Start by Trying to Write Applications

There's a tendency for new programmers to want to write complete applications that a non-technical user can use. You might want to write a makeSunset() application that goes out and fetches a picture for a user and generates a sunset for them. Building good user interfaces that anyone can use is hard work. Start out more slowly. It's hard enough to make a method that just does something to a picture. You can work on user interfaces later. ◼

Even larger methods, like makeSunset(), do "one and only one thing." The method makeSunset() makes a sunset-looking picture. It does that *by* decreasing green and decreasing blue. It calls two other methods to do that. What we end up with is a *hierarchy* of goals—the "one and only one thing" that is being done. makeSunset() does its one thing, by asking two other methods to do their one thing. We call this *hierarchical decomposition* (breaking down a problem into smaller parts, and then breaking down those smaller parts until you get something that you can easily program), and it's very powerful for creating complex programs out of pieces that you understand. This is also called *top-down refinement or problem decomposition*.

4.3.6 Variable Name Scope

Names in methods are *completely* separate from names in the interactions pane and also from names in other methods. We say that they have different *scope*. Scope is the area where a name is known by the computer. Variables declared inside of a method have method scope and only apply inside that method. That is why we can use the same variable names in several methods. Variables declared inside the Interactions Pane are known inside the Interactions Pane until it is reset. This is why you get Error: Redefinition of 'picture' when you declare a variable that is already declared in the Interactions Pane.

The *only* way to get any data (pictures, sounds, filenames, numbers) from the interactions pane into a method is by passing it in as input to the method. Within the method, you can use any names you want—names that you first define within the method (like `pixel` in the last example) or names that you use to stand for the input data (like `fileName`) *only* exist while the method is running. When the method is done, those variable names literally do not exist anymore.

This is really an advantage. Earlier, we said that naming is very important to computer scientists: We name everything, from data to methods to classes. But if each name could mean one and only one thing *ever*, we'd run out of names. In natural language, words mean different things in different contexts (e.g., "What do you mean?" and "You are being mean!"). A method is a different context—names can mean something different than they do outside of that method.

Sometimes, you will compute something inside a method that you want to return to the interactions pane or to a calling method. We've already seen methods that output a value, like `FileChooser.pickAFile()` which outputs a filename. If you created a `Picture` object using `new Picture(fileName)` inside a method, you should return it so that it can be used. You can do that by using the `return` keyword.

The name that you give to a method's input can be thought of as a *placeholder*. Whenever the placeholder appears, imagine the input data appearing instead. So, in a method like:

Program 10: General Change Red by a Passed Amount

```
/**
 * Method to change the red by an amount
 * @param amount the amount to change the red by
 */
public void changeRed(double amount)
{
  Pixel[] pixelArray = this.getPixels();
  Pixel pixel = null;
  int value = 0;
  int i = 0;

  // loop through all the pixels
  while( i < pixelArray.length)
  {
    // get the current pixel
    pixel = pixelArray[i];

    // get the value
    value = pixel.getRed();

    /* set the red value to the original value
     * times the passed amount
     */
    pixel.setRed((int) (value * amount));
```

```
      // increment i
      i++;
   }
}
```

■

When you call (invoke) the method changeRed with a specific amount such as picture.changeRed(0.7); it will decrease the red by 30%. In the method changeRed the input parameter amount is set to 0.7. This is similar to declaring a variable inside the method like this double amount = 0.7;. Just like any variable declared in the method the parameter amount is known inside the method. It has method scope.

Call changeRed with an amount less than one to decrease the amount of red in a picture. Call changeRed with an amount greater than one to increase the amount of red in a picture. Remember that the amount of red must be between 0 and 255. If you try to set the amount of red less than 0 it will be set to 0. If you try to set the amount of red greater than 255 it will be set to 255.

We've talked about different ways of writing the same method—some better, some worse. There are others that are pretty much equivalent, and others that are much better. Let's consider a few more ways that we can write methods.

We can pass in more than one input at a time. Consider the following:

Program 11: Change all Pixel Colors by the Passed Amounts

```
/**
 * Method to change the color of each pixel in the picture
 * object by passed in amounts.
 * @param redAmount the amount to change the red value
 * @param greenAmount the amount to change the green value
 * @param blueAmount the amount to change the blue value
 */
public void changeColors(double redAmount,
                         double greenAmount,
                         double blueAmount)
{
  Pixel[] pixelArray = this.getPixels();
  Pixel pixel = null;
  int value = 0;
  int i = 0;

  // loop through all the pixels
  while( i < pixelArray.length)
  {
    // get the current pixel
    pixel = pixelArray[i];

    // change the red value
    value = pixel.getRed();
    pixel.setRed((int) (redAmount * value));
```

```java
        // change the green value
        value = pixel.getGreen();
        pixel.setGreen((int) (greenAmount * value));

        // change the blue value
        value = pixel.getBlue();
        pixel.setBlue((int) (blueAmount * value));

        // increment i
        i++;
      }
    }
```

We could use this method as shown below:

```java
> String fName = "C:/intro-prog-java/mediasources/beach-smaller.jpg";
> Picture picture = new Picture(fName);
> picture.changeColors(1.0,0.7,0.7);
> picture.show();
```

The above code would have the same result as makeSunset(). It keeps the red values the same and decreases the green and blue values 30%. That's a pretty useful and powerful method.

Recall seeing in Program 7 (page 108) this code:

```java
/**
 * Method to clear the blue from the picture (set
 * the blue to 0 for all pixels)
 */
public void clearBlue()
{
  Pixel[] pixelArray = this.getPixels();
  Pixel pixel = null;
  int index = 0;

  // loop through all the pixels
  while (index < pixelArray.length)
  {
    // get the current pixel
    pixel = pixelArray[index];

    // set the blue on the pixel to 0
    pixel.setBlue(0);

    // increment index
    index++;
  }
}
```

We could also write that same algorithm like this:

```
/**
 * Method to clear the blue from the picture (set
 * the blue to 0 for all pixels)
 */
public void clearBlue2()
{
  Pixel[] pixelArray = this.getPixels();
  int i = 0;

  // loop through all the pixels
  while(i < pixelArray.length)
  {
      pixelArray[i].setBlue(0);
      i++;
  }
}
```

It's important to note that this method achieves the *exact same* thing as the earlier method did. Both set the blue channel of all pixels to zero. An advantage of the second method is that it is shorter and doesn't require a variable declaration for a pixel. However, it may be harder for someone to understand. A shorter method isn't necessarily better.

4.3.7   Using a For Loop

You may have had the problem that you forgot to declare the index variable before you tried to use it in your `while` loop. You may also have had the problem of forgetting to increment the index variable before the end of the loop body. This happens often enough that another kind of loop is usually used when you want to loop a set number of times. It is called a *for loop*.

A for loop executes a command or group of commands in a block. A for loop allows for declaration and/or initialization of variables before the loop body is first executed. A for loop continues executing the loop body while the continuation test is true. After the end of the body of the loop and before the continuation test one or more variables can be changed.

The syntax for a for loop is:

```
for (initialization area; continuation test; change area)
{
  /* commands in body of the loop */
}
```

Let's talk through the pieces here.

- First comes the required Java keyword `for`.

- Next we have a required opening parenthesis.

- Next is the initialization area. You can declare and initialize variables here. For example, you can have `int i=0` which declares a variable **i** of the primitive type `int` and initializes it to 0. You can initialize more than one variable here by separating the initializations with commas. You are not required to have any initializations here.

- Next comes the required semicolon.
- Next is the continuation test. This holds an expression that returns true or false. When this expression is true the loop will continue to be executed. When this test is false the loop will finish and the statement following the body of the loop will be executed.
- Next comes the required semicolon.
- Next is the change area. Here you usually increment or decrement variables, such as i++ to increment i. The statements in the change area actually take place after each execution of the body of the loop.
- Next is the required closing parenthesis.

If you just want to execute one statement (command) in the body of the loop, it can just follow on the next line. It is normally indented to show that it is part of the for loop. If you want to execute more than one statement in the body of the for loop, you will need to enclose the statements in a block (a set of open and close curly braces).

Common Bug: Change Loop Variables in One Place!
When you specify how to change the loop variables in the change area of the for loop this will actually happen at the end of the body of the loop. So don't also change the loop variables in the loop or you will change them twice and probably not get the desired result.

Compare the flowchart (Figure 4.22) for a for loop with the flowchart for a while loop (Figure 4.16). They look the same because for loops and while loops *execute in the same way* even though the code looks different. Any code can be written using either. The syntax of the for loop just makes it easier to remember to declare a variable for use in the loop and to change it each time through the loop since all of that is written at the same time that you write the test. To change clearBlue() to use a for loop simply move the declaration and initialization of the index variable i to be done in the initialization area and the increment of i to be done in the change area.

Program 12: Another Clear Blue Method

```
/**
 * Method to clear the blue from the picture (set
 * the blue to 0 for all pixels)
 */
public void clearBlue3()
{
  Pixel[] pixelArray = this.getPixels();

  // loop through all the pixels
```

```java
        for (int i=0; i < pixelArray.length; i++)
            pixelArray[i].setBlue(0);
}
```

■

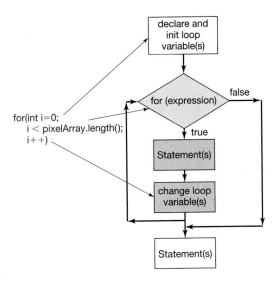

FIGURE 4.22
Flowchart of a for loop.

4.3.8 Lightening and Darkening

To lighten or darken a picture is pretty simple. It's the same pattern as we saw previously, but instead of changing a color component, you change the overall color. Here's lightening and then darkening as methods. Figure 4.23 shows the lighter and darker versions of the original picture seen earlier.

Program 13: Lighten the Picture

```java
/**
 * Method to lighten the colors in the picture
 */
public void lighten()
{
  Pixel[] pixelArray = this.getPixels();
  Color color = null;
  Pixel pixel = null;

  // loop through all the pixels
  for (int i = 0; i < pixelArray.length; i++)
  {
    // get the current pixel
    pixel = pixelArray[i];
```

```
    // get the current color
    color = pixel.getColor();

    // get a lighter color
    color = color.brighter();

    // set the pixel color to the lighter color
    pixel.setColor(color);
  }
}
```

Program 14: Darken the Picture

```
/**
 * Method to darken the color in the picture
 */
public void darken()
{
  Pixel[] pixelArray = this.getPixels();
  Color color = null;
  Pixel pixel = null;

  // loop through all the pixels
  for (int i = 0; i < pixelArray.length; i++)
  {
    // get the current pixel
    pixel = pixelArray[i];

    // get the current color
    color = pixel.getColor();

    // get a darker color
    color = color.darker();

    // set the pixel color to the darker color
    pixel.setColor(color);
  }
}
```

FIGURE 4.23
Original picture, lightened picture, and darkened picture.

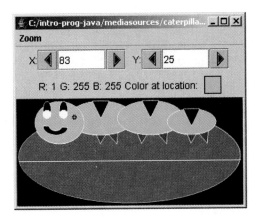

FIGURE 4.24
Negative of the image.

4.3.9   Creating a Negative

Creating a *negative image* of a picture is much easier than you might think at first. Let's think it through. What we want is the opposite of each of the current values for red, green, and blue. It's easiest to understand at the extremes. If we have a red component of 0, we want 255 instead. If we have 255, we want the negative to have a zero.

Now let's consider the middle ground. If the red component is slightly red (say, 50), we want something that is almost completely red—where the "almost" is the same amount of redness in the original picture. We want the maximum red (255), but 50 less than that. We want a red component of $255 - 50 = 205$. In general, the negative should be $255 - original$. We need to compute the negative of each of the red, green, and blue components, then create a new negative color, and set the pixel to the negative color.

Here's the program that does it, and you can see from the image that it really does work (Figure 4.24).

Program 15: Create the Negative of the Original Picture

```java
/**
 * Method to negate the picture
 */
public void negate()
{
  Pixel[] pixelArray = this.getPixels();
  Pixel pixel = null;
  int redValue, blueValue, greenValue = 0;

  // loop through all the pixels
  for (int i = 0; i < pixelArray.length; i++)
  {
    // get the current pixel
    pixel = pixelArray[i];
```

```
            // get the current red, green, and blue values
            redValue = pixel.getRed();
            greenValue = pixel.getGreen();
            blueValue = pixel.getBlue();

            // set the pixel's color to the new color
            pixel.setColor(new Color(255 - redValue,
                                     255 - greenValue,
                                     255 - blueValue));
        }
    }
```

■

4.3.10 Converting to Grayscale

Converting to grayscale is a fun program. It's short, not hard to understand, and yet has such a nice visual effect. It's a really nice example of what one can do easily yet powerfully by manipulating pixel color values.

Recall that the resultant color is gray whenever the red component, green component, and blue component have the same value. That means that our RGB encoding supports 256 levels of gray from, $(0, 0, 0)$ (black) to $(1, 1, 1)$ through $(100, 100, 100)$ and finally $(255, 255, 255)$. The tricky part is figuring out what the replicated value should be.

What we want is a sense of the *intensity* of the color. It turns out that it's pretty easy to compute: We average the three component colors. Since there are three components, the formula for intensity is:

$$\frac{(red + green + blue)}{3}$$

This leads us to the following simple program and Figure 4.25.

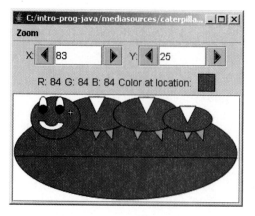

FIGURE 4.25
Color picture converted to grayscale.

Program 16: Convert to Grayscale

```java
/**
 * Method to change the picture to grayscale
 */
public void grayscale()
{
  Pixel[] pixelArray = this.getPixels();
  Pixel pixel = null;
  int intensity = 0;

  // loop through all the pixels
  for (int i = 0; i < pixelArray.length; i++)
  {
    // get the current pixel
    pixel = pixelArray[i];

    // compute the intensity of the pixel (average value)
    intensity = (int) ((pixel.getRed() + pixel.getGreen() +
                    pixel.getBlue()) / 3);

    // set the pixel color to the new color
    pixel.setColor(new Color(intensity,intensity,intensity));

  }
}
```

This is an overly simply notion of grayscale. Below is a program that takes into account how the human eye perceives *luminance*. Remember that we consider blue to be darker than red, even if there's the same amount of light reflected off. So we *weight* blue lower, and red more, when computing the average.

Program 17: Convert to Grayscale with More Careful Control of Luminance

```java
/**
 * Method to change the picture to grayscale with luminance
 */
public void grayscaleWithLuminance()
{
  Pixel[] pixelArray = this.getPixels();
  Pixel pixel = null;
  int luminance = 0;
  double redValue = 0;
  double greenValue = 0;
  double blueValue = 0;

  // loop through all the pixels
  for (int i = 0; i < pixelArray.length; i++)
  {
```

```
        // get the current pixel
        pixel = pixelArray[i];

        // get the corrected red, green, and blue values
        redValue = pixel.getRed() * 0.299;
        greenValue = pixel.getGreen() * 0.587;
        blueValue = pixel.getBlue() * 0.114;

        // compute the intensity of the pixel (average value)
        luminance = (int) (redValue + greenValue + blueValue);

        // set the pixel color to the new color
        pixel.setColor(new Color(luminance,luminance,luminance));

    }
}
```

4.4 CONCEPTS SUMMARY

In this chapter we have introduced arrays, loops, and comments.

4.4.1 Arrays

Arrays are used to store many pieces of data of the same type. They allow you to quickly access a particular item in the array using an index. If you couldn't use an array, you would have to create a separate variable name for each piece of data.

To declare a variable that refers to an array, use the type followed by open '[' and close ']' square brackets and then the variable name.

```
Pixel[] pixelArray;
```

This declares an array of `Pixel` objects. The value stored at each position in the array is a reference to a `Pixel` object.

Arrays are objects, and you can find out how large an array is by getting its length.

```
pixelArray.length
```

Notice that this isn't a method call (there are no parentheses). This accesses a public read-only field.

You can get an element of the array using `arrayReference[index]`. Where the index values can range from 0 to `arrayReference.length-1`.

```
pixel = pixelArray[i];
```

4.4.2 Loops

Loops are used to execute a block of statements while a boolean expression is true. Most loops have variables that change during the loop which eventually cause the boolean expression to be false and the loop to stop. Loops that never stop are called infinite loops.

We introduced three types of loops in this chapter: `for-each`, `while` and `for`. The `while` loop is usually used when you don't know how many times a loop needs to execute and for loops are used when you do know how many times the loop needs to execute. The for-each loop was introduced in Java 5 (1.5). It loops through all of the elements of an array.

The while loop has the keyword while followed by a boolean expression and then a block of statements between an open and close curly brace. If the boolean expression is true, the body of the loop will be executed. If the boolean expression is false, execution will continue after the body of the loop (after the close curly brace). If you just want to execute one statement in the body of the loop, then you don't need the open and close curly braces, but you should indent the statement.

```
while (boolean expression)
{
   statement1;
   statement2;
   ...
}
```

If you use a while loop to execute a block of statements a set number of times you will need to declare a variable before the while and that variable will need to be changed in the body of the loop. You may also need to declare other variables that you use in the loop before the while. Don't declare variables inside the loop because you will use more memory that way.

```
int index = 0;

// loop through all the pixels
while(index < pixelArray.length)
{
  // get the current pixel
  pixel = pixelArray[index];

  // do something to the pixel

  // increment the index
  index++;
}
```

The for loop does the same thing as a while loop, but it lets you declare the variables that you need for the loop, specify the boolean expression to test, and specify how to change the loop variables all in one place. This means you are less likely to forget to do each of these things.

```
// loop through all the pixels
for (int index = 0; index < pixelArray.length; index++)
{
  // get the current pixel
  pixel = pixelArray[index];

  // do something to the pixel

}
```

4.4.3 Comments

Comments are text that the programmer adds to the code to explain the code. The compiler ignores the comments when it translates the code into a form that the computer understands.

There are several types of comments in Java. To tell the compiler to ignore all text till the end of the current line use //.

```
// get the current pixel
pixel = pixelArray[index];
```

To tell the compiler to ignore several lines use a starting /* and ending */.

```
/* set the red value to the original value
 * times the passed amount
 */
pixel.setRed((int) (value * amount));
```

To put special comments in that can be parsed out by the javadoc utility to make html documentation use a starting /** followed by an ending */.

```
/**
 * Method to change the red by an amount
 * @param amount the amount to change the red by
 */
```

OBJECTS AND METHODS SUMMARY

In this chapter, we talk about several kinds of encodings of data (or objects).

Color	An object that holds red, green, and blue values, each between 0 and 255.
Picture	Pictures are encodings of images, typically coming from a JPEG file or a bitmap (.bmp) file.
Pixel	A pixel is a dot in a Picture object. It has a color (red, green, and blue) and an (x, y) position associated with it. It remembers its own Picture object so that a change to the pixel changes the real dot in the picture.

Picture Methods

getHeight()	This method returns the height of the Picture object in pixels.
getPixel(int x, int y)	This method takes an x position and a y position (two numbers), and returns the Pixel object at that location in the Picture object it is invoked on.
getPixels()	Returns a one-dimensional array of Pixel objects in the Picture object it is invoked on.
getWidth()	This method returns the width of the Picture object in pixels.
writePictureTo(String fileName)	This method takes a file name (a string) as input, then writes the Picture object to the file as a JPEG. (Be sure to end the filename in ".jpg" or ".bmp" for the operating system to understand it well.)

Pixel Methods

getColor()	Returns the Color object for the Pixel object.
getRed(), getGreen(), getBlue()	Each method returns the value (between 0 and 255) of the amount of redness, greenness, and blueness (respectively) in the Pixel object.
getX(), getY()	This method returns the *x* or *y* (respectively) position of where that Pixel object is in the picture.
setColor(Color color)	This method takes a Color object and sets the color for the Pixel object.
setRed(int value), setGreen(int value), setBlue(int value)	Each method takes a value (between 0 and 255) and sets the redness, greenness, or blueness (respectively) of the Pixel object to the given value.

Color Methods

new Color(int red,int green, int blue)	Takes three inputs: the red, green, and blue values (in that order), then creates and returns a Color object.
darker(),brighter()	The methods return a slightly darker or lighter (respectively) version of the Color object.

ColorChooser Methods

ColorChooser.pickAColor()	Displays a window with ways to pick a color. Find the color you want, and the method will return the Color object that you picked.

There are a bunch of *constants* that are useful in this chapter. These are variables with pre-defined values. These values are colors: Color.black, Color.white, Color.blue, Color.red, Color.green, Color.gray, Color.darkGray, Color.pink, Color.yellow, Color.orange, Color.lightGray, Color.magenta, Color.cyan. You can also use Color.BLACK, Color.WHITE, and so on. Notice that these are not method calls but are public class variables (fields) so they can be accessed using *ClassName.fieldName*.

PROBLEMS

4.1 What is meant by each of the following?

- Pixel
- Kilobyte
- RGB
- Loop

- HSV
- Flowchart
- Infinite loop
- Variable scope
- Array
- Matrix
- JPEG
- Column-major order
- Pixelization
- Luminance

4.2 Why don't we see red, green, and blue spots at each position in our picture?

4.3 Why is the maximum value of any color channel 255?

4.4 The color encoding we're using is "RGB". What does that mean, in terms of the amount of memory required to represent color? Is there a limit to the number of colors that we can represent? Can we represent *enough* colors in RGB?

4.5 Program 5 (page 97) is obviously too much color reduction. Write a version that only decreases the red by 10%, and one that reduces red by 20%. Which seems to be more useful? Note that you can always repeatedly reduce the redness in a picture, but you don't want to have to do it *too* many times, either.

4.6 Each of the below is equivalent to Program 6 (page 106). Test them and convince yourself that they are equivalent. Which do you prefer and why?

```
/**
 * Method to increase the amount of red by 1.3
 */
public void increaseRed2()
{
  Pixel[] pixelArray = this.getPixels();
  int value = 0;

  // loop through all the pixels
  for (int i = 0; i < pixelArray.length; i++)
  {
    // set the red value to 1.3 times what it was
    value = pixelArray[i].getRed();
    pixelArray[i].setRed((int) (value * 1.3));
  }
}
```

```
/**
 * Method to increase the amount of red by 1.3
 */
public void increaseRed3()
{
  Pixel[] pixelArray = this.getPixels();
  Pixel pixel = null;
  int red = 0;
  int green = 0;
  int blue = 0;
  int newRed = 0;

  // loop through all the pixels
  for (int i = 0; i < pixelArray.length; i++)
  {
    // get the current pixel
    pixel = pixelArray[i];

    // get the color values
    red = pixel.getRed();
    green = pixel.getGreen();
    blue = pixel.getBlue();

    // calculate the new red value
    newRed = (int) (red * 1.3);

    // set the pixel color to the new color
    pixel.setColor(new Color(newRed,green,blue));
  }
}
```

4.7 Change any of the methods that used a while loop to use a for loop. Compile and run the changed method and make sure it still works.

4.8 Change a variable name in any of the given methods. Make sure you change all instances of the variable name to the new name. Compile and run the changed method and make sure it still works.

4.9 Write new methods like Program 7 (page 108) to clear red and green. For each of these, which would be the most useful in actual practice? How about combinations of these?

4.10 Write a method to keep just the blue color. This means to set all the green and red values to zero. Write a method to keep just the red color. Write a method to keep just the green color.

4.11 Write a new method to *maximize* blue (i.e., setting it to 255) instead of clearing it use Program 7 (page 108) as a starting point. Is this useful? Would the red or green versions be useful?

4.12 Write a method that modifies the red, green, and blue values of a picture by different amounts. Try it out on different pictures to see if you get any nice results.

4.13 How do we get the height from a `Picture` object?

4.14 How do we get the width from a `Picture` object?

4.15 How many pixels are in a picture with a width of 200 and a height of 100?

4.16 How many pixels are in a picture with a width of 640 and a height of 480?

4.17 How do you get an array of `Pixel` objects from a `Picture` object?

4.18 How do you get the red value from a `Pixel` object?

4.19 How do you set the red value in a `Pixel` object?

4.20 There is more than one way to compute the right grayscale value for a color value. The simple method that we use in Program 16 (page 123) may not be what your grayscale printer uses when printing a color picture. Compare the color (relatively unconverted by the printer) grayscale image using our simple algorithm in with what your printer produces when you print the image. How do the two pictures differ?

TO DIG DEEPER

A wonderful book on how vision works, and how artists have learned to manipulate it, is *Vision and Art: The Biology of Seeing* by Margaret Livingstone [21].

5 Modifying Pixels in a Matrix

Chapter Learning Objectives

The media learning goals for this chapter are:

- To mirror pictures, horizontally or vertically.
- To compose pictures into one another and create collages.
- To blend two pictures.
- To rotate pictures.
- To scale pictures smaller and larger.

The computer science goals for this chapter are:

- To use nested loops for processing elements of a matrix (a two-dimensional array).
- To initialize and change multiple variables in a `for` loop.
- To develop some debugging strategies, specifically, using print statements to explore executing code.
- To break long methods into smaller pieces.
- To show how to return a value from a method.
- To use method overloading.

5.1 COPYING PIXELS

We can only get so far in our image processing with `getPixels()` before we need to know *where* a pixel is. For example, if we want to copy just part of a picture to another picture, we will need to know the x and y values to start with and end at.

5.1.1 Looping Across the Pixels with a Nested Loop

We can't use a single `for` loop if we want to keep track of the x and y values for a pixel. We have to use *two* `for` loops—one to move horizontally across the columns, and the other to move vertically to get every pixel. The method `getPixels()` did this inside itself, to make it easier to write simple picture manipulations. But if you want to access each individual pixel, you'll need to use two loops, one for each dimension of the picture. The inner loop will be *nested* inside the outer loop, literally, inside its block.

Your loops will look something like this:

```
// loop through the columns (x direction)
for (int x = 0; x < getWidth(); x++)
{
  // loop through the rows (y direction)
  for (int y = 0; y < getHeight(); y++)
  {
    // get the current pixel at this x and y position
    pixel = getPixel(x,y);

    // do something to the color

    // set the new color
    pixel.setColor(aColor);
  }
}
```

This will process all the y values from top to bottom in the first column and then all the y values in the next column and so on until all the pixels are processed.

You could also process all the x values in the top row and then all the x values in the next row and so on using this:

```
// loop through the rows (y direction)
for (int y = 0; y < getHeight(); y++)
{
  // loop through the columns (x direction)
  for (int x = 0; x < getWidth(); x++)
  {
    // get the current pixel at this x and y position
    pixel = getPixel(x,y);

    // do something to the color

    // set the new color
    pixel.setColor(aColor);
  }
}
```

Does it matter which way you process the pixels? Not if all you are trying to do is process all the pixels. Both of these loops will process all the pixels in a picture. For example, here's Program 13 (page 119), but using explicit pixel references.

Program 18: Lighten the Picture Using Nested Loops

```
/**
 * Method to lighten the colors in the picture
 */
public void lighten2()
```

```
{
  Color color = null;
  Pixel pixel = null;

  // loop through the columns (x direction)
  for (int x = 0; x < getWidth(); x++)
  {
    // loop through the rows (y direction)
    for (int y = 0; y < getHeight(); y++)
    {
      // get pixel at the x and y location
      pixel = getPixel(x,y);

      // get the current color
      color = pixel.getColor();

      // get a lighter color
      color = color.brighter();

      // set the pixel color to the lighter color
      pixel.setColor(color);
    }
  }
}
```

■

Let's walk through (trace) how it would work. Imagine that we just executed
`picture.lighten2()`.

1. The code `picture.lighten2()` executes the object method in the Picture class `public void lighten2()`. The method is implicitly passed the current picture object (you can refer to the current picture object using the keyword `this`).

2. The code `Color color = null;` and `Pixel pixel = null;` declares the variables color (an object of the Color class) and pixel (an object of the Pixel class). Both of these are initialized to `null` (not referring to any object yet). These variables will be needed when we are looping through the pixels. We could declare these in the for loop but then they would be redeclared each time through the loop. It is better to declare them once before the loop and change them each time through the loop.

3. The code `for (int x = 0; x < getWidth(); x++)` declares a variable x of type `int` which will be initialized to 0 and then a check will be made to see if x is less than the width of the current Picture object. If x is less than the width, then the body of this for loop will be executed. After the body of the loop has been executed one time the value in x will be incremented and the continuation condition will be tested again.

4. The code `for (int y = 0; y < getHeight(); y++)` declares a variable y of type `int` which will be initialized to 0. The test checks that y is less than the height of the current Picture object. If y is less than the height then

the body of this `for` loop will be executed. After the body has executed the value in y will be incremented and the continuation condition will be tested again.

5. The code `pixel = getPixel(x,y);` sets the variable `pixel` to refer to the `Pixel` object at the given x and y location in the picture.

6. The code `color = pixel.getColor();` sets the variable `color` to refer to the `Color` object at the current pixel.

7. Next comes `color = color.brighter();`. This creates a new lighter (brighter) `Color` object based on the original `Color` object and sets the variable `color` to refer to that new `Color` object.

8. The code `pixel.setColor(color);` sets the current pixel's color to be the lighter color.

9. Each time we reach the end of the inner `for` loop, the y value will be incremented by 1 and then the value of y will be compared to the height of the picture. If the value of y is less than the height, the statements in the body of the loop will be executed again. If the value of y is equal or greater than the height, execution will jump to the next statement (the outer loop).

10. Each time we reach the end of the outer `for` loop the x value will be incremented by 1 and then the value of x will be compared to the width of the picture. If the x value is less than the width of the picture, the commands in the loop body will be executed. If the value of x is equal or greater than the width of the picture, execution will continue at the statement following the body of the loop.

5.1.2 Mirroring a Picture

Let's start out with an interesting effect that is only occasionally useful, but it is fun. Let's mirror a picture along its vertical axis. In other words, imagine that you have a mirror, and you place it on a picture so that the left side of the picture shows up in the mirror. That's the effect that we're going to implement. We'll do it in a couple of different ways.

First, let's think through what we're going to do. We want to copy the pixel in the first column and first row $(0, 0)$ to the pixel in the last column and first row $(width - 1, 0)$. We will copy the pixel in the second column and first row $(1, 0)$ to the second to last column and first row $(width - 2, 0)$. We will continue to do this until we reach the middle of the picture $(width/2)$. Remember that the index for the last column is one less than the width so each time through the loop we are copying from the (x, y) to $(width - 1 - x, y)$.

What if we have an even number of pixels? The smallest even number of pixels is two. The `mirrorPoint` would be $(2/2 = 1)$. The first time through the loop this would copy from $(0, 0)$ to $(width - 1 - 0, 0)$ which is $(1, 0)$. Then x would increment and the inner loop would stop since x isn't less than the `mirrorPoint` (Figure 5.1).

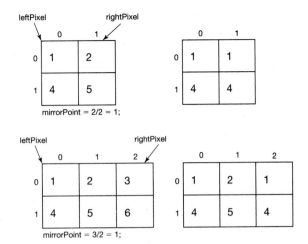

FIGURE 5.1
Once we pick a mirror point, we can just walk x halfway and copy from (x, y) to (width −
1 − x, y).

What if we have an odd number of pixels? We don't want to copy the middle pixel.
Let's try it with three pixels. The `mirrorPoint` would be $(3/2 = 1)$. Remember that
integer division results in an integer result and the fractional part is thrown away.
The first time through the loop this would copy from $(0, 0)$ to $(\text{width} − 1 − 0, 0)$
which is $(2, 0)$. Then x would increment and the inner loop would stop since x
wouldn't be less than the `mirrorPoint`.

Take a look at Figure 5.1 to convince yourself that we'll actually reach every pixel
(except the middle one if there are an odd number of pixels) using this scheme. Here's
the actual program.

Program 19: Mirror Pixels in a Picture along a Vertical Line

```
/**
 * Method to mirror around a vertical line in the middle
 * of the picture based on the width
 */
public void mirrorVertical()
{
  int width = this.getWidth();
  int mirrorPoint = width / 2;
  Pixel leftPixel = null;
  Pixel rightPixel = null;

  // loop through all the rows
  for (int y = 0; y < getHeight(); y++)
  {
    // loop from 0 to the middle (mirror point)
    for (int x = 0; x < mirrorPoint; x++)
    {
      leftPixel = getPixel(x, y);
```

```
            rightPixel = getPixel(width - 1 - x, y);
            rightPixel.setColor(leftPixel.getColor());
        }
    }
}
```

■

We'd use it like this, and the result appears in Figure 5.2.

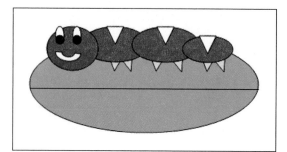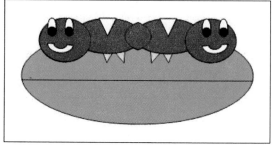

FIGURE 5.2
Original picture (left) and mirrored along the vertical axis (right).

```
> String fileName =
  "C:/intro-prog-java/mediasources/caterpillar.jpg";
> Picture picture = new Picture(fileName);
> picture.show();
> picture.mirrorVertical();
> picture.repaint();
```

Can we mirror horizontally? Sure!

Program 20: Mirror Pixels Horizontally, Top-to-Bottom

```
/**
 * Method to mirror around a horizontal line in the middle
 * based on the height. It copies the top mirrored to
 * the bottom
 */
public void mirrorHorizontal()
{
  int height = this.getHeight();
  int mirrorPoint = height / 2;
  Pixel topPixel = null;
  Pixel bottomPixel = null;

  // loop through the columns
  for (int x=0; x < getWidth(); x++)
  {
    // loop from 0 to just before the mirror point
```

```
      for (int y=0; y < mirrorPoint; y++)
      {
        topPixel = getPixel(x,y);
        bottomPixel = getPixel(x,height - 1 - y);
        bottomPixel.setColor(topPixel.getColor());
      }
    }
}
```

We'd use it like this, and the result appears in Figure 5.3.

```
> String fName =
  "C:/intro-prog-java/mediasources/redMotorcycle.jpg";
> System.out.println(fName);
C:/intro-prog-java/mediasources/redMotorcycle.jpg
> Picture picture = new Picture(fName);
> picture.show();
> picture.mirrorHorizontal();
> picture.repaint();
```

FIGURE 5.3
A motorcycle mirrored horizontally, top to bottom (left) and bottom to top (right).

Now this last method copies from the top of the picture onto the bottom (see Figure 5.3). You can see that we're getting the color from topPixel which is from (x,y)—that will always be *above* mirrorPoint since smaller values of *y* are nearer the top of the picture. To copy from the bottom up, simply change the color at the top pixel to the color of the bottom pixel (Figure 5.3).

Program 21: Mirror Pixels Horizontally, Bottom-to-Top

```
/**
 * Method to mirror around a horizontal line in the middle
 * based on the height of the picture.  It copies the bottom
 * to the top.
 */
```

```
public void mirrorHorizontalBottomToTop()
{
  int height = this.getHeight();
  int mirrorPoint = height / 2;
  Pixel topPixel = null;
  Pixel bottomPixel = null;

  // loop through the columns
  for (int x=0; x < getWidth(); x++)
  {
    // loop from 1 to just before the mirror point
    for (int y=0; y < mirrorPoint; y++)
    {
      topPixel = getPixel(x,y);
      bottomPixel = getPixel(x,height - 1 - y);
      topPixel.setColor(bottomPixel.getColor());
    }
  }
}
```

We'd use it like this, and the result appears in Figure 5.3.

```
> String fName =
  "C:/intro-prog-java/mediasources/redMotorcycle.jpg";
> Picture picture = new Picture(fName);
> picture.show();
> picture.mirrorHorizontalBottomToTop();
> picture.repaint();
```

Mirroring usefully

While mirroring is probably mostly used for interesting effects, occasionally it has some more serious (but still fun!) purposes. Mark took a picture of the Temple of Hephaistos which is in the ancient agora in Athens, Greece, when traveling to a conference (Figure 5.4). By sheer luck, Mark got the pediment dead horizontal. The Temple of Hephaistos had its pediment damaged. Mark wondered if he could "fix" it by mirroring the good part onto the broken part.

This time we don't want to mirror one-half of the picture onto the other half. We just want to mirror the pixels from the good side of the pediment on the left onto the bad side on the right. We also don't want to mirror all the pixels in the y direction. We just need the pixels from the top of the pediment to the bottom of the pediment. We can use the explorer to find out the value for those pixels (Figure 5.5). The pediment starts at x=13 and the middle is at x=276. The highest part of the pediment is at y=27 and it ends at y=97.

How do we mirror just a small part of a picture? Well, we still need a point to mirror around. We will use 276 for that instead of half the width like we did in the method mirrorVertical(). Let's start by copying the mirrorVertical() method and changing the name to mirrorTemple() and set the mirror point to the value 276. We just want to copy from x=13 to x<276. We can start y at the top of the pediment

FIGURE 5.4
Temple of Hephaistos from the ancient agora in Athens, Greece.

FIGURE 5.5
Coordinates where we need to do the mirroring.

27 (instead of 0) and copy while it is less than 97 (instead of the height of the picture). Then we will copy from the pixel at (x, y) to a pixel at the mirror point plus the distance from the mirror point to the current x (mirrorPoint + (mirrorPoint − x)).

Program 22: Mirror Part of a Picture Vertically

```
/**
 * Method to mirror part of the temple picture around a
 * vertical line at a mirror point
 */
public void mirrorTemple()
{
  int mirrorPoint = 276;
  Pixel leftPixel = null;
  Pixel rightPixel = null;
```

```
  // loop through the rows
  for (int y = 27; y < 97; y++)
  {
    // loop from 1 to just before the mirror point
    for (int x = 13; x < mirrorPoint; x++)
    {
      leftPixel = getPixel(x, y);
      rightPixel = getPixel(mirrorPoint + (mirrorPoint - x), y);
      rightPixel.setColor(leftPixel.getColor());
    }
  }
}
```

To use this method try this.

```
> String fileName = "C:/intro-prog-java/mediasources/temple.jpg";
> Picture picture = new Picture(fileName);
> picture.explore();
> picture.mirrorTemple();
> picture.explore();
```

The final picture is in Figure 5.6—it worked pretty well! Of course, it is possible to tell that it was digitally manipulated. For example, if you check the shadows, you can see that the sun must have been on the left and the right at the same time.

You may be tired of typing the full path name to each file. You can save the name of the directory that has your media in it and then use

```
FileChooser.getMediaPath(fileName)
```

to get the full path name.

FIGURE 5.6
The manipulated temple.

The method `FileChooser.getMediaPath(fileName)` generates a complete path for you by returning a string with the saved directory name followed by the base file name. The default media directory is "c:/intro-prog-java/mediasources/". If you wish to use a different media directory you should execute

`FileChooser.setMediaPath(directory)`

first! Using `FileChooser.setMediaPath(directory)` lets you specify the place (directory) where you store your media.

The temple example is a good one to ask ourselves about. If you really understand, you can answer questions like "What's the *first* pixel to be mirrored in this method?" and "How many pixels get copied anyway?" You should be able to figure these out by thinking through the program—pretend you're the computer and execute the program in your mind.

If that's too hard, you can insert `System.out.println()` statements, but you might change the ending values on the loops so that it won't take too long to finish:

```
/**
 * Method to mirror part of the temple picture around a
 * vertical line at a mirror point
 */
public void mirrorTemple()
{
  int mirrorPoint = 276;
  Pixel leftPixel = null;
  Pixel rightPixel = null;

  // loop through the rows
  for (int y = 27; y < 28; y++)
  {
    // loop from 13 to just before the mirror point
    for (int x = 13; x < 17; x++)
    {
      System.out.println("Copying color from " +
                  x + " to " +
                  (mirrorPoint + (mirrorPoint - x)));
      leftPixel = getPixel(x, y);
      rightPixel = getPixel(mirrorPoint + (mirrorPoint - x), y);
      rightPixel.setColor(leftPixel.getColor());
      count = count + 1;
    }
  }
}
```

This will loop through the first four pixels. When we run this we get the following:

```
> String fileName = "C:/intro-prog-java/mediasources/temple.jpg";
> Picture picture = new Picture(fileName);
> picture.mirrorTemple();
Copying color from 13 to 539
Copying color from 14 to 538
Copying color from 15 to 537
Copying color from 16 to 536
```

It starts copying at $x = 13$ to *mirrorPoint* + (*mirrorPoint* − *x*) which is $276 + (276 − 13) = 539$. Next it increments x and copies from $x = 14$ to $276 + (276 − 14) = 538$. Each time through the loop x will increment and the distance from the `mirrorPoint` to x will decrease.

How many pixels did we process? We can have the computer figure that one out, too. Just add a count that starts at 0 and increment it each time we copy a pixel. After the loop finishes print out the value of count.

```
/**
 * Method to mirror part of the temple picture around a
 * vertical line at a mirror point
 */
public void mirrorTemple()
{
  int mirrorPoint = 276;
  Pixel leftPixel = null;
  Pixel rightPixel = null;
  int count = 0;

  // loop through the rows
  for (int y = 27; y < 97; y++)
  {
    // loop from 13 to just before the mirror point
    for (int x = 13; x < mirrorPoint; x++)
    {
      leftPixel = getPixel(x, y);
      rightPixel = getPixel(mirrorPoint + (mirrorPoint - x), y);
      rightPixel.setColor(leftPixel.getColor());
      count = count + 1;
    }
  }
  System.out.println("We copied " + count + " pixels");
}
```

This one comes back with `We copied 18410 pixels`. Where did that number come from? You can calculate how many times you execute the commands in a for loop with $end − start + 1$. We copy 70 rows of pixels (y goes from 27 to 96 (because of the <97) which is $96 − 27 + 1 = 70$). We copy 263 columns of pixels (x goes from 13 to <276 which is $275 − 13 + 1 = 263$). $70 * 263$ is $18,410$.

5.2 COPYING AND TRANSFORMING PICTURES

We can even copy from one picture to another. We're going to end up keeping track of a *source* picture that we take pixels from and a *target* picture that we're going to set pixels in. Actually, we don't copy the pixels—we simply make the pixels in the target the same color as the pixels in the source. Copying pixels requires us to keep track of multiple index variables: The (x, y) position in the source and the (x, y) in the target.

What's exciting about copying pixels is that making some small changes in how we deal with the index variables leads to not only *copying* the image but *transforming* it. In this section, we're going to talk about copying, cropping, rotating, and scaling pictures.

```
> FileChooser.getMediaPath("temple.jpg")
"C:/intro-prog-java/mediasources/temple.jpg"
> String fileName = FileChooser.getMediaPath("temple.jpg");
> Picture temple = new Picture(fileName);
```

Our target will be the paper-sized JPEG file in the mediasources directory, which is 7 × 9.5 inches, which will fit on a 9 × 11.5 inch lettersize piece of paper with one inch margins.

```
> String paperFile = FileChooser.getMediaPath("7inx95in.jpg");
> Picture paperPicture = new Picture(paperFile);
> paperPicture.show();
> System.out.println(paperPicture.getWidth());
504
> System.out.println(paperPicture.getHeight());
684
```

5.2.1 Copying

To copy a picture we simply make sure that we increment sourceX and targetX variables (the source and target index variables for the X axis) together, and the sourceY and targetY variables together. We can initialize more than one variable in the initialization area of a for loop and change more than one variable in the change area.

Here's a program for copying a picture of Katie to the current picture.

Program 23: Copying a Picture to the Current Picture

```
/**
 * Method to copy the picture of Katie to the
 * upper left corner of the current picture
 */
public void copyKatie()
{
  String sourceFile =
    FileChooser.getMediaPath("KatieFancy.jpg");
  Picture sourcePicture = new Picture(sourceFile);
  Pixel sourcePixel = null;
  Pixel targetPixel = null;

  // loop through the columns
  for (int sourceX = 0, targetX=0;
       sourceX < sourcePicture.getWidth();
       sourceX++, targetX++)
  {
    // loop through the rows
    for (int sourceY = 0, targetY =0;
         sourceY < sourcePicture.getHeight();
```

```
                    sourceY++, targetY++)
    {
      // set the target pixel color to the source pixel color
      sourcePixel = sourcePicture.getPixel(sourceX,sourceY);
      targetPixel = this.getPixel(targetX,targetY);
      targetPixel.setColor(sourcePixel.getColor());
    }
  }
}
```

■

To use this method create a picture from the file that has a blank paper-sized picture. The picture of Katie will be copied to the top-left corner of the blank picture Figure 5.7.

```
> String fileName = FileChooser.getMediaPath("7inx95in.jpg");
> Picture targetPicture = new Picture(fileName);
> targetPicture.show();
> targetPicture.copyKatie();
> targetPicture.show();
```

This method copies a picture of Katie to the canvas (blank picture) (Figure 5.7). Here's how it works:

- The first two lines are just setting up the source (sourcePicture).
- Then we have the declaration of variables to keep track of the target and source pixels.

FIGURE 5.7
Copying a picture to a canvas.

- Next comes the loop for managing the x index variables, sourceX for the source picture and targetX for the target (current) picture. The for loop declares both variables and initializes them to 0. You can have more than one variable declared and initialized in the initialization area of a for loop, just separate them with commas. Next the continuation test checks if the sourceX is less than the width of the source picture. Finally, in the change area, we increment both the sourceX and targetX variables each time after the statements in the body of the loop have been executed. You can change more than one variable in the change area as long as you separate the changes with commas. The for loop for looping through the columns is:

```
for (int sourceX = 0, targetX=0;
     sourceX < sourcePicture.getWidth();
     sourceX++, targetX++)
```

- Inside the loop for the X variables is the loop for the Y variables. It has a very similar structure, since it's goal is to keep targetY and sourceY in synch in exactly the same way.

```
for (int sourceY = 0, targetY=0;
     sourceY < sourcePicture.getHeight();
     sourceY++, targetY++)
```

It's inside the Y loop that we actually get the color from the source pixel and set the corresponding pixel in the target (current picture) to the same color.

Of course, we don't have to copy from $(0, 0)$ in the source to $(0, 0)$ in the target. We can easily copy to another location in the target picture. All we have to do is to change where the target X and Y coordinates *start*. The rest stays exactly the same (Figure 5.8).

Program 24: Copy Elsewhere into the Current Picture

```
/**
 * Method to copy the picture of Katie to (100,100) in the
 * current picture
 */
public void copyKatieMidway()
{
  String sourceFile =
    FileChooser.getMediaPath("KatieFancy.jpg");
  Picture sourcePicture = new Picture(sourceFile);
  Pixel sourcePixel = null;
  Pixel targetPixel = null;

  // loop through the columns
  for (int sourceX = 0, targetX=100;
       sourceX < sourcePicture.getWidth();
       sourceX++, targetX++)
  {
```

```
    // loop through the rows
    for (int sourceY = 0, targetY =100;
         sourceY < sourcePicture.getHeight();
         sourceY++, targetY++)
    {
      // set the target pixel color to the source pixel color
      sourcePixel = sourcePicture.getPixel(sourceX,sourceY);
      targetPixel = this.getPixel(targetX,targetY);
      targetPixel.setColor(sourcePixel.getColor());
    }
  }
}
```

■

To try this method create the target picture from the blank paper-sized picture file, invoke the method on it, and show the result. The picture of Katie will be copied with the upper left corner at (100, 100).

```
> String fileName = FileChooser.getMediaPath("7inx95in.jpg");
> Picture targetPicture = new Picture(fileName);
> targetPicture.copyKatieMidway();
> targetPicture.show();
```

Similarly, we don't have to copy a *whole* picture. *Cropping* is taking only part of a picture out of the whole picture. Digitally, that's just a matter of changing your start and end coordinates. To grab just Katie's face out of the picture, we only have

FIGURE 5.8
Copying a picture midway into a canvas.

FIGURE 5.9
Copying part of a picture onto a canvas.

to figure out the upper-left corner of a rectangle enclosing her face and use that as the starting values for sourceX and sourceY. We also need to determine the bottom-right corner of the rectangle enclosing her face and use that as the stopping x and y values (Figure 5.9). We can use the picture explorer to determine these values. The upper-left corner of the rectangle enclosing the face is at (70, 3), and the bottom-right corner is at (135, 80).

Program 25: Cropping a Picture onto a Canvas

```
/**
 * Method to copy just Katie's face to the current picture
 */
public void copyKatiesFace()
{
  String sourceFile =
    FileChooser.getMediaPath("KatieFancy.jpg");
  Picture sourcePicture = new Picture(sourceFile);
  Pixel sourcePixel = null;
  Pixel targetPixel = null;

  // loop through the columns
  for (int sourceX = 70, targetX = 100;
       sourceX < 135; sourceX++, targetX++)
```

```
    {
      // loop through the rows
      for (int sourceY = 3, targetY = 100;
           sourceY < 80; sourceY++, targetY++)
      {
        // set the target pixel color to the source pixel color
        sourcePixel = sourcePicture.getPixel(sourceX,sourceY);
        targetPixel = this.getPixel(targetX,targetY);
        targetPixel.setColor(sourcePixel.getColor());
      }
    }
  }
```

■

To try this method, create the target picture from the blank paper-sized picture file, invoke the method on it, and show the result. Just Katie's face will be copied to the target picture with the upper-left corner at (100, 100).

```
> String fileName = FileChooser.getMediaPath("7inx95in.jpg");
> Picture targetPicture = new Picture(fileName);
> targetPicture.copyKatiesFace();
> targetPicture.show();
```

Try to copy part of another picture to the blank paper-sized picture file. What do you need to change and what can stay the same?

How does that work?

Let's look at a small example to see what's going on in the copying program. We start out with a source and a target, and copy from x = 0, y = 0 to x = 3, y = 1.

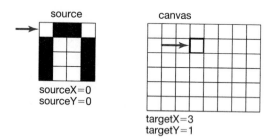

We then increment both the sourceY and targetY, and copy again.

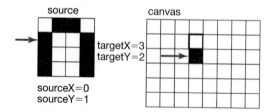

We continue down the column, incrementing both Y index variables.

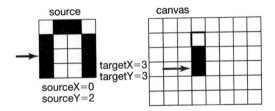

When done with that column, we increment the X index variables and move on to the next column, until we copy every pixel.

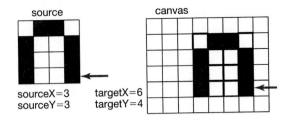

5.2.2   Creating a Collage

In the mediasources folder are a couple images of flowers (Figure 5.10), each 100 pixels wide. Let's make a *collage* of them, by combining several of our effects to create different flowers. We'll copy them all into the blank image 640x480.jpg. All we really have to do is to copy the pixel colors to the right places.

FIGURE 5.10
Flowers in the mediasources folder.

Program 26: Creating a Collage by Copying Flowers

```
/**
 * Method to copy flower pictures to create a collage.
 * All the flower pictures will be lined up near the
 * bottom of the current picture (5 pixels from the bottom)
 */
```

```
public void copyFlowers()
{

  // create the flower pictures
  Picture flower1Picture =
    new Picture(FileChooser.getMediaPath("flower1.jpg"));
  Picture flower2Picture =
    new Picture(FileChooser.getMediaPath("flower2.jpg"));

  // declare the source and target pixel variables
  Pixel sourcePixel = null;
  Pixel targetPixel = null;

  // save the heights of the two pictures
  int flower1Height = flower1Picture.getHeight();
  int flower2Height = flower2Picture.getHeight();

  /* copy the first flower picture to 5 pixels from the bottom
   * left corner of the current picture
   */
  for (int sourceX = 0, targetX = 0;
      sourceX < flower1Picture.getWidth();
      sourceX++, targetX++)
  {
    for (int sourceY = 0,
        targetY = this.getHeight() - flower1Height - 5;
        sourceY < flower1Picture.getHeight();
        sourceY++, targetY++)
    {
      sourcePixel = flower1Picture.getPixel(sourceX,sourceY);
      targetPixel = this.getPixel(targetX,targetY);
      targetPixel.setColor(sourcePixel.getColor());
    }
  }

  // copy the flower2 picture starting with x = 100
  for (int sourceX = 0, targetX = 100;
      sourceX < flower2Picture.getWidth();
      sourceX++, targetX++)
  {
    for (int sourceY = 0,
        targetY = this.getHeight() - flower2Height - 5;
        sourceY < flower2Picture.getHeight();
        sourceY++, targetY++)
    {
      sourcePixel = flower2Picture.getPixel(sourceX,sourceY);
      targetPixel = this.getPixel(targetX,targetY);
      targetPixel.setColor(sourcePixel.getColor());
    }
  }

  // copy the flower1 negated to x = 200
```

```
flower1Picture.negate();
for (int sourceX = 0, targetX = 200;
     sourceX < flower1Picture.getWidth();
     sourceX++, targetX++)
{
  for (int sourceY = 0,
       targetY = this.getHeight() - flower1Height - 5;
       sourceY < flower1Picture.getHeight();
       sourceY++, targetY++)
  {
    sourcePixel = flower1Picture.getPixel(sourceX,sourceY);
    targetPixel = this.getPixel(targetX,targetY);
    targetPixel.setColor(sourcePixel.getColor());
  }
}

// clear the blue in flower 2 picture and add at x=300
flower2Picture.clearBlue();
for (int sourceX = 0, targetX = 300;
     sourceX < flower2Picture.getWidth();
     sourceX++, targetX++)
{
  for (int sourceY = 0,
       targetY = this.getHeight() - flower2Height - 5;
       sourceY < flower2Picture.getHeight();
       sourceY++, targetY++)
  {
    sourcePixel = flower2Picture.getPixel(sourceX,sourceY);
    targetPixel = this.getPixel(targetX,targetY);
    targetPixel.setColor(sourcePixel.getColor());
  }
}

// copy the negated flower 1 to x=400
for (int sourceX = 0, targetX = 400;
     sourceX < flower1Picture.getWidth();
     sourceX++, targetX++)
{
  for (int sourceY = 0,
       targetY = this.getHeight() - flower1Height - 5;
       sourceY < flower1Picture.getHeight();
       sourceY++, targetY++)
  {
    sourcePixel = flower1Picture.getPixel(sourceX,sourceY);
    targetPixel = this.getPixel(targetX,targetY);
    targetPixel.setColor(sourcePixel.getColor());
  }
}
}
```

Here's how we run the collage (Figure 5.11):

```
> String fileName = FileChooser.getMediaPath("7inx95in.jpg");
```

```
> Picture targetPicture = new Picture(fileName);
> targetPicture.copyFlowers();
> targetPicture.show();
```

This method is long and repetitive, which makes it hard to read. One of the ways to improve it is to pull out pieces of code that perform the same task and make these new methods. Each time we add a new picture to our canvas, the only things changing are the picture to be added and the `targetX`. The `targetY` is always calculated the same way as the height of the canvas minus the height of the picture being copied minus 5.

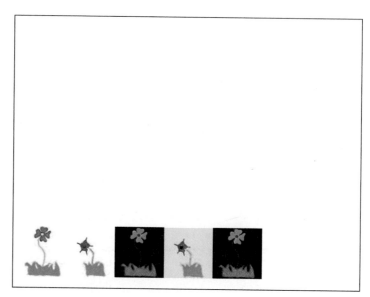

FIGURE 5.11
Collage of flowers.

Let's write a new more general method that is passed the picture to copy and the x location to start copying it to. For the y location let's put it 5 pixels from the bottom of the current picture.

Program 27: General Copy Method

```
/**
 * Method that will copy all of the passed source picture into
 * the current picture object starting with the left corner
 * given by xStart.  It will put the sourcePicture at 5 pixels
 * from the bottom of this picture
 * @param sourcePicture the picture object to copy
 * @param xStart the x position to start the copy in the target
 */
public void copyPictureTo(Picture sourcePicture,
                          int xStart)
```

```
{
  Pixel sourcePixel = null;
  Pixel targetPixel = null;

  // loop through the columns
  for (int sourceX = 0, targetX = xStart;
       sourceX < sourcePicture.getWidth();
       sourceX++, targetX++)
  {
    // loop through the rows
    for (int sourceY = 0,
         targetY = this.getHeight() -
                     sourcePicture.getHeight() - 5;
         sourceY < sourcePicture.getHeight();
         sourceY++, targetY++)
    {
      sourcePixel = sourcePicture.getPixel(sourceX,sourceY);
      targetPixel = this.getPixel(targetX,targetY);
      targetPixel.setColor(sourcePixel.getColor());
    }
  }

}

/**
 * Method to copy two flowers in a pattern to the
 * bottom (5 pixels from bottom) of the current picture
 */
public void copyFlowersBetter()
{

  // create the flower pictures
  Picture flower1Picture =
    new Picture(FileChooser.getMediaPath("flower1.jpg"));
  Picture flower2Picture =
    new Picture(FileChooser.getMediaPath("flower2.jpg"));

  // copy the first flower picture to near the
  // bottom left corner of the canvas
  this.copyPictureTo(flower1Picture,0);

  /* copy the flower2 picture starting with
   * x = 100 in the canvas
   */

  this.copyPictureTo(flower2Picture,100);

  // copy the flower1 negated to x = 200 in the canvas
  flower1Picture.negate();
  this.copyPictureTo(flower1Picture,200);

  /* clear the blue in flower 2 picture and
   * add at x=300 in the canvas
   */
```

```
      flower2Picture.clearBlue();
      this.copyPictureTo(flower2Picture,300);

      // copy the negated flower 1 to x=400
      this.copyPictureTo(flower1Picture,400);
    }
```

The method `copyFlowersBetter` is much easier to read and understand now. And we now have a method `copyPictureTo` which is easy to reuse.

We can even make a more general copy method, which takes both the starting x and starting y values for the target picture and copies the passed source picture into the current picture with the source picture's upper-left corner at the passed starting x and y values in the target.

```
/**
 * Method that will copy all of the passed source picture into
 * the current picture object starting with the left corner
 * given by xStart, yStart
 * @param sourcePicture the picture object to copy
 * @param xStart the x position to start the copy into on the
 * target
 * @param yStart the y position to start the copy into on the
 * target
 */
public void copyPictureTo(Picture sourcePicture,
                          int xStart,
                          int yStart)
{
  Pixel sourcePixel = null;
  Pixel targetPixel = null;

  // loop through the columns
  for (int sourceX = 0, targetX = xStart;
       sourceX < sourcePicture.getWidth();
       sourceX++, targetX++)
  {
    // loop through the rows
    for (int sourceY = 0,
         targetY = yStart;
         sourceY < sourcePicture.getHeight();
         sourceY++, targetY++)
    {
      sourcePixel = sourcePicture.getPixel(sourceX,sourceY);
      targetPixel = this.getPixel(targetX,targetY);
      targetPixel.setColor(sourcePixel.getColor());
    }
  }

}
```

Notice that you can have two methods with the same names (copyPictureTo) and you don't have any trouble when you compile. How can that be? Java allows you to have many methods with the same method name as long as the parameters are different. The first copyPictureTo method took a Picture object and an int. The second copyPictureTo method took a Picture object, and two int values. So the two methods have a different number of parameters. Having more than one method with the same name but different parameters is called *overloading*. It doesn't really matter what you name the parameters. What matters is the types. Two methods with the same name are allowed if the number of parameters is different, or the types of the parameters are different, or the order of the parameter types is different. A *method signature* is the method name and the parameter list. So the method signatures need to be different in order for a method to be overloaded. The return type is not part of the method signature. Having two methods with the same name and same parameter list but different return types is not allowed.

5.2.3 Blending Pictures

When we create collages by copying, any overlap typically means that one picture shows *over* another. The last picture painted on is the one that appears. But it doesn't have to be that way. We can *blend* pictures by multiplying their colors and adding them. This gives us the effect of *transparency*.

We know that 100% of something is the whole thing. 50% of one and 50% of another would also add up to 100%. In the program below, we blend a picture of the two sisters with an overlap of 50 (the width of Katie minus 150) columns of pixels (Figure 5.12) onto the current picture.

FIGURE 5.12
Blending the picture of Katie and Jenny.

Program 28: Blending Two Pictures

```java
/**
 * Method to blend two sisters together onto the current
 * picture
 */
public void blendPictures()
{

  // create the sister pictures
  Picture katiePicture =
    new Picture(FileChooser.getMediaPath("KatieFancy.jpg"));
  Picture jennyPicture =
    new Picture(FileChooser.getMediaPath("JenParty.jpg"));

  // declare the source and target pixel variables
  Pixel katiePixel = null;
  Pixel jennyPixel = null;
  Pixel targetPixel = null;

  /* declare the target x and source x since we will need
   * the values after the for loop
   */
  int sourceX = 0;
  int targetX = 0;

  // copy the first 150 pixels of katie to the canvas
  for (; sourceX < 150; sourceX++, targetX++)
  {
    for (int sourceY=0, targetY=0;
         sourceY < katiePicture.getHeight();
         sourceY++, targetY++)
    {
      katiePixel = katiePicture.getPixel(sourceX,sourceY);
      targetPixel = this.getPixel(targetX,targetY);
      targetPixel.setColor(katiePixel.getColor());
    }
  }

  /* copy 50% of katie and 50% of jenny till
   * the end of katie's width
   */
  for (; sourceX < katiePicture.getWidth();
       sourceX++, targetX++)
  {
    for (int sourceY=0,targetY=0;
         sourceY < katiePicture.getHeight();
         sourceY++, targetY++)
    {
      katiePixel = katiePicture.getPixel(sourceX,sourceY);
      jennyPixel =
        jennyPicture.getPixel(sourceX - 150,sourceY);
```

```
          targetPixel = this.getPixel(targetX,targetY);
          targetPixel.setColor(
                new Color((int) (katiePixel.getRed() * 0.5 +
                                 jennyPixel.getRed() * 0.5),
                          (int) (katiePixel.getGreen() * 0.5 +
                                 jennyPixel.getGreen() * 0.5),
                          (int) (katiePixel.getBlue() * 0.5 +
                                 jennyPixel.getBlue() * 0.5)));
        }
      }

      // copy the rest of Jenny
      sourceX = sourceX - 150;
      for (; sourceX < jennyPicture.getWidth();
           sourceX++, targetX++)
      {
        for (int sourceY = 0, targetY = 0;
             sourceY < jennyPicture.getHeight();
             sourceY++, targetY++)
        {
          jennyPixel = jennyPicture.getPixel(sourceX,sourceY);
          targetPixel = this.getPixel(targetX,targetY);
          targetPixel.setColor(jennyPixel.getColor());
        }
      }
    }
```

To try this out, create a picture object using the blank 640 by 480 file and invoke the method on that. Show the result.

```
> String fileName = FileChooser.getMediaPath("640x480.jpg");
> Picture picture = new Picture(fileName);
> picture.blendPictures();
> picture.show();
```

Making it Work Tip: Optional Parts of the for Loop

Notice that we are missing the initialization area in the for loops in the method blendPictures(). Also notice that we moved the declaration of sourceX and sourceY outside the loops. This is because we want to keep the values around after the first loop ends. The initialization area of a for loop is optional (the ';' is not optional). In fact, the initialization area, continuation test, and change area are all optional. You could code a for loop as for (;;) but that isn't terribly useful. It would execute the body of the loop forever. This is one way to create an infinite loop.

5.2.4   Rotation

Transformations to the image occur by using the index variables differently or incrementing them differently, but otherwise keeping the same program. Let's rotate Katie 90 degrees to the left. What does that mean? Let's try it with something simple first. You can write some numbers in a table on a piece of paper and then rotate it left and

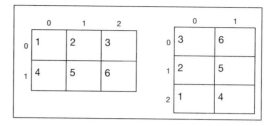

FIGURE 5.13
Rotating some numbers in a table to the left 90 degrees.

then read the new table to see where the old numbers were moved to (Figure 5.13). Notice that the columns become the rows and the rows the columns but it isn't as simple as just using the source x for the target y and the source y for the target x.

Value (0, 0) in the source moves to (0, 2) in the target. Value (0, 1) in the source moves to (1, 2) in the target. Value (1, 0) in the source moves to (0, 1) in the target. Value (1, 1) in the source moves to (1, 1) in the target. Value (2, 0) in the source moves to (0, 0) in the target. Value (2, 1) in the source moves to (1, 0) in the target. So the first column values move into the bottom row and the last column values move into the top row. Also notice that the target x value is the same as the source y value.

We will do the rotation by looping through the pixels in the usual way and getting the source pixel in the usual way, but the target pixel's x value will be the source y and the target pixel's y value will be width of the source picture—1—the source x (Figure 5.14).

Program 29: Rotating a Picture Left 90 Degrees

```
/**
 * Method to copy the picture of Katie but rotate
 * her left 90 degrees on the current picture
 */
public void copyKatieLeftRotation()
{
  String sourceFile =
    FileChooser.getMediaPath("KatieFancy.jpg");
  Picture sourcePicture = new Picture(sourceFile);
  Pixel sourcePixel = null;
  Pixel targetPixel = null;

  // loop through the columns
  for (int sourceX = 0;
      sourceX < sourcePicture.getWidth();
      sourceX++)
  {
    // loop through the rows
    for (int sourceY = 0;
        sourceY < sourcePicture.getHeight();
        sourceY++)
```

```
        {
          // set the target pixel color to the source pixel color
          sourcePixel = sourcePicture.getPixel(sourceX,sourceY);
          targetPixel = this.getPixel(sourceY,
                    sourcePicture.getWidth() - 1 - sourceX);
          targetPixel.setColor(sourcePixel.getColor());
        }
      }
    }
```

To try this out, create a picture from the blank paper-sized file and then invoke the method on it. Show the result (see Figure 5.14).

```
> String fileName = FileChooser.getMediaPath("7inx95in.jpg");
> Picture picture = new Picture(fileName);
> picture.copyKatieLeftRotation();
> picture.show();
```

How does that work?

Rotating starts with the same source and target, and even the same variable values, but since we *use* the target X and Y differently, we get a different effect.

FIGURE 5.14
Copying a picture to a blank page rotated to the left 90 degrees.

Now, as we increment the Y variables, we're moving *down* the source, but *across* the target from left to right. As we increment the X variables we're moving *across* the source but *up* the target.

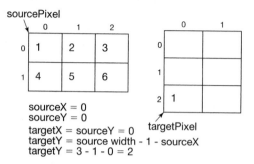

The source x and source y are both 0. The target x is equal to the source y thus it is also 0. But, the target y is equal to the width of the source picture minus 1 minus the source x. The width of the source picture is 3, which means that the target y is $3 - 1 - 0$, which is 2. Thus we copy the color of the source pixel at $(0, 0)$ to the target pixel at $(0, 2)$.

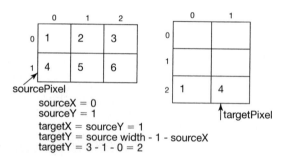

The source y is incremented by the inner loop to 1 and tested against the height of the source picture (2). Since it is less than the height we do the body of the inner loop. Now the source x is 0 and the source y is 1. The target x is equal to the source y which means it is 1. The target y is equal to the width of the source picture minus 1 minus the source y. The width of the source picture is 3, thus the target y is $3 - 1 - 0$, which is 2. Thus we copy the color of the source pixel at $(0, 1)$ to the target pixel at $(1, 2)$.

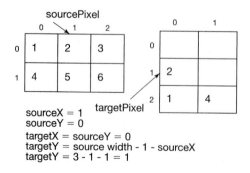

The source y is incremented by the inner loop to 2 and tested against the height of the source picture (2). Since it is not less than the height the inner loop finishes and the source x is incremented to 1 by the outer loop. The inner loop starts and sets the source y to 0. Now the source x is 1 and the source y is 0. The target x is equal to the source y, which means that it is also 0. The target y is equal to the width of the source picture minus 1 minus the source y. The width of the source picture is 3, thus the target y is $3 - 1 - 1$ which is 1. Thus we copy the color of the source pixel at $(1, 0)$ to the target pixel at $(0, 1)$.

The inner loop will increment source y and so the next color will be copied from $(1, 1)$ to $(1, 1)$. Then, the inner loop will stop again and source x will be incremented by 1 to 2. The next color will be copied from $(2, 0)$ to $(0, 0)$. The inner loop will increment source y so the next color will be copied from $(2, 1)$ to $(1, 0)$. At this point source x will be incremented to 3 which is not less than the width of the source picture (3) and the nested loop will stop.

5.2.5 Scaling

A very common transformation for pictures is to scale them. Scaling up means to make them larger, and scaling them down makes them smaller. It's common to scale a 1-megapixel or 3-megapixel picture down to a smaller size to make it easier to use on the Web or to send via e-mail. Smaller pictures require less disk space, and thus less network bandwidth, and thus are faster to upload or download.

Scaling a picture requires the use of *sampling* which we'll also use with sounds later. To scale a picture *smaller* we are going to take *every other* pixel when copying from the source to the target. To scale a picture *larger* we are going to take *every pixel twice*.

Scaling the picture down is the easier method. We will use a picture of one of the CS graduate students at Georgia Tech, Jakita N. Owensby (`jakita.jpg`). Her picture is 768 (width) by 768 (height). Instead of incrementing the source X and Y variables by 1, we simply increment by 2. We divide the amount of space by 2, since we'll fill half as much room—our width will be 768/2 and the height will be 768/2. The result is a smaller picture of Jakita on the blank 640 by 480 picture (Figure 5.15).

FIGURE 5.15
Scaling the picture of Jakita (a CS graduate student at Georgia Tech) down.

Program 30: Scaling a Picture Down (Smaller)

```
/**
 * Method to copy the picture of Jakita but smaller
 * (half as big) to the current picture
 */
public void copyJakitaSmaller()
{
  Picture jakitaPicture =
    new Picture(FileChooser.getMediaPath("jakita.jpg"));
  Pixel sourcePixel = null;
  Pixel targetPixel = null;

  // loop through the columns
  for (int sourceX = 0, targetX=0;
       sourceX < jakitaPicture.getWidth();
       sourceX+=2, targetX++)
  {
    // loop through the rows
    for (int sourceY=0, targetY=0;
         sourceY < jakitaPicture.getHeight();
         sourceY+=2, targetY++)
    {
      sourcePixel = jakitaPicture.getPixel(sourceX,sourceY);
      targetPixel = this.getPixel(targetX,targetY);
      targetPixel.setColor(sourcePixel.getColor());
    }
  }

}
```

∎

To try this out create a picture object using the blank 640 by 480 file and invoke the method on that. Show the result.

```
> Picture p = new Picture(FileChooser.getMediaPath("640x480.jpg"));
> p.copyJakitaSmaller();
> p.show();
```

Scaling up the picture (making it larger) is a little trickier. We want to take every pixel twice. What we're going to do is to increment the source index variables by 0.5. Now, we can't reference pixel 1.5. But if we reference (int) 1.5 we'll get 1 again, and that'll work. The sequence of 1, 1.5, 2, 2.5... will become 1,1,2,2... The result is a larger form of the picture (Figure 5.16). Let's try this on rose.jpg which is 320 by 240 so scaling it up will result in a picture that is 640 by 480.

Program 31: Scaling the Picture Up (Larger)

```
/**
 * Method to copy a flower but scaled to 2x normal size
 * onto the current picture
 */
```

```
public void copyFlowerLarger()
{
  Picture flowerPicture =
    new Picture(FileChooser.getMediaPath("rose.jpg"));
  Pixel sourcePixel = null;
  Pixel targetPixel = null;

  // loop through the columns
  for (double sourceX = 0, targetX=0;
       sourceX < flowerPicture.getWidth();
       sourceX = sourceX + 0.5, targetX++)
  {
    // loop through the rows
    for (double sourceY=0, targetY=0;
         sourceY <  flowerPicture.getHeight();
         sourceY = sourceY + 0.5, targetY++)
    {
      sourcePixel =
        flowerPicture.getPixel((int) sourceX,(int) sourceY);
      targetPixel = this.getPixel((int) targetX,(int) targetY);
      targetPixel.setColor(sourcePixel.getColor());
    }
  }

}
```

To try this out create a picture object using the blank 640 by 480 file and invoke the method on that. Show the result.

```
> String fileName = FileChooser.getMediaPath("640x480.jpg");
> Picture picture = new Picture(fileName);
> picture.copyFlowerLarger();
> picture.show();
```

FIGURE 5.16
Scaling up a picture.

How did that work?

We start from the same place as the original code for copying a picture. Say we are copying from the source picture starting at $(0, 0)$ and copying to the target picture starting at $(3, 1)$. First we will copy the color of the pixel at $(0, 0)$ in the source picture to $(3, 1)$ in the target picture.

source

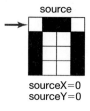

sourceX=0
sourceY=0

canvas

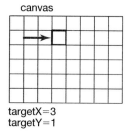

targetX=3
targetY=1

When we increment `sourceY` by 0.5, the actual value will be 0.5 but the `(int)` value is 0 so we end up referring to the same pixel in the source, but the target has moved on to the next pixel. So we will copy the color of the pixel at $(0, 0)$ to $(3, 2)$.

source

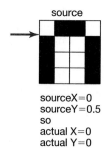

sourceX=0
sourceY=0.5
so
actual X=0
actual Y=0

canvas

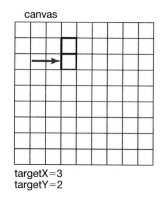

targetX=3
targetY=2

When we increment `sourceY` a second time by 0.5, it will now equal 1.0, so we now move on to the next pixel in the source. So we will copy the color of the pixel at $(0, 1)$ to $(3, 3)$.

source

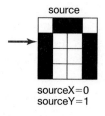

sourceX=0
sourceY=1

canvas

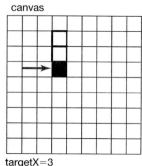

targetX=3
targetY=3

Again, when the `sourceY` is incremented by 0.5, the actual value will be 1.5, but the (`int`) of that is 1, so we will copy from (0, 1) to (3, 4).

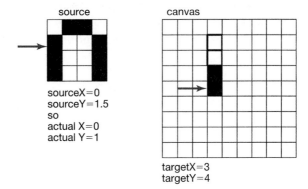

And eventually, we cover every pixel. Notice that the end result is degraded—it's choppier than the original. Each pixel is copied four times: twice in the x direction and twice in the y direction.

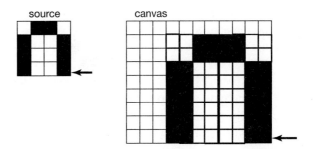

This would work fine for scaling up by a factor of 2. What if we wanted to scale up by a factor of 3? We could add 1/3 each time through the loop but what is 1/3? It is represented in a double as 0.3333333333333333. Casting this to `int` would give us 0 for the source. When we add the factor to `sourceX` we would get 0.6666666666666666. This would also result in 0 when we cast to `int`. When we next add the factor we should get 0.9999999999999999 which is still less than one and thus the cast to `int` would still result in 0. So we would copy the source pixel four times instead of three times. So this approach won't work as a general algorithm. It will work for scaling up a picture by an even amount but not by an odd amount.

You might want to be able to scale up a picture without always using the canvas picture as a target picture. One way to create a `Picture` object is to pass in a width and height: `new Picture(width,height)`. This will create a blank picture of the passed width and height (both specified in pixels). `new Picture(640,480)` would create a picture object that is 640 pixels wide by 480 pixels tall—just like the canvas.

Here is a more general method that will scale up the current picture object by some passed number of times. It creates a new `Picture` object of the desired width and height. It loops through all the source pixels and for each source pixel it copies it the passed number of times in both the x and y direction to the target picture. The hard part is determining the x and y values for the target picture. The source pixel at $(0, 0)$ should be copied to the target picture $(0, 0)$, $(0, 1)$, $(0, 2)$, $(1, 0)$, $(1, 1)$, $(1, 2)$, $(2, 0)$, $(2, 1)$, $(2, 2)$. The source pixel at $(1, 0)$ should be copied to $(0, 3)$, $(0, 4)$, $(0, 5)$, $(1, 3)$, $(1, 4)$, $(1, 5)$, $(2, 3)$, $(2, 4)$, $(2, 5)$. The target x and y is based on the source x and y times the number of times each pixel is copied plus the current x and y indices.

source

	0	1
0	1	2
1	3	4

target

	0	1	2	3	4	5
0	1	1	1	2	2	2
1	1	1	1	2	2	2
2	1	1	1	2	2	2
3	3	3	3	4	4	4
4	3	3	3	4	4	4
5	3	3	3	4	4	4

Since this method creates a picture object that it changes, we want to be able to return this object so that we can refer to it again. How do we return something from a method? Well, we need to say what type of thing we are returning and then we have to actually return it. You specify the type of thing that the method returns in the method declaration. Up to now we have been using the keyword void to say that the method doesn't return anything. So, change the void to be the type of thing that you are returning. Since this method will return an object of the Picture class the type is Picture. At the end of the method use the keyword return followed by what you want to return. The compiler will check that the type of the thing you actually return matches the type you used in the method declaration. If it doesn't you will get a compile error.

Program 32: General Scale Up Method

```
/**
 * Method to create a new picture that is scaled up by the
 * passed number of times.
 * @return the new scaled up picture
 */
public Picture scaleUp(int numTimes)
{
  Picture targetPicture =
    new Picture(this.getWidth() * numTimes,
                this.getHeight() * numTimes);
  Pixel sourcePixel = null;
  Pixel targetPixel = null;
  int targetX = 0;
  int targetY = 0;

  // loop through the source picture columns
  for (int sourceX = 0;
       sourceX < this.getWidth();
       sourceX++)
```

```
    {
      // loop through the source picture rows
      for (int sourceY=0;
          sourceY < this.getHeight();
          sourceY++)
      {
        // get the source pixel
        sourcePixel = this.getPixel(sourceX,sourceY);

        // loop copying to the target y
        for (int indexY = 0; indexY < numTimes; indexY++)
        {
          // loop copying to the target x
          for (int indexX = 0; indexX < numTimes; indexX++)
          {
            targetX = sourceX * numTimes + indexX;
            targetY = sourceY * numTimes + indexY;
            targetPixel = targetPicture.getPixel(targetX,
                                                  targetY);
            targetPixel.setColor(sourcePixel.getColor());
          }
        }
      }
    }

    return targetPicture;

  }
```

■

Since the method `scaleUp` returns the resulting scaled `Picture` object we had better save a reference to the `Picture` object to be able to refer to it again.

```
> Picture p = new Picture(FileChooser.getMediaPath("flower1.jpg"));
> p = p.scaleUp(2);
> p.explore();
```

Since this method creates a new `Picture` object and copies the scaled picture into that new `Picture` object and then returns the new `Picture` object if you want to see the result you will have to save a reference to the resulting picture. You can reuse variables like p, but realize that you will no longer have a reference to the original `Picture` object. Of course, you could have declared a new variable to hold the scaled picture. It would also be of type `Picture`.

```
> String fileName = FileChooser.getMediaPath("flower1.jpg");
> Picture origPicture = new Picture(fileName);
> Picture scaledPicture = origPicture.scaleUp(2);
> scaledPicture.show();
> origPicture.show();
```

5.3 CONCEPTS SUMMARY

This chapter introduced two-dimensional arrays, nested loops, working with multiple variables in a `for` loop, returning a value from a method, and method overloading.

5.3.1 Two-Dimensional Arrays

Pixels are stored in a two-dimensional array. A two-dimensional array is similar to seating in an auditorium. You can find your seat based on the row and chair number. You can access a location in a two-dimensional array by specifying an x and y. All indices start with 0.

5.3.2 Nested Loops

To process all of the pixels in a picture and track the x and y location of each pixel you need to use a nested loop. Nested loops are loops inside of loops. You can either loop through the rows and then the columns (y and then x) or loop through the columns and then the rows (x and then y).

```
// loop through the rows (y direction)
for (int y = 0; y < this.getHeight(); y++)
{
  // loop through the columns (x direction)
  for (int x = 0; x < this.getWidth(); x++)
  {
    // get the current pixel at this x and y position
    pixel = this.getPixel(x,y);

    // do something to the color

    // set the new color
    pixel.setColor(aColor);
  }
}
```

To restrict the area that you are looping through, use different values for starting and stopping the loop. To loop through a rectangular area starting with the pixel at (startX, startY) at the upper-left corner of the rectangular area and ending with the pixel at (endX, endY) as the bottom-right corner of the rectangular area, use:

```
// loop through the rows (y direction)
for (int y = startY; y <= endY; y++)
{
  // loop through the columns (x direction)
  for (int x = startX; x <= endX; x++)
  {
    // get the current pixel at this x and y position
    pixel = this.getPixel(x,y);

    // do something to the color

    // set the new color
    pixel.setColor(aColor);
  }
}
```

You can declare more than one variable in a loop. This is useful when you copy from one picture to another. Use variables to represent the source picture x and y values and use other variables to represent the target picture x and y values. You can change how the source and target pixel are used in order to rotate the picture.

```
// loop through the columns
for (int sourceX = 0, targetX = 0;
     sourceX < sourcePicture.getWidth();
     sourceX++, targetX++)
{
  // loop through the rows
  for (int sourceY = 0, targetY = 0;
       sourceY < sourcePicture.getHeight();
       sourceY++, targetY++)
  {
    sourcePixel = sourcePicture.getPixel(sourceX,sourceY);
    targetPixel = this.getPixel(targetX,targetY);
    targetPixel.setColor(sourcePixel.getColor());
  }
}
```

By changing the initial and ending values of sourceX, sourceY, targetX, and targetY you can change what part of the source picture you want to copy and where you want it to go on the target picture. Using this you can clip and create collages.

If you change the amount you increment or decrement a loop variable by, you can scale a picture up or down.

5.3.3   Returning a Value from a Method

To declare a method you specify the visibility for the method, the type of thing it returns, the name of the method, and the parameter list inside parentheses. This is followed by the body of the method which is inside of an open and close curly brace.

```
visibility returnType name(parameterList)
{
  // statements in method

  // return a value
  return valueToReturn;
}
```

Methods that do not return any value use the keyword void as the return type. Methods that do return a value use the type of that value for the return type and then have a return keyword in them that is followed by the thing to return. Remember that a type is any of the primitive types or the name of a class.

Here is an example public method declaration that doesn't return anything and the name of the method is mirrorVertical and it doesn't take any parameters.

```
public void mirrorVertical()
```

Here is an example public method declaration that returns an object of the class Picture.

```
public Picture scaleUp(int numTimes)
```

Notice that it gives a return type of `Picture`. The body of the method must have the keyword `return` in it and it must return an object that is an instance of the class `Picture`.

5.3.4 Method Overloading

A class can have more than one method with the same name as long as the parameter list is different. The methods can take a different number of parameters, or the types of the parameters can be different, or the order of the types can be different. You can't have two methods with the same name and the same number of parameters with the same types in the same order.

```
public void copyPictureTo(Picture sourcePicture, int xStart)
public void copyPictureTo(Picture sourcePicture, int xStart,
                          int yStart)
```

Notice that there are two method declarations with the same name but one takes two parameters and one takes three. The compiler will check that a method exists that takes the same number and type of parameters. If the compiler can't find a method with the same number, type, and order of parameters it will report that the method doesn't exist.

```
> p.copyPictureTo();
Error: No 'copyPictureTo' method in 'Picture'
```

OBJECTS AND METHODS SUMMARY

Here are the methods used or introduced in this chapter:

`new Picture(int width, int height)`	Creates a new `Picture` object with the given width and height. All pixels are white.
`getMediaPath(String fileName)`	Returns the full path name with the media directory followed by the passed file name. This is a class method on the `FileChooser` class. The default media directory is "c:/intro-prog-java/mediasources/".
`setMediaPath(String directory)`	Sets the media directory to use when getting a full path using `getMediaPath(String fileName)`. This is a class method on the `FileChooser` class.

PROBLEMS

5.1 What do the following mean?

- Overloading
- Nested Loop
- Debug

- Rotate
- Scale
- Parameter
- void
- return

5.2 Modify any of the methods from the last chapter to use a nested loop. Run it to make sure it still works.

5.3 Take a picture of a person and mirror just their top part to their bottom part (two heads, with one at either end).

5.4 Take a picture of a person and mirror it so that the person looks like conjoined twins.

5.5 Create a new method that will blend two pictures with 10% from just the first picture and a 80% overlap and then 10% from just the last picture. It helps if the two pictures are the same width and height.

5.6 Create a new method that will blend two pictures with 20% from just the first picture and a 60% overlap and then 20% from just the last picture. It helps if the two pictures are the same width and height.

5.7 Modify Program 5 (page 97) to take the amount to reduce red by as a parameter.

5.8 Modify Program 22 (page 139) to be more general by passing in the start and stop x and y and the mirror point in x.

5.9 Convert the method `copyFlowerLarger()` (Program 31 (page 162)) to a method that can scale any picture up to twice the original width and height. It should return a new picture object created using
`new Picture(this.getWidth() * 2,this.getHeight() * 2)`.

5.10 Write a method to flip a picture over so that things that were on the left are now on the right. You probably want to create a new picture and copy the pixels from a passed-in picture to the new picture. Return the new picture.

5.11 Modify Program 29 (page 158) in this chapter to take the source picture to rotate and to create a new picture of just the needed size. Return the new picture.

5.12 Write a method to mirror a picture around a horizontal line from (0, height-1) to (width-1, height-1). Be aware that this will double the height of the picture.

5.13 Write a method to mirror a picture around a vertical line from (width-1, 0) to (width-1, height-1). Be aware that this will double the width of the picture.

5.14 Try to mirror a picture around a diagonal line from (0, 0) to (width-1, height-1). Try to mirror a picture around a diagonal line from (0, height-1) to (width-1, 0).

5.15 Write a method to rotate a picture to the right by 90 degrees.

5.16 Write a method to rotate a picture to the right by 180 degrees.

5.17 All of our copy methods copy rectangular areas. Try to write a copy method that copies a triangular area. Write one that copies a circular area.

5.18 We've seen that if you increment the source picture index by 2 while incrementing the target picture index by 1 for each copied pixel, you end up with the source being scaled down onto the target. What happens if you increment the target picture index by 2 as well? What happens if you increment both the source and target by 0.5 and use `int` to get just the integer part?

5.19 Write a method named `createCollage` to create a collage of the same image at least four times onto the `7x95in.jpg` blank JPEG. (You are welcome to add additional images, too.) One of those four copies can be the original picture. The other three should be modified forms. You can do any of scaling, cropping, or rotating the image; creating a negative of the image; shifting or altering colors on the image; and making it darker or lighter.

After composing your image, *mirror it*. You can do it vertically or horizontally (or otherwise), in any direction—just make sure that your four base images are visible still after mirroring.

Your single method should make all of this happen—all of the effects and compositing must occur from the single function `createCollage`. Of course, it is perfectly okay to *use* other functions, but make it so that a tester of your program need only to call `setMediaPath()` and put all your input pictures in her mediasources directory, create a `Picture` object from the blank paper-sized file, and then execute `createCollage()`—and will expect to have a collage generated and returned.

5.20 Think about how the grayscale algorithm works. Basically, if you know the *luminance* of anything visual (e.g., a small image, a letter), you can replace a pixel with that visual element in a similar way to create a collage image. Try implementing that. You'll need 256 visual elements of increasing lightness, all of the same size. You'll create a collage by replacing each pixel in the original image with one of these visual elements.

TO DIG DEEPER

The bible of computer graphics is *Introduction to Computer Graphics* [11]. It's highly recommended.

CHAPTER 6

Conditionally Modifying Pixels

Chapter Learning Objectives

The media learning goals for this chapter are:

- To replace one color with another in a picture.
- To do simple edge detection.
- To replace several colors in a picture: sepia-toned.
- To replace a range of colors with one color: posterizing.
- To average nearby pixels when scaling up for a smoother result: blur.
- To replace the background in a picture.

The computer science goals for this chapter are:

- To conditionally execute a statement or block of statements using `if`.
- To use a conditional with two possible results: `if` and `else`.
- To use a conditional with greater than two possible results: `if`, `else if`, and `else`.
- To introduce the *not* operator.
- To combine boolean expressions with *and* and *or*.

6.1 CONDITIONAL PIXEL CHANGES

So far we have been processing all of the pixels in the same way. But what if we want to process the pixels in different ways? For example, we might want to turn someone's hair a different color, or get rid of "red-eye" in a picture, or even reduce the number of colors in a picture.

We need something that executes a block of code only if some condition (expression) is true. We know that computers can compare values to see if they are equal, less than, or greater than (and combinations of these) and return `true` or `false`. We have used this with loops by continuing a loop while the index is less than the length of the array as in: `while(index < pixelArray.length)`. This will execute the loop while the expression (`index < pixelArray.length`) is true.

Try the following in the interactions pane:

```
> 0 < 20
true
> 30 < 20
false
> 20 < 20
false
> 20 <= 20
true
```

One way to conditionally execute code in Java is with an `if (expression)`. The `if` is a keyword that means that if the expression in the parentheses evaluates to `true` then execute the following statement or block of statements. If it is false just skip the execution of that statement or block of statements (Figure 6.1) So, we can check whether the color at the current pixel is close to a particular color and if so execute a statement or block of statements (in curly braces).

Here is an example `if` statement with just a single statement indented on the next line following the `if`. We usually indent statements following an `if` to show that they are part of the statement and will not always be executed. Java doesn't care about the indentation, but it makes it easier for people to read and understand.

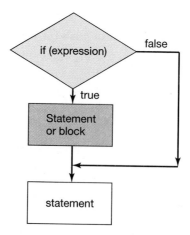

FIGURE 6.1
Flowchart of an `if` statement.

```
boolean flag = true;
if (flag)
    System.out.println("flag is true");
System.out.println(flag);
```

Let's try the following in the interactions pane:

```
> int x = 30;
> if (x < 40) System.out.println("x is less than 40");
x is less than 40
> if (x > 40) System.out.println("x is greater than 40");
> System.out.println(x);
30
```

Notice that since x **is** less than 40, the string saying so was output. However, since x **is not** greater than 40, the string saying x is greater than 40 was not output. We do see the output from the next statement `System.out.println(x)` since execution jumps to the statement following an `if` when the expression is false.

6.1.1 Comparing Colors

What does it mean to compare two colors? How can the computer tell if the color at the current pixel is "red"? The distance between two colors is the Cartesian distance between the colors as points in a three-dimensional space, where red, green, and blue are the three dimensions. Recall that the distance between two points (x_1, y_1) and (x_2, y_2) is:

$$\sqrt{(x_1 - x_2)^2 + (y_1 - y_2)^2}$$

The similar measure for two colors $(red_1, green_1, blue_1)$ and $(red_2, green_2, blue_2)$ is:

$$\sqrt{(red_1 - red_2)^2 + (green_1 - green_2)^2 + (blue_1 - blue_2)^2}$$

However, you won't have to code this. The `Pixel` class has an object method `colorDistance(Color color)` which returns the distance between the color in the current `Pixel` object and the passed color. The hard part is determining what "close enough" is for two colors.

6.1.2 Replacing Colors

Here's a program that tries to replace the brown color with red. Mark used the picture explorer to figure out roughly what the RGB values were for Katie's brown hair, then wrote a program to look for colors close to that, and then increased the redness of those pixels. Mark played a lot with the value that he used for distance (here, 50.0) and the amount of redness increased (here, 100% increase). However, this approach turned part of the couch and carpet red too (Figure 6.2).

FIGURE 6.2
Increasing reds in the browns.

Program 33: Color Replacement: Turn Brown into Red

```java
/**
 * Method to turn the brown in a picture
 * into red
 */
public void turnBrownIntoRed()
{
  Color brown = new Color(42,25,15);
  Pixel[] pixels = this.getPixels();
  Pixel pixel = null;

  // loop through the pixels
  for (int i=0; i<pixels.length; i++)
  {
    // get the current pixel
    pixel = pixels[i];

    // check if in distance to brown and if so double the red
    if (pixel.colorDistance(brown) < 50.0)
      pixel.setColor(new Color((int) (pixel.getRed() * 2.0),
                               pixel.getGreen(),
                               pixel.getBlue()));
  }
}
```

To use this method to turn Katie into a redhead, first create a `Picture` object from the file "KatieFancy.jpg". Then invoke the method `turnBrownIntoRed` on that `Picture` object and show or explore the result.

```
> String fileName = FileChooser.getMediaPath("KatieFancy.jpg");
> Picture picture = new Picture(fileName);
> picture.turnBrownIntoRed();
> picture.explore();
```

Notice that we can use a simple `for` loop through the one-dimensional array of `pixels` for this. We don't care where the pixels are in the two-dimensional array in this method. Of course, we could have used nested `for` loops instead to loop through all the pixels.

What this method is doing is looping through all the pixels in the current picture and for each pixel checking if the distance between the color in the current pixel is less than 50 away from the color brown (defined as red=42, green=25, blue=15). If the distance between the current color and the defined brown is less than 50, the red value at the current pixel is doubled. If the distance is equal to or greater than 50, the pixel color is not changed.

With the picture explorer we can also figure out the coordinates just around Katie's face, and then just do the browns near her face. The effect isn't too good, though it's clear that it worked. The line of redness is too sharp and rectangular (Figure 6.3).

Program 34: Color Replacement in a Rectangular Area

```
/**
 * Method to turn brown to red inside of
 * a rectangular area
 */
public void turnBrownToRedInRectangle()
{
  Color brown = new Color(42,25,15);
  Pixel pixel = null;

  // loop through the x values
  for (int x=63; x < 125; x++)
  {
    for (int y=6; y < 76; y++)
    {

      // get the current pixel
      pixel = this.getPixel(x,y);

      // check if in dist to brown and if so double the red
      if (pixel.colorDistance(brown) < 50.0)
        pixel.setColor(new Color((int) (pixel.getRed() * 2.0),
                                 pixel.getGreen(),
                                 pixel.getBlue()));
    }
  }
}
```

To use this method to turn Katie's hair red, first create a `Picture` object from the file "KatieFancy.jpg". Then invoke the method `turnBrownIntoRedInRectangle` on that `Picture` object and show the result (see Figure 6.3).

```
> String fileName = FileChooser.getMediaPath("KatieFancy.jpg");
> Picture picture = new Picture(fileName);
> picture.turnBrownIntoRedInRectangle();
> picture.explore();
```

We put the values for the range right inside the method

```
turnBrownIntoRedInRectangle()
```

this meant that we didn't need to pass any parameters to specify the range but it makes the method less reusable. If we want to use it to change a different picture, we would have to edit the method to change the range and then recompile. The method would be easier to reuse if we specified the range when we invoke the method. We can also pass in the distance to check for between brown and the current color.

FIGURE 6.3
On left the couch color changes, on right the couch color doesn't change.

Program 35: Color Replacement with Passing in the Range

```
/**
 * Method to turn brown to red in a rectangular area
 * specified
 * by startX, endX-1, startY, endY-1
 * @param startX the starting location to check in x
 * @param endX the last pixel checked is one less than
 * this in x
 * @param startY the starting location to check in y
 * @param endY the last pixel checked is one less than
 * this in y
 */
public void turnBrownToRedInRectangle(int startX, int endX,
                                      int startY, int endY,
                                      double distance)
{
  Color brown = new Color(42,25,15);
  Pixel pixel = null;

  // loop through the x values
  for (int x=startX; x < endX; x++)
  {
    for (int y=startY; y < endY; y++)
    {

      // get the current pixel
      pixel = this.getPixel(x,y);

      /* check if in distance to brown is less than
       * the passed distance and if so double the red
       */
      if (pixel.colorDistance(brown) < distance)
        pixel.setColor(new Color((int) (pixel.getRed() * 2.0),
                                 pixel.getGreen(),
                                 pixel.getBlue()));
    }
  }
}
```

Can you think of any other things that you could do to make this method easier to reuse? What if we want to change something other than brown? What if we want to change the old color by increasing the green?

6.1.3   Reducing Red-Eye

"Red-eye" is the effect where the flash from the camera bounces off the back of the subject's eyes. Reducing red-eye is a really simple matter. We find the pixels that are "pretty close" to red (a distance from red of 167 works well), then change those pixels' color to a replacement color.

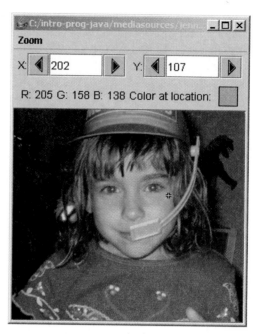

FIGURE 6.4
Finding the range of where Jenny's eyes are red.

We probably don't want to change the whole picture. In the Figure 6.4, we can see that Jenny is wearing a red dress—we don't want to wipe out that red, too. We'll fix that by only changing the *area* where Jenny's eyes are. Using the picture explorer, we find the upper-left and lower-right corners of her eyes. Those points were (109, 91) and (202, 107).

Program 36: Remove Red-Eye

```
/**
 * Method to remove red-eye from the current picture object
 * in the rectangle defined by startX, startY, endX, endY.
 * The red will be replaced with the passed newColor
 * @param startX the top left corner x value of a rectangle
 * @param startY the top left corner y value of a rectangle
 * @param endX the bottom right corner x value of a
 * rectangle
 * @param endY the bottom right corner y value of a
 * rectangle
 * @param newColor the new color to use
 */
public void removeRedEye(int startX, int startY, int endX,
                         int endY, Color newColor)
{
  Pixel pixel = null;
```

```
/* loop through the pixels in the rectangle defined by the
   startX, startY, and endX and endY */
for (int x = startX; x < endX; x++)
{
  for (int y = startY; y < endY; y++)
  {
    // get the current pixel
    pixel = getPixel(x,y);

    // if the color is near red then change it
    if (pixel.colorDistance(Color.red) < 167)
      pixel.setColor(newColor);
  }
}
}
```

We call this method with:

```
> String fileName =
    "c:/intro-prog-java/mediasources/jenny-red.jpg";
> Picture jennyPicture = new Picture(fileName);
> jennyPicture.removeRedEye(109,91,202,107,java.awt.Color.black);
> jennyPicture.explore();
```

to replace the red with black—certainly other colors could be used for the replacement color. The result was good, and we can check that the eye really does now have all-black pixels (Figure 6.5).

FIGURE 6.5
After fixing red-eye.

6.2 SIMPLE EDGE DETECTION: CONDITIONALS WITH TWO OPTIONS

What if we want to look for areas of high contrast between a pixel and the pixel below it? If the contrast is high, we can make the pixel black, and if the difference is low, we can make the pixel white. This is a simple form of edge detection. It results in a picture that looks like a pencil sketch.

What does high contrast mean? It means that the difference between the two colors is high. One way to calculate this is to average the red, green, and blue values in the top pixel and subtract this from the average of the red, green, and blue values in the bottom pixel. If the absolute value of the difference is greater than some amount, then there is high contrast. If there is high contrast set the top pixel color to black and if not set it to white.

6.2.1 Negation

You have seen a way to execute a statement or block of statements if some condition is true using an `if`. But how do you execute a statement or block of statements if a condition is false? One way is to use an `if` but negate the condition using the `'!'` (*logical not*) operator.

```
> !true
false
> !false
true
```

So if we wanted to check whether a value was less than 20 and if it is print out "Yes, the value is less than 20" and if it isn't print out "No, this value is not less than 20" we could test for the value being less than 20 and also test for the value being not less than 20 using the `'!'` operator.

```
> int x = 30;
> if (x < 20) System.out.println("Yes, the value is less than 20");
> if (! (x < 20)) System.out.println("No, not less than 20");
No, not less than 20
```

6.2.2 Testing for Both Conditions

Another way to test that a value isn't less than 20 is to test whether it is greater or equal to 20.

```
> int x = 30;
> if (x < 20) System.out.println("Yes, the value is less than 20");
> if (x >= 20) System.out.println("No, not less than 20");
No, not less than 20
```

The problem with this approach is that we have to run both tests every time. But if the first test is true, there is no reason to run the second test (x can't be both less than 20 and greater or equal to 20). We would like a way to say that if the first test is true, execute one statement or block of statements, and if it is false, then execute a different statement or block of statements.

6.2.3 Conditionals with Two Options

The way to do this is with if (expression) and else. As before, the if part will execute the statement or block of statements following the if when the expression is true. But, if we add an else this will also execute the statement or block of statements following the else when the expression following the if is false (Figure 6.6). And it will also mean that the else is skipped if the if test was true.

To enter the following in DrJava's interaction pane, use SHIFT-ENTER after the if statement to let DrJava know that there will be a following else.

```
> int x = 30;
> if (x < 20) System.out.println("Yes, the value is less than 20");
else System.out.println("No, this value is not less than 20");

No, this value is not less than 20
```

As you can see, the statement following the if didn't execute, but the statement following the else did. Try the same thing but this time give x a value less than 20.

```
> x = 15;
> if (x < 20) System.out.println(
      "Yes, the value is less than 20");
else System.out.println("No, this value is not less than 20");

Yes, the value is less than 20
```

Notice that this time the statement following the if did execute but the statement following the else did not.

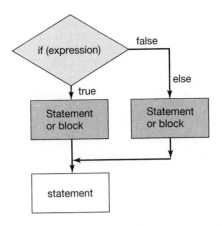

FIGURE 6.6
Flowchart of an if with an else.

6.2.4 Simple Edge Detection

To do simple edge detection, we will loop through the pixels with the outer loop incrementing y from 0 to less than picture height-1. Usually we have been looping

while y is less than the height, so why stop at height-1? We are comparing the value
at a y position with the pixel below it so the last y value that still has another row
below it is at height-2.

The inner loop will increment x from 0 to less than the picture width. The top
pixel will be set to the pixel at the current x and y location. The bottom pixel will be
set to the pixel at the current x but y+1. We will compare the absolute value of the
difference between the intensities (average of color values), and if it is less than some
passed limit, we will change the top pixel color to white, and otherwise we will set
the top pixel color to black. The Pixel class has an object method getAverage()
that returns the average of the three color values.

Program 37: Edge Detection

```
/**
 * Method to do a simple edge detection by comparing the
 * absolute value of the difference between the color
 * intensities (average of the color values) between a
 * pixel and the pixel below it. If the absolute value
 * of the difference between the color intensities is
 * less than a passed amount the top pixel color
 * will be set to white.  Otherwise it is set to black.
 * @param amount if the absolute value of the differences
 * in the color average is less than this
 * set the color to white, else black
 */
public void edgeDetection(double amount) {
  Pixel topPixel = null;
  Pixel bottomPixel = null;
  double topAverage = 0.0;
  double bottomAverage = 0.0;
  int endY = this.getHeight() - 1;

  /* loop through y values from 0 to height - 1
   * (since compare to below pixel) */
  for (int y = 0; y < endY; y++) {

    // loop through the x values from 0 to width
    for (int x = 0; x < this.getWidth(); x++) {

      // get the top and bottom pixels
      topPixel = this.getPixel(x,y);
      bottomPixel = this.getPixel(x,y+1);

      // get the color averages for the two pixels
      topAverage = topPixel.getAverage();
      bottomAverage = bottomPixel.getAverage();

      /* check if the absolute value of the difference
       * is less than the amount */
      if (Math.abs(topAverage - bottomAverage) < amount) {
        topPixel.setColor(Color.WHITE);
```

```
        // else set the color to black
        } else {
          topPixel.setColor(Color.BLACK);
        }
      }
    }
  }
```

To execute this method and see the result (Figure 6.7) use:

```
> String fileName = FileChooser.getMediaPath("butterfly1.jpg");
> Picture p = new Picture(fileName);
> p.explore();
> p.edgeDetection(10);
> p.explore();
```

 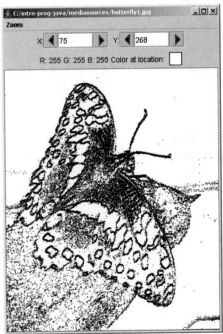

FIGURE 6.7
Original picture and after edge detection.

Making it Work Tip: Using Curly Braces

You may have noticed that the method `edgeDetection` shows the starting curly braces at the end of the line instead of on a new line as shown in the previous methods. Java doesn't care if the curly braces are at the end of a line or on a new line. Some programmers prefer one to another. It is often easier to see that you forgot a curly brace if it is by itself on a new line. However, the Java guidelines say to put the opening curly brace at the end of a line and the closing one on a new line.

You may also notice that we are using curly braces after the if and else even though there is only one statement to be executed, so they aren't really needed. It is good practice to have them even if they aren't needed because the code is easier to read and change.

∎

6.3 SEPIA-TONED AND POSTERIZED PICTURES: USING MULTIPLE CONDITIONALS TO CHOOSE THE COLOR

We handled the case of having two different ways to process the pixels using an if and else. What if we have more than two ways that we want to process some pixels? For example, what if we wanted to do one thing if a value is less than some number, another thing if it is equal and yet a third if it is greater than the number? We could check for each of these conditions with an if as shown below:

```
> int y = 10;
> if (y < 10) System.out.println("y is less than 10");
> if (y == 10) System.out.println("y is equal to 10");
y is equal 10
> if (y > 10) System.out.println("y is greater than 10");
```

This works but results in some unnecessary checking. Notice that y was equal to 10 and so that was printed out but it still executed the next statement which checked if y was greater than 10. But, can y be equal to 10 and greater than 10? What would have happened if y was less than 10? It would have printed out a string saying that y is less than 10 and then still checked if y was equal or greater than 10. We need something to say that if the previous test was true, execute that and then skip to the end of all the checks. We have seen a way to do this for two possibilities (true or false) using if and else. One way to handle three or more possibilities is with if, else if and else (Figure 6.8). You can use as many else if statements as needed. You are not required to have a final else.

```
> int y = 2;
> if (y < 10) System.out.println("Y is less than 10");
  else if (y == 10) System.out.println("y is equal to 10");
  else System.out.println("y is greater than 10");
y is less than 10
```

So far, we've done color modification by simply saying "This color replaces that color." We can be more sophisticated in our color swapping. We can look for a range of colors, by using if, else if, and else, and replace the color with some function of the original color or a specific color. The results are quite interesting.

For example, we might want to generate sepia-toned prints. Older prints sometimes have a yellowish tint to them. We could just do an overall color change, but the end result isn't aesthetically pleasing. By looking for different kinds of color—highlights, middle ranges, and shadows—and treating them differently, we can get a better effect (Figure 6.9).

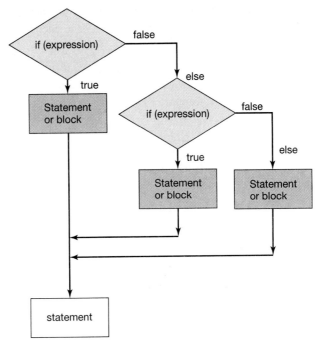

FIGURE 6.8
Flowchart of an `if`, `else if`, and an `else`.

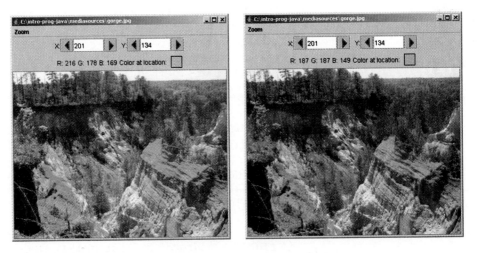

FIGURE 6.9
Original scene (left) and using our sepia-tone program.

The way we do this is to first convert the picture to gray, both because older prints were in shades of gray, and because it makes it a little easier to work with. We then look for high, middle, and low ranges of color, and change them separately. We want to make the shadows (darkest grays) a bit darker. We want to make most of the picture (middle grays) into a brownish color. We want to make the highlights (lightest grays) a bit yellow. Recall that yellow is a mixture of red and green, so one way to make things yellow is to increase the red and green. Another way is to reduce the amount of blue. The advantage to reducing the blue is that you don't have to worry about increasing a value past 255 which is the maximum.

Program 38: Convert a Picture to Sepia-Tones

```java
/**
 * Method to change the current picture to a sepia
 * tint (modify the middle colors to a light brown and
 * the light colors to a light yellow and make the
 * shadows darker)
 */
public void sepiaTint()
{
  Pixel pixel = null;
  double redValue = 0;
  double greenValue = 0;
  double blueValue = 0;

  // first change the current picture to grayscale
  this.grayscale();

  // loop through the pixels
  for (int x = 0; x < this.getWidth(); x++)
  {
    for (int y = 0; y < this.getHeight(); y++)
    {
      // get the current pixel and color values
      pixel = this.getPixel(x,y);
      redValue = pixel.getRed();
      greenValue = pixel.getGreen();
      blueValue = pixel.getBlue();

      // tint the shadows darker
      if (redValue < 60)
      {
        redValue = redValue * 0.9;
        greenValue = greenValue * 0.9;
        blueValue = blueValue * 0.9;
      }

      // tint the midtones a light brown
      // by reducing the blue
      else if (redValue < 190)
      {
        blueValue = blueValue * 0.8;
      }

      // tint the highlights a light yellow
      // by reducing the blue
      else
```

```
      {
        blueValue = blueValue * 0.9;
      }

      // set the colors
      pixel.setRed((int) redValue);
      pixel.setGreen((int) greenValue);
      pixel.setBlue((int) blueValue);
    }
  }
}
```

Try this method out by:

```
> Picture picture = new Picture(Picture.getMediaPath("gorge.jpg"));
> picture.show();
> picture.sepiaTint();
> picture.repaint();
```

Posterizing is a process of converting a picture to a smaller number of colors. We're going to do that by looking for specific ranges of color, then setting the color to *one* value in that range. The result is that we reduce the number of colors in the picture (Figure 6.10).

FIGURE 6.10
Reducing the colors (right) from the original (left).

Program 39: Posterizing a Picture

```java
/**
 * Method to posterize (reduce the number of colors) in
 * the picture.  The number of reds, greens, and blues
 * will be 4.
 */
public void posterize()
{
  Pixel pixel = null;
  int redValue = 0;
  int greenValue = 0;
  int blueValue = 0;

  // loop through the pixels
  for (int x = 0; x < this.getWidth(); x++) {
    for (int y = 0; y < this.getHeight(); y++) {

      // get the current pixel and colors
      pixel = this.getPixel(x,y);
      redValue = pixel.getRed();
      greenValue = pixel.getGreen();
      blueValue = pixel.getBlue();

      // check for red range and change color
      if (redValue < 64)
        redValue = 31;
      else if (redValue < 128)
        redValue = 95;
      else if (redValue < 192)
        redValue = 159;
      else
        redValue = 223;

      // check for green range
      if (greenValue < 64)
        greenValue = 31;
      else if (greenValue < 128)
        greenValue = 95;
      else if (greenValue < 192)
        greenValue = 159;
      else
        greenValue = 223;

      // check for blue range
      if (blueValue < 64)
        blueValue = 31;
      else if (blueValue < 128)
        blueValue = 95;
      else if (blueValue < 192)
        blueValue = 159;
```

```
      else
        blueValue = 223;

      // set the colors
      pixel.setRed(redValue);
      pixel.setGreen(greenValue);
      pixel.setBlue(blueValue);
    }
  }
}
```

■

What's really going on here, though, is setting up (a) a bunch of *levels*, then (b) setting the value of red, green, or blue to the midpoint of that level. We can do this more generally using mathematics to compute the ranges for a desired number of levels and picking the midpoint. We need to check whether the current value is in the range and if so set it to the midpoint of the range.

How do we check whether a value is in a range? If we call the bottom of the range `bottomValue` and the top of the range `topValue`, then we could use this math notation `bottomValue <= testValue < topValue`. However in Java we need to write it `bottomValue <= testValue && testValue < topValue`. The two ampersands (`'&&'`) mean 'and'. If your mother says that you have to set the table *and* sweep the floor, how many jobs do you have to do? The answer is two, or both of them. If she says that you can set the table *or* sweep the floor, how many jobs do you have to do then? The answer is one, or just one of the two. Similarly if in Java you have `if (expression && expression)` then both expressions must be true for the body of the `if` to be executed. And, if you have `if (expression || expression)` then only one of the two expressions must be true for the body of the `if` to be executed. The `||` means `'or'`.

Below is the program for a flexible number of levels, and Figure 6.11 shows a couple of examples.

Program 40: Posterize by Levels

```
/**
 * Method to posterize (reduce the number of colors) in
 * the picture
 * @param numLevels the number of color levels to use
 */
public void posterize(int numLevels)
{
  Pixel pixel = null;
  int redValue = 0;
  int greenValue = 0;
  int blueValue = 0;
  int increment = (int) (256.0 / numLevels);
  int bottomValue, topValue, middleValue = 0;

  // loop through the pixels
  for (int x = 0; x < this.getWidth(); x++) {
    for (int y = 0; y < this.getHeight(); y++) {
```

```
            // get the current pixel and colors
            pixel = this.getPixel(x,y);
            redValue = pixel.getRed();
            greenValue = pixel.getGreen();
            blueValue = pixel.getBlue();

            // loop through the number of levels
            for (int i = 0; i < numLevels; i++)
            {
              // compute the bottom, top, and middle values
              bottomValue = i * increment;
              topValue = (i + 1) * increment;
              middleValue = (int) ((bottomValue + topValue - 1)
                                    / 2.0);

              /* check if current values are in current range and
               * if so set them to the middle value
               */
              if (bottomValue <= redValue &&
                  redValue < topValue)
                pixel.setRed(middleValue);
              if (bottomValue <= greenValue &&
                  greenValue < topValue)
                pixel.setGreen(middleValue);
              if (bottomValue <= blueValue &&
                  blueValue < topValue)
                pixel.setBlue(middleValue);
            }
          }
        }
      }
```

FIGURE 6.11
Pictures posterized to two levels (left) and four levels (right).

Computer Science Idea: Overloading

Notice that we now have two methods called `posterize`. One method doesn't take any parameters, and the other that takes the number of levels. In Java you are allowed to have more than one method with the same name as long as the parameters are different. This is called *overloading*. You can have a different number of parameters as in this case. You can also use different types and/or orders for the parameters. It means that you can have several methods that have the same behavior but operate on different parameters. It certainly is easier than coming up with new names for methods that do that same thing. ■

6.4 HIGHLIGHTING EXTREMES

What if we want to highlight the lightest and darkest areas of a picture? Would we highlight areas that are less than some amount from white **and** less than the same amount from black? Is there any color that is close to both white and black? No, we would want to replace the color at all pixels that have a distance from white **or** a distance from black less than some amount. We used `'&&'` to mean 'and' in the last program. In this program we will use `'||'` to mean 'or'.

Program 41: Highlight Extremes

```
/**
 * Method to replace the pixel colors in the current
 * picture object that have a color distance less than
 * the passed amount to white or black with the passed
 * replacement color
 * @param replacementColor the new color to use
 */
public void highlightLightAndDark(double amount,
                                  Color replacementColor) {
  Pixel pixel = null;

  // loop through all the pixels in the x direction
  for (int x = 0; x < getWidth(); x++) {

    // loop through all the pixels in the y direction
    for (int y = 0; y < getHeight(); y++) {

      // get the current pixel
      pixel = getPixel(x,y);

      // if the distance from white or black is less than the
      // passed amount use the replace color instead
      if (pixel.colorDistance(Color.white) < amount ||
          pixel.colorDistance(Color.black) < amount) {
        pixel.setColor(replacementColor);
      }
    }
  }
}
```

You can use this as follows and see the result in Figure 6.12:

```
> String fileName = Picture.getMediaPath("butterfly1.jpg");
> Picture picture = new Picture(fileName);
> picture.explore();
> picture.highlightLightAndDark(50.0,java.awt.Color.yellow);
> picture.explore();
```

FIGURE 6.12
Original picture (left) and light or dark areas highlighted (right).

6.5 COMBINING PIXELS: BLURRING

When we make pictures larger (scaling them up), we usually get rough edges: Sharp steps to lines, which we call *pixelation*. We can reduce pixelation by *blurring* the image. What we do is set each pixel to an *average* of pixels around it. In this example, we go through all pixels (note the large loop that surrounds everything) and then in the X and Y dimensions, compute the average of the pixels to either side of the pixel. It takes a picture, and a number (`size`) of pixels to compute the average.

Of course we need to be careful not to try and access pixels beyond the allowed values of the two-dimensional array of pixels. Try this in the interactions pane:

```
> String fileName = FileChooser.getMediaPath("caterpillar.jpg");
> Picture p = new Picture(fileName);
```

```
> System.out.println(p.getWidth());
329
> System.out.println(p.getHeight());
150
> p.getPixel(330,160);
java.lang.ArrayIndexOutOfBoundsException: Coordinate out of
bounds!
  at sun.awt.image.ByteInterleavedRaster.getDataElements
    (Unknown Source)
  at java.awt.image.BufferedImage.getRGB(Unknown Source)
  at SimplePicture.getBasicPixel(SimplePicture.java:247)
  at Pixel.setValuesFromPictureAndLocation(Pixel.java:137)
  at Pixel.<init>(Pixel.java:57)
  at SimplePicture.getPixel(SimplePicture.java:270)
  at sun.reflect.NativeMethodAccessorImpl.invoke0(Native Method)
  at sun.reflect.NativeMethodAccessorImpl.invoke(Unknown Source)
  at sun.reflect.DelegatingMethodAccessorImpl.invoke
    (Unknown Source)
  at java.lang.reflect.Method.invoke(Unknown Source)
```

The java.lang.ArrayIndexOutOfBoundsException tells us that we tried to access an array element that was outside the allowed indices. If this happens when our program is executing, the program will stop and report the exception. This is called a run-time exception because it happens when the program is running rather than at compile time.

So how do we check that the index values are acceptable? We know that the x indices range from 0 to width − 1 and the y indices range from 0 to height − 1. So we can use

```
x >= 0 && x < this.getWidth() && y >= 0 && y < this.getHeight().
```

Program 42: A Simple Blur

```
/**
 * Method to blur the pixels
 * @param numPixels the number of pixels to average in all
 * directions so if the numPixels is 2 then we will average
 * all pixels in the rectangle defined by 2 before the
 * current pixel to 2 after the current pixel
 */
public void blur(int numPixels)
{
  Pixel pixel = null;
  Pixel samplePixel = null;
  int redValue = 0;
  int greenValue = 0;
  int blueValue = 0;
  int count = 0;
```

```
        // loop through the pixels
        for (int x=0; x < this.getWidth(); x++) {
          for (int y=0; y < this.getHeight(); y++) {

            // get the current pixel
            pixel = this.getPixel(x,y);

            // reset the count and red, green, and blue values
            count = 0;
            redValue = greenValue = blueValue = 0;

            /* loop through pixel numPixels before x to
             * numPixels after x
             */
            for (int xSample = x - numPixels;
                 xSample <= x + numPixels;
                 xSample++) {
              for (int ySample = y - numPixels;
                   ySample <= y + numPixels;
                   ySample++) {

                /* check that we are in the range of acceptable
                 * pixels
                 */
                if (xSample >= 0 && xSample < this.getWidth() &&
                    ySample >= 0 && ySample < this.getHeight()) {
                  samplePixel = this.getPixel(xSample,ySample);
                  redValue = redValue + samplePixel.getRed();
                  greenValue = greenValue + samplePixel.getGreen();
                  blueValue = blueValue + samplePixel.getBlue();
                  count = count + 1;
                }
              }
            }

            // use average color of surrounding pixels
            Color newColor = new Color(redValue / count,
                                       greenValue / count,
                                       blueValue / count);
            pixel.setColor(newColor);
          }
        }
      }
```

Here is how to use this method:

```
> Picture p = new Picture(
    FileChooser.getMediaPath("flower1.jpg"));
> p = p.scaleUp(2);
> p.explore();
> p.blur(2);
> p.explore();
```

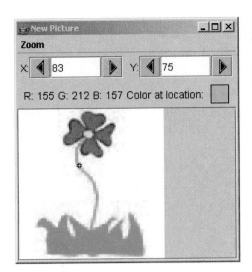
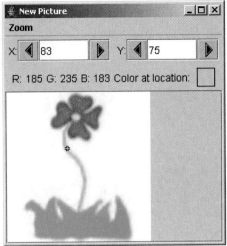

FIGURE 6.13
Making the flower bigger, then blurring to reduce pixelation.

Figure 6.13 shows the flower from the collage made bigger, then blurred. You can see the pixelation in the bigger version—the sharp, blocky edges. With the blur, some of that pixelation goes away. More careful blurs take into account regions of colors (so that edges between colors are kept sharp), and thus are able to reduce pixelation without removing sharpness.

6.6   BACKGROUND SUBTRACTION

Let's imagine that you have a picture of someone, and a picture of where they stood without them there (Figure 6.14). Could you *subtract* the background of the person (i.e., figure out where the colors are close), and then replace it with another another background? Say, of the moon (Figure 6.15)?

FIGURE 6.14
A picture of a child (Katie), and her background without her.

FIGURE 6.15
A new background, the moon.

Program 43: Subtract the Background and Replace it with a New One

```
/**
 * Method to replace the background in the current picture
 * with the background from another picture
 * @param oldBackground a picture with the old background
 * to replace
 * @param newBackground a picture with the new background
 * to use
 */
public void swapBackground(Picture oldBackground,
                           Picture newBackground)
{
  Pixel currPixel = null;
  Pixel oldPixel = null;
  Pixel newPixel = null;

  // loop through the columns
  for (int x=0; x<getWidth(); x++)
  {

    // loop through the rows
    for (int y=0; y<getHeight(); y++)
    {

      // get the current pixel and old background pixel
      currPixel = this.getPixel(x,y);
      oldPixel = oldBackground.getPixel(x,y);
```

```
    /* if the distance between the current pixel color
     * and the old background pixel color is less
     * than the 15 then swap in the new background pixel
     */
    if (currPixel.colorDistance(oldPixel.getColor()) < 15.0)
    {
      newPixel = newBackground.getPixel(x,y);
      currPixel.setColor(newPixel.getColor());
    }
  }
 }
}
```

■

To test whether we can replace an old background with a new background, try:

```
> String fileName = FileChooser.getMediaPath("kid-in-frame.jpg");
> Picture p = new Picture(fileName);
> fileName = FileChooser.getMediaPath("bgframe.jpg");
> Picture oldBg = new Picture(fileName);
> fileName = FileChooser.getMediaPath("moon-surface.jpg");
> Picture newBg = new Picture(fileName);
> p.swapBackground(oldBg,newBg);
> p.show();
```

We can, but the effect isn't as good as we would like (Figure 6.16). Our daughter's top color was too close to the color of the wall. And though the light was dim, the shadow is definitely having an effect here.

Barb tried the same thing with a picture of two of our kids in front of a wall. Barb should have used a tripod (really critical to get the pixels to line up). The two original pictures (Figure 6.17) weren't all that comparable. The background swap

FIGURE 6.16
Katie on the moon.

FIGURE 6.17
Two kids in front of a wall, and a picture of the wall.

(with the bridge scene) didn't change all that much! We changed the threshold value to 50, and finally got *some* pretty good swapping (Figure 6.18).

FIGURE 6.18
Swapping a country bridge for the wall, using background subtraction, with a threshold of 50.

```
> String fileName = FileChooser.getMediaPath("twoKidsWall.jpg");
> Picture p = new Picture(fileName);
> Picture oldBg = new Picture(
   FileChooser.getMediaPath("wall2.jpg"));
> Picture newBg = new Picture(
   FileChooser.getMediaPath("bridge.jpg"));
> p.swapBackground(oldBg,newBg);
> p.show();
```

Making it Work Tip: Add an Input Parameter to Generalize a Method

Notice that we changed the threshold from 15.0 to 50.0 for the second test of the swapBackground(oldBG,newBG) method. A better thing to do would be to change the method to take the threshold distance as another input parameter swapBackground(oldBG,newBG,threshold). This means we won't have to keep changing the method each time we want to change the threshold, which means the method can be used in more situations.

■

Program 44: Better Swap Background

```java
/**
 * Method to replace the background in the current picture
 * with the background from another picture
 * @param oldBackground a picture with the old background
 * to replace
 * @param newBackground a picture with the new background
 * to use
 * @param threshold if the distance between the current
 * pixel color and the background pixel color is less
 * than this amount use the new background pixel color
 */
public void swapBackground(Picture oldBackground,
                           Picture newBackground,
                           double threshold)
{
  Pixel currPixel = null;
  Pixel oldPixel = null;
  Pixel newPixel = null;

  // loop through the columns
  for (int x=0; x<getWidth(); x++)
  {

    // loop through the rows
    for (int y=0; y<getHeight(); y++)
    {

      // get the current pixel and old background pixel
      currPixel = this.getPixel(x,y);
      oldPixel = oldBackground.getPixel(x,y);
```

```
        /* if the distance between the current pixel color
         * and the old background pixel color is less than
         * the threshold then swap in the new background
         * pixel
         */
        if (currPixel.colorDistance(oldPixel.getColor()) <
                                 threshold)
        {
          newPixel = newBackground.getPixel(x,y);
          currPixel.setColor(newPixel.getColor());
        }
      }
    }
  }
```

To make this work pass the threshold too when invoking `swapBackground`:

```
> Picture p = new Picture(
  FileChooser.getMediaPath("twoKidsWall.jpg"));
> Picture oldBg = new Picture(
  FileChooser.getMediaPath("wall2.jpg"));
> Picture newBg = new Picture(
  FileChooser.getMediaPath("bridge.jpg"));
> p.swapBackground(oldBg,newBg,50);
> p.show();
```

6.7 CHROMAKEY

The way that weatherpersons appear to be in front of a weather map that changes, is that they actually stand before a background of a fixed color (usually blue or green), then subtract that color. This is called *chromakey*. Mark took our son's blue sheet, attached it to the entertainment center, then took a picture of himself in front of it, using a timer on a camera (Figure 6.19).

FIGURE 6.19
Mark in front of a blue sheet.

Mark tried a new way to test for "blueness." If the blue value was greater than the sum of the red and green values then the color was "blue."

Program 45: Chromakey: Replace all Blue with the New Background

```
/**
 * Method to do chromakey using a blue background
 * @param newBg the new background image to use to replace
 * the blue from the current picture
 */
public void chromakey(Picture newBg)
{
  Pixel currPixel = null;
  Pixel newPixel = null;

  // loop through the columns
  for (int x=0; x<getWidth(); x++)
  {

    // loop through the rows
    for (int y=0; y<getHeight(); y++)
    {

      // get the current pixel
      currPixel = this.getPixel(x,y);

      /* if the color at the current pixel is mostly blue
       * (blue value is greater than red and green
       * combined), then use new background color
       */
      if (currPixel.getRed() + currPixel.getGreen() <
          currPixel.getBlue())
      {
        newPixel = newBg.getPixel(x,y);
        currPixel.setColor(newPixel.getColor());
      }
    }
  }
}
```

The effect is really quite striking (Figure 6.20). Do note the "folds" in the lunar surface, though. The really cool thing is that this program works for any background that's the same size as the image (Figure 6.21). To put Mark on the moon and on the beach, try this:

```
> String fileName = FileChooser.getMediaPath("blue-mark.jpg");
> Picture mark = new Picture(fileName);
> fileName = FileChooser.getMediaPath("moon-surface.jpg");
```

```
> Picture newBg = new Picture(fileName);
> mark.chromakey(newBg);
> mark.explore();
> mark = new Picture(
  FileChooser.getMediaPath("blue-mark.jpg"));
> newBg = new Picture(FileChooser.getMediaPath("beach.jpg"));
> mark.chromakey(newBg);
> mark.explore();
```

FIGURE 6.20
Mark on the moon.

FIGURE 6.21
Mark on the beach.

There's another way of writing this code, which is shorter but does the same thing.

Program 46: Chromakey, Shorter

```java
/**
 * Method to do chromakey using a blue background
 * @param newBg the new background image to use to replace
 * the blue from the current picture
 */
public void chromakeyBlue(Picture newBg)
{
  Pixel[] pixelArray = this.getPixels();
  Pixel currPixel = null;
  Pixel newPixel = null;

  // loop through the pixels
  for (int i = 0; i < pixelArray.length; i++)
  {
    // get the current pixel
    currPixel = pixelArray[i];

    /* if the color at the current pixel is mostly blue
     * (blue value is greater than green and red
     * combined), then use new background color
     */
    if (currPixel.getRed() + currPixel.getGreen() <
        currPixel.getBlue())
    {
      newPixel = newBg.getPixel(currPixel.getX(),
                                currPixel.getY());
      currPixel.setColor(newPixel.getColor());
    }

  }
}
```

Making it Work Tip: When Do You Need a Different Method Name?

Notice that we used a different name for the new shorter method. We couldn't have used the same name and had both methods in our Picture class since the parameters are the same. Methods can be overloaded (use the same name) as long as the parameters are different (in number, or order, or type).

You don't really want to do chromakey with a common color, like red—something that there's a lot of in your face. If you do, some of the person's face will be swapped. This is why moviemakers and weather people use blue or green backgrounds.

6.8   CONCEPTS SUMMARY

We have covered boolean expressions, conditionally executing code using `if` and `else`, combining boolean expressions using "and" (&&) and "or" (||) and method overloading.

6.8.1   Boolean Expressions

A boolean expression is one that results in `true` or `false`. The values `true` and `false` are reserved words in Java. Here are some example boolean expressions.

```
> int x = 20;
> System.out.println(x <= 30);
true
> System.out.println(x > 30);
false
> System.out.println(x == 20);
true
> System.out.println(x != 20);
false
```

Notice that to check for a variable having a value we use `==` not `=`. The `=` is used to assign a value to a variable, not check for equality. To check for inequality use `!=`.

6.8.2   Combining Boolean Expressions

You can combine boolean expressions with the Java operators **&&** to represent "and" and **||** to represent "or". When you use **&&** both boolean expressions must be true in order for it to return true. If the first boolean expression isn't true the second won't even be tested. This is called short-circuit evaluation. When you use **||**, only one boolean expression must be true in order for it to return true. With **||**, if the first boolean expression is true, the second won't be evaluated. If the first boolean expression is false, the second one will still be evaluated.

```
> int x = 3;
> int y = 5;
> System.out.println(x < 5 && y < 6);
true
> System.out.println(x > 5 && y < 6);
false
> System.out.println(x < 5 && y > 6);
false
> System.out.println(x > 5 && y > 6);
false
> System.out.println(x > 5 || y < 6);
true
```

6.8.3   Conditional Execution

To conditionally execute one statement, use the `if` keyword followed by a boolean expression inside an open and close parenthesis. Put the statement that you only want executed if the boolean expression is true on a new line and indent it. If the boolean expression is false, then execution will continue with the next statement.

```
if (boolean expression)
    // statement to execute if the boolean expression is true
    statement
// next statement
statement
```

To conditionally execute a block of statements, use the `if` keyword followed by a boolean expression inside of an open and close parenthesis. Put the statements to be executed when the boolean expression is true inside of an open and close curly brace. Indent the statements to make it easier to visually see that these statements will only be executed if the boolean expression is true. If the boolean expression is false, execution will continue with the statement following the close curly brace.

```
if (boolean expression)
{
    statements
}
```

If you want to execute one block of statements if the boolean expression is true and another if it is false, use the `else` keyword as well. Put the statements that you want to execute when the boolean expression is true inside of an open and close curly brace after the `if (boolean Expression)`. Next, add the keyword `else` and put the statements that you want executed when the boolean expression is false inside of an open and close curly brace.

```
if (boolean expression)
{
 statements
}
 else
{
 statements
}
```

If you have 3 or more options use nested `if`s and `else`s.

```
if (boolean expression)
{
    statements
}
else if (boolean expression)
{
    statements
}
else
{
    statements
}
```

If you have four options, start with an `if (boolean expression)` and have two `else if (boolean expression)` and a final `else`. The last `else` is optional.

PROBLEMS

6.1   What are each of the following:

- Conditional execution

- Short circuit evaluation

- A boolean expression

- Chromakey
- Sepia-tint
- Posterize
- Edge detection
- Blurring

6.2   Try doing chromakey (page 203) in a range—grab something out of its background where the something is only in one part of a picture. For example, put a halo around someone's head, but don't mess with the rest of their body.

6.3   Try doing edge detection (page 184) in a range. Change just part of a picture by passing in the start x, start y, end x, and end y.

6.4   Try doing sepia-tint (page 188) in a range. Change just part of a picture by passing in the start x, start y, end x, and end y.

6.5   Modify the general copy method copyPictureTo on page 152 in Chapter 5 to stop looping if it is past the width of either the source picture or the current picture.

6.6   Write a method to copy all but the white pixels from one picture to another. Use this to put the robot in robot.jpg on the moon in moon-surface.jpg.

6.7   Start with a picture of someone you know, and make some specific color changes to it:

- Turn the skin green.
- Turn the eyes red.
- Turn the hair orange.

Of course, if you're friend's skin is already green, or eyes red, or hair orange–choose different target colors.

6.8   Which of the methods below removes all the blue from every pixel of a picture that already has a blue value of more than 100?

1. A only
2. D only
3. B and C
4. C and D
5. None
6. All

What do the other ones do?

A.
```java
public void blueOneHundred()
{
    Pixel p = null;

    for (int x = 0; x < 100; x++)
    {
```

```
      for (int y=0; y < 100; y++)
      {
        p = getPixel(x,y);
        p.setBlue(100);
      }
    }
  }
```

B.

```
  public void blueChange()
  {
    Pixel[] pixelArray = getPixels();
    Pixel pixel = null;

    for (int i = 0; i < pixelArray.length; i++)
    {
      pixel = pixelArray[i];
      if (pixel.getBlue() > 0)
      {
        pixel.setBlue(100);
      }
    }
  }
```

C.

```
  public void clearSomeBlue() {
      Pixel[] pixelArray = getPixels();
      Pixel pixel = null;

    for (int i = 0; i < pixelArray.length; i++)
    {
      pixel = pixelArray[i];
      if (pixel.colorDistance(Color.BLUE) > 100)
        pixel.setBlue(0);
    }
  }
```

D.

```
  public void setBlue() {
      Pixel[] pixelArray = getPixels();
      Pixel pixel = null;

    for (int i = 0; i < pixelArray.length; i++)
    {
      pixel = pixelArray[i];
      if (pixel.getBlue() > 100)
        pixel.setBlue(0);
    }
  }
```

6.9   What is the result from the following:

```
boolean value1 = true;
boolean value2 = false;
if (value1 && value2)
    System.out.println("first if is true");
if (value1 || value2)
    System.out.println("second if is true");
if (value1 && !value2)
    System.out.println("third if is true");
if (value1 || !value2)
    System.out.println("fourth if is true");
if (!value1 && value2)
    System.out.println("fifth if is true");
if (!value1 || value2)
    System.out.println("sixth if is true");
if (!value1 && !value2)
    System.out.println("seventh if is true");
if (!value1 || !value2)
    System.out.println("eighth if is true");
```

6.10   Write the method to turn the lightest areas of a picture gray to simulate a fog.

6.11   Write the method to turn the darkest areas of a picture green.

6.12   Write a method to lighten the darkest areas of a picture.

6.13   Write a method to darken the lightest areas of a picture.

6.14   Write a method to turn the pixels with an average color < 85 green, pixels with an average color < 170 red, and the rest of the pixels blue.

6.15   Write another method to blur the picture (Program 42 (page 195)) but this time make a copy of the picture first and use the values from the copy to determine the new value for a pixel. To make a copy of a picture, just create a new picture passing in the old one `Picture copy = new Picture(oldPicture);`.

6.16   Write other edge detection methods (page 184). Try comparing the current pixel intensity with the one on the right. Try comparing the current pixel to the average of the pixels to the right and below.

6.17   What would the output from the following be:

```
int x = 30;
for (int i=x; i < 40; i++)
{
  if (i < 35)
    System.out.println("i is less than 35");
  else if (i == 35)
    System.out.println("i is 35");
  else
    System.out.println("i is greater than 35");
}
```

6.18 What would the output from the following be:

```
boolean continue = true;
int count = 0;
int max = 20;
while (continue)
{
    System.out.println(count);
    count++;
    max++;
    if (count > 10 && max > 40)
        continue = false;
}
```

6.19 What would the output from the following be:

```
boolean continue = true;
int count = 0;
int max = 20;
while (continue)
{
    System.out.println(count);
    count++;
    max++;
    if (count > 10 || max > 40)
        continue = false;
}
```

6.20 Write a method to do green or red chromakey (page 203).

7 Drawing

7.1 DRAWING USING THE GRAPHICS CLASS

7.2 PROGRAMS AS SPECIFYING DRAWING PROCESS

7.3 USING GRAPHICS2D FOR ADVANCED DRAWING

7.4 CONCEPTS SUMMARY

Chapter Learning Objectives

The media learning goals for this chapter are:

- To be able to draw simple shapes (lines, ovals, rectangles, arcs) on existing pictures.
- To draw text on a picture.
- To create pictures by drawing them.
- To use the Java2D API for more complicated drawing.

The computer science goals for this chapter are:

- To understand the difference between vector and bitmapped image formats.
- To be able to choose when one should write a program for a task versus using existing applications software.
- To promote reuse by working with existing classes.
- To start using the Java API to explore classes and packages.
- To introduce the concept of inheritance.
- To introduce the concepts of interfaces and constants.

7.1 DRAWING USING THE GRAPHICS CLASS

Professional photographers have a problem in that it is easy for people to scan pictures and print many copies of them. How can they allow people to see proofs of pictures, but discourage people from using their pictures without paying for them? One way that professional photographers protect their images is to put some text on them. People can still scan the picture and make copies, but it is obvious that the picture is stolen. The text also hides some of the picture so people are more likely to pay for pictures without the text.

How can you add text to a picture? We know that this is just a matter of setting pixel values to whatever we want, but setting individual pixel values to draw a line

FIGURE 7.1
Adding a grid of lines to a picture (barbara.jpg).

or a circle or some letters is hard. Here's an example that creates a grid of lines on a picture (Figure 7.1). It works by simply setting all the pixels in a line to black! The gap between the lines is 20 pixels.

Program 47: Draw Lines by Setting Pixels

```java
/**
 * Method to draw a grid on a picture
 */
public void drawGrid()
{
  Pixel pixel = null;

  // Draw the horizontal lines
  for (int y = 20; y < this.getHeight(); y+=20)
  {
    for (int x = 0; x < this.getWidth(); x++)
    {
      pixel = this.getPixel(x,y);
      pixel.setColor(Color.black);
    }
  }

  // draw the vertical lines
  for (int x = 20; x < this.getWidth(); x+=20)
  {
    for (int y = 0; y < this.getHeight(); y++)
```

```
      {
        pixel = this.getPixel(x,y);
        pixel.setColor(Color.black);
      }
    }
  }
```

To test this method create a `Picture` object and then invoke the method on the `Picture`.

```
> String fileName = FileChooser.getMediaPath("barbara.jpg");
> Picture pictureObj = new Picture(fileName);
> pictureObj.show();
> pictureObj.drawGrid();
> pictureObj.repaint();
```

This method first draws the horizontal lines by setting y to a value of 20 and incrementing y by 20, while x starts at 0 and is incremented by 1. Next the method draws the vertical lines by setting x to 20 and incrementing x by 20 while y starts at 0 and is incremented by 1. To draw more lines, decrease the start and increment values, and to draw fewer lines, increase the start and increment values.

Making it Work Tip: Working with Color Objects

You may notice that this program is using the predefined `Color` object (object of the `Color` class) `Color.black`. Remember that Java pre-defines for you a bunch of colors: `Color.black`, `Color.white`, `Color.blue`, `Color.red`, `Color.green`, `Color.gray`, `Color.lightGray`, `Color.darkGray`, `Color.yellow`, `Color.orange`, `Color.pink`, `Color.magenta`, and `Color.cyan`. You can use any of these when you need a color. You can also create a `Color` object by providing the red, green, and blue values (between 0 and 255) using `new Color(red,green,blue)`. For example, to create a pure black color you would use `new Color(0,0,0)`, and to create a pure white color, you would use `new Color(255,255,255)`.

We can imagine drawing anything we want like this, by simply setting individual pixels to whatever colors we want. We could draw rectangles or circles, simply by figuring out what pixels need to be what color. We could even draw letters—by setting the appropriate pixels to the appropriate colors, we could make any letter we want. While we could do it, it would involve a lot of work to do all the math for all the different shapes and letters. That's work that lots of people want done, so instead, the basic drawing has been built into Java for you.

7.1.1 Drawing with Graphics Methods

Most modern programming languages with graphics libraries provide ways to draw a variety of shapes and text. In Java the `Graphics` class in the `java.awt` package has a number of methods that allow you to draw simple shapes and text. These graphics methods work similar to painting. First you pick a color to use to paint with, and then you can paint several shapes using that color. If one shape is drawn over another, it will cover the shape underneath.

Computer Science Idea: Packages

A package is a collection of related classes. Java defines a large number of classes and it would be overwhelming if they weren't grouped into packages. Some common packages are java.lang, which has the basics of the Java language in it, java.awt, which has the original graphics classes in it, and java.io, which contains classes used for input and output. ∎

- setColor(Color color) sets the color to use for drawing.
- drawLine(int x1, int y1, int x2, int y2) draws a line from position $(x1, y1)$ to $(x2, y2)$ using the current color.
- drawRect(int x1, int y1, int w, int h) draws the outline of a rectangle with the upper-left corner at $(x1, y1)$, a width of w, and a height of h using the current color.
- fillRect(int x1, int y1, int w, int h) draws a filled (solid) rectangle with the upper-left corner at $(x1, y1)$, a width of w, and a height of h using the current color.
- drawOval(int x1, int y1, int w, int h) draws the outline of an oval with the upper-left corner of the enclosing rectangle at $(x1, y1)$, the width of the enclosing rectangle is w and the height of the enclosing rectangle is h using the current color.
- fillOval(int x1, int y1, int w, int h) draws a filled (solid) oval with the upper-left corner of an enclosing rectangle at $(x1, y1)$, the width of the enclosing rectangle is w and the height of the enclosing rectangle is h using the current color.
- drawArc(int x1, int y1, int w, int h, int startAngle, int arcAngle) draws an outline of an arc that is part of an oval that fits in the enclosing rectangle at $(x1, y1)$, the width of the enclosing rectangle is w and the height of the enclosing rectangle is h. The arc starts at the given *startAngle* and extends *arcAngle* degrees (where 0 degrees is at the 3 o'clock position on a clock and 45 degrees goes through the upper-right corner of the enclosing rectangle). The ending angle is the *startAngle* plus *arcAngle*.
- fillArc(int x1, int y1, int w, int h, int startAngle, int arcAngle) draws a filled arc that is part of an oval that fits in the enclosing rectangle at $(x1, y1)$, the width of the enclosing rectangle is w and the height of the enclosing rectangle is h. The arc starts at the given *startAngle* and extends *arcAngle* degrees (where 0 degrees is at the 3 o'clock position on a clock and 45 degrees goes through the upper-right corner of the enclosing rectangle). The ending angle is the *startAngle* plus *arcAngle*.

- `drawPolygon(int[] xArray, int[] yArray, int numPoints)` draws the outline of a closed polygon using the x values in *xArray* and the y values in *yArray* using the current color.
- `fillPolygon(int[] xArray, int[] yArray, int numPoints)` draws a filled closed polygon using the x values in *xArray* and the y values in *yArray* using the current color.

Making it Work Tip: Use the Java API

Java is a large language, and it is nearly impossible to know every method for every class. Use the application program interface (API) documentation to see the methods that are available for a class. If you look at the documentation for the `Graphics` class in the `java.awt` package, you will see *all* of the methods defined for that class. We are only showing some of the most commonly used methods here. To view the API documentation go to: `http://java.sun.com/`. Find the specification for the version of the language that you are using. Click on the package in the top-left window frame, and then click on the class name in the bottom-left window frame. The documentation for that class will appear on the right. Scroll down to "Method Summary" (Figure 7.2). This gives an alphabetical listing of all of the methods defined in that class. ■

We can use these commands to add simple shapes to existing pictures. What would it look like if a mysterious red box washed up on the shore of a beach? We

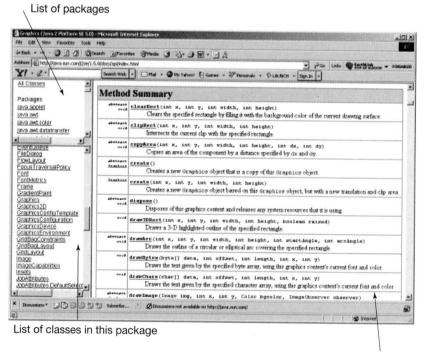

List of packages

List of classes in this package

Documentation for the class: Graphics

FIGURE 7.2
Viewing the Java API for java.awt.Graphics.

FIGURE 7.3
A box washed up on the shore of the beach.

will need to get a Graphics object to use for the drawing. We can get one from a Picture object using the method getGraphics(). When you draw, you set the color using setColor(Color color) and then do any drawing commands. We can make a box appear on a picture of a beach with this method (Figure 7.3).

Program 48: Adding a Box

```
/**
 * Method to add a solid red rectangle to the current picture
 */
public void addBox()
{

  // get the graphics context from the picture
  Graphics g = this.getGraphics();

  // set the color to red
  g.setColor(Color.red);

  // draw the box as a filled rectangle
  g.fillRect(150,200,50,50);
}
```

Execute this method using:

```
> String fileName = FileChooser.getMediaPath("beach-smaller.jpg");
> Picture p = new Picture(fileName);
> p.addBox();
> p.show();
```

This method isn't very reusable. The only way to change it to work for other rectangles is to modify the color and rectangle information and then recompile. If we want this to work on any rectangle, then we will want to pass parameters to make the method more general.

Program 49: General Draw Box

```java
/**
 * Method to draw a filled box on the current picture
 * @param color the color to draw the box with
 * @param topLeftX the top left x coordinate of the box
 * @param topLeftY the top left y coordinate of the box
 * @param width the width of the box
 * @param height the height of the box
 */
public void drawBox(Color color, int topLeftX, int topLeftY,
                    int width, int height)
{
  // get the graphics context for drawing
  Graphics g = this.getGraphics();

  // set the current color
  g.setColor(color);

  // draw the filled rectangle
  g.fillRect(topLeftX,topLeftY,width,height);
}
```

We could use this more general method to generate the same picture by:

```java
> Picture p =
  new Picture(FileChooser.getMediaPath("beach-smaller.jpg"));
> p.drawBox(java.awt.Color.red,150,200,50,50);
> p.show();
```

The advantage of the method drawBox over the method addBox is that it can be used to draw any rectangle of any color on any picture.

Below is another example of using the simple drawing commands (Figure 7.4).

Program 50: An Example of Using Drawing Commands

```java
/**
 * Method to show different drawing capabilities.  It
 * will draw a string, a line, a filled rectangle, the
 * outline of a rectangle, the outline of an oval,
 * and a filled arc.
 */
public void drawExample()
{

  // get the graphics object to use for drawing
  Graphics graphics = this.getGraphics();

  // start with a black color
  graphics.setColor(Color.black);
```

```
      /* draw the string with an upper left corner
       * at x=10, y=75
       */
      graphics.drawString(
         "This is a test of drawing a string on a picture",
                          10,75);

      // draw a line from (10,20) to (300,50)
      graphics.drawLine(10,20,300,50);

      // set the color to yellow
      graphics.setColor(Color.yellow);

      /* draw a filled rectangle (filled with yellow) at
       * upper left (0,200) with a width of 300 and
       * height 250
       */
      graphics.fillRect(0,200,300,250);

      // set the color back to black
      graphics.setColor(Color.black);

      /* draw the outline of a rectangle with the upper
       * left at (10,210) and a width of 200 and a height
       * of 100
       */
      graphics.drawRect(10,210,200,100);

      /* draw an oval enclosed by a rectangle with the top
       * left corner at (400,10) and a width of 200 and a
       * height of 100
       */
      graphics.drawOval(400,10,200,100);

      /* draw an arc which is part of an oval enclosed by
       * a rectangle with the top left corner at (400,300)
       * a width of 200, and a height of 150.  The arc
       * starts at 0 (3 o'clock position) and goes 180
       * degrees counter-clockwise to the 9 o'clock position
       */
      graphics.fillArc(400,300,200,150,0,180);
   }
```

To try this out create a picture from the blank 640 by 480 file. Then invoke the method `drawExample()` on the picture.

```
> Picture p = new Picture(FileChooser.getMediaPath("640x480.jpg"));
> p.drawExample();
> p.show();
```

How would you draw a simple face (Figure 7.5)? You could draw an oval for the head. You could use filled ovals for the eyes. You could use arcs for the mouth and eyebrows.

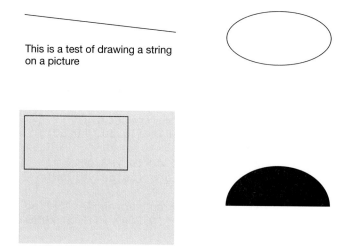

This is a test of drawing a string
on a picture

FIGURE 7.4
An example drawn picture.

Program 51: An Example of Using Oval and Arc Drawing Commands

```
/**
 * Method to draw a face to demonstrate drawing
 * ovals and arcs
 */
public void drawFace()
{
  // get the graphics object to use for drawing
  Graphics graphics = this.getGraphics();

  // start with a black color
  graphics.setColor(Color.black);

  // draw the oval for the face
  graphics.drawOval(130,50,380,380);

  // draw the ovals for the eyes
  graphics.fillOval(225,155,40,40);
  graphics.fillOval(375,155,40,40);

  // draw the arcs for the eyebrows
  graphics.drawArc(225,145,40,40,45,90);
  graphics.drawArc(375,145,40,40,45,90);

  // draw the arc for the mouth
  graphics.drawArc(190,85,255,255,-45,-90);
}
```

To try this, create a picture from the blank 640 by 480 file. Then invoke the method drawFace() on the picture.

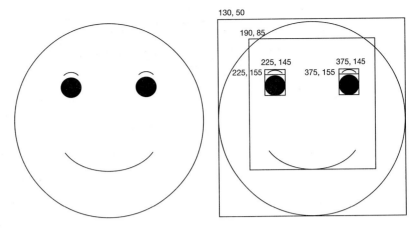

FIGURE 7.5
A drawn face (left) and the face with enclosing rectangles (right).

```
> Picture p = new Picture(
    FileChooser.getMediaPath("640x480.jpg"));
> p.drawFace();
> p.show();
```

Making it Work Tip: Drawing Ovals and Arcs

Notice that to draw an oval or arc you give the upper-left corner of the enclosing rectangle, not the upper-left corner of the oval or arc (Figure 7.5). Arcs specify the starting angle, but not the ending angle. The ending angle is the starting angle added to the arc angle. Graph paper and a protractor can help you plan your drawing. ■

7.1.2 Vector and Bitmap Representations

Here's a thought: Which of these is smaller—the picture (Figure 7.4) or Program 50 (page 218)? The picture, on my disk, is about 31 kilobytes (a *kilobyte* is a thousand bytes). The program is less than 2 kilobytes. What if you just saved the program and not the pixels? That's what a *vector representation* for graphics is about.

Vector-based graphical representations are basically executable programs that generate the picture when desired. Vector-based representations are used in Postscript, Flash, and AutoCAD. When you make a change to an image in Flash or AutoCAD, you are actually making a change to the underlying representation—essentially, you're changing the program, like the one in Program 50 (page 218). The program is then executed again to make the image appear. But thanks to Moore's Law, that execution-and-new-display occurs so fast that it feels like you're changing the picture.

Font definitions languages like Postscript and TrueType actually define miniature programs (or equations) for each and every letter or symbol. When you want the letter or symbol at a particular size, the program is run to figure out which pixels should be set to what values. (Some actually specify more than one color to create the effect of smoother curves.) Because the programs are written to handle the desired font size as an input, the letters and symbols can be generated at any size.

Bitmap graphical representations, on the other hand, store every individual pixel, or some compressed representation of the pixels. Formats like BMP, GIF, and JPEG are essentially bitmap representations. GIF and JPEG are compressed representations—they don't represent each and every pixel with 24 bits. Instead, they use some techniques to represent the same information but with fewer bits.

What does *compression* mean? It means that various techniques have been used to make the file smaller. Some compression techniques are *lossy compression*—some detail is lost, but hopefully the least significant (perhaps even invisible to the human eye, or ear) detail. Other techniques like *lossless compression* lose no detail, but still scrunch the file. One of the lossless techniques is *run length encoding* (RLE).

Imagine that you've got a long line of yellow pixels in a picture, surrounded by some blue pixels. Something like this:

B B Y Y Y Y Y Y Y Y B B

What if you encoded this, not as a long line of pixels, but as something like:

B B 9 Y B B

In words, you encode "blue, blue, then 9 yellows, then blue and blue." Since each of those yellow pixels takes 24 bits (3 bytes for red, green and blue), but recording "9" takes just a single byte, there's a huge savings. We say that we're encoding the *length* of the *run* of yellows–thus, run length encoding. That's just one of the compression methods used to make pictures smaller.

There are several benefits to vector-based representations over bitmap representations. If you can represent the picture you want to send (say, over the Internet) using a vector-based representation, it's much smaller than sending all the pixels—in a sense, vector notation is already compressed. Essentially, you're sending the *instructions* for how to make the picture, rather than sending the picture itself. For very complex images, however, the instructions can be as long as the image itself (imagine sending all the directions on how to paint the *Mona Lisa*!), so there is no benefit. But when the images are simple enough, representations like those used in Flash make for faster upload and download times than sending the same information as JPEG images.

The real benefit of vector-based notations comes when you want to change the image. Let's say that you're working on an architectural drawing, and you extend a line in your drawing tool. If your drawing tool is only working with bitmapped images (sometimes called a *painting tool*) then all you have are more pixels on the screen that are adjacent to the other pixels on the screen representing the line. There's nothing in the computer that says that all those pixels represent a line of any kind—they're just pixels. But if your drawing tool is working with vector-based representations (sometimes called a *drawing tool*), then extending a line means that you're changing an underlying representation of a line.

Why is that important? The underlying representation is actually a *specification* of the drawing, and it can be used anywhere that a specification is needed. Imagine taking the drawing of a part, then actually running the cutting and stamping machines based on that drawing. This happens regularly in many shops, and it's possible because the drawing isn't just pixels—it's a specification of the lines and their relationships, which can then be scaled and used to determine the behavior of machines.

You might be wondering, "But how could we *change* the program? Can we write a program that would essentially re-type the program or parts of the program?" Yes, we can, and we'll do that in the chapter on text (Chapter 12).

7.1.3 Drawing Text (Strings)

In order to add text to an image we can use the `java.awt.Graphics` method `drawString(String str, int x, int y)`. This will draw the passed string at the passed x and y position. However, the x and y values are not the top left corner as is usual with the drawing methods. The x and y values give the baseline of the string which is the line on which you would write the string if you were using lined paper (Figure 7.6).

When you use the `drawString` method, the string will be drawn in the current color and *font*. The font specifies what the characters in the string will look like, what style will be used (bold, italic, plain), and how big the characters will be. You have seen that you can set the color using `setColor(Color colorObj)`. You can also set the font using `setFont(Font fontObj)`.

To create a `Font` object you specify the font name, style, and size: `new Font(String name, int style, int size)`. You can always use any of Dialog, DialogInput, Monospaced, Serif, or SansSerif for font names. You can get an array of all of the available font names using:

```
> import java.awt.*;
> GraphicsEnvironment env =
    GraphicsEnvironment.getLocalGraphicsEnvironment();
> String[] nameArray = env.getAvailableFontFamilyNames();
> for (int i=0; i < nameArray.length; i++)
    System.out.println(nameArray[i]);
```

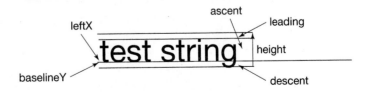

FIGURE 7.6
Shows font information including the baseline.

The method to draw a passed string on the current picture at the passed x and y is:

Program 52: Draw a String on a Picture

```java
/**
 * Method to draw a string on the current picture
 * @param text the string to draw
 * @x the x location to start at
 * @y the y location of the baseline
 */
public void drawString(String text, int x, int y)
{

    // get the graphics object
    Graphics g = this.getGraphics();

    // set the color
    g.setColor(Color.black);

    // set the font
    g.setFont(new Font("Arial",Font.BOLD,24));

    // draw the string
    g.drawString(text,x,y);
}
```

To use this program, you can use the picture explorer to determine where you want the baseline of the string to be and then use the drawString method to draw the string on the picture. Our son, Matthew, took a picture of a kitten on a trip to Greece. Let's add a string that explains the picture near the bottom of the picture (Figure 7.7).

FIGURE 7.7
Drawing a string on a picture.

FIGURE 7.8
Drawing a string centered on a picture.

```
> Picture p = new Picture(FileChooser.getMediaPath("kitten.jpg"));
> p.explore();
> p.drawString("Matt's picture of a kitten in Greece",67,283);
> p.explore();
```

The string isn't quite in the center of the picture. What if we want it to be in the center as it is in Figure 7.8? How could we calculate the starting x position for the string such that the resulting string is centered? We know that the center of the picture horizontally is at half the width of the picture (int) (picture.getWidth() * 0.5). If we subtract half the length of the string in pixels from the center of the picture that would center the string. How do we calculate the length of the string in pixels? The length of the string depends on the number of characters in the string but also on the font used to draw the string.

To get information about the length of the string in the number of pixels drawn we can use the FontMetrics class which is in package java.awt. To get a FontMetrics object use g.getFontMetrics() where g is a Graphics object. The FontMetrics class contains methods for getting information about the display of a font. For example, we can get the length in pixels of a string using the method stringWidth(String str). We could get the height in pixels of a string drawn in the current font using the method getHeight(). We could get the length of the descent (part of a character like 'p' below the baseline) using getDescent().

Program 53: Drawing a String Centered Horizontally on a Picture

```
/**
 * Method to draw a horizontally centered string
 * on the current picture
 * @param text the string to draw
 * @y the y location of the baseline
 */
public void drawHorizontalCenteredString(String text,
                                         int y)
{

  // get the graphics object
  Graphics g = this.getGraphics();

  // create the font object
  Font font = new Font("Arial",Font.BOLD,24);

  // set the color
  g.setColor(Color.black);

  // set the font
  g.setFont(font);

  // get the font metrics
  FontMetrics fontMetrics = g.getFontMetrics();

  // get the width of the string
  int strWidth = fontMetrics.stringWidth(text);

  // calculate the center of the picture
  int center = (int) (this.getWidth() * 0.5);

  // draw the string centered in x
  g.drawString(text,
               center - (int) (strWidth * 0.5),
               y);
}
```

7.2 PROGRAMS AS SPECIFYING DRAWING PROCESS

Another thing we can do with drawing is create pictures that are exactly specified—things that might be too hard to do by hand. Take, for example, Figure 7.9.

This is a rendering of a famous optical illusion, and it's not as effective as the famous ones—but it's simple to understand how this version works. Our eyes tell us that the left half of the picture is lighter than the right half, even though the end quarters are exactly the same shade of gray. The effect is caused by the sharp boundary between the middle quarters, where one moves (left-to-right) from gray to white, and the other moves black to gray.

The image in Figure 7.9 is a carefully defined and created picture. It would be very hard to do with pencil and paper. It would be possible to do with something

FIGURE 7.9
A programmed grayscale effect.

like Photoshop, but it wouldn't be easy. Using the graphics methods in this chapter, however, we can easily specify exactly what that picture should be.

Program 54: Draw the Gray Effect

```
/**
 * Method to draw a gray effect picture on the
 * current picture
 */
public void drawGrayEffect()
{

  // create a medium gray color to use
  Color medGray = new Color(100,100,100);

   // Do 100 columns of medium gray
   for (int x = 0; x < 100; x++)
     for (int y = 0; y < 100; y++)
       this.getPixel(x,y).setColor(medGray);

   /* Do 100 columns of gray starting at medium
    * gray and getting lighter
    */
   for (int x=100, grayLevel=100;
        x < 200;
        x++,grayLevel++)
     for (int y=0; y < 100; y++)
       this.getPixel(x,y).setColor(
             new Color(grayLevel,grayLevel,grayLevel));

   // Do 100 columns starting at black and getting lighter
   for (int x=200, grayLevel=0; x < 300; x++, grayLevel++)
     for (int y=0; y < 100; y++)
        this.getPixel(x,y).setColor(
             new Color(grayLevel,grayLevel,grayLevel));

   // Do 100 columns of medium gray
   for (int x=300; x < 400; x++)
     for (int y=0; y < 100; y++)
        this.getPixel(x,y).setColor(medGray);
}
```

To use this method, create a picture of the file that has a blank 640 by 480 picture in it. Invoke the method on that picture.

```
> Picture p = new Picture(FileChooser.getMediaPath("640x480.jpg"));
> p.drawGrayEffect();
> p.show();
```

Graphics methods are very good at drawings that are repeated where the positions of lines and shapes and the selection of colors can be made by mathematical relationships.

Program 55: Draw the Picture in Figure 7.10

```
/**
 * Method to draw a picture with a succession of
 * filled rectangles with the top left corner the
 * darkest and the bottom right the lightest on
 * the current picture
 */
public void drawFilledRectangles()
{
  Graphics g = this.getGraphics();
  Color color = null;

  // loop 25 times
  for (int i = 25; i > 0; i--)
  {
    color = new Color(i * 10, i * 5, i);
    g.setColor(color);
    g.fillRect(0,0,i*10,i*10);
  }
}
```

FIGURE 7.10
Nested colored rectangles.

To use this method create a picture of the file that has a blank 640 by 480 picture in it. Invoke the method on that picture.

```
> Picture p = new Picture(FileChooser.getMediaPath("640x480.jpg"));
> p.drawFilledRectangles();
> p.show();
```

Program 56: Draw the Picture in Figure 7.11

```
/**
 * Method to draw a picture with a succession of
 * rectangles on the current picture
 */
public void drawRectangles()
{
  Graphics g = this.getGraphics();
  Color color = null;

  // loop 25 times
  for (int i = 25; i > 0; i--)
  {
    g.setColor(Color.black);
    g.drawRect(i,i,i*3,i*4);
    g.drawRect(100+i*4,100+i*3,i*8,i*10);
  }
}
```

To use this method, create a picture of the file that has a blank 640 by 480 picture in it. Invoke the method on that picture.

```
> Picture p = new Picture(FileChooser.getMediaPath("640x480.jpg"));
> p.drawRectangles();
> p.show();
```

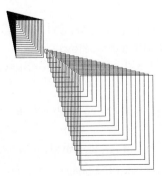

FIGURE 7.11
Nested outlined rectangles.

7.2.1 Why Do We Write Programs?

Why do we write programs, especially to draw pictures? Couldn't we draw pictures like these in Photoshop or Visio? Certainly we can, but we'd have to know *how*, and that's not easy knowledge to come by. Could we *teach* you how to do this in Photoshop? Probably, but that may take a lot of effort—Photoshop isn't simple.

But if we *give* you these methods (programs), you can create the picture anytime you want. What's more, by giving you the methods, We're giving you the *exact* definition that you can go and change for yourself.

> **Computer Science Idea: We Write Programs to Encapsulate and Communicate Process**
> The reason why we write programs is to exactly specify a process and to communicate it to others.
> ■

Imagine that you have some process to communicate. It doesn't have to be drawing—imagine that it's a financial process (such that you could do it in a spreadsheet or in a program like Quicken) or something that you do with text (such as laying out text for a book or a brochure). If you can do something by hand, you should just do it. If you need to *teach* someone else to do it, consider writing a program to do it. If you need to explain to *lots* of people how to do it, definitely use a program. If you want lots of people to be able to do the process themselves, without someone having to teach them something first, write a program and give the people the program.

7.3 USING GRAPHICS2D FOR ADVANCED DRAWING

We have used the `java.awt.Graphics` object to draw simple shapes like lines, rectangles, ovals, arcs, and polygons. The `Graphics` object is like a painter who picks up a brush with the color you set and paints a shape with it. If you ask the painter to paint another shape over a previous one the new shape will cover the original shape. But, what if we want to use a thicker "brush" when we draw? What if we want shapes to combine rather than occlude? What if we want to treat our shapes as objects?

The `java.awt.Graphics` class is okay for simple drawing but lacks many advanced features. However, the class `java.awt.Graphics2D` which is part of the Java 2D API can be used for more advanced drawing. Some of the capabilities of a `Graphics2D` object are:

- You can set the width of the brush (pen). You can also set the style of the brush to do different types of dashed lines.

- You can rotate, translate, scale, or shear what you are drawing.

- You can fill a shape with more than just a solid color. You can fill a shape with a gradient or a texture.

- You can change what happens when objects overlap.

- You can clip objects so that only the part visible inside the clipping area is drawn. This is like using a stencil.
- You can set rendering hints to make your curves smoother using anti-aliasing if it is available.

7.3.1   Setting the Brush Width

To use these advanced features you will need a Graphics2D object. To get a Graphics2D object you must cast the Graphics object to a Graphics2D object using Graphics2D g2 = (Graphics2D) graphics. All Graphics objects that you get are really Graphics2D objects, so this is allowed.

You can set the brush options using setStroke. You set the color, gradient, or texture to use for painting with the method setPaint(Paint p). Instead of methods that draw shapes the Graphics2D class has you create objects and either draw them to draw the outline or fill them to fill with the current paint information. Here is a simple program that draws a red x on the current picture using a brush (stroke) with the specified width.

Program 57: Draw an X on a Picture

```
/**
 * Method to add two crossed lines to a picture.
 * One line will go from the top left corner to the
 * bottom right corner.  The other will go from the
 * bottom left corner to the top right corner.
 */
public void drawWideX(Color color, float width)
{
  // get the Graphics2D object
  Graphics graphics = this.getGraphics();
  Graphics2D g2 = (Graphics2D) graphics;

  // set the color and brush width
  g2.setPaint(color);
  g2.setStroke(new BasicStroke(width));

  // get the max x and y values
  int maxX = getWidth() - 1;
  int maxY = getHeight() - 1;

  // draw the lines
  g2.draw(new Line2D.Double(0,0,maxX,maxY));
  g2.draw(new Line2D.Double(0,maxY,maxX,0));
}
```

You can use this program to add a wide red 'X' to a picture, as shown in Figure 7.12.

FIGURE 7.12
Drawing a red X on a picture.

```
> String fileName = FileChooser.getMediaPath("grayMotorcycle.jpg");
> Picture p = new Picture(fileName);
> p.drawWideX(java.awt.Color.red,5);
> p.show();
```

Making it Work Tip: Creating and Drawing Shapes with Graphics2D

Notice that we created a Line2D.Double object and then asked the Graphics2D object named g2 to draw this object. This is different from how we drew shapes using the Graphics class. With the Graphics2D class you create geometric objects and either draw or fill them.

The Line2D.Double probably looks strange to you. This is actually the name of a class in the java.awt.geom package. Even though java.awt.geom and java.awt both start the same they are different packages. If you imported all classes in the package java.awt using the wildcard '*' you still wouldn't have imported the classes in the java.awt.geom package. You need at least two import statements if you are using classes from both of these packages.

■

7.3.2   Copying Pictures by Drawing Images

Both the Graphics and Graphics2D classes have methods for drawing images. You can use these methods to copy a picture to the current picture object. You don't have to copy the colors pixel by pixel. The method to do this is drawImage.

There are many methods with the name drawImage. Recall that method overloading allows methods with the same name as long as the parameters are different. Look at the API for the Graphics class to see all the drawImage methods. Which method would you use to copy all the pixels in one image (picture) to another at a particular location?

Notice that the drawImage methods take an Image object not a Picture object. The Picture class is one we created, but it contains a method that will get you an Image object: getImage().

So, to copy a picture to the current picture object you need to get the Graphics object to use to draw on the current picture. You can do this using the method getGraphics(). Next draw the Image that you get from the passed Picture (using the method getImage()) at the passed x and y location using the method drawImage(Image img, int x, int y, ImageObserver observer). What is an ImageObserver? It is an object that wants to be notified as the image is changed. It can be null to say that no object wants to be notified.

Program 58: Copy a Picture to this Picture

```java
/**
 * Method to copy the passed picture into the current
 * picture at the given x and y position in the
 * current picture
 * @param source the picture to copy
 * @param x the x of the upper left corner to copy to
 * @param y the y of the upper left corner to copy to
 */
public void copy(Picture source, int x, int y)
{
  // get the graphics object
  Graphics g = this.getGraphics();

  // copy the image
  g.drawImage(source.getImage(),x,y,null);
}
```

You can use this program to copy a turtle to the beach (Figure 7.13) using:

```
> Picture p1 = new Picture(FileChooser.getMediaPath("beach.jpg"));
> p1.explore();
> Picture p2 = new Picture(FileChooser.getMediaPath("turtle.jpg"));
> p1.copy(p2,194,304);
> p1.show();
```

Now change the copy method to use a Graphics2D object. Will it still compile? Try it and see. Does the Graphics2D class have the drawImage method?

Program 59: Copy a Picture to this Picture Using Graphics2D

```java
/**
 * Method to copy the passed picture into the current
 * picture at the given x and y position in the current
 * picture
 * @param source the picture to copy
 * @param x the x of the upper left corner to copy to
 * @param y the y of the upper left corner to copy to
 */
```

```
public void copy2D(Picture source, int x, int y)
{
  // get the graphics object
  Graphics g = this.getGraphics();
  Graphics g2 = (Graphics2D) g;

  // copy the image
  g2.drawImage(source.getImage(),x,y,null);
}
```

Why does this work? The class `Graphics2D` *inherits* from the class `Graphics`. What does that mean? Have you heard of children inheriting features or abilities from their parents like eye color, hair color, or musical ability? A child class inherits from a parent class. What can it inherit? Classes don't have eye color, but they do define data (fields) and behavior (methods). A child class inherits data (fields) and behavior (methods).

Unlike people, classes inherit *all* of the fields and methods of the parent class and they can only have *one* parent. An object of a child class can invoke public methods that are defined in a parent class just as if they were defined in the child class. An object of a child class can also access any public fields in a parent class as if they were defined in the child class.

What about private fields and methods? While these are inherited, they can not be directly accessed by a child object, nor should they be. The standard way to work with private fields is to provide public methods that can modify or access the private fields, but keep the data in a valid state. Private methods are only meant to

FIGURE 7.13
Drawing a turtle on a beach.

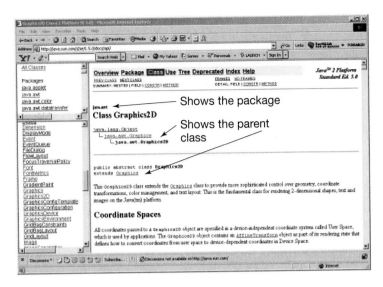

FIGURE 7.14
Documentation for Graphics2D.

be used inside the class they are defined in, so you wouldn't want a child directly using them.

How can we tell that the class `Graphics2D` inherits from the class `Graphics`? If you look at the API for `Graphics2D` (Figure 7.14) you will see that the API starts with the package name. On the next line is the class name. Following that is the ancestor tree of the class. It shows all the ancestors of the class starting with `java.lang.Object`. The class `java.awt.Graphics2D` class inherits from the class `java.awt.Graphics` which inherits from the class `java.lang.Object`. You can also tell who the parent class is by finding the class name given after the `extends` keyword in the class declaration.

Making it Work Tip: Object is the Top Ancestor

All classes inherit from the class `java.lang.Object`, and it is the only class that doesn't inherit from another class. Even if a class doesn't specify in the class definition the class it inherits from using the extends keyword it will inherit from `Object`. ∎

7.3.3 General Scaling

We have shown how to scale an image up by copying the same pixel more than once. We have shown how to scale an image down by skipping every other pixel. The methods that we wrote would double the size of the original image or reduce it by half. But, what if we want to scale up in x and down in y? What if we want to scale to a specific size? The `Graphics2D` class provides ways to handle scaling using an `AffineTransform` object in package `java.awt.geom` to handle the transformation. Here is a program that will scale a picture by the passed x and y factors.

Program 60: General Scale Method

```
/**
 * Method to create a new picture by scaling the current
 * picture by the given x and y factors
 * @param xFactor the amount to scale in x
 * @param yFactor the amount to scale in y
 * @return the resulting picture
 */
public Picture scale(double xFactor, double yFactor)
{
    // set up the scale transform
    AffineTransform scaleTransform = new AffineTransform();
    scaleTransform.scale(xFactor,yFactor);

    // create a new picture object that is the right size
    Picture result = new Picture((int) (getWidth() * xFactor),
                                 (int) (getHeight() * yFactor));

    // get the graphics 2d object to draw on the result
    Graphics graphics = result.getGraphics();
    Graphics2D g2 = (Graphics2D) graphics;

    // draw the current image onto the result image scaled
    g2.drawImage(this.getImage(),scaleTransform,null);

    return result;
}
```

You can use the `scale` method to create a new picture from the original picture by scaling up or down by any amount in x and/or y (Figure 7.15).

```
> Picture p = new Picture(
    FileChooser.getMediaPath("mattDoor.jpg"));
> Picture p1 = p.scale(2.0,0.5);
> p1.show();
```

FIGURE 7.15
Original picture and picture scaled up two times in x and down by half in y.

Making it Work Tip: Build from Working Parts

Earlier we wrote a method to scale a picture by copying colors from a source picture to a target picture pixel by pixel. Here we are using classes defined as part of the Java language to do that work for us. There are many classes in Java available for you to use. When you start solving a problem, you don't have to create everything you need from scratch. Instead, you can assemble your solution from classes that already exist. This is one of the goals of object-oriented programming: make things reusable by encapsulating related data and methods in classes. ■

7.3.4 Shearing

One of the effects that is easy to do with an `java.awt.geom.AffineTransform` object is to shear the image. Shearing by 1.0 in x moves each row over by the y index amount. So the first row, with a y index of 0, starts at (0, 0). The second row, with a y index of 1, starts at (1, 1). The third row, with a y index of 2, starts at (2, 2). The last row's x will start at (*height* − 1, *height* − 1). To figure out how big our new picture will need to be no matter what the amounts we are shearing by are, use a method in the Picture class, the `getTranslationEnclosingRectangle(AffineTransform trans)` method, which takes an `AffineTransform` object and returns a rectangle that will enclose the picture that results from applying that `AffineTransform` object to the current `Picture` object.

Program 61: General Shear Method

```
/**
 * Method to create a new picture by shearing the current
 * picture by the given x and y factors
 * @param xFactor multiplier to use to shift in x
 * direction based on y index
 * @param yFactor multiplier to use to shift in y
 * direction based on x index
 * @return the resulting picture
 */
public Picture shear(double xFactor, double yFactor)
{
  // set up the shear transform
  AffineTransform shearTransform = new AffineTransform();
  shearTransform.shear(xFactor,yFactor);
  Rectangle2D rect =
    getTranslationEnclosingRectangle(shearTransform);

  /* create a new picture object big enough to hold the
   * result
   */
  Picture result = new Picture(
                  (int) (Math.ceil(rect.getWidth())),
                  (int) (Math.ceil(rect.getHeight())));
```

```
// get the graphics 2d object from the result
Graphics graphics = result.getGraphics();
Graphics2D g2 = (Graphics2D) graphics;

/* save the current transformation and set-up to
 * center the new image
 */
AffineTransform savedTrans = g2.getTransform();
AffineTransform centerTrans = new AffineTransform();
centerTrans.translate(0 - rect.getX(), 0 - rect.getY());
g2.setTransform(centerTrans);

// draw the current image onto the result image sheared
g2.drawImage(this.getImage(),shearTransform,null);

// reset g2 transformation to the saved one
g2.setTransform(savedTrans);

return result;
}
```

You can use the shear method to create a new picture from the original picture by shearing by any amount in x and/or y (Figure 7.16).

FIGURE 7.16
Picture sheared by 1.0 in x.

```
> Picture p = new Picture(
   FileChooser.getMediaPath("mattDoor.jpg"));
> Picture p1 = p.shear(1.0,0.0);
> p1.show();
```

7.3.5 Drawing with a GradientPaint

Instead of just filling with a solid color, you can fill with a blend of two colors (a gradient). You have to specify the two colors and the rectangular area where they transition from one color to another in the coordinates of the shapes you are drawing.

What if you want to add a sun that changes color from yellow at the top to red at the bottom to a picture? You can create a `java.awt.GradientPaint` object and set that to be the paint using the method `setPaint(Paint p)`. A `GradientPaint` object is a kind of `Paint` object because the class `GradientPaint` implements the `Paint` *interface*.

7.3.6   Interfaces

What is an interface? An interface in Java is a special kind of class that only has abstract methods (methods with just a method declaration and no body) and perhaps some constants defined in it.

You can compare two strings and find out if one is less than, equal to, or greater than another because the `String` class implements the `java.lang.Comparable` interface. This means that the `String` class provides the code for the `compareTo(Object o)` method which returns an integer less than 0 if one string is less than the other, the integer 0 if the strings contain the same characters, and an integer greater than zero if one string is greater than the other. It compares the characters in the strings alphabetically. Take a look at the `java.lang.Comparable` interface for an example of an interface. Also see `java.lang.String` for an example of a class implementing an interface.

Even though a class can only inherit from one parent class a class can implement many interfaces. An object of a class that implements an interface is said to be of the interface type.

> ### Computer Science Idea: Constants
>
> Constants are variables that are declared with the keyword `final` which means that the value of the variable can't change. Constants are usually also declared with the keyword `static` so that they are allocated in the object that defines the class and not in each object of the class. You don't need each object of a class to have a copy of a constant. Constants are usually `public` so that other classes can use them.
>
> The convention in Java is to name constants with all capital letters and use `'_'` between words (like `AlphaComposite.SRC_OVER`). If a constant is defined with the keyword `static` it can be referred to using `ClassName.CONSTANT_NAME`.

So even though the class `GradientPaint` inherits from `java.lang.Object` it implements the interface `java.awt.Paint` and so objects of `GradientPaint` can be passed to methods that expect objects of the type `Paint`. The classes `Color` and `TexturePaint` also implement the `Paint` interface which is why they can also be passed to the method `setPaint(Paint p)`.

> ### Computer Science Idea: Interface
>
> An interface is a boundary between two things. You use a user interface to communicate with the computer. You may be familiar with the USB interface. It allows several different types of devices to communicate with a computer. You can hook up a mouse, a camera, or a disk drive, and the computer will know how to communicate with the device because each uses the same interface.

Program 62: Using a Gradient Paint

```
/**
 * Method to add a gradient painted sun to the current picture
 * @param x the x location for the upper left corner of the
 * rectangle enclosing the sun
 * @param y the y location for the upper left corner of the
 * rectangle enclosing the sun
 * @param width the width of the enclosing rectangle
 * @param height the height of the enclosing rectangle
 */
public void drawSun(int x, int y, int width, int height)
{

  // get the graphics2D object for this picture
  Graphics g = this.getGraphics();
  Graphics2D g2 = (Graphics2D) g;

  // create the gradient for painting from yellow to red with
  // yellow at the top of the sun and red at the bottom
  float xMid = (float) (width / 0.5 + x);
  GradientPaint gPaint = new GradientPaint(xMid, y,
                                           Color.yellow,
                                           xMid, y + height,
                                           Color.red);

  // set the gradient and draw the ellipse
  g2.setPaint(gPaint);
  g2.fill(new Ellipse2D.Double(x,y,width,height));
}
```

You can use this program to add a sun to the beach (Figure 7.17).

FIGURE 7.17
A beach with a sun that is filled with a gradient from yellow to red.

```
> Picture p = new Picture(FileChooser.getMediaPath("beach.jpg"));
> p.drawSun(201,80,40,40);
> p.show();
```

7.3.7   Blending Pictures Using AlphaComposite

In the `blendPictures` method on page 156 we blended two pictures by multiply-ing the pixel color values by 0.5 and adding them. It is also possible to use an `AlphaComposite` object from package `java.awt` to do blending or transparency effects. The default is to replace the color at overlapping pixels with the new color. To modify this default you can get an `AlphaComposite` object that speci-fies how you want to handle overlapping pixels in the source and destination using the class method `AlphaComposite.getInstance(int rule, float alpha)` that returns an `AlphaComposite` object to handle the overlap. For the rule you can use one of the predefined constants such as `SRC_OVER` which draws the new pixels on top of the old pixels. The `alpha` value can be between 0.0 and 1.0 where 0.0 is fully transparent (invisible) and 1.0 is fully opaque. If we use an `alpha` value of 0.5 we will achieve the same effect as the method `blendPictures` without having to loop through all the pixels and calculate the resulting color.

To overlap two pictures, we will draw the part of the first picture before a given overlap point using one of the `drawImage` methods inherited from `Graphics` that specifies the rectangular area to draw to and the rectangular area to draw from. We will draw the first part using an `AlphaComposite` that uses an alpha value of 1.0 (opaque) so that it replaces any previous pixel color. Next we will draw the parts of the two pictures that overlap using an alpha value of 0.5 so that it uses half the color from the image being drawn and half the color from the current image. Finally we will draw the part of the second picture that is after the overlapping area using an alpha value of 1.0 (opaque).

Program 63: Overlap Pictures Using AlphaComposite

```
/**
 * Method to overlap one picture with another
 * horizontally on top of the current picture.  First
 * the part of the first picture before the overlap
 * will be displayed, next to that will be the overlapping
 * region up to the end of the first picture, after that
 * is the remainder of the second picture
 * @param p1 the first picture to display
 * @param p2 the second picture to display
 * @param startOverlap the x position where the overlap begins
 */
public void overlapPictures(Picture p1,
                            Picture p2,
                            int startOverlap)
```

```
            {
                int amountOverlap = p1.getWidth() - startOverlap;

                // get the Graphics2D object
                Graphics g = this.getGraphics();
                Graphics2D g2 = (Graphics2D) g;

                // draw p1 up to overlap point
                g2.setComposite(
                    AlphaComposite.getInstance(AlphaComposite.SRC_OVER,
                                                        (float) 1.0f));
                g2.drawImage(p1.getImage(),
                          0,0,startOverlap,p1.getHeight(),
                          0,0,startOverlap,p1.getHeight(),
                          null);

                // draw p1 in the overlap area (replace background)
                g2.drawImage(p1.getImage(),
                          startOverlap,0,p1.getWidth(),p1.getHeight(),
                          startOverlap,0,p1.getWidth(),p1.getHeight(),
                          null);

                // set the composite to blend the old and new pixels
                // 50%
                g2.setComposite(
                    AlphaComposite.getInstance(AlphaComposite.SRC_OVER,
                                                        0.5f));

                g2.drawImage(p2.getImage(),
                          startOverlap,0,p1.getWidth(),p2.getHeight(),
                          0,0,amountOverlap,p2.getHeight(),null);

                // draw p2 after the overlap
                g2.setComposite(
                    AlphaComposite.getInstance(AlphaComposite.SRC_OVER,
                                                        (float) 1.0f));
                g2.drawImage(p2.getImage(),
                          p1.getWidth(),0,p2.getWidth() + startOverlap,
                          p2.getHeight(), amountOverlap, 0, p2.getWidth(),
                          p2.getHeight(),null);

            }
```

To use this program to overlap two pictures (Figure 7.18), do:

```
> String fileName = FileChooser.getMediaPath("KatieFancy.jpg");
> Picture p1 = new Picture(fileName);
> Picture p2 = new Picture(
    FileChooser.getMediaPath("JenParty.jpg"));
> Picture p3 = new Picture(
    FileChooser.getMediaPath("640x480.jpg"));
> p3.overlapPictures(p1,p2,150);
> p3.show();
```

FIGURE 7.18
Two pictures with a horizontal overlap.

You can experiment with the alpha amount that you use in the method `getInstance`. If you specify 0.5, then half of the source color values will be combined with half of the target color values. If you specify 1.0, then the source color will replace the target color. If you use 0.25, then only 0.25 of the source color will be combined with 0.75 of the target color.

7.3.8   Clipping

You can create one shape and then use that shape as a stencil to limit what is shown when you draw other shapes or images. Only the area inside of the stencil will be seen. This is called *clipping*.

Let's create a stencil from an ellipse and then draw the beach using that stencil to clip the image of the beach. The only part of the beach that will be visible is the part inside the ellipse (Figure 7.19).

FIGURE 7.19
Clip picture using an ellipse.

Program 64: Clip an Image to an Ellipse

```
/**
 * Method to clip the picture to an ellipse
 * @return a new picture with the image clipped
 * to an ellipse
 */
public Picture clipToEllipse()
{
  int width = this.getWidth();
  int height = this.getHeight();
  Picture result = new Picture(width,height);

  // get the graphics2D object for this picture
  Graphics g = result.getGraphics();
  Graphics2D g2 = (Graphics2D) g;

  // create an ellipse to use for clipping
  Ellipse2D.Double ellipse =
      new Ellipse2D.Double(0,0,width,height);

  // use the ellipse for clipping
  g2.setClip(ellipse);

  // draw the image
  g2.drawImage(this.getImage(),0,0,width,
               height,null);

  // return the result
  return result;
}
```

To use this program try the following:

```
> Picture p = new Picture(FileChooser.getMediaPath("beach.jpg"));
> Picture p2 = p.clipToEllipse();
> p2.show();
```

7.4 CONCEPTS SUMMARY

In this chapter we discussed packages, using predefined Java classes, inheritance, and interfaces.

7.4.1 Packages

A package is a group of related classes. Classes that are basic to the Java language are in java.lang like the System class. Classes that are used for graphics are in java.awt like the Color class. Classes that are used for input and output are in java.io like the File class.

The full name for a class is *packageName.ClassName*. You don't have to use the full name for any class in the package java.lang. You don't have to use the full name for classes in packages other than java.lang if you use a import statement. You can import a class by using the keyword import and then the full name of the class.

```
> import java.awt.Color;
```

You can also import all classes in a package.

```
> import java.awt.*;
```

When you use classes in packages other than java.lang in methods you will either need to use the full class name or add import statements before the class definition.

```
import java.awt.*;
import java.awt.font.*;
import java.awt.geom.*;
import java.text.*;

/**
 * A class that represents a picture.  This class inherits from
 * SimplePicture and allows the student to add functionality to
 * the Picture class.
 *
 * Copyright Georgia Institute of Technology 2004
 * @author Barbara Ericson ericson@cc.gatech.edu
 */
public class Picture extends SimplePicture
```

7.4.2 Predefined Java Classes

There are a large number of predefined classes in Java. The API contains the documentation for all the classes in a version of Java. The documentation tells you important information about each class such as what methods it has. The documentation is organized by packages. There are classes for doing graphical user interfaces (in packages `javax.swing` and `java.awt`). There are classes for doing input and output (in package `java.io`). There are classes for doing work with databases (in package `java.sql`). There are classes for doing work with sound (in package `javax.sound`). There are classes for working with lists, sets, and maps (`java.util`).

It is easier and faster to build on what exists rather than write your own classes. Even if what you need isn't part of Java, someone else may have written something similar.

7.4.3 Inheritance

When one class inherits from another it gets all the data (fields) and behavior (methods) from that class. This means that if `Graphics2D` inherits from `Graphics` it understands the same public messages as `Graphics`. The API for a class shows what class it inherits from as well as all methods that are inherited and what class they are inherited from.

7.4.4 Interfaces

A Java class can inherit from only one class, but it can implement several interfaces. An interface defines how classes will communicate without worrying about what types they actually are. An object of a class that implements an interface can be declared with the interface name as the type. So if a `GradientPaint` object implements the `Paint` *interface* it can be passed as a parameter to methods that take objects of the type `Paint`. The API for a class shows what interfaces it implements.

OBJECTS AND METHODS SUMMARY

In this chapter we have talked about several kinds of objects.

AffineTransform	java.awt.geom	An object that knows how to do transformations, such as rotation, scaling, and shearing.
AlphaComposite	java.awt	An object that knows how to combine overlapping pixels.
BasicStroke	java.awt	An object that knows how to draw the outlines of shapes in different widths, with different kinds of joins between lines, and possibly using dashes.

Ellipse2D.Double	java.awt.geom	An object that represents an ellipse with coordinates that can be of the type double.
Graphics	java.awt	An object that knows how to draw or fill simple shapes.
Graphics2D	java.awt	An object that can handle more complicated drawing.
Line2D.Double	java.awt.geom	An object that represents a line with coordinates that can be of the type double.

Picture Methods

| getGraphics() | Returns a Graphics object that can be used to draw on the current picture. |
| getImage() | Returns an Image object that can be used by drawImage methods in Graphics or Graphics2D. |

Graphics Methods

drawArc(int x1, int y1, int w, int h, int startAngle, int arcAngle)	Draws the outline of an arc which is part of an oval that fits in an enclosing rectangle with an upper-left corner at $(x1, y1)$, a width of w, and a height of h. The arc will start at the given startAngle and end at *startAngle + arcAngle*.
drawImage(Image image, int x, int y, ImageObserver observer)	Draws the passed image with the top-left corner at (x, y). The observer is the object to be notified as more of the image is drawn.
drawImage(Image image, int dx1, int dy1, int dx2, int dy2, int sx1, sy1, sx2, sy2, ImageObserver observer)	Draws the area from the passed image that is inside the rectangle defined by $(sx1, sy1)$ and $(sx2, sy2)$ into the rectangle defined by $(dx1, dy1)$ and $(dx2, dy2)$ in the destination. The observer is the object to be notified as more of the image is drawn.
drawLine(int x1, int y1, int x2, int y2)	Draws a line from position $(x1, y1)$ to $(x2, y2)$.
drawOval(int x1, int y1, int w, int h)	Draws the outline of an oval that fits in an enclosing rectangle with an upper-left corner at $(x1, y1)$, a width of w, and a height of h.
drawPolygon(int[] xArray, int[] yArray, int numPoints)	Draws the outline of a closed polygon with the points of the polygon given in the x and y arrays.
drawRect(int x1, int y1, int w, int h)	Draws the outline of a rectangle with the upper-left corner at $(x1, y1)$, a width of w, and a height of h.

`fillArc(int x1, int y1, int w, int h, int startAngle, int arcAngle)`	Draws a filled arc which is part of an oval that fits in an enclosing rectangle with an upper-left corner at $(x1, y1)$, a width of w, and a height of h. The arc will start at the given startAngle and end at *startAngle + arcAngle*.
`fillOval(int x1, int y1, int w, int h)`	Draws a filled oval that fits in an enclosing rectangle with an upper-left corner at $(x1, y1)$, a width of w, and a height of h.
`fillPolygon(int[] xArray, int[] yArray, int numPoints)`	Draws a filled closed polygon with the points of the polygon given in the x and y arrays.
`fillRect(int x1, int y1, int w, int h)`	Draws a rectangle filled with the current color with an upper-left corner at $(x1, y1)$, a width of w, and a height of h.
`setClip(Shape clip)`	Sets the shape to use as a stencil to limit what is shown.
`setColor(Color colorObj)`	Sets the color to draw with.
`setFont(Font fontObj)`	Sets the font to use for drawing strings.

Graphics2D Methods

`draw(Object obj)`	Draw the outline of the passed object.
`drawImage(Image image, AffineTransform xform, ImageObserver observer)`	Draws the passed `Image` object after applying the passed `AffineTransform` object to it and notifies the `ImageObserver` as more of the rendered image is available.
`getFontRenderContext()`	Returns a `FontRenderContext` object that contains rendering hints and device information, such as the dots-per-inch.
`getTransform()`	Returns the current `AffineTransform` object that represents all current transformations (rotations, translations, scaling, etc).
`fill(Object obj)`	Draw the passed object filled with the current paint type.
`setComposite(Composite comp)`	Set the `Composite` object that specifies how to handle overlapping pixels.
`setPaint(Paint paint)`	Sets the color, gradient, or texture to use when painting.
`setStroke(Stroke s)`	Set the brush (pen) to the one defined by the passed `Stroke` object.
`setTransform(AffineTransform transform)`	Sets the current transformation object to the passed `AffineTransform` object.

PROBLEMS

7.1 What are each of the following:

- Compression
- A constant
- Vector graphics
- Bitmapped graphics
- A package
- Inheritance
- An interface

7.2 Use the Java API to answer the following questions:

- What method of the String class would help you check if a string ends with a certain sequence of characters?
- What method of the String class would tell you the first position of a character in a String object?
- What method of the String class would tell you the last position of a character in a String object?
- What method of the String class removes extra spaces before and after the other characters?

7.3 Use the Java API to answer the following questions:

- What methods of the String class are inherited?
- What class does the String class inherit from?
- What class does the Math class inherit from?
- What class does the Integer class inherit from?
- What interfaces are in the package java.lang?
- Which classes implement the Comparable interface?
- What interfaces does the String class implement?

7.4 Which of the following use bitmapped graphics:

- JPEG
- Flash
- BMP
- GIFF
- Postscript
- AutoCAD

7.5 Using the drawing tools presented here, draw a house—just go for the simple child's house with one door, two windows, walls, and a roof.

7.6 Create a method that will add a cartoon type word balloon to your picture.

7.7 Put a cabana on the beach. Draw the house from the previous exercise on the beach where we put the mysterious box previously.

7.8 Now use your house to draw a town with dozens of houses at different sizes. You'll probably want to modify your house method to draw at an input coordinate, then change the coordinate where each house is drawn.

7.9 Draw a rainbow—use what you know about colors, pixels, and drawing operations to draw a rainbow. Is this easier to do with our drawing methods or by manipulating individual pixels? Why?

7.10 Modify the method `drawFace` to take the width and height of the desired face and calculate the positions based on the desired width and height.

7.11 Draw glasses on a picture of a person who doesn't normally wear glasses.

7.12 Draw a hat on someone in a picture.

7.13 Draw a weight over someone in a picture.

7.14 Draw a string on a picture at the top of the picture and centered horizontally. You will need to use the `FontMetrics` class to get the height of the string in pixels in order to determine where the baseline should be so that the string is visible. You should also subtract the descent from the height.

7.15 Create another method that takes the text, x, y, font and color to use when you draw a string. Rewrite the old `drawString()` method to call this new method.

7.16 Create a method that draws an X across the current picture using dashed lines.

7.17 Create a method that draws bars across the current picture using thick lines.

7.18 Write a general rotate method that takes the degrees to rotate the current `Picture` object and returns a new `Picture` object. Use the `Affine-Transform.rotate(double radians)` method to do this. You will need to use the general `Math.toRadians(int degrees)` method to translate the degrees to radians.

7.19 Write a method to draw a text string rotated 90 degrees to the right down the right side of the picture.

7.20 Write a method to overlap two pictures vertically using an `AlphaComposite` object.

7.21 Write a method to clip an image to a triangle or star shape.

PART 3 SOUNDS

8 Modifying All Samples in a Sound

Chapter Learning Objectives

The media learning goals for this chapter are:

- To understand how we digitize sounds, and the limitations of human hearing that allow us to digitize sounds.
- To use the Nyquist theorem to determine the sampling rate necessary for digitizing a desired sound.
- To manipulate the volume of a sound.
- To create (and avoid) clipping.

The computer science goals for this chapter are:

- To understand and use a one-dimensional array as a data structure.
- To use the formula that n bits result in 2^n possible patterns in order to figure out the number of bits needed to save values.
- To debug sound programs (methods).
- To use iteration (with `while` and `for` loops) for manipulating sounds.
- To use conditionals when manipulating sounds.

8.1 HOW SOUND IS ENCODED

There are two parts to understanding how sound is encoded and manipulated.

- First, what are the physics of sound? How is it that we hear a variety of sounds?
- Next, how can we then map these sounds into the numbers of a computer?

8.1.1 The Physics of Sound

Physically, sounds are waves of air pressure. When something makes a sound, it makes ripples in the air just like stones or raindrops dropped into a pond cause

FIGURE 8.1
Raindrops causing ripples in the surface of the water, just as sound causes ripples in the air.

ripples in the surface of the water (Figure 8.1). Each drop causes a wave of pressure to pass over the surface of the water, which causes visible rises in the water, and less visible but just as large depressions in the water. The rises are increases in pressure and the lows are decreases in pressure. Some of the ripples we see are actually ones that arise from *combinations* of ripples—some waves are the sums and interactions from other waves.

We call these increases in air pressure *compressions* and decreases in air pressure *rarefactions*. It's these compressions and rarefactions that lead to our hearing. The shape of the waves, their *frequency*, and their *amplitude* all impact how we perceive sound.

The simplest sound in the world is a *sine wave* (Figure 8.2). In a sine wave, the compressions and rarefactions arrive with equal size and regularity. In a sine wave, one compression plus one rarefaction is called a *cycle*. The distance from the zero point to the greatest pressure (or least pressure) is called the *amplitude*.

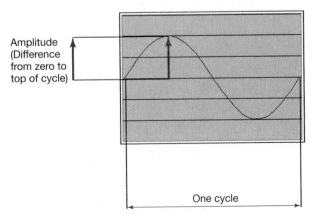

Amplitude
(Difference
from zero to
top of cycle)

One cycle

FIGURE 8.2
One cycle of the simplest sound, a sine wave.

Formally, amplitude is measured in *Newtons per meter-squared* (N/m^2). That's a rather hard unit to understand in terms of perception, but you can get a sense of the amazing range of human hearing from this unit. The smallest sound that humans typically hear is $0.0002N/m^2$, and the point at which we sense the vibrations in our entire body is $200N/m^2$! In general, amplitude is the most important factor in our perception of *volume*: If the amplitude rises, we typically perceive the sound as being louder. Other factors like air pressure factor into our perception of increased volume, too. Ever notice how sounds sound different on very humid days as compared with very dry days?

When we perceive an increase in volume, we say that we're perceiving an increase in the *intensity* of sound. Intensity is measured in watts per meter-squared (W/m^2). (Yes, those are watts just like the ones you're referring to when you get a 60-watt light bulb—it's a measure of power.) The intensity is proportional to the square of the amplitude. For example, if the amplitude doubles, intensity quadruples.

Human perception of sound is not a direct mapping from the physical reality. The study of the human perception of sound is called *psychoacoustics*. One of the odd facts about psychoacoustics is that most of our perception of sound is *logarithmically* related to the actual phenomena. Intensity is an example of this. A change in intensity from $0.1W/m^2$ to $0.01W/m^2$ sounds the *same* to us (as in the same amount of volume change) as a change in intensity of $0.001W/m^2$ to $0.0001W/m^2$.

We measure the change in intensity in *decibels* (dB). That's probably the unit that you most often associate with volume. A decibel is a logarithmic measure, so it matches the way we perceive volume. It's always a ratio, a comparison of two values. $10 * log_{10}(I_1/I_2)$ is the change in intensity in decibels between I_1 and I_2. If two amplitudes are measured under the same conditions, we can express the same definition as amplitudes: $20 * log_{10}(A_1/A_2)$. If $A_2 = 2 * A_1$ (i.e., the amplitude doubles), the difference is roughly 6 dB.

When decibel is used as an absolute measurement, it's in reference to the threshold of audibility at *sound pressure level* (SPL): 0 dB SPL. Normal speech has an intensity of about 60 dB SPL. Shouted speech is about 80 dB SPL.

How often a cycle occurs is called the *frequency*. If a cycle is short, then there can be lots of them per second. If a cycle is long, then there are fewer of them. As the frequency increases we perceive that the *pitch* increases. We measure frequency in *cycles per second* (cps) or *Hertz* (Hz).

All sounds are periodic: there is always some pattern of rarefaction and compression that leads to cycles. In a sine wave, the notion of a cycle is easy. In natural waves, it's not so clear where a pattern repeats. Even in the ripples in a pond, the waves aren't as regular as you might think. The time between peaks in waves isn't always the same: it varies. This means that a cycle may involve several peaks-and-valleys until it repeats.

Humans hear between 2 Hz and 20,000 Hz (or 20 kilohertz, abbreviated 20 kHz). Again, as with amplitudes, that's an enormous range! To give you a sense of where music fits into that spectrum, the note A above middle C is 440 Hz in traditional, *equal temperament* tuning (Figure 8.3).

FIGURE 8.3
The note A above middle C is 440 Hz.

Like intensity, our perception of pitch is almost exactly proportional to the log of the frequency. We really don't perceive absolute differences in pitch, but the *ratio* of the frequencies. If you heard a 100 Hz sound followed by a 200 Hz sound, you'd perceive the same pitch change (or *pitch interval*) as a shift from 1,000 Hz to 2,000 Hz. Obviously, a difference of 100 Hz is a lot smaller than a change of 1,000 Hz, but we perceive it to be the same.

In standard tuning, the ratio in frequency between the same notes in adjacent octaves is 2:1. Frequency doubles each octave. We told you earlier that A above middle C is 440 Hz. You know then that the next A up the scale is 880 Hz.

How we think about music is dependent upon our cultural standards, but there are some universals. Among these universals are the use of pitch intervals (e.g., the ratio between notes C and D remains the same in every octave), the relationship between octaves remains constant, and the existence of four to seven main pitches (not considering sharps and flats here) in an octave.

What makes the experience of one sound different from another? Why is it that a flute playing a note sounds *so* different than a trumpet or a clarinet playing the same note? We still don't understand everything about psychoacoustics and what physical properties influence our perception of sound, but here are some of the factors that lead us to perceiving different sounds (especially musical instruments) as distinct.

- Real sounds are almost never single frequency sound waves. Most natural sounds have *several* frequencies in them, often at different amplitudes. These additional frequencies are sometimes called *overtones*. When a piano plays the note C, for example, part of the richness of the tone is that the notes E and G are *also* in the sound, but at lower amplitudes. Different instruments have different overtones in their notes. The central tone, the one we're trying to play, is called the *fundamental*.

- Instrument sounds are not continuous with respect to amplitude and frequency. Some come slowly up to the target frequency and amplitude (like wind instruments), while others hit the frequency and amplitude very quickly and then the volume fades while the frequency remains pretty constant (like a piano).

- Not all sound waves are represented well by sine waves. Real sounds have funny bumps and sharp edges. Our ears can pick these up, at least in the first few waves. We can do a reasonable job synthesizing with sine waves, but

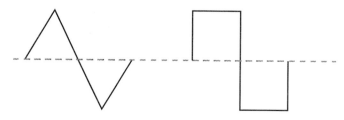

FIGURE 8.4
Some synthesizers using triangular (or *sawtooth*) or square waves.

synthesizers sometimes also use other kinds of wave forms to get different kinds of sounds (Figure 8.4).

8.1.2 Exploring Sounds

On your CD, you will find the *MediaTools* application with documentation for how to get it started. The MediaTools application contains tools for sound, graphics, and video. Using the sound tools, you can actually observe sounds as they're coming into your computer's microphone to get a sense of what louder and softer sounds look like, and what higher and lower pitched sounds look like.

The basic sound editor looks like Figure 8.5. You can record sounds, open WAV files on your disk, and view the sounds in a variety of ways. (You will need a microphone on your computer to record sounds!)

To view sounds, click the RECORD VIEWER button, then the RECORD button. (Hit the STOP button to stop recording.) There are three kinds of views that you can make of the sound.

The first is the *signal view* (Figure 8.6). In the signal view, you're looking at the sound raw—each increase in air pressure results in a rise in the graph, and each decrease in sound pressure results in a drop in the graph. Note how rapidly the wave changes! Try making some softer and louder sounds so that you can see how the look of the representation changes. You can always get back to the signal view from another view by clicking the SIGNAL button.

The second view is the *spectrum view* (Figure 8.7). The spectrum view is a completely different perspective on the sound. In the previous section, you read that natural sounds are often actually composed of several different frequencies at once.

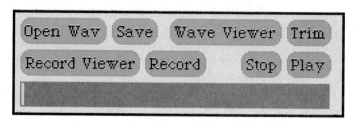

FIGURE 8.5
Sound editor main tool.

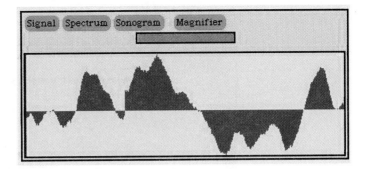

FIGURE 8.6
Viewing the sound signal as it comes in.

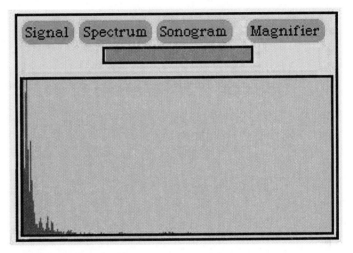

FIGURE 8.7
Viewing the sound in a spectrum view.

The spectrum view shows these individual frequencies. This view is also called the *frequency domain*.

Frequencies increase in the spectrum view from left to right. The height of a column indicates the amount of energy (roughly, the volume) of that frequency in the sound. Natural sounds look like Figure 8.8 with more than one *spike* (rise in the graph). (The smaller rises around a spike are often seen as *noise*.)

The technical term for how a spectrum view is generated is called a *Fourier transform*. A Fourier transform takes the sound from the *time domain* (rises and falls in the sound over time) into the frequency domain (identifying which frequencies are in a sound, and the energy of those frequencies, over time). The specific technique being used in the MediaTools signal view is a *Fast Fourier Transform* (or *FFT*), a very common way to do Fourier transforms quickly on a computer so that we can get a real time view of the changing spectra.

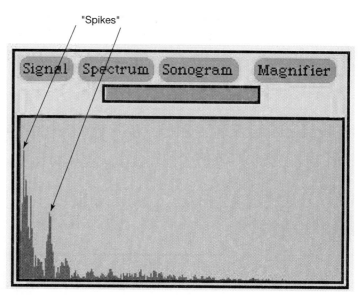

FIGURE 8.8
Viewing a sound in spectrum view with multiple "spikes".

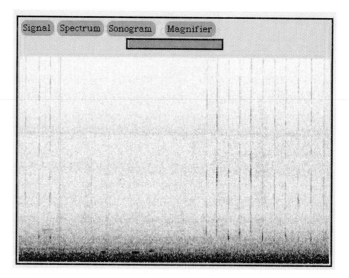

FIGURE 8.9
Viewing the sound signal in a sonogram view.

The third view is the *sonogram view* (Figure 8.9). The sonogram view is very much like the spectrum view in that it's describing the frequency domain, but it presents these frequencies over time. Each column in the sonogram view, sometimes called a *slice* or *window (of time)*, represents all the frequencies at a given moment in time. The frequencies increase in the slice from lower (bottom) to higher (top). The *darkness* of the spot in the column indicates the amount of energy of that frequency in the input sound at the given moment. The sonogram view is great for studying how sounds change over time, e.g., how the sound of a piano key being struck changes as the note fades, or how different instruments differ in their sounds, or in how different vocal sounds differ.

Making it Work Tip: Explore Sounds!
You really should try these different views on real sounds. You'll get a much better understanding of sound and what the manipulations we're doing in this chapter are doing to the sounds.

8.1.3   Encoding Sounds

You just read about how sounds work physically and how we perceive them. To manipulate these sounds on a computer and to play them back on a computer, we have to digitize them. To digitize sound means to take this flow of waves and turn it into numbers. We want to be able to capture a sound, perhaps manipulate it, and then play it back (through the computer's speakers) and hear what we captured—as exactly as possible.

The first part of the process of digitizing a sound is handled by the computer's hardware—the physical machinery of the computer. If a computer has a microphone and the appropriate sound equipment (like a SoundBlaster sound card on Windows computers), then it's possible, at any moment, to measure the amount of air pressure against that microphone as a single number. Positive numbers correspond to rises in pressure, and negative numbers correspond to rarefactions. We call this an *analog-to-digital conversion (ADC)*—we've moved from an analog signal (a continuously changing sound wave) to a digital value. This means that we can get an instantaneous measure of the sound pressure, but it's only one step along the way. Sound is a continuous changing pressure wave. How do we store that in our computer?

By the way, playback systems on computers work essentially the same in reverse. The sound hardware does a *digital-to-analog conversion (DAC)*, and the analog signal is then sent to the speakers. The DAC process also requires numbers representing pressure.

If you've had some calculus, you've got some idea of how we might do that. You know that we can get close to measuring the area under a curve with more and more rectangles whose height matches the curve (Figure 8.10). With that idea, it's pretty clear that if we capture enough of those microphone pressure readings, we capture the wave. We call each of those pressure readings a *sample*—we are literally "sampling" the sound at that moment. But how many samples do we need? In integral calculus, you compute the area under the curve by (conceptually) having an infinite number of rectangles. While computer memories are growing larger and larger all the time, we still can't capture an infinite number of samples per sound.

Mathematicians and physicists wondered about these kinds of questions long before there were computers, and the answer to how many samples we need was actually computed long ago. The answer depends on the highest *frequency* you want to capture. Let's say that you don't care about any sounds higher than 8,000 Hz. The

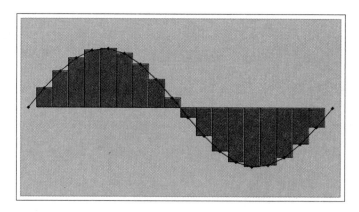

FIGURE 8.10
Area under a curve estimated with rectangles.

Nyquist theorem says that we would need to capture 16,000 samples per second to completely capture and define a wave whose frequency is less than 8,000 cycles per second.

Computer Science Idea: Nyquist Theorem

To capture a sound of at most n cycles per second, you need to capture $2n$ samples per second. ∎

This isn't just a theoretical result. The Nyquist theorem influences applications in our daily life. It turns out that human voices don't typically get over 4,000 Hz. That's why our telephone system is designed around capturing 8,000 samples per second. That's why playing music through the telephone doesn't really work very well. The limits of (most) human hearing is around 22,000 Hz. If we were to capture 44,000 samples per second, we would be able to capture any sound that we could actually hear. CD's are created by capturing sound at 44,100 samples per second—just a little bit more than 44 kHz for technical reasons and for a fudge factor.

We call the rate at which samples are collected the *sampling rate*. Most sounds that we hear in daily life are well within the range of the limits of our hearing. You can capture and manipulate sounds in this class at a sampling rate of 22 kHz (22,000 samples per second), and it will sound quite reasonable. If you use a too low sampling rate to capture a high-pitched sound, you'll still hear something when you play the sound back, but the pitch will sound strange.

Typically, each of these samples are encoded in two bytes (16 bits). Though there are larger *sample sizes*, 16 bits works perfectly well for most applications. CD-quality sound uses 16 bit samples.

In 16 bits, the numbers that can be encoded range from $-32,768$ to $32,767$. These aren't magic numbers—they make perfect sense when you understand the encoding. These numbers are encoded in 16 bits using a technique called *two's complement notation*, but we can understand it without knowing the details of that technique.

We've got 16 bits to represent positive and negative numbers. Let's set aside one of those bits (remember, it's just 0 or 1) to represent whether we're talking about a positive (0) or negative (1) number. We call that the *sign bit*. That leaves 15 bits to represent the actual value. How many different patterns of 15 bits are there? We could start counting:

```
000000000000000
000000000000001
000000000000010
000000000000011
. . .
111111111111110
111111111111111
```

That looks forbidding. Let's see if we can figure out a pattern. If we've got two bits, there are four patterns: 00, 01, 10, 11. If we've got three bits, there are eight patterns: 000, 001, 010, 011, 100, 101, 110, 111. It turns out that 2^2 is four, and 2^3 is eight. Play with four bits. How many patterns are there? $2^4 = 16$. It turns out that we can state this as a general principle.

Computer Science Idea: 2^n Patterns in *n* Bits

If you have *n* bits, there are 2^n possible patterns in those *n* bits.

$2^{15} = 32,768$. Why is there one more value in the negative range than the positive? Zero is neither negative nor positive, but if we want to represent it as bits, we need to define some pattern as zero. We use one of the positive range values (where the sign bit is zero) to represent zero, so that takes up one of the 32,768 patterns.

The sample size is a limitation on the amplitude of the sound that can be captured. If you have a sound that generates a pressure greater than 32,767 (or a rarefaction greater than −32,768), you'll only capture up to the limits of the 16 bits. If you were to look at the wave in the signal view, it would look like somebody took some scissors and *clipped* off the peaks of the waves. We call that effect *clipping* for that very reason. If you play (or generate) a sound that's clipped, it sounds bad—it sounds like your speakers are breaking.

There are other ways of digitizing sound, but this is by far the most common. The technical term for this way of encoding sound is *pulse coded modulation (PCM)*. You may encounter that term if you read further in audio or play with audio software.

What this means is that a sound in a computer is a long list of numbers, each of which is a sample in time. There is an ordering in these samples: If you played the samples out of order, you wouldn't get the same sound at all. The most efficient way to store an ordered list of data items on a computer is with an *array*. An array is literally a sequence of bytes right next to one another in memory. We call each value in an array an *element*. We introduced arrays in Section 4.1.

We can easily store the samples that make up a sound in an array. Think of each two bytes as storing a single sample. The array will be large—for CD-quality

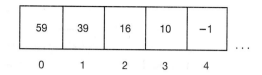

FIGURE 8.11
A depiction of the first five elements in a real sound array.

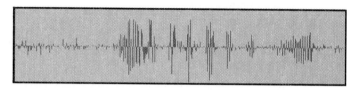

FIGURE 8.12
A sound recording graphed in the MediaTools.

sounds, there will be 44,100 elements for every second of recording. A minute long recording will result in an array with 26,460,000 elements.

Each array element has a number associated with it, called its *index*. The index numbers start at 0 and increase sequentially. The first one is 0, the second one is 1, and so on. It may sound strange to say the index for the first array element is 0, but this is basically a measure of the distance from the first element in the array. Since the distance from the first element to itself is 0, the index is 0. You can think about an array as a long line of boxes, each one holding a value and each box having an index number on it (Figure 8.11).

Using the MediaTools, you can graph a sound file (Figure 8.12) and get a sense of where the sound is quiet (small amplitudes), and loud (large amplitudes). This is actually important if you want to manipulate the sound. For example, the gaps between recorded words tend to be quiet—at least quieter than the words themselves. You can pick out where words end by looking for these gaps, as in Figure 8.12.

You will soon read about how to read a file containing a recording of a sound into a *sound object*, view the samples in that sound, and change the values of the sound array elements. By changing the values in the array, you change the sound. Manipulating a sound is simply a matter of manipulating elements in an array.

8.2   MANIPULATING SOUNDS

Now that we know how sounds are encoded, we can manipulate sounds using Java programs. Here's what we'll need to do.

1. We'll need to get a filename of a WAV file, and make a Sound object from it. You already saw how to do that in Section 3.6.5.

2. You will often get the samples of the sound as an array. Sample objects are easy to manipulate, and they know that when you change them, they should automatically change the original sound. You'll read first about manipulating

the samples to start with, then about how to manipulate the sound samples from within the sound itself.

3. Whether you get the sample objects out of a sound or just deal with the samples in the sound object, you will then want to do something to the value at the sample.

4. You may then want to write the sound back out to a new file, to use elsewhere. (Most sound editing programs know how to deal with audio.)

8.2.1   Opening Sounds and Manipulating Samples

You have already seen how to pick a file with `FileChooser.pickAFile()` and then make a Sound object (object of the class Sound) with `new Sound(fileName)`. Here's an example of doing that in DrJava.

```
> String fileName = FileChooser.pickAFile();
> Sound sound1 = new Sound(fileName);
> System.out.println(sound1);
Sound file: preamble.wav number of samples: 421110
```

What `new Sound(fileName)` does is to scoop up all the bytes from the file name provided as input, dump them into memory, and place a big sign on them saying, "This is a sound object (an object of the class Sound)!" When you execute `Sound sound1 = new Sound(fileName)`, you are saying, "Create an object variable called `sound1` that refers to the Sound object created from the information in the file with a file name given by the variable `fileName`." When you use `sound1` as input to methods, you are saying "Use that sound object over there (yeah, the one referred to by the variable `sound1`) as input to this method."

You can get the samples from a sound using `getSamples()`. The method `getSamples()` must be invoked on a Sound object and returns an array of all the samples as `SoundSample` objects (objects of the class `SoundSample`). When you execute this method, it may take quite a while before it finishes—longer for longer sounds, shorter for shorter sounds.

```
> SoundSample[] sampleArray = sound1.getSamples();
> System.out.println(sampleArray.length);
421110
```

The method `getSamples()` is making an array of `SoundSample` *objects* out of the samples in the Sound object. An *object* is more than just a simple value–for example, a `SoundSample` object knows what Sound object it came from and what its index is. You will read more about objects later, but take it at face value now that `getSamples()` provides you with a bunch of sample objects that you can manipulate—and, in fact, makes manipulation pretty easy. You can get the value of a `SoundSample` object by using `getValue()`, and you set the value of a `SoundSample` object with `setValue(value)`.

But before we get to the manipulations, let's look at some other ways to get and set samples. We can ask the sound to give us the value of a specific sample at a specific index, by using the method `getSampleValueAt(index)` on a Sound object.

```
> System.out.println(sound1.getSampleValueAt(0));
36
> System.out.println(sound1.getSampleValueAt(1));
29
```

What numbers can we use as index values? We can use anything between 0 and the number of samples minus 1. We can get the number of samples using getLength(). Notice the error that we get below if we try to get a sample past the end of the array.

```
> System.out.println(sound1.getLength());
421110
> sound1.getSampleValueAt(500000);
You are trying to access the sample at index: 500000, but the last
valid index is at 421109
```

We can similarly change sample values in a Sound object with

setSampleValueAt(index)

This method changes the value of the sample at the passed index. We can then check it again with getSampleValueAt().

```
> System.out.println(sound1.getSampleValueAt(0));
36
> sound1.setSampleValueAt(0,12);
> System.out.println(sound1.getSampleValueAt(0));
12
```

What do you think would happen if we then played this sound? Would it really sound different than it did before, now that we've turned the first sample from the number 36 to the number 12? Not really. To explain why not, let's find out what the sampling rate is for this sound, by using the method getSamplingRate().

```
> String fileName = FileChooser.getMediaPath("preamble.wav");
> Sound aSound = new Sound(fileName);
> System.out.println(aSound.getSamplingRate());
22050.0
```

To make some of our manipulations easier, we're going to be using

FileChooser.setMediaPath(String directory)

and

FileChooser.getMediaPath(String baseFileName)

Using setMediaPath(String directory) will *set* a media directory (folder), and then getMediaPath(String baseFileName) will reference media files within that directory. This makes it much easier to reference media files—you don't have to spell out the whole path. The method getMediaPath takes a base file name as an argument, and will return the directory set by setMediaPath with the passed file name added to the end of the directory name. The default for the media directory is c:/intro-prog-java/mediasources/. If you have your media in another directory, you will need to use setMediaPath before you can use getMediaPath.

```
> FileChooser.setMediaPath("c:/intro-prog-java/mediasources/");
The media directory is now c:/intro-prog-java/mediasources/
> System.out.println(FileChooser.getMediaPath("barbara.jpg"));
c:/intro-prog-java/mediasources/barbara.jpg
> System.out.println(FileChooser.getMediaPath("croak.wav"));
c:/intro-prog-java/mediasources/croak.wav
```

Common Bug: It's not a File, it's a String

Just because getMediaPath returns something that looks like a path doesn't mean that a file really exists at that location. You have to know the right base name and enter it correctly. If you put in a base file name of a file that doesn't exist you'll get a path to a non-existent file. The method getMediaPath will warn you if the file doesn't exist.

```
> FileChooser.getMediaPath("blahblah.wav");
There is no file named blahblah.wav in directory
c:/intro-prog-java/mediasources/
```

The sound that we're manipulating in this example (a recording of Mark reading part of the U.S. Constitution's preamble) has a sampling rate of 22,050 samples per second. Changing one sample changes 1/22,050 of the first second of that sound. If you can hear that, you have amazingly good hearing—and we will have some doubts about your truthfulness!

Obviously, to make a significant manipulation to the sound, we have to manipulate hundreds if not thousands of samples. We're certainly not going to do that by typing thousands of lines like this:

```
> aSound.setSampleValueAt(0,12);
> aSound.setSampleValueAt(1,24);
> aSound.setSampleValueAt(2,100);
> aSound.setSampleValueAt(3,99);
> aSound.setSampleValueAt(4,-1);
```

We need to take advantage of the computer executing our program, by telling it to go do something hundreds or thousands of times. That's the topic for the next section.

But we will end this section by talking about how to write your results back out to a file. Once you've manipulated your sound and want to save it out to use elsewhere, you use write(String fileName) which takes a filename as input. Be sure that your file ends with the extension ".wav" if you're saving a sound so that your operating system knows what to do with it (what type of data is in it)!

```
> Sound aSound = new Sound(FileChooser.pickAFile());
> System.out.println(aSound.getFileName());
c:\intro-prog-java\mediasources\preamble.wav
> aSound.write("c:\\intro-prog-java\\mediasources\\preamble.wav");
```

Common Bug: Saving a File Quickly—and How to Find it Again!
What if you don't know the whole path to a directory of your choosing? You don't have to specify anything more than the base name.

```
> aSound.write("new-preamble.wav")
```

The problem is finding the file again! In what directory did it get saved? This is a pretty simple bug to resolve. The default directory (the one you get if you don't specify a path) is wherever DrJava is. You can also use

```
FileChooser.getMediaPath("new-preamble.wav");
```

to get the full name of the media directory and base file name.

You'll probably figure out when playing sounds a lot that if you use `play()` a couple times in quick succession, you'll mix the sounds. How do you make sure that the computer plays only a single sound and then waits for that sound to end? You use something called `blockingPlay()`. That works the same as `play()`, but it waits for the sound to end so that no other sound can interfere while it's playing.

8.2.2   Using MediaTools for Looking at Sounds

The MediaTools for manipulating sounds that you read about earlier can also be used to study sound files. Any WAV file on your computer can be opened and studied within the sound tools.

Using the MediaTools Application

Your CD contains a `mediasources` directory on it. Most of the examples in the book use the media in this directory. You'll probably want to drag the `mediasources` folder onto your hard disk so that you can use it there. The default media directory is `c:/intro-prog-java/mediasources` so that would be a good place to put it. If you put it somewhere else just use

```
FileChooser.setMediaPath(directory)
```

in the DrJava Interactions Pane to set the directory to use a different directory.

From the basic sound editor tool in the MediaTools application, click on FILE to get the option to open a WAV file (Figure 8.13). The MediaTools' open file dialog will then appear. Find a WAV file by clicking on the directories on the left until you find one that contains the WAV files you want on the right (Figure 8.14), then click OK.

You will then be shown the file in the sound editor view (Figure 8.15). The sound editor lets you explore a sound in many ways (Figure 8.16). As you scroll through the sound and change the *sound cursor* (the red/blue line in the graph) position, the INDEX changes to show you which sound array element you're currently looking at, and the VALUE shows you the value at that index. You can also fit the whole

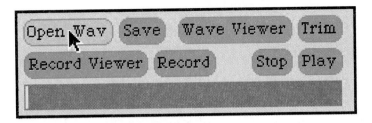

FIGURE 8.13
The sound editor open menu in MediaTools application.

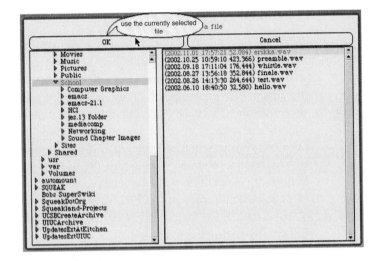

FIGURE 8.14
MediaTools application open file dialog.

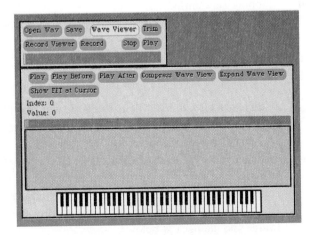

FIGURE 8.15
A sound opened in the editor in MediaTools application.

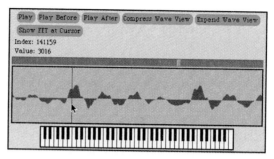

FIGURE 8.16
Exploring the sound in the editor in MediaTools application.

sound into the graph to get an overall view (COMPRESS WAVE VIEW button) which necessarily "skips" some samples in the view, or get back to the expanded view where every sample is visible with the EXPAND WAVE VIEW button. You can set the cursor (via the scrollbar or by dragging in the graph window), then play the sound before (PLAY BEFORE button) or after the cursor (PLAY AFTER)—a good way to hear what part of the sound corresponds to what index positions. You can even "play" your recorded sound as if it were an instrument—try pressing the piano keys across the bottom of the editor. Keys to the right shift the sound to a higher frequency—something we'll be learning to do a bit later. Clicking the SHOW FFT AT CURSOR button presents an FFT view of the sound.

8.2.3 Introducing Loops

The problem of wanting to do something similar a great many times is a common one in computing: How do we get the computer to do something over-and-over again? We need to get the computer to *loop* or *iterate*. Java has commands especially for looping (iterating).

Starting with Java version 5.0 (1.5) there is a new way of looping through all members of an array using a for-each loop. We first introduced this loop in Section 4.3.1. The syntax is

```
for (Type variableName : array)
```

You can read this as, "for each element in the array execute the body of the loop." The first time through the loop the variableName will refer to the first element of the array (the one at index 0). The second time through the loop the variableName will refer to the second element of the array (the one at index 1). The last time through the loop the variableName will refer to the last element of the array (the one at index (length −1)). The code to loop through all the SoundSample objects in an array of SoundSample objects and set the value of each sample to its original value (no change) is below:

```
public void doNothing()
{
  SoundSample[] sampleArray = this.getSamples();
  int value = 0;
```

```
// loop through all the samples in the array
for (SoundSample sample : sampleArray)
{
  value = sample.getValue();
  sample.setValue(value);
}
}
```

As you can see, the for-each loop makes it easy to loop through *all* the elements of an array. You can use the for-each loop whenever you want to process all the elements of an array and you don't need to know the current index in the body of the loop.

If you are not using Java 1.5, you may want to start with a while loop. Even if you are using Java 1.5, there are things you can do with a while loop that you can't do with a for-each loop. A while loop executes some commands while a test returns true. In order for the loop to stop there must be some way for the test to end up false. We introduced the while loop in Section 4.3.2.

The way that we will manipulate a sound is to change the values in the samples that make up the sound. We want to loop through all the samples in a sound and do something to each value. One way to do that is to loop through all the elements of the array of samples. We are going to use the getSamples() method we saw earlier to provide our array.

For example, here is the while loop that simply sets each sample to its own value (a particularly useless exercise, but it'll get more interesting in just a couple pages).

```
public void doNothing()
{
  SoundSample[] sampleArray = this.getSamples();
  SoundSample sample = null;
  int index = 0;
  int value = 0;

  // loop through all the samples in the array
  while (index < sampleArray.length)
  {
    sample = sampleArray[index];
    value = sample.getValue();
    sample.setValue(value);
    index++;
  }
}
```

Let's talk through this code.

- The first statement gets the array of SoundSample objects from the current Sound object using the method getSamples() and declares a variable sampleArray which refers to it. The this means the current Sound object that was implicitly passed to the method. You could leave off the this and the compiler would add it.

- The next statement declares a variable `sample` that can refer to a `SoundSample` object but is set to `null` to show that it doesn't reference any object yet.
- Next a primitive variable `index` is declared and initialized to 0.
- The primitive variable `value` is declared and initialized to 0.
- The code `while (index < sampleArray.length)` tests if the value of `index` is less than the length of the array of `SoundSample` objects. If it is, the body of the loop will be executed. If not, execution will continue with the first statement following the body of the loop.
- The first statement in the body of the loop sets the variable `sample` to refer to the `SoundSample` object at the value of `index` in the array `sampleArray`. Since index starts off with a value of 0 this will refer to the first `SoundSample` object in the array the first time through the loop.
- The space reserved for the variable `value` is set to the value of the `SoundSample` object referred to by `sample`.
- Next, the value of the `SoundSample` object referred to by `sample` is set to the contents of `value`. Since the contents of the variable `value` is the value for this `SoundSample` object there will be no change. It just sets the sample value to the original value.
- Finally, the value in `index` is incremented by one. Then execution will jump back to the `while` test again.

Here's the exact same code (it would work *exactly* the same), but with different variable names.

```java
SoundSample[] a = this.getSamples();
SoundSample s = null;
int i = 0;
int v = 0;

// loop through all the samples in the array
while (i < a.length)
{
  s = a[i];
  v = s.getValue();
  s.setValue(v);
  i++;
}
```

What's the difference? These are slightly easier to confuse variable names. `a` and `s` are not as obvious as to what they are naming as `sampleArray` and `sample`. Java doesn't care which we use, and the single-character variable names are clearly easier to type. But the longer variable names make it easier to understand your code. It is best to try to make your code easier for humans to understand.

You may have wondered do we need the variable `v`? We could combine the two statements into one.

```java
SoundSample[] a = this.getSamples();
SoundSample s = null;
```

```
int i = 0;

// loop through all the samples in the array
while (i < a.length)
{
  s = a[i];
  s.setValue(s.getValue());
  i++;
}
```

Now that we see how to get the computer to do thousands of commands without writing thousands of individual lines, let's do something useful with this.

Making it Work Tip: Keep Sounds Short
Longer sounds take up more memory and will process more slowly.

Common Bug: Windows and WAV Files
The world of WAV files isn't as compatible and smooth as one might like. WAV files created with other applications (such as Windows Recorder) *may* not play in DrJava, and DrJava WAV files may not play in all other applications (e.g., WinAmp 2). Some tools like Apple QuickTime Player Pro (http://www.apple.com/quicktime) are good at reading *any* WAV file and being able to export a new one that most any other application can read. Some WAV files are encoded using MP3, which means they are really MP3 files. You can convert these using Sound.convert(origFileName, convertedFileName) where origFileName and convertedFileName are the full names (include path information).

8.3   CHANGING THE VOLUME OF SOUNDS

Earlier, we said that the amplitude of a sound is the main factor in the volume. This means that if we increase the amplitude, we increase the volume. Or if we decrease the amplitude, we decrease the volume.

Don't get confused here—changing the amplitude doesn't reach out and twist up the volume knob on your speakers. If your speaker's volume (or computer's volume) is turned down, the sound will never get very loud. The point is getting the sound itself louder. Have you ever watched a movie on TV where, without changing the volume on the TV, sound becomes so low that you can hardly hear it? (Marlon Brando's dialogue in the movie *The Godfather* comes to mind.) That's what we're doing here. We can make sounds *shout* or *whisper* by tweaking the amplitude.

8.3.1   Increasing Volume

Here's a method that doubles the amplitude of an input sound.

Program 65: Increase an Input Sound's Volume

```java
/**
 * Method to double the volume (amplitude) of the sound
 */
public void increaseVolume()
{
  SoundSample[] sampleArray = this.getSamples();
  SoundSample sample = null;
  int value = 0;
  int index = 0;

  // loop through all the samples in the array
  while (index < sampleArray.length)
  {
    sample = sampleArray[index];
    value = sample.getValue();
    sample.setValue(value * 2);
    index++;
  }
}
```

Go ahead and type the above into your DrJava definitions pane before the last curly brace in the Sound.java class. Click COMPILE ALL to get DrJava to compile it. Follow along the example below to get a better idea of how this all works.

To use this program, you have to create a sound first and invoke this method on it. Don't forget that you can't type this code in and have it work as-is: Your path names may be different than what is shown here!

```
> String f = "c:/intro-prog-java/mediasources/gettysburg10.wav";
> Sound s = new Sound(f);
> s.play();
> s.explore();
> s.increaseVolume();
> s.play();
> s.explore();
```

In the interactions pane we create a variable f which refers to a String object that holds the name of a file. We create the variable s which refers to a Sound object created from the file using new Sound(f). We ask this Sound object to play using s.play(). We then open an explorer on the sound to see what it looks like graphically using s.explore(). We next increase its volume using s.increaseVolume(). This implicitly passes the Sound object to the method increaseVolume(). So the code this.getSamples() in the method increaseVolume() means to get them from the implicitly passed Sound object (the one referred to by variable s).

> **Computer Science Idea: Changing Memory Doesn't Change the File**
>
> If you create another Sound object from the same file, will you get the original sound or the sound with volume increased? You will get the original sound. The Sound object s was created by reading the file data into memory. The change to the Sound object was done in memory, but the file wasn't changed. If you want to save your changes write them out to a file using the method *soundObj*.write(String fileName); where soundObj is the name of the Sound object and fileName is the full path name of the file. So to save the changed Sound object above use s.write("gettyLouder.wav");. This will create a new file with the changed sound in it.   ∎

8.3.2 Did that Really Work?

Now, is it really louder, or does it just seem that way? We can check it in several ways. You could always make the sound even louder by evaluating increaseVolume on our sound a few more times—eventually, you'll be totally convinced that the sound is louder. But there are ways to test even more subtle effects.

If you compare graphs of the two sounds using the sound explorer, you will find that the graph of the sound does have greater amplitude after increasing it using our method. Check it out in Figure 8.17.

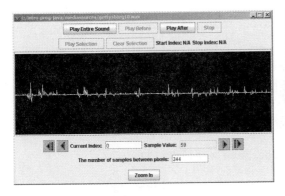 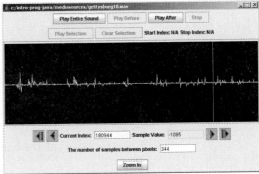

FIGURE 8.17
Comparing the graphs of the original sound (left) and the louder one (right).

Maybe you're unsure that you're really seeing a larger wave in the second picture. You can use a sound explorer to check the individual sample values. You can actually already see that in Figure 8.17—see that the first value (index number 0) is 59 in the original sound and 118 in the second sound. You can also check the value at any index using the sound explorer. Just click on a location and the value will be displayed for that location. To check the same location in the second explorer just type in the desired current index and it will show the value at that index. You'll see that the louder sound really does have double the value of the same sample in the original sound (Figure 8.18).

Finally, you can always check for yourself from within DrJava. If you've been following along with the example,[1] then the variable s is the now louder sound.

---

[1]What? You haven't? You *should*! It'll make much more sense if you try it yourself!

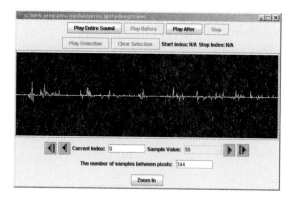 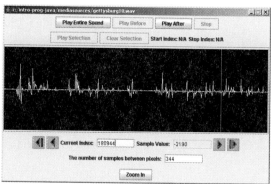

FIGURE 8.18
Comparing specific samples in the original sound (left) and the louder one (right).

f should still be the filename of the original sound. Go ahead and make a new sound object which is the *original* sound—that is named below as sOrig (for *sound original*). Check any sample that you want—it's always true that the louder sound has twice the value than the original sound.

```
> System.out.println(s);
 Sound file:
c:/intro-prog-java/mediasources/gettysburg10-louder.wav number of
samples: 220568
> System.out.println(f);
c:/intro-prog-java/mediasources/gettysburg10.wav
> Sound sOrig = new Sound(f);
> System.out.println(s.getSampleValueAt(0));
118
> System.out.println(sOrig.getSampleValueAt(0));
59
> System.out.println(s.getSampleValueAt(1));
78
> System.out.println(sOrig.getSampleValueAt(1));
39
> System.out.println(s.getSampleValueAt(999));
-80
> System.out.println(sOrig.getSampleValueAt(999));
-40
```

You can see from the last value that even negative values become *more* negative. That's what's meant by "increasing the amplitude." The amplitude of the wave goes in *both* directions. We have to make the wave larger in both the positive and negative dimensions.

It's important to do what you just read in this chapter: *Doubt* your programs. Did that *really* do what we wanted it to do? The way you check is by *testing*. That's what this section is about. You just saw several ways to test:

- By looking at the result overall (like with the graphs created by the explorer),
- By checking pieces of the results (like with the explorer or MediaTools), and

- By writing additional code statements that check the results of the original program.

Figuring out how it worked

Let's walk through the code, slowly, and consider how this program worked.

```
/**
 * Method to double the volume (amplitude) of the sound
 */
public void increaseVolume()
{
  SoundSample[] sampleArray = this.getSamples();
  SoundSample sample = null;
  int value = 0;
  int index = 0;

  // loop through all the samples in the array
  while (index < sampleArray.length)
  {
    sample = sampleArray[index];
    value = sample.getValue();
    sample.setValue(value * 2);
    index++;
  }
}
```

Recall our picture of the samples in a sound array.

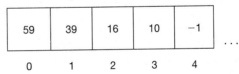

This is what `sound.getSamples()` would return: An array of `SoundSample` objects. The `while` loop allows us to walk through each sample, one at a time. The name (variable) `sample` will refer to each `SoundSample` object in turn.

The variable `index` starts out with a value of 0. This is less than the length of the array `sampleArray` so the body of the loop is executed. The variable `sample` is changed to refer to the first `SoundSample` object (the one at index 0).

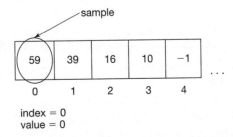

The variable `value` will take on the value of 59 when `value=sample.get Value()` is executed. The value stored at that `SoundSample` object will be set to value times 2 (59 * 2 = 118).

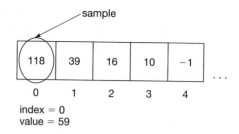

index = 0
value = 59

The value in variable `index` will be incremented by 1 ($0 + 1 = 1$). That's the end of the first pass through the body of the `while` loop. The loop will then start over. The test that `index` is less than the length of the array of samples will happen again. Since it is still less the body of the loop will be executed (statements inside the open and close curly braces). The variable `sample` will be changed to refer to the second item in the array (the one at index 1).

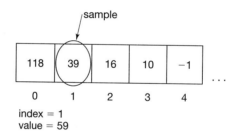

index = 1
value = 59

Again, the variable `value` is set to the value of the `SoundSample` object. The value of the `SoundSample` object is set to twice the amount held in the variable `value`.

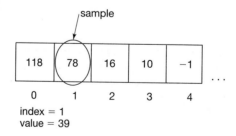

index = 1
value = 39

This is what it will look like after five times through the loop.

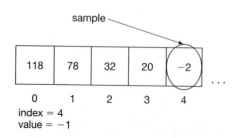

index = 4
value = −1

But really, the `while` loop *keeps* going through all the samples—tens of thousands of them! Thank goodness it's the *computer* executing this program!

What you have just read in this section is called *tracing* the program. We slowly went through how each step in the program was executed. We drew pictures to describe the data in the program. We used numbers, arrows, equations, and even plain English to explain what was going on in the program. This is the single most important technique in programming. It's part of *debugging*. Your program will *not* always work. Absolutely, guaranteed, without a shadow of a doubt—you will write code that does not do what you want. But the computer *will* do *SOMETHING*. How do you figure out what it *is* doing? You debug, and the most significant way to do that is by tracing the program.

8.3.3 Decreasing Volume

Decreasing volume, then, is the reverse of the previous process.

Program 66: Decrease an Input Sound's Volume

```
/**
 * Method to halve the volume (amplitude) of the sound.
 */
public void decreaseVolume()
{
  SoundSample[] sampleArray = this.getSamples();
  SoundSample sample = null;
  int value = 0;
  int index = 0;

  // loop through all the samples in the array
  while (index < sampleArray.length)
  {
    sample = sampleArray[index];
    value = sample.getValue();
    sample.setValue((int) (value * 0.5));
    index++;
  }
}
```

- Our method is called on a Sound object. The Sound object is implicitly passed to the method and is accessed using the keyword `this`. You can leave off the `this` on `this.getSamples()` since it is understood to be invoked on the current object.

- The variable `sample` will refer to a different `SoundSample` object each time through the loop.

- Each time `sample` refers to a new `SoundSample` object, we will get the *value* of that `SoundSample` object. We put that in the variable `value`.

- We then set the value held by the SoundSample object to 50% of its current value, by multiplying value by 0.5, and setting the sample value to that. However, because the value is an integer and the result of a computation with a floating point value (0.5) is a floating point number we must cast to integer using (int) (value * 0.5) to let the compiler know we realize that we will be throwing away the fractional part.

We can use it like this.

```
> String f = FileChooser.pickAFile();
> System.out.println(f);
C:\intro-prog-java\mediasources\gettysburg10-louder.wav
> Sound sound1 = new Sound(f);
> System.out.println(sound1);
Sound file:
C:\intro-prog-java\mediasources\gettysburg10-louder.wav number of
samples: 220568
> sound1.play();
> sound1.decreaseVolume();
> sound1.play();
```

We can even do it again, and lower the volume even further.

```
> sound1.decreaseVolume();
> sound1.play();
```

8.3.4 Using a for Loop

Have you ever forgotten to declare the variable index? If you did the method wouldn't compile. Did you ever forget to increment the variable index? If you did the loop would never end until you hit RESET. Because of these problems, programmers typically use a for loop instead of a while loop when they want to execute a block of commands a set number of times. A for loop is equivalent to a while loop (means the same thing to the computer). The for loop is just less error prone for a programmer (though it can be harder for a beginner to understand). We introduced for loops in Section 4.3.7.

A for loop looks like this: for (*initialization*; *test*; *change*). The initialization area lets you declare and initialize variables for use in the loop, the test is where you test if the loop should continue, and the change area is where you change the value of counters or indices used in the loop. For example, see the following new version of the method decreaseVolume which has been modified to use a for loop instead of a while loop.

Program 67: Decrease an Input Sound's Volume Using a for Loop

```
/**
 * Method to halve the volume (amplitude) of the sound.
 */
public void decreaseVolume2()
{
```

```
    SoundSample[] sampleArray = this.getSamples();
    SoundSample sample = null;
    int value = 0;
    // int index = 0;

    // loop through all the samples in the array
    // while (index < sampleArray.length)
    for (int index = 0; index < sampleArray.length; index++)
    {
      sample = sampleArray[index];
      value = sample.getValue();
      sample.setValue((int) (value * 0.5));
      // index++;
    }
  }
}
```

■

We have used the to-end-of-line comment '//' to comment out some lines of code to show the difference between the while and for loops. Notice that what is different is that we don't declare and initialize the index before the loop, it is done in the initialization part of the for statement. We also don't increment the index as the last statement in the loop. This is moved to the change area in the for statement. So we have replaced three lines of code with one and made it more likely that we will remember to declare variables for use in the loop and change them. However, what really happens during execution *is the same thing* as what happened during the while loop. The declarations and initializations done in the initialization part of the for loop will actually take place before the first test. The change of the loop variables will actually take place after each execution of the loop body and before the next test.

8.3.5 Making Sense of Methods

The lessons that we learned when writing picture methods (from Section 4.3.5) apply to sound methods as well. We want to write methods that do one and only one thing. We want to write methods that can be reused.

We can write methods that take an input value. For example, here's a program to changeVolume. It accepts a factor that is multiplied by each sample value. This method can be used to increase or decrease the amplitude (and thus, the volume).

Program 68: Change a Sound's Volume by a Given Factor

```
/**
 * Method to change the volume (amplitude) of the sound
 * by multiplying the current values in the sound by
 * the passed factor.
 * @param factor the factor to multiply by
 */
public void changeVolume(double factor)
{
  SoundSample[] sampleArray = this.getSamples();
```

```
      SoundSample sample = null;
      int value = 0;

      // loop through all the samples in the array
      for (int i = 0; i < sampleArray.length; i++)
      {
        sample = sampleArray[i];
        value = sample.getValue();
        sample.setValue((int) (value * factor));
      }
    }
```

■

This program is clearly more flexible than increaseVolume(). Does that make it better? Certainly it is for some purposes (e.g., if you were writing software to do general audio processing), but for other purposes, having separate and clearly named methods for increasing and decreasing volume may be better. Of course, you could modify increaseVolume() and decreaseVolume() to call changeVolume() with the appropriate factor. Remember that software is written for humans—write software that is understandable for the people who will be reading and using your software.

We are reusing the name sample a lot. We have used it in several methods in the Sound class. *That's okay.* Names can have different meanings depending on their context. Variables declared in a method have meaning only inside that method. Methods can even use the same variable names as other methods. You can even use the same variable names that you use in your methods in the interactions pane. This is a different *context*. If you create a variable in a method context (like value in Program 68 above), then that variable won't exist when you get back out to the interactions pane. We can return values from a method context back out to the interactions pane (or a calling method) by using return, which we'll talk more about later.

8.4   NORMALIZING SOUNDS

If you think about it, it seems strange that the last two methods work! We can just multiply these numbers representing a sound—and the sound seems (essentially) the same to our ears just louder? The way we experience a sound depends less on the specific numbers than on the *relationship* between them. Remember that the overall shape of the sound waveform is dependent on *many* samples. In general, if we multiply all the samples by the same multiplier, we only effect our sense of volume (intensity), not the sound itself. (We'll work to change the sound itself in future sections.)

A common operation that people want to do with sounds is to make them as **LOUD AS POSSIBLE**. That's called *normalizing*. It's not really hard to do, but it takes more lines of code than we've used previously and a few more variables, but we can do it. Here's the algorithm, in English, that we need to tell the computer to do.

- We have to figure out what the largest sample in the sound is. If it's already at the maximum value (the allowed range is −32,768 to 32,767, so the maximum allowed positive value is 32,767), then we can't really increase the volume and still get what seems like the same sound. Remember that we have to multiply all the samples by the same multiplier.

   It's an easy (*algorithm*) to find the largest value—sort of a *sub-program* within the overall normalizing program. Define a name (say, `largest`) and assign it a small value (0 works). Now, check all the samples. If you find a sample with an absolute value larger than the `largest`, save that as the value for `largest`. Keep checking the samples, comparing to the *new* largest. Eventually, the very largest value in the array will be in the variable `largest`.

   To do this, we'll need a way of figuring out the maximum value of two values. We can use an `if (value > largest)` to check if the current value is greater than the current largest and if so set that value to the largest. We can also save the index of that value so that we can check it with the sound explorer.

- Next, we need to figure out what value to multiply all the samples by. We want the largest value to become 32,767. Thus, we want to figure out a *multiplier* such that (*multiplier*)(*largest*) = 32,767.

   Solve for the multiplier: *multiplier* = 32,767/*largest*. The multiplier will need to be a floating point number (have a decimal component), so we need to convince Java that not everything here is an integer. Turns out that that's easy—use 32,767.0. Simply stick on ".0".

- Now, loop through all the samples, as we did for `increaseVolume`, and multiply the sample by the multiplier.

Here's a program to normalize sounds.

Program 69: Normalize the Sound to a Maximum Amplitude

```
/**
 * Method to normalize (make as loud as possible) a sound.
 */
public void normalize()
{
  int largest = 0;
  int maxIndex = 0;
  SoundSample[] sampleArray = this.getSamples();
  SoundSample sample = null;
  int value = 0;

  // loop comparing the absolute value of the current value
  // to the current largest
  for (int i = 0; i < sampleArray.length; i++)
  {
    sample = sampleArray[i];
    value = Math.abs(sample.getValue());
    if (value > largest)
```

```
        {
          largest = value;
          maxIndex = i;
        }
    }

    // now calculate the multiplier to multiply by
    double multiplier = 32767.0 / largest;

    // print out the largest value and the multiplier
    System.out.println("The largest value was " + largest +
                          " at index " + maxIndex);
    System.out.println("The multiplier is " + multiplier);

    /* loop through all the samples and multiply by the
     * multiplier
     */
    for (int i = 0; i < sampleArray.length; i++)
    {
      sample = sampleArray[i];
      sample.setValue((int) (sample.getValue() * multiplier));
    }
}
```

There are several notational items to note about this program.

- There is more than one loop in this method. That is okay. We can even use the same variable i in each loop. Since the variable is declared in the initialization area of the for loop, it is only known in that loop. So, when we declare i again in the second loop it is seen as a new variable and not an attempt to declare the same variable more than once.

- There are System.out.println() statements in there! These statements can be *really* useful. First, they give you some feedback that the program is running—a useful thing in long-running programs. Second, they show you what it's finding, which can be interesting. Third, it's a terrific testing method and a way to debug your programs. Let's imagine that the printout showed that the multiplier was less than 1.0. We know that that kind of multiplier *decreases* volume. You should suspect that something went wrong.

Here's how to run this program:

```
> Sound s = new Sound(FileChooser.getMediaPath("preamble.wav"));
> s.explore();
> s.normalize();
The largest value was 10216 at index 179377

The multiplier is 3.207419733750979
> s.play();
> s.explore();
```

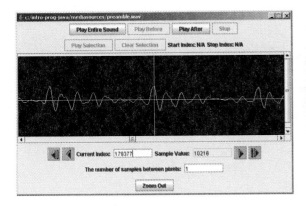 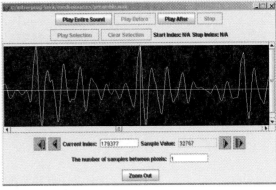

FIGURE 8.19
Comparing the original sound with the normalized one.

Exciting, huh? Obviously, the interesting part is hearing the much louder volume, which is awfully hard to do in a book. So please try it now if you haven't yet. But you can see from Figure 8.19 that the values have increased.

8.4.1 Generating Clipping

Earlier, we talked about *clipping*, what happens when the normal curves of the sound are broken by the limitations of the sample size. One way of generating clipping is to keep increasing the volume. Another way is to explicitly force clipping.

What if you *only* had the largest and smallest possible sample values? What if all positive values (including zero), were the *maximum* value (32,767) and all negative values were the minimum value (−32,768)? Try this program, particularly on sounds with words in them.

Program 70: Set All Samples to Extreme Values

```java
/**
 * Method to set all the sample values to the
 * maximum positive value if they were positive
 * (including 0) and the minimum negative
 * value if they were negative.
 */
public void forceToExtremes()
{

  SoundSample[] sampleArray = this.getSamples();
  SoundSample sample = null;

  // loop through the sample values
  for (int i = 0; i < sampleArray.length; i++)
  {
    // get the current sample
    sample = sampleArray[i];
```

```
    // if the value was positive (or zero) set it to the
    // maximum positive value
    if (sample.getValue() >= 0)
      sample.setValue(32767);

    // else force to max negative value
    else
      sample.setValue(-32768);
  }
}
```

Here's how to run this program:

```
> Sound s = new Sound(FileChooser.getMediaPath("preamble.wav"));
> s.play();
> s.explore();
> s.forceToExtremes();
> s.play();
> s.explore();
```

Look at Figure 8.20 and see that all the values have been set to extremes. When you play the sound back, you'll hear a bunch of awful noises. That's clipping. The really amazing thing is that you can *still* make out the words in sounds that you manipulate with this method. Our ability to decipher words from noise is incredibly powerful.

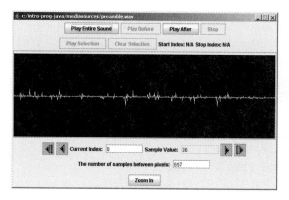 

FIGURE 8.20
Comparing the original sound with one with all values set to extremes.

8.5 CONCEPTS SUMMARY

In this chapter we worked with one-dimensional arrays, while loops, for loops, and conditionals.

8.5.1 Arrays

Arrays are used to store many pieces of data of the same type. They allow you to quickly access a particular item in the array using an index. If you couldn't use an array, you would have to create a separate variable name for each piece of data.

To declare a variable that refers to an array use the type followed by open '[' and close ']' square brackets and then the variable name.

```
SoundSample[] sampleArray;
```

This declares an array of SoundSample objects. The value stored at each position in the array is a reference to a SoundSample object.

Arrays are objects and you can find out how large an array is using:

```
arrayReference.length
```

Notice that this isn't a method call but instead it accesses a public field.

You can get an element of the array using arrayReference[index]. Where the index values can range from 0 to arrayReference.length-1.

8.5.2 Loops

Loops are used to execute a block of statements while a boolean expression is true. Most loops have variables that change during the loop which eventually cause the boolean expression to be false and the loop to stop. Loops that never stop are called infinite loops.

We used three types of loops in this chapter: for-each, while, and for. The while loop is usually used when you don't know how many times a loop needs to execute and the for and for-each loops are usually used when you do know how many times the loop will execute.

The for-each loop was introduced in Java 1.5 and loops through all the elements of an array one at a time.

```
SoundSample[] sampleArray = this.getSamples();
int value = 0;

// loop through all the samples in the array
for (SoundSample sample : sampleArray)
{
  value = sample.getValue();
  // do something to the value
  sample.setValue(value);
}
```

This declares a variable sample that is of the type SoundSample and each time through the loop the sample variable will refer to a different element of the array until all the elements have been processed.

The while loop has the keyword while followed by a boolean expression and then a block of statements between an open and close curly brace. If the boolean expression is true, the body of the loop will be executed. If the boolean expression is false, execution will continue after the body of the loop (after the close curly brace). If you just want to execute one statement in the body of the loop, then you don't need the open and close curly braces, but you should indent the statement.

```
while (boolean expression)
{
  statement1;
  statement2;
  ...
}
```

If you use a while loop to execute a block of statements a set number of times, you will need to declare a variable before the while and that variable will need to be changed in the body of the loop. You may also need to declare other variables that you use in the loop before the while. Don't declare variables inside the loop because you will use more memory that way.

```
SoundSample[] sampleArray = this.getSamples();
SoundSample sample = null;
int index = 0;
int value = 0;

// loop through all the samples in the array
while (index < sampleArray.length)
{
  sample = sampleArray[index];
  value = sample.getValue();
  // do something to the value
  sample.setValue(value);
  index++;
}
```

The for loop does the same thing as a while loop, but it lets you declare the variables that you need for the loop, specify the boolean expression to test, and specify how to change the loop variables all in one place. This means you are less likely to forget to do each of these things.

```
SoundSample[] sampleArray = this.getSamples();
SoundSample sample = null;
int value = 0;

// loop through all the samples in the array
for (int index = 0; index < sampleArray.length; index++)
{
  sample = sampleArray[index];
  value = sample.getValue();
  // do something to the value
  sample.setValue(value);
}
```

8.5.3 Conditional Execution

To conditionally execute one statement use the if keyword followed by a boolean expression inside of an open and close parenthesis. Put the statement that you only want executed if the boolean expression is true on a new line and indent it. If the boolean expression is false, execution will continue with the next statement.

```
if (boolean expression)
   // statement to execute if the boolean expression is true
   statement
// next statement
statement
```

To conditionally execute a block of statements, use the `if` keyword followed by a boolean expression inside of an open and close parenthesis. Put the statements to be executed when the boolean expression is true inside of an open and close curly brace. Indent the statements to make it easier to visually see that these statements will only be executed if the boolean expression is true. If the boolean expression is false, execution will continue with the statement following the close curly brace.

```
if (boolean expression)
{
   statements
}
```

If you want to execute one block of statements if the boolean expression is true, and another if it is false, use the `else` keyword as well. Put the statements that you want to execute when the boolean expression is true inside of an open and close curly brace after the `if(booleanExpression)`. Next, add the keyword `else` and put the statements that you want executed when the boolean expression is false inside of an open and close curly brace.

```
if (boolean expression)
{
 statements
}
else
{
 statements
}
```

OBJECTS AND METHODS SUMMARY

In this chapter, we talk about several kinds of encodings of data (or objects).

Sound	Sound objects are encodings of sounds, typically coming from a WAV file.
SoundSample	An object that represents a sample in a sound. The value of a sample is between −32,768 and 32,767 representing the voltage that a microphone would generate at a given instant when recording a sound. The length of the instant is typically either 1/44,100 of a second (for CD-quality sound) or 1/22,050 of a second (for good enough sound on most computers). A SoundSample object remembers what sound it came from, so if you change its value, it knows to go back and change the right sample value in the sound.

Here are the methods used or introduced in this chapter:

Math Methods

Math.abs(number)	Takes a number and returns it as a positive number.

FileChooser Methods

FileChooser.getMediaPath(String fileName)	Takes a filename as input, and returns the full path name of the file with the media directory before the filename.
FileChooser.pickAFile()	Lets the user pick a file and returns the complete path name as a string.
FileChooser.setMediaPath(String directory)	Takes a directory as input and sets the directory name to be what is added to the passed filename using getMediaPath.

Sound Methods

blockingPlay()	Plays the Sound object it is invoked on, and makes sure that no other sound plays at the exact same time. (Compare two blockingPlay's with two play's right after each other.)
getLength()	Returns the number of samples in the Sound object it is invoked on.
getSamples()	Returns an array of SoundSample objects for the Sound object it is invoked on.
getSampleValueAt(int index)	Takes an index (an integer value), and returns the value of the sample at that index for the Sound object it is invoked on.
getSamplingRate()	Returns the number representing the number of samples in each second for the Sound object it is invoked on.
play()	Plays the Sound object it is invoked on.
setSampleValueAt(int index, int value)	Takes an index, and a value, and sets the value of the sample at the given index in the Sound object it was invoked on to the given value.
write(String fileName)	Takes a filename (a string) and writes the sound in the Sound object it is invoked on to that file as a WAV file. (Make sure that the filename ends in ".wav" if you want the operating system to treat it right.)

SoundSample Methods

getValue()	Returns the value for the SoundSample object it is invoked on.
setValue(int value)	Sets the value for the SoundSample object it is invoked on to be the passed value.

PROBLEMS

8.1 What are each of the following:

- Clipping
- Normalize
- Amplitude
- Frequency
- Rarefactions
- WAV
- Iterate
- for-each loop
- A sine wave

8.2 Modify Program 65 (page 272) to use a for loop. If you are using Java 1.5 or above modify it to use a for-each loop.

8.3 If you are using Java 1.5 or above modify Program 7 (page 108) to use a for-each loop.

8.4 In Section 8.3.1, we walked through how Program 65 (page 272) worked. Draw the pictures to show how Program 66 (page 277) works, in the same way.

8.5 Create a new method that will halve the volume of the positive values and double the volume of the negative values. You can use Program 65 (page 272) as a starting point.

8.6 What will be output from the following code:

```java
public void test1()
{
  int x = 0;
  while (x < 3)
  {
    x = x + 1;
    System.out.println(x);
  }
}
```

8.7 What will be output from the following code:

```
public void test2()
{
  int x = 3;
  while (x > 0)
  {
    x = x + 1;
    System.out.println(x);
  }
}
```

8.8 What will be output from the following code:

```
public void test3()
{
  int x = 2;
  while (x >= 2)
  {
    x = x + 1;
    System.out.println(x);
  }
  System.out.println("x is " + x);
}
```

8.9 What will be output from the following code:

```
public void test4()
{
  int x = 2;
  int y = 0;
  while (x < 10 && y < 1)
  {
    x = x + 1;
    y = y + 1;
    System.out.println(x + ", " + y);
  }
}
```

8.10 What will be output from the following code:

```
public void test5() {
  int x = 2;
  int y = 0;
  while (x < 10 || y < 1)
  {
    x = x + 1;
    y = y + 1;
    System.out.println(x + ", " + y);
  }
}
```

8.11 What will be output from the following code:

```
public void test6() {
```

```
    int x = 12;
    int y = 0;
    while (x < 10 && y < 1)
    {
        x = x + 1;
        y = y + 1;
        System.out.println(x + ", " + y);
    }
}
```

8.12 What will be output from the following code:

```
public void test7() {
    int x = 12;
    int y = 0;
    while (x < 10 || y < 1)
    {
        x = x + 1;
        y = y + 1;
        System.out.println(x + ", " + y);
    }
}
```

8.13 What will be output from the following code:

```
public void test8() {
    int x = 12;
    int y = 0;
    while (x !< 10 || y < 1)
    {
        x = x + 1;
        y = y + 1;
        System.out.println(x + ", " + y);
    }
}
```

8.14 What will be output from the following code:

```
public void test9()
{
    int x = 12;
    int y = 0;
    while (!(x < 10 || y < 1))
    {
        x = x + 1;
        y = y + 1;
        System.out.println(x + ", " + y);
    }
}
```

8.15 What will be output from the following code:

```
public void test10()
{
```

```
int x = 2;
int y = 0;
while (!(x < 10 && y < 1))
{
    x = x + 1;
    y = y + 1;
    System.out.println(x + ", " + y);
}
}
```

8.16 In method `normalize` on page 281, we found the largest value in the sound. Write a method that will find the smallest value in the sound and print it out.

8.17 What happens if you increase a volume too far? Explore that by creating a Sound object, then increase the volume once, and again, and again. Does it always keep getting louder? Or does something else happen? Can you explain why?

8.18 Instead of multiplying samples by a multiplier (like 2 or 0.5), try *adding* a value to them. What happens to a sound if you add 100 to every sample? What happens if you add 1,000 to every sample?

8.19 Try sprinkling in some specific values into your sounds. What happens if you set the value of a few hundred samples in the middle of a sound to 32,767? Or a few hundred −32,768? Or a bunch of zeroes? What happens to the sound?

8.20 Open up the SONOGRAM view and say some vowel sounds. Is there a distinctive pattern? Do "Oh's" always sound the same? Do "Ah's"? Does it matter if you switch speakers—are the patterns the same?

8.21 Get a couple of different instruments and play the same note on them into MediaTool application's sound editor with the sonogram view open. Are all "C's" made equal? Can you *see* some of why one sound is different than another?

8.22 Try out a variety of WAV files as instruments, using the piano keyboard in the MediaTools application sound editor. What kinds of recordings work best as instruments?

TO DIG DEEPER

There are many wonderful books on psychoacoustics and computer music. One of Mark's favorites for understandability is *Computer Music: Synthesis, Composition, and Performance* by Dodge and Jerse [8]. The bible of computer music is Curtis Roads's massive *The Computer Music Tutorial* [24].

9

Modifying Samples Using Ranges

Chapter Learning Objectives

The media learning goals for this chapter are:

- To manipulate parts of a sound differently.
- To create a sound clip.
- To splice sounds together to make sound compositions.
- To reverse sounds.
- To mirror sounds.

The computer science goals for this chapter are:

- To return a value from a method.
- To use ranges in iteration.
- To change more than one variable in a loop.
- To identify algorithms that cross media boundaries.

9.1   MANIPULATING DIFFERENT SECTIONS OF A SOUND DIFFERENTLY

Manipulating all of the samples in a sound in the same way can be useful, but really interesting effects come from chopping up sounds and manipulating them differentially: Some words this way, other sounds that way. How would you do that? We need to be able to loop through *portions* of the sample, without walking through the whole thing. This turns out to be an easy thing to do, but we need to manipulate samples somewhat differently (e.g., we have to use our `for` loop in a slightly different way).

Recall that each sample has an index number, and that we can get each individual sample value with `getSampleValue(int index)` (with an index number as input). We can set any sample with `setSampleValue(int index, int value)` (with inputs of an index number, and a new value). That's how we can manipulate samples without using `getSamples()` and `SoundSample` objects. But we still don't want to have to write code like:

```
sound.setSampleValue(0,12);
sound.setSampleValue(1,28);
```

Not for tens of thousands of samples! So we will continue to use a `for` loop. However, if we are not processing the entire sound in the same way, the index value that we start at won't necessarily be 0, and the last index value won't necessarily be the length of the sound minus 1.

What if we want to *increase* the sound for the first half of the sound, then *decrease* it in the second half. How could we do that? First we will need to calculate the halfway point. We can determine that by dividing the length of the sound by 2. Since the length and 2 are both integers, the result will also be an integer, so no casting is needed (any values after the decimal point will be thrown away). We will need two loops. One loop will start at the beginning of sound (0) and loop till the halfway point. The second loop will start at the halfway point and loop to the end of the sound (length − 1).

Program 71: Increase the Volume then Decrease

```
/**
 * Method to increase the first half of the sound
 * (double it) and then decrease the
 * second half (half it).
 */
public void increaseAndDecrease()
{
  int half = this.getLength() / 2;
  int value = 0;

  // loop through the first half of the sound
  for (int i = 0; i < half; i++)
  {
    // get the current value
    value = this.getSampleValueAt(i);

    // set the value to 2x the original
    this.setSampleValueAt(i,value * 2);
  }

  // loop through the second half of the sound
  for (int i = half; i < this.getLength(); i++)
  {

    // get the current value
    value = this.getSampleValueAt(i);
```

```
    // set the value to half the original
    this.setSampleValueAt(i,(int) (value * 0.5));
  }

}
```

■

There are two loops in increaseAndDecrease(), each of which deals with one half of the sound.

- The first loop deals with the samples from 0 to halfway through the sound. Those samples all get multiplied by 2, to double their amplitude.
- The second loop goes from halfway through to the end of the sound. Here, we multiply each sample by 0.5 thus decreasing the sound by 50%.

Another Way of Writing Array References

It's worth pointing out that in many languages, square brackets ([ ]) are standard notations for manipulating arrays. It works that way in Java. For any array, array[index] returns the index-th element in the array. The number inside the square brackets is always an index variable, but it's sometimes referred to as a *subscript*, because of the way that mathematicians refer to the *i*-th element of *a*, e.g., a_i.

Let's demonstrate how to get the elements at various index values.

```
> Sound sound = new Sound(FileChooser.getMediaPath("croak.wav"));
> SoundSample[] sampleArray = sound.getSamples();
> System.out.println(sampleArray[0]);
Sample at index 0 has value 0
> System.out.println(sampleArray[1]);
Sample at index 1 has value 0
> System.out.println(sampleArray[8000]);
Sample at index 8000 has value 512
```

9.2   CREATE A SOUND CLIP

Sometimes a sound is too long and you want just part of it. This can happen when you record a sound. There may be silence before and after the actual sound. Or, you may want to pull one word out of a sound. You can "clip" a sound just as we clipped a picture by copying just part of the sound. What if we want to pull the "This" out of the sound thisisatest.wav? How can we tell where it ends? Open an explorer on the sound using sound.explore();. Click at the first flat area after the first non-flat area (silence should have values near 0). Click the PLAY BEFORE button to play the part of the sound before the current index. You can use the arrow buttons to change the current index as well. Using the explorer we see that the word "this" ends at about 8,500 (Figure 9.1).

So to copy just part of a sound into another sound we will need to create a new Sound object. One of the ways to make a new Sound object is to tell it how many

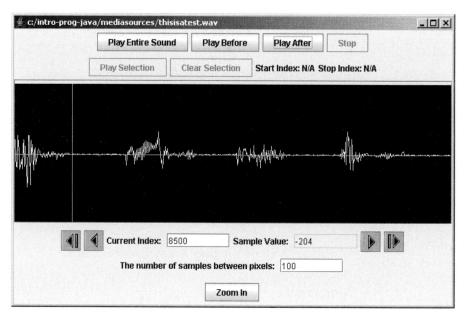

FIGURE 9.1
Exploring the "This is a test" to find the end of the first word.

samples it will have. To calculate the number of samples we can subtract the ending value from the starting value and add 1.

We can then create a new sound and loop copying from the start to the end from the source Sound object into the target Sound object starting at the beginning of the target sound. We have to make sure to increment both the index in the source and the index in the target. If we forget to increment the source index, we will copy the same source sample over and over, and if we fail to increment the target index, we will copy to the same place in the target over and over.

We need to return our new sound object in order to be able to refer to it again. To return something from a method, we need to specify the type of the thing that will be returned in the method declaration (replacing the void keyword). We also need to use the keyword return followed by what we want to return.

Program 72: Create a Sound Clip

```java
/**
 * Method to create a new sound by copying just part of
 * the current sound to a new sound
 * @param start the index to start the copy at (inclusive)
 * @param end the index to stop the copy at (inclusive)
 * @return a new sound with just the samples from start to
 * end in it
 */
public Sound clip(int start, int end)
{
  // calculate the number of samples in the clip
```

```
  int lengthInSamples = end - start + 1;
  Sound target = new Sound(lengthInSamples); // hold clip
  int value = 0;          // holds the current sample value
  int targetIndex = 0;   // index in target sound

  // copy from start to end from source into target
  for (int i = start; i <= end; i++, targetIndex++)
  {
    value = this.getSampleValueAt(i);
    target.setSampleValueAt(targetIndex,value);
  }

  return target;
}
```

Notice that we said that we would return a Sound object from this method by saying that the type of thing returned is from the class Sound. At the end of the method, we use the keyword return followed by the variable that refers to the new Sound object. So in order to refer to this new Sound object again, we will need to declare a variable and set the value of that variable to refer to the returned Sound object.

```
> Sound test = new
Sound(FileChooser.getMediaPath("thisisatest.wav"));
> test.explore();
> Sound s1 = test.clip(0,8500);
> s1.play();
> s1.explore();
```

Use the explorer on the original sound and the clipped sound. Change the number of samples between pixels to be 100 in the clipped sound. Then compare the sample values. Convince yourself that the clipped sound does have the same values as the original (Figure 9.2).

9.3   SPLICING SOUNDS

Splicing sounds is a term that dates back to when sounds were recorded on tape, so juggling the order of things on the tape involved literally cutting the tape into segments and then gluing it back together in the right order. That's "splicing". When everything is digital, it's *much* easier.

To splice sounds, we simply have to copy elements around in the array. It's easiest to do this with two (or more) arrays, rather than copying within the same array. Splicing lets you create all kinds of sounds, speeches, nonsense, and art.

The easiest kind of splice to do is when the sounds are in separate files. All that you need to do is to copy each sound, in order, into a target sound. You need to keep track of the next index in the target sound. Here's a method that creates the start of a sentence "Guzdial is ..." (readers are welcome to complete the sentence).

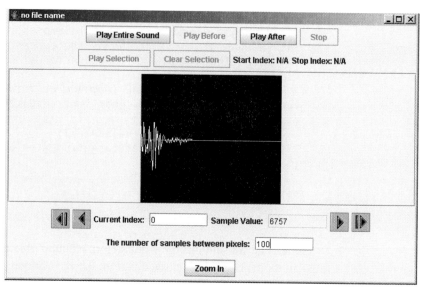

FIGURE 9.2
Exploring the sound clip.

Program 73: Splice Words into a Single Sentence

```
/**
 * Method to splice two sounds together with some silence
 * between them into the current sound
 */
public void splice() {
  Sound sound1 =
    new Sound(FileChooser.getMediaPath("guzdial.wav"));
  Sound sound2 =
    new Sound(FileChooser.getMediaPath("is.wav"));
  int targetIndex = 0; // the starting place on the target
  int value = 0;

  // copy all of sound 1 into the current sound (target)
  for (int i = 0;
       i < sound1.getLength();
       i++, targetIndex++)
  {
    value = sound1.getSampleValueAt(i);
    this.setSampleValueAt(targetIndex,value);
  }

  // create silence between words by setting values to 0
  for (int i = 0;
       i < (int) (this.getSamplingRate() * 0.1);
       i++, targetIndex++)
  {
    this.setSampleValueAt(targetIndex,0);
  }
```

```
    // copy all of sound 2 into the current sound (target)
    for (int i = 0;
         i < sound2.getLength();
         i++, targetIndex++)
    {
      value = sound2.getSampleValueAt(i);
      this.setSampleValueAt(targetIndex,value);
    }
  }
}
```
■

To test this we need a "blank" sound that the two sounds will be copied to. You can use the file "sec3silence.wav" for this. It holds 3 seconds of silence, which should be more than enough.

```
> String silence = FileChooser.getMediaPath("sec3silence.wav");
> Sound target = new Sound(silence);
> target.play();
> target.splice();
> target.play();
```

There are three loops in this method `splice`, each of which copies one segment into the current (target) sound—a segment being either a word or a silence between words.

- The method starts by creating sound objects for the word "Guzdial" (`sound1`) and the word "is" (`sound2`).
- Notice that we set `targetIndex` (the index for the target sound) equal to 0 *before* the first loop. We then increment it in every loop, but we never again set it to a specific value. That's because `targetIndex` is always the index for the *next empty sample* in the target sound. Because each loop follows the previous one, we just keep tacking samples onto the end of the current sound (the target).
- In the first loop, we copy each and every sample from `sound1` into the current sound `this`. We have the index i go from 0 to one before the length of `sound1`. We get the sample value at index i from `sound1`, then set the sample value at `targetIndex` in the current sound to that value. We then increment both i and `targetIndex`.
- In the second loop, we create 0.1 seconds of silence. Since `getSamplingRate()` gives us the number of samples in one second of the current sound, 0.1 times that tells us the number of samples in 0.1 seconds. We don't get any source value here—we simply set the `targetIndex`-th sample to 0 (for silence), then increment the `targetIndex`.
- Finally, we copy in all the samples from `sound2`, just like the first loop where we copied in `sound1`.

The more common kind of splicing is when the words are in the middle of an existing sound, and you need to pull them out from there. The first thing to do in splicing like that is to figure out the index numbers that delimit the pieces you're interested in. Using the explorer, that's pretty easy to do.

- Open an explorer using `sound.explore()`.
- Click the mouse button to choose a current position and then play the sound before or after that current position.
- Or, select part of the sound by clicking the mouse when the cursor points to a place to start and dragging the mouse to the end of an area of interest. This selection will highlight and you can play the selection.

Using exactly this process, Mark found the ending points of the first few words in `preamble10.wav`. (He assumed that the first word starts at the index 0, though that might not always be true for every sound.)

Word	Ending index
We	15,730
the	17,407
People	26,726
of	32,131
the	33,413
United	40,052
States	55,510

Writing a loop that copies things from one array to another requires a little bit of juggling. You need to think about keeping track of two indices: where you are in the array that you're copying *from*, and where you are in the array that you're copying *to*. These are two different variables, tracking two different indexes. But they both increment in the same way.

Below is the method that changes the preamble from "We the people of the United States" to "We the UNITED people of the United States."

Program 74: Splice the Preamble to have United People

Be sure to set the media path before trying this on your computer.

```
/**
 * Method to splice "We the " then "United" then
 * "people of the United States" into the current
 * sound
 */
public void splicePreamble()
{
  String file = FileChooser.getMediaPath("preamble10.wav");
  Sound source = new Sound(file);
  int targetIndex = 0; // start copying to first sample value
  int value = 0;
```

```
    // loop copying the "We the " into the current sound
    for (int sourceIndex = 0;
         sourceIndex < 17407;
         sourceIndex++, targetIndex++)
    {
      value = source.getSampleValueAt(sourceIndex);
      this.setSampleValueAt(targetIndex,value);
    }

    // loop copying the "united" into the current sound
    for (int sourceIndex = 33414;
         sourceIndex < 40052;
         sourceIndex++,targetIndex++)
    {
      value = source.getSampleValueAt(sourceIndex);
      this.setSampleValueAt(targetIndex,value);
    }

    // copy the "people of the United States"
    for (int sourceIndex = 17408;
         sourceIndex < 55510;
         sourceIndex++, targetIndex++)
    {
      value = source.getSampleValueAt(sourceIndex);
      this.setSampleValueAt(targetIndex,value);
    }
  }
```

```
> String silence = FileChooser.getMediaPath("sec3silence.wav");
> Sound target = new Sound(silence);
> target.play();
> target.splicePreamble();
> target.play();
```

The first loop copies the words "We the" into the current sound. The second loop copies the word "united" into the current sound. The last loop copies the words "people of the United States" into the current sound. Notice that the value of `targetIndex` is set to 0 at the beginning, so we start copying at the beginning of the current sound. In each loop we increment `targetIndex` but we never reset its value, so it always points to the next place in the current sound to copy to.

Figure 9.3 shows the original `preamble10.wav` file in the left sound explorer, and the new spliced one (saved with `write(String fileName)`) on the right.

Let's see if we can figure out what's going on mathematically. Recall the table back on page 300. First we copy the range from 0 to 17,406 to the target sound. This means we copied 17,407 pixels ($17,406 - 0 + 1 = 17,407$). After the first loop, the value of `targetIndex` will be 17,407. Next we copy the range from 33,414 to 40,051 which means we copy ($40,051 - 33,414 + 1 = 6,638$) 6,638 pixels. After the

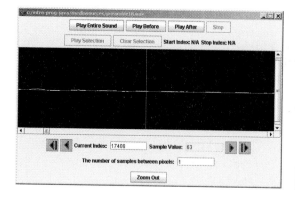 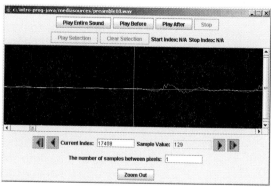

FIGURE 9.3
Comparing the original sound (left) to the spliced sound (right).

second loop, the value of `targetIndex` will be 24,045 ($17{,}407 + 6{,}638 = 24{,}045$). Next we copy the range from 17,408 to 55,509 which is ($55{,}509 - 17{,}408 + 1 = 38{,}102$) pixels. The total number of copied pixels is ($17{,}407 + 6{,}638 + 38{,}102 = 62{,}147$). The value of `targetIndex` will be 62,147 after the last loop. You can add `System.out.println("Target index is " + targetIndex);` after each loop to check that this is correct.

Program 75: Splice Preamble and Show Target Index

```java
/**
 * Method to splice "We the " then "United" then
 * "people of the United States" into the current
 * sound
 */
public void splicePreamble()
{
  String file = FileChooser.getMediaPath("preamble10.wav");
  Sound source = new Sound(file);
  int targetIndex = 0; // start copying to first sample value
  int value = 0;

  // loop copying the "We the " into the current sound
  for (int sourceIndex = 0;
       sourceIndex < 17407;
       sourceIndex++, targetIndex++)
  {
    value = source.getSampleValueAt(sourceIndex);
    this.setSampleValueAt(targetIndex,value);
  }

  // print the value of the target index
  System.out.println("Target index is " + targetIndex);

  // loop copying the "united" into the current sound
  for (int sourceIndex = 33414;
       sourceIndex < 40052;
```

```
                    sourceIndex++,targetIndex++)
  {
    value = source.getSampleValueAt(sourceIndex);
    this.setSampleValueAt(targetIndex,value);
  }

  // print the value of the target index
  System.out.println("Target index is " + targetIndex);

  // copy the "people of the United States"
  for (int sourceIndex = 17408;
       sourceIndex < 55510;
       sourceIndex++, targetIndex++)
  {
    value = source.getSampleValueAt(sourceIndex);
    this.setSampleValueAt(targetIndex,value);
  }

  // print the value of the target index
  System.out.println("Target index is " + targetIndex);
}
```

We can also use the explorer to check that the last copied pixel is at 62,146 by checking the value at 62,147. It should still be 0, as should all the values from that index to the end of the sound.

Each of the loops that copies part of the preamble sound into the current sound is very similar. To make a general splice method we will pass in the Sound object to copy from, the starting index to use in that passed sound, the index to stop before in the passed sound, and the place to start the copy to in current sound.

Program 76: General Splice Method

```
/**
 * Method to copy part of the passed sound into this sound at
 * the given start index
 * @param source the source sound to copy from
 * @param sourceStart the starting index to copy from in the
 * source (the copy will include this)
 * @param sourceStop the ending index (the copy won't include
 * this)
 * @param targetStart the index to start copying into
 */
public void splice(Sound source,
                   int sourceStart,
                   int sourceStop,
                   int targetStart)
{
  // loop copying from source to target
  for (int sourceIndex = sourceStart,
       targetIndex = targetStart;
```

```
                 sourceIndex < sourceStop &&
                     targetIndex < this.getLength();
                 sourceIndex++, targetIndex++)
             this.setSampleValueAt(targetIndex,
                 source.getSampleValueAt(sourceIndex));
      }
```

This new object method can be used to splice "united" in the phrase "We the people of the United States" as shown below:

Program 77: Using the General Splice Method

```
/**
 * Method to splice the preamble into the current sound so that
 * it says We the United people of the United States
 */
public void splicePreamble2()
{
  Sound preamble =
    new Sound(FileChooser.getMediaPath("preamble10.wav"));

  // first splice the "we the" into the current sound
  this.splice(preamble,0,17407,0);

  // now splice the "united" into the current sound
  this.splice(preamble,33414,40052,17407);

  /* now splice the "people of the United States" into
   * the current sound
   */
  this.splice(preamble,17408,55510,24045);
}
```

You can execute this new method using the following:

```
> String fileName = FileChooser.getMediaPath("sec3silence.wav");
> Sound target = new Sound(fileName);
> target.splicePreamble2();
> target.explore();
```

Compare the sound created using the `splicePreamble` method versus the sound created using the `splicePreamble2` method. They should result in exactly the same sound. Why should we try to write general methods? Take a look at `splicePreamble2`. It is much easier to read than `splicePreamble`. We want general methods because they are easier to reuse and make our programs smaller and easier to understand.

9.4 REVERSING A SOUND

In the splicing example, we copied the samples from the words just as they were in the original sound. We don't have to always go in the same order. We can reverse the words—or make them faster, slower, louder, or softer. For an example, here's a method that reverses a sound so that you can play it backward.

Program 78: Reverse a Sound

```
/**
 * Method to reverse the current sound.
 */
public void reverse()
{
  Sound orig = new Sound(this.getFileName());
  int length = this.getLength();

  // loop through the samples
  for (int targetIndex = 0, sourceIndex = length - 1;
       targetIndex < length && sourceIndex > 0;
       targetIndex++, sourceIndex--)
    this.setSampleValueAt(targetIndex,
                          orig.getSampleValueAt(sourceIndex));

}
```

This method first creates another Sound object from the same file as the current Sound object. This will make a copy of the original sound. Next the method saves the length of the current Sound object. Then it loops.

The loop initializes the value of `targetIndex` to 0, and the value of `sourceIndex` to the length of the sound minus 1. It loops while `targetIndex` is less than the length of the sound and the `sourceIndex` is greater than 0. It increments `targetIndex` by 1 after the body of the loop and it decrements the value of `sourceIndex` by one each time through the loop.

Why does it start `sourceIndex` at the length of the sound minus 1 and decrement it each time through the loop? Remember that the last valid index is at the length minus 1, which is why the `sourceIndex` starts with this value. So we copy from the end of the source sound (length − 1) to the beginning of the target sound (0) during the first execution of the loop. The second time through the loop we copy from the next to last sound sample in the source (length − 2) to the second position in the target (1). We will keep looping until the `targetIndex` equals the length of the sound.

To use this method to reverse a sound try (Figure 9.4):

```
> Sound s = new Sound(FileChooser.getMediaPath("croak.wav"));
> s.play();
> s.explore();
> s.reverse();
> s.play();
> s.explore();
```

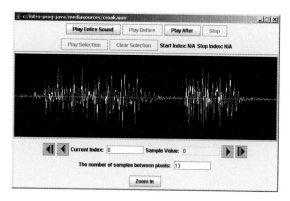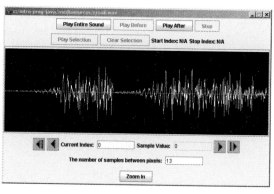

FIGURE 9.4
Comparing the original sound (left) to the reversed sound (right).

9.5 MIRRORING A SOUND

Once we know how to play sounds forward and backward, *mirroring* the sound is the exact same process as mirroring pictures! Compare this to Program 19 (page 135). Do you see that this is the same *algorithm*, though we're dealing with a different medium?

Program 79: Mirror a Sound, Front to Back

```
/**
 * Method to mirror a sound front to back
 */
public void mirrorFrontToBack()
{
  int length = this.getLength(); // save the length
  int mirrorPoint = length / 2; // mirror around this
  int value = 0; // hold the current value

  // loop from 0 to mirrorPoint
  for (int i = 0; i < mirrorPoint; i++) {
    value = this.getSampleValueAt(i);
    this.setSampleValueAt(length - 1 - i,value);
  }
}
```

To use this method try:

```
> Sound s = new Sound(FileChooser.getMediaPath("croak.wav"));
> s.explore();
> s.mirrorFrontToBack();
> s.explore();
```

The length of the sound in the file "croak.wav" is 8,808, so the mirror point is at 4,404. Use the explorer to check the values on either side of the mirror point (Figure 9.5).

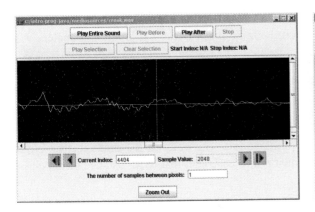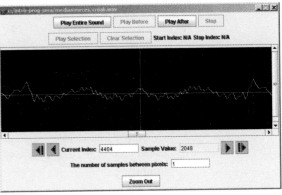

FIGURE 9.5
Comparing the mirror point in the original sound (left) to the mirrored sound (right).

9.6   CONCEPTS SUMMARY

This chapter covered working with ranges in loops and how to return a value from a method.

9.6.1   Ranges in Loops

To limit the range of a loop, change the starting value and/or ending value. For example, to create a new sound from just part of an original sound you can change the start and end values for the loop. This was seen in Program 72 (page 296).

```
// copy from start to end from source into target
for (int i = start; i <= end; i++, targetIndex++)
{
  value = this.getSampleValueAt(i);
  target.setSampleValueAt(targetIndex,value);
}
```

9.6.2   Returning a Value from a Method

To declare a method you specify the visibility for the method, the type of thing it returns, the name of the method, and the parameter list inside parentheses. This is followed by the body of the method which is inside of an open and close curly brace.

Methods that do not return any value use the keyword void as the returnType. If the method has a return type other than the keyword void it must contain a return statement in the method that returns a value of that type. Remember that a type is any of the primitive types or the name of a class.

```
visibility returnType name(parameterList)
{
 // statements in method

 // return a value
 return valueToReturn;
}
```

Here is an example public method declaration that doesn't return anything. The name of the method is mirrorFrontToBack and it doesn't take any parameters.

```
public void mirrorFrontToBack()
```

Here is an example public method declaration that returns an object of the class Sound.

```
public Sound echo(int delay, int numEchoes)
```

Notice that it gives a return type of Sound. The body of the method must have the keyword return in it, and it must return an object that is an instance of the class Sound.

```
return echoSound;
```

PROBLEMS

9.1 What does each of the following mean:

- Clip
- Splice
- Reverse
- Mirror

9.2 What will be output from the following code:

```
public void test1()
{
  for (int x = 5; x > 0; x--)
  {
    System.out.println(x);
  }
}
```

9.3 What will be output from the following code:

```
public void test2()
{
  for (int x = 0; x < 10; x = x + 2)
  {
    System.out.println(x);
  }
}
```

9.4 What will be output from the following code:

```
public void test3()
{
  for (int x = 1; x < 10; x = x + 2)
  {
    System.out.println(x);
  }
}
```

9.5 Would this compile? If not, what change do you need to make so that it will compile?

```
public void test()
{
    System.out.println("In Test");
}
```

9.6 Would this compile? If not, what change do you need to make so that it will compile?

```
public int test2(int x)
{
    System.out.println("In Test2");
}
```

9.7 Would this compile? If not, what change do you need to make so that it will compile?

```
public void test3(int x)
{
    return "In Test3";
}
```

9.8 Would this compile? If not, what change do you need to make so that it will compile?

```
public String test4(int x)
{
    return x * 4;
}
```

9.9 How many times will this loop execute?

```
for (int i = 5; i <= 10; i++)
    System.out.println(i);
```

9.10 How many times will this loop execute?

```
for (int i = 1; i <= 10; i++)
    System.out.println(i);
```

9.11 How many times will this loop execute?

```
for (int i = 0; i < 10; i++)
    System.out.println(i);
```

9.12 Rewrite Program 71 (page 294) so that two input values are provided to the method: the sound, and a *percentage* of how far into the sound to go before dropping the volume.

9.13 Rewrite Program 71 (page 294) so that you normalize the first second of a sound, then slowly decrease the sound in steps of 1/5 for each following second. (How many samples are in a second? getSamplingRate() is the number of samples per second for the given sound.)

9.14 Try rewriting Program 71 (page 294) so that you have a linear increase in volume to halfway through the sound, then linearly decrease the volume down to zero in the second half.

9.15 I think that if we're going to say "We the UNITED people" in the splice method (Program 74 (page 300)), the "UNITED" should be emphasized—it should be really loud. Change the method so that the word "united" is maximally loud (normalized) in the phrase "united people."

9.16 Try using a stopwatch to time the execution of the methods in this chapter. Time from hitting return on the command until the next prompt appears. What is the relationship between execution time and the length of the sound? Is it a linear relationship, i.e., longer sounds take longer to process and shorter sounds take less time to process? Or is it something else? Compare the individual methods. Does normalizing a sound take longer than raising (or lowering) the amplitude a constant amount? How much longer? Does it matter if the sound is longer or shorter?

9.17 Make an audio collage. Make it at least five seconds long, and include at least two different sounds (e.g., sounds from different files). Make a copy of one of those different sounds and modify it using any of the techniques described in this chapter (e.g., mirroring, splicing, and volume manipulations). Splice together the original two sounds and the modified sound to make the complete collage.

9.18 Compose a sentence that no one ever said, by combining words from other sounds into a grammatically correct new sound. Write a method named `audio-Sentence` to generate a sentence out of individual words. Use at least three words in your sentence! You can use the words in the `mediasources` folder on your CD or record your own words. Be sure to include a tenth (1/10) of a second pause between the words. (Hint 1: Remember that zeroes for the sample values generate silence or pause.) (Hint 2: Remember that the sampling rate is the number of samples per second. From there, you should be able to figure out how many samples need to set to zero to generate a 1/10 of a second pause.) Be sure to access your sounds in your Media Folder using `getMediaPath` so that it will work for users of your program as long as they first execute `setMediaPath`.

9.19 Write a method called `erasePart` to set all the samples in the 2nd second of "thisisatest.wav" to 0's—essentially making the 2nd second go silent. (Hint: Remember that `getSamplingRate()` tells you the number of samples in a single second in a sound.) Play and return the partially erased sound.

9.20 We've seen a method that reverses a sound and a method that can process samples by index number. Write a method called `reverseLastHalf` that reverses just the second half of the current sound. For example, if the sound said "MarkBark" the returned sound should say "MarkkraB."

9.21 Write a method similar to Program 79 (page 306) that mirrors from back to front.

TO DIG DEEPER

When you are using the MediaTools application, you are actually using a programming language called *Squeak*, developed initially and primarily by Alan Kay, Dan Ingalls, Ted Kaehler, John Maloney, and Scott Wallace [19]. Squeak is now open-source,[1] and is an excellent cross-platform multimedia tool. There is a book *Squeak: Object-Oriented Design with Multimedia Applications* that introduces Squeak, including its sound capabilities [14], and another book on *Squeak, Open Personal Computing for Multimedia* [16] that includes a chapter on *Siren*, a variation of Squeak by Stephen Pope especially designed for computer music exploration and composition.

---

[1]http://www.squeak.org

10 Making Sounds by Combining Pieces

Chapter Learning Objectives

The media learning goals for this chapter are:

- To blend sounds so that one fades into another.
- To create echoes.
- To change the frequency (pitch) of a sound.
- To create sounds that don't exist in nature by composing more basic sounds (sine waves).
- To choose between sound formats such as MIDI and MP3 for different purposes.

The computer science goals for this chapter are:

- To explain blending as an algorithm that crosses media boundaries.
- To build programs from multiple methods.
- To introduce class (static) methods.
- To introduce private (helper) methods.

10.1   COMPOSING SOUNDS THROUGH ADDITION

Creating sounds digitally that didn't exist previously is lots of fun. Rather than simply moving around samples or multiplying them, we actually change their values—add waves together. The result are sounds that never existed until you made them.

In physics, adding sounds involves issues of canceling waves out and enforcing other factors. In math, it's about matrices. In computer science, it's the easiest process in the world! Let's say that you've got a sound, source, that you want to add in to the current Sound object. *Simply add the values at the same index numbers!* That's it!

```
// loop through all of the source
for (int i = 0; i < source.getLength(); i++) {

    // add source sound value and this sound value
    value = this.getSampleValueAt(i) +
            source.getSampleValueAt(i);

    // set the value in this sound to the new value
    this.setSampleValueAt(i,value);
}
```

10.2   BLENDING SOUNDS

In this example, we take two sounds—someone saying "Aah!" and a bassoon instrument sound of C in the fourth octave—and *blend* the two sounds. The way we do

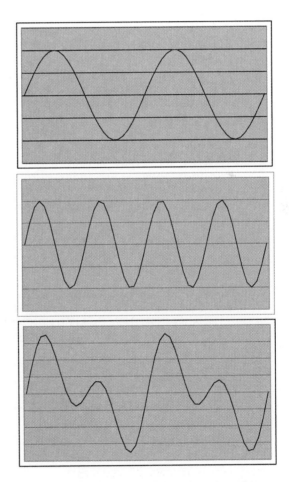

FIGURE 10.1
The top and middle waves are added together to create the bottom wave.

this is to first copy part of the first sound, "Aah!", then copy 50% of each sound, and then copy the rest of the second sound (Figure 10.1). This is very much like mixing 50% of each sound at a mixing board. It's also very much like the way that we blended pictures in Program 28 (page 156)!

Program 80: Blending Two Sounds

```
/**
 * Method to overlap or blend two sounds.  Start
 * by copying the first 20,000 samples from sound1 into
 * the current sound then copy the sum of half of sound1
 * and half of sound2 for the next 20,000 samples and
 * end with the next 20,000 samples from sound2.
 */
public void blendSounds() {
  Sound sound1 =
    new Sound(FileChooser.getMediaPath("aah.wav"));
  Sound sound2 =
    new Sound(FileChooser.getMediaPath("bassoon-c4.wav"));
  int value = 0;

  // copy the first 20,000 samples from sound1 into target
  for (int index=0; index < 20000; index++)
    this.setSampleValueAt(index,
                          sound1.getSampleValueAt(index));

  // copy the next 20,000 samples from sound1 and blend that
  // with the first 20,000 samples from sound2
  for (int index = 0; index < 20000; index++)
  {
    value = (int) ((sound1.getSampleValueAt(index + 20000) *
                    0.5) +
                   (sound2.getSampleValueAt(index) * 0.5));
    this.setSampleValueAt(index + 20000,value);
  }

  // copy the next 20,000 samples from sound2 into the target
  for (int index=20000; index < 40000; index++)
    this.setSampleValueAt(index + 20000,
                          sound2.getSampleValueAt(index));
}
```

Common Bug: Set the Media Folder First!

If you're going to write code that uses `FileChooser.getMediaPath(String baseName)`, you'll need to execute `FileChooser.setMediaPath(String directory)` first.

Like blending the picture (Program 28 (page 156)), there are loops in this method for each segment of the blended sound.

- We start by creating the `sound1` and `sound2` sounds for blending. The length of these sounds is over 40,000 samples, but we're just going to use the first 40,000 as an example.

- In the first loop, we simply get 20,000 samples from `sound1` and copy them into the current sound `this`. Notice that we're not using a separate index variable for the `target`—instead, we're using the same index variable, `index`, for both sounds since we are copying from 0 to 19,999 from `sound1` into 0 to 19,999 in the current sound.

- In the next loop, we copy 20,000 samples from both `sound1` and `sound2` blended into the current sound. We get a sample from each of `sound1` and `sound2`, then multiply each by 0.5 and add the results together. The result is a sample that represents 50% of each. Notice that we are using one index variable here as well but adding 20,000 to the value of that for determining the index of `sound1` and the current sound. So we blend values from `sound1` starting at index 20,000 and from `sound2` starting at index 0 and the blended values go into the current sound starting at index 20,000.

- Finally, we copy another 20,000 samples from `sound2`. The result sounds like "Aah," first, then half of each, then just a bassoon note. Notice that we start the index at 20,000 for the next place to copy from `sound2`. This means we need to add 20,000 to that value for the index in the current sound (since there are already 40,000 values in the current sound).

To create the blended sound, first create a sound using the file that has 3 seconds of silence. Then explore it to see what it looks like before the blending (Figure 10.2). Next, blend the two sounds into the silent sound. Finally, explore the new sound.

```
> String fileName = FileChooser.getMediaPath("sec3silence.wav");
> Sound target = new Sound(fileName);
> target.explore();
> target.blendSounds();
> target.explore();
```

10.3   CREATING AN ECHO

Creating an echo effect is similar to the splicing method (Program 74 (page 300)) that we saw in the last chapter, but involves actually creating sounds that didn't exist before. We do that by actually *adding* wave forms. What we're doing here is adding samples from a `delay` number of samples away into the sound, but multiplied by 0.6 so that they're fainter.

Program 81: Make a Sound and a Single Echo of It

```
/**
 * Method to add an echo to a sound
 * @param delay the number of samples before the echo starts
 */
```

```java
public void echo(int delay)
{
  // make a copy of the original sound
  Sound s = new Sound(this.getFileName());
  int value = 0;

  // loop from delay to end of sound
  for (int i = delay; i < this.getLength(); i++)
  {

    /* get the value back by delay samples from the
     * copy of the sound and make it fainter
     */
    value = (int) (s.getSampleValueAt(i-delay) * 0.6);

    /* set the value at the current index to the sum
     * of the current value and the echo
     */
    this.setSampleValueAt(i,
                          this.getSampleValueAt(i) +
                          value);
  }
}
```

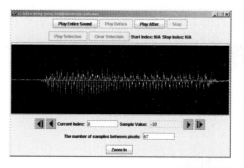
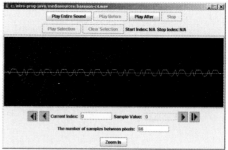
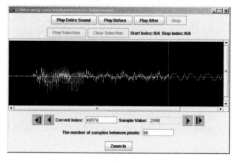

FIGURE 10.2

The original "ahh" sound, the original bassoon note, and the blended sound.

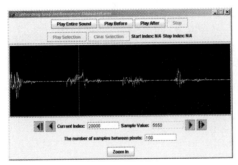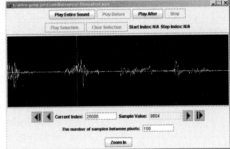

FIGURE 10.3
The original "This is a test" sound (left), and the sound with an echo (right).

How it Works

The echo method takes a delay: the number of samples before the echo starts. Try this with different amounts of delay. With low values of delay, the echo will sound more like *vibrato*. Higher values (try 10,000 or 20,000) will give you a real echo.

- This method creates a copy of the current sound s. This is where we'll get the original, unadulterated samples for creating the echo. (You could try this without creating a copy to get some interesting layered echoes.)
- Next we declare a variable value to hold a value of a sample.
- Our loop starts with the index i being set to the passed delay and continues through the rest of the sound.
- The echoed sound is delay samples back, so i-delay is the sample we need. We multiply it by 0.6 to make it softer in volume.
- We then add the echoed sample to the current sample at i and set it in the current Sound object.

Try this method on sounds with words in them (Figure 10.3).

```
> String fileName = FileChooser.getMediaPath("thisisatest.wav");
> Sound sound = new Sound(fileName);
> sound.explore();
> sound.echo(20000);
> sound.explore();
```

10.3.1   Creating Multiple Echoes

This method actually lets you set the number of echoes that you get. You can generate some amazing effects in this way.

Program 82: Creating Multiple Echoes

```
/**
 * Method to create multiple echoes of the current sound
 * @param delay the number of samples before the echo starts
```

```
 * @param numEchoes the number of echoes desired
 * @return a new sound with the echoes in it
 */
public Sound echo(int delay, int numEchoes)
{
  int soundLength = this.getLength();
  Sound echoSound = new Sound(numEchoes * delay + soundLength);
  int value = 0;
  int echoIndex = 0;
  int echoValue = 0;
  double echoAmplitude = 1; // to start

  // copy the original sound
  echoSound.splice(this,0,soundLength,0);

  /* loop starting with 1 to create the first echo at the
   * right place and end when = the number of echoes
   */
  for (int echoCount = 1; echoCount <= numEchoes; echoCount++)
  {
    // decrease the volume (amplitude) of the echo
    echoAmplitude = echoAmplitude * 0.6;

    // echo the whole sound
    for (int i = 0; i < soundLength; i++)
    {
      echoIndex = i + (delay * echoCount);
      echoValue = (int) (this.getSampleValueAt(i) *
                         echoAmplitude);
      echoSound.setSampleValueAt(echoIndex,echoValue +
                 echoSound.getSampleValueAt(echoIndex));
    }
  }
  return echoSound;
}
```

To try out this method, create a Sound object, and then invoke this method on the Sound object. Be sure to save the resulting Sound.

```
> Sound sound = new Sound(FileChooser.getMediaPath("croak.wav"));
> Sound echo = sound.echo(8000,5);
> echo.play();
```

10.4 HOW SAMPLING KEYBOARDS WORK

Sampling keyboards are keyboards that use recordings of sounds (e.g., pianos, harps, trumpets) to create music by playing those sound recordings in the desired pitch. Modern music and sound keyboards (and synthesizers) allow musicians to record sounds in their daily lives and turn them into "instruments" by shifting the frequency of the original sounds. How do the synthesizers do it? It's not really complicated. The interesting part is that it allows you to use any sound you want as an instrument.

Sampling keyboards use huge amounts of memory to record lots of different instruments at different pitches. When you press a key on the keyboard, the recording *closest* in pitch to the note you pressed is selected, then the recording is shifted to exactly the pitch you requested.

This first method works by creating a sound that *skips* every other sample. You read that right—after being so careful to treat all the samples the same, we're now going to skip half of them! In the mediasources directory, you'll find a sound named c4.wav. This is the note C, in the fourth octave of a piano, played for one second. It makes a good sound to experiment with, though really, any sound will work.

Program 83: Double the Frequency of a Sound

```
/**
 * Method to double the frequency of a sound by taking
 * every second sample.  The result will be a higher
 * sound.
 */
public void doubleFreq()
{
  // make a copy of the original sound
  Sound s = new Sound(this.getFileName());

  /* loop through the sound and increment target index
   * by one but source index by 2 and set target value
   * to the copy of the original sound
   */
  for (int sourceIndex=0, targetIndex = 0;
       sourceIndex < this.getLength();
       sourceIndex=sourceIndex+2, targetIndex++)
     this.setSampleValueAt(targetIndex,
                           s.getSampleValueAt(sourceIndex));

  // clear out the rest of this sound
  for (int i = this.getLength() / 2;
       i < this.getLength();
       i++)
     this.setSampleValueAt(i,0);

}
```

Here's how to use the double frequency method (Figure 10.4).

```
> Sound s = new Sound(FileChooser.getMediaPath("c4.wav"));
> s.explore();
> s.doubleFreq();
> s.explore();
```

This method starts like the other ones in this chapter by making a copy of the sound. Then it loops through the sound but it increments the index that keeps the

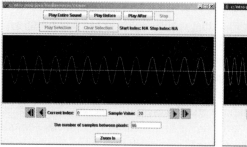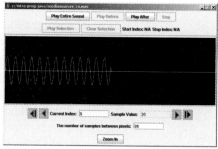

FIGURE 10.4
The original sound (left), and the sound with the frequency doubled (right).

position in the source sound `sourceIndex` by 2 and the index that keeps the position in the target sound `targetIndex` by 1. This will copy the sample value at `sourceIndex` 0 to `targetIndex` 0, then `sourceIndex` 2 to `targetIndex` 1, then `sourceIndex` 4 to `targetIndex` 2, and so on. Since the resulting sound will be half as long as it was the second loop just fills the rest of the sound with zeroes.

Try it![1] You'll see that the sound really does double in frequency with the result that it sounds higher!

How did that happen? It's not really all that complicated. Think of it like this: the frequency of the original sound is really the number of cycles that pass by in a certain amount of time. If you skip every other sample, the new sound has just as many cycles, but has them in half the amount of time!

Now let's try the other way: Let's take every sample twice! What happens then?

To do this, we need to use a cast to "throw away" the fractional part of a floating point number using a cast to integer. To cast a floating point number to an integer number, use `(int)`.

```
> System.out.println((int)0.5)
0
> System.out.println((int)1.5)
1
```

Here's the method that *halves* the frequency. The for loop moves the value of the variable `targetIndex` along the length of the sound. The `sourceIndex` is now being incremented—but only by 0.5! The effect is that we'll take every sample in the source twice. The `sourceIndex` will be 0.0, 0.5, 1.0, 1.5, and so on, but because we're using the `(int)` of that value, we'll take samples 0, 0, 1, 1, and so on.

Program 84: Half the Frequency

```
/**
 * Method to halve the frequency of a sound by taking
 * each sample twice.  The result will be a lower
 * sound.
 */
```

[1] You are now trying this out as you read, aren't you?

```
public void halveFreq()
{
  // make a copy of the original sound
  Sound s = new Sound(this.getFileName());

  /* loop through the sound and increment target index
   * by one but source index by 0.5 and set target value
   * to the copy of the original sound
   */
  for (double sourceIndex=0, targetIndex = 0;
       targetIndex < this.getLength();
       sourceIndex=sourceIndex+0.5, targetIndex++)
    this.setSampleValueAt((int) targetIndex,
            s.getSampleValueAt((int) sourceIndex));

}
```

■

This method first creates a copy of the sound. Then it loops through the sound incrementing the sourceIndex by 0.5 and the targetIndex by 1. We get a sample value from source at the *integer* value using ((int)) of the sourceIndex. We set the target at the *integer* value using ((int)) of the targetIndex to the sample value that we got from the copy of the sound. We then add 0.5 to the sourceIndex. This means that the sourceIndex, the first few times through the loop, will take on the values 0.0, 0.5, 1.0, 1.5, 2.0, 2.5, and so on. But the integer part of this sequence is 0, 0, 1, 1, 2, 2, and so on. The result is that we take each sample from the source sound *twice*.

Think about what we're doing here. Imagine that the 0.5 above were actually 0.75 or 3.0. Would this work? The for loop would have to change, but essentially the idea is the same in all these cases. We are *sampling* the source data to create the target data. Using a *sample index* of 0.5 slows down the sound and halves the frequency. A sample index larger than one speeds up the sound and increases the frequency.

Let's try to generalize this sampling with the method below. (Note that this one *won't* work right!)

Program 85: Changing the Frequency of a Sound: BROKEN!

```
/**
 * Method to change the frequency of a sound by the
 * passed factor
 * @param factor the amount to increment the source
 * index by.  A number greater than 1 will increase the
 * frequency and make the sound higher
 * while a number less than one will decrease the
 * frequency and make the sound lower.
 */
public void changeFreq(double factor)
{
    // make a copy of the original sound
```

```
Sound s = new Sound(this.getFileName());

/* loop through the sound and increment the target index
 * by one but increment the source index by the factor
 */
for (double sourceIndex=0, targetIndex = 0;
     targetIndex < this.getLength();
     sourceIndex=sourceIndex+factor, targetIndex++)
{
  this.setSampleValueAt((int) targetIndex,
          s.getSampleValueAt((int) sourceIndex));
}

}
```

■

Here's how we could use this:

```
> s = new Sound(FileChooser.getMediaPath("c4.wav"));
> s.explore();
> s.changeFreq(0.75);
> s.explore();
```

That will work really well! But what if the factor for sampling is *MORE* than 1.0?

```
> String fileName = FileChooser.getMediaPath("Elliot-hello.wav");
> Sound hello = new Sound(fileName);
> hello.changeFreq(1.5);
You are trying to access the sample at index: 54759, but the last
valid index is at 54757.
```

Why? What's happening? Here's how you could see it: Print out the sourceIndex just before the setSampleValueAt. You'd see that the sourceIndex becomes *larger* than the source sound! Of course, that makes sense. If each time through the loop, we increment the targetIndex by 1, but we're incrementing the sourceIndex by *more than one*, we'll get past the end of the source sound before we reach the end of the target sound. But how do we avoid it?

Here's what we want to happen: If the sourceIndex ever gets equal to or larger than the length of the source, we want to reset the sourceIndex—probably back to 0. The key word here is *if*.

As you may recall from Section 6.1, we can tell Java to make decisions based on a *test*. We use an if statement to execute a group of statements if a test evaluates to true. In this case, the test is sourceIndex >= s.getLength(). We can test on <, >, == (for equality), != (for inequality, not-equals) and even <= and >=. An if statement can take a block of statements, just as while and for do. The block defines the statements to execute if the *test* in the if statement is true. In this case, our block is simply sourceIndex = 0;. The block of statements is defined inside of an open curly brace '{' and a close curly brace '}'. If you just have one statement that you want to execute, it doesn't *have* to be in a block, but it is better to keep it in a block.

The method below generalizes this and allows you to specify how much to shift the samples by.

Program 86: Changing the Frequency of a Sound

```
/**
 * Method to change the frequency of a sound
 * by the passed factor
 * @param factor the amount to increment the source
 * index by.  A number greater than 1 will increase the
 * frequency and make the sound higher
 * while a number less than one will decrease the frequency
 * and make the sound lower.
 */
public void changeFreq2(double factor)
{
   // make a copy of the original sound
   Sound s = new Sound(this.getFileName());

   /* loop through the sound and increment the target index
    * by one but increment the source index by the factor
    */
   for (double sourceIndex=0, targetIndex = 0;
        targetIndex < this.getLength();
        sourceIndex=sourceIndex+factor, targetIndex++)
   {
     if (sourceIndex >= s.getLength())
     {
       sourceIndex = 0;
     }
     this.setSampleValueAt((int) targetIndex,
             s.getSampleValueAt((int) sourceIndex));
   }

}
```

■

We can actually set the factor so that we get whatever frequency we want. We call this factor the *sampling interval.* For a desired frequency f_0, the sampling interval should be:

$$samplingInterval = (sizeOfSourceSound)\frac{f_0}{samplingRate}$$

This is how a keyboard synthesizer works. It has recordings of pianos, voices, bells, drums, whatever. By *sampling* those sounds at different sampling intervals, it can shift the sound to the desired frequency.

The last method of this section plays a single sound at its original frequency, then at two times, three times, four times, and five times the frequency. We need to use blockingPlay to let one sound finish playing before the next one starts. Try it with play and you'll hear the sounds collide as they're generated faster than the computer can play them.

Program 87: Playing a Sound in a Range of Frequencies

```
/**
 * Method to play a sound 5 times and each time increase the
 * frequency.  It doesn't change the original sound.
 */
public void play5Freq()
{
  Sound s = null;

  // loop 5 times but start with 1 and end at 5
  for (int i = 1; i < 6; i++)
  {
    // reset the sound
    s = new Sound(this.getFileName());

    // change the frequency
    s.changeFreq(i);

    // play the sound
    s.blockingPlay();
  }
}
```

■

To use this method, try:

```
> Sound s = new Sound(FileChooser.getMediaPath("c4.wav"));
> s.play5Freq();
```

This method loops with the value of i starting at 1 and ending before it is 6. This will loop five times. Why start at 1 instead of 0? What would happen if we used a factor of 0 to change the frequency? We would end up with silence for the first sound.

10.4.1   Sampling as an Algorithm

You should recognize similarity between the halving recipe (method) Program 84 (page 320) and the recipe for scaling a picture up (larger) Program 31 (page 162). To halve the frequency, we take each sample twice by incrementing the source index by 0.5 and using the casting (int) to get the integer part of that. To make the picture larger, we take each pixel twice, by adding 0.5 to the source index variable and using the casting on that. These two methods are using the same *algorithm*. The details of pictures vs. sounds aren't critical. The point is that the same basic process is being used in each.

We have seen other algorithms that cross media boundaries. Obviously, our increasing red and increasing volume methods (and the decreasing versions) are essentially doing the same things. The way that we blend pictures or sounds is the same. We take the component color channels (pixels) or samples (sounds) and add them using percentages to determine the amount from each that we want in the final product. As long as the percentages total 100%, we'll get a reasonable output that reflects the input sounds or pictures at the correct percentages.

Identifying algorithms like these is useful for several reasons. If we understand the algorithm in general (e.g., when it's slow and when it's fast, what it works for and what it doesn't, what the limitations are), then the lessons learned apply in the specific picture or sound instances. The algorithms are also useful for designers to know. When you are designing a new program, you can keep in mind the algorithms that you know so that you can use them when they apply.

When we double or halve the sound frequency, we are also shrinking and doubling the length of the sound (respectively). You might want a target sound whose length is *exactly* the length of the sound, rather than have to clear out extra stuff from a longer sound. You can do that with new Sound(int lengthInSamples). new Sound(44000) returns a new empty sound of 44,000 samples.

10.5   ADDITIVE SYNTHESIS

Additive synthesis creates sounds by adding sine waves together. We saw earlier that it's really pretty easy to add sounds together. With additive synthesis, you can shape the waves yourselves, set their frequencies, and create "instruments" that never existed.

10.5.1   Making Sine Waves

Let's figure out how to produce a set of samples to generate a sound at a given frequency and amplitude.

From trigonometry, we know that if we take the sine of the radians from 0 to 2π, we'll get a circle. Spread that over time, and you get a sine wave. In other words, if you took values from 0 to 2π, computed the sine of each value, and graphed the computed values, you'd get a sine wave. From your math courses, you know that there's an infinity of numbers between 0 and 1. Computers don't handle infinity very well, so we'll actually only take *some* values between 0 to 2π.

To create the following graph, Mark filled 20 rows (a totally arbitrary number) of a spreadsheet with values from 0 and 2π (about 6.28). Mark added about 0.314 (6.28/20) to each preceding row. In the next column, he took the sine of each value in the first column, then graphed it.

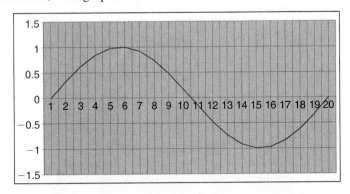

Let's say that we want to create a sound at a given frequency, say 440 Hz. This means that we have to fit an entire cycle like the above into 1/440 of a second. (440 cycles per second, means that each cycle fits into 1/440 second, or 0.00227 seconds.) Mark made the above picture using 20 values. Call it 20 *samples*. How many samples do we have to chop up the 440 Hz cycle into? That's the same question as: How many samples must go by in 0.00227 seconds? We know the sampling rate—that's the number of samples in one second. Let's say that it's 22,050 samples per second (our default sampling rate). Each sample is then (1/22,050) 0.0000453 seconds. How many samples fit into 0.00227? That's 0.00227/0.0000453, or about 50. What we just did here mathematically is:

$$interval \ = \ 1/frequency$$
$$samplesPerCycle \ = \ \frac{interval}{1/samplingRate} = (samplingRate)(interval)$$

Now let's spell this out in Java code. To get a waveform at a given frequency, say 440 Hz, we need 440 of these waves in a single second. Each one must fit into the interval of 1/*frequency*. The number of samples that needs to be produced during the interval is the sampling rate divided by the frequency, or interval $(1/f) *$ (*sampling rate*). Call that the *samplesPerCycle*.

At each entry of the sound *sampleIndex*, we want to:

- Get the fraction of *sampleIndex/samplesPerCycle*.
- Multiply that fraction by 2π. That's the number of radians we need. Take the *sin* of (*sampleIndex/samplesPerCycle*) $* 2\pi$.
- Multiply the result by the desired amplitude, and put that in the sample value at `sampleIndex`.

10.5.2   Creating Sounds Using Static Methods

All of the methods that we have written work with an *existing* object. But if the method we want to write this time *creates* the object, there won't be a current object to modify. How can we invoke this method if we don't have an object of the class to invoke it on? We can use a *class method*. A class method is also called a `static` method.

Class methods can be called using *ClassName.methodName(parameterList)*. Recall that when a class definition is compiled it creates a file (*ClassName*.class) that contains all the information in the class definition in a form that the computer can understand. When you use a class name for the first time in your code or in the interactions pane, Java looks for that file and loads the definition of that class. It also creates an object that represents that class.

We have been using new *Class(parameterList)* to create new objects of the class by asking that object that represents the class to create an object for us. Now we will use *ClassName.methodName(parameterList)* to ask the object that represents the class to create an object of that class and return it.

How do we make a method a class method? We add the keyword `static` to it, usually after the visibility (i.e., `public`, `private`). Now when you hear "static" you may think of noise on your radio or that something won't move. But in Java "static" means something that exists in the object that represents the class. So why not use "class" instead of "static"? The keyword `class` is used in Java to define new classes. But when you see the keyword `static` think `class`. So the keyword `static` in a method declaration tells you that the method is a "class" method.

To build sounds, there are some *silent* sounds in the media sources. Our sine wave generator will use the one second of silence sound to build a sine wave of one second. We'll provide an amplitude as input—that will be the *maximum* amplitude of the sound. (Since sine generates between −1 and 1, the range of amplitudes will be between −*amplitude* and *amplitude*.)

Program 88: Generate a Sine Wave at a Given Frequency and Amplitude

```java
/**
 * Method to create a one second sine wave sound with the
 * given frequency and maximum amplitude
 * @param freq the desired frequency
 * @param maxAmplitude the maximum amplitude
 * @return the new sound
 */
public static Sound createSineWave(int freq, int maxAmplitude)
{
  Sound s =
    new Sound(FileChooser.getMediaPath("sec1silence.wav"));
  double samplingRate = s.getSamplingRate();
  double rawValue = 0;
  int value = 0;
  double interval = 1.0 / freq; // length of cycle in seconds
  double samplesPerCycle = interval * samplingRate;
  double maxValue = 2 * Math.PI;

  // loop through the length of the sound
  for (int i = 0; i < s.getLength(); i++)
  {
    // calculate the value between -1 and 1
    rawValue = Math.sin((i / samplesPerCycle) * maxValue);

    // multiply by the desired max amplitude
    value = (int) (maxAmplitude * rawValue);

    // set the value at this index
    s.setSampleValueAt(i,value);
  }
  return s;
}
```

Notice that this method creates an object of the Sound class and returns it. In order to be able to refer to this Sound object again be sure to set a variable to refer to

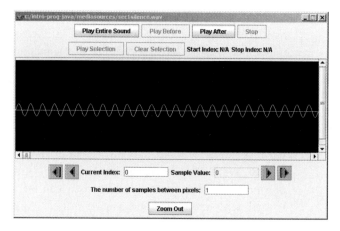

FIGURE 10.5
The sine wave with a frequency of 880 and a maximum amplitude of 4,000.

it. We can invoke any class method using *ClassName.methodName(parameterList)*.
Let's build a sine wave of 880 Hz at an amplitude of 4,000 (Figure 10.5).

```
> Sound s = Sound.createSineWave(880,4000);
> s.explore();
```

10.5.3   Adding Sine Waves Together

Now let's add sine waves together. As we said at the beginning of the chapter, that's
pretty easy: Just add the samples at the same indices together. Here's a method that
adds one sound into a second sound.

Program 89: Add Two Sounds Together

```java
/**
 * Method to add the passed sound to this sound
 * @param source the sound to combine with this one
 */
public void add(Sound source)
{
  int value = 0; // holder for new value

  // loop through all of the source
  for (int i = 0; i < source.getLength(); i++)
  {

    // add source sound value and this sound value
    value = this.getSampleValueAt(i) +
            source.getSampleValueAt(i);

    // set the value in this sound to the new value
    this.setSampleValueAt(i,value);
  }
}
```

How are we going to use this method to add together sine waves? We need both of them at once? Turns out that it's easy:

Let's add together 440 Hz, 880 Hz (twice 440), and 1,320 Hz (880 + 440), and we'll increase the amplitudes. We'll double the amplitude each time: 2,000, then 4,000, then 8,000. We'll add them all up into a sound called sound440. At the end, we generate a 440 Hz sound so that we can listen to them both and compare.

```
> Sound s440 = Sound.createSineWave(440,2000);
> Sound s880 = Sound.createSineWave(880,4000);
> Sound s1320 = Sound.createSineWave(1320,8000);
> s440.add(s880);
> s440.add(s1320);
> s440.explore();
> Sound orig440 = Sound.createSineWave(440,2000);
> orig440.explore();
```

Common Bug: Beware of Adding Amplitudes Past 32,767

When you add sounds, you add their amplitudes too. A maximum of 2,000 + 4,000 + 8,000 will never be greater than 32,767, but do worry about that. Remember what happened when the amplitude got too high in the last chapter.

10.5.4   Checking our Result

How do we know if we really got what we wanted? We can test our code by using the sound tools in the MediaTools. First we save out a sample wave (just 440 Hz) and the combined wave.

```
> orig440.write(FileChooser.getMediaPath("just440.wav"));
> s440.write(FileChooser.getMediaPath("combined440.wav"));
```

Open up each of these in turn in the sound editor. Right away, you'll notice that the wave forms look very different (Figure 10.6). That tells you that we did *something* to the sound, but what?

The way to really check your additive synthesis is with a fast fourier transform (FFT). Generate the FFT for each signal. You'll see that the 440 Hz signal has a single spike (Figure 10.7). That's what you'd expect—it's supposed to be a single sine wave. Now, look at the combined wave form's FFT (Figure 10.8). It's what it's supposed to be! You see three spikes there, and each succeeding one is double the height of the last one.

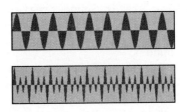

FIGURE 10.6
The raw 440 Hz signal on top, then the 440 + 880 + 1,320 Hz signal on the bottom.

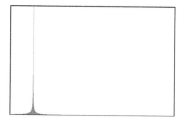

FIGURE 10.7
FFT of the 440 Hz sound.

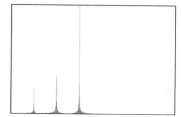

FIGURE 10.8
FFT of the combined sound.

10.5.5 Square Waves

We don't have to just add sine waves. We can also add *square waves*. These are literally square-shaped waves, moving between +1 and −1. The FFT will look very different, and the *sound* will be very different. It can actually be a much richer sound.

Try this method instead of the sine wave generator and see what you think. Note the use of an `if` statement to swap between the positive and negative sides of the wave halfway through a cycle.

Program 90: Square Wave Generator for Given Frequency and Amplitude

```
/**
 * Method to generate a 1 second sound with square waves
 * with the passed frequency and maximum amplitude.
 * @param freq the desired frequency
 * @param maxAmplitude the maximum amplitude
 * @return the created sound
 */
public static Sound createSquareWave(int freq,
                                     int maxAmplitude)
{
  Sound s =
    new Sound(FileChooser.getMediaPath("sec1silence.wav"));
  double samplingRate = s.getSamplingRate();
  int value = 0;
  double interval = 1.0 / freq; // length of cycle in seconds
  double samplesPerCycle = interval * samplingRate;
  double samplesPerHalfCycle = (int) (samplesPerCycle / 2);
```

```
      // loop through the length of the sound
    for (int soundIndex = 0, sampleCounter = 0;
          soundIndex < s.getLength();
          soundIndex++, sampleCounter++)
  {
    // check if in first half of cycle
    if (sampleCounter < samplesPerHalfCycle)
      value = maxAmplitude;
    else
    {
      // make the value negative
      value = maxAmplitude * -1;

      /* if the sample counter is greater than the
       * samples per cycle reset it to 0
       */
      if (sampleCounter > samplesPerCycle)
          sampleCounter = 0;
    }

    // set the value
    s.setSampleValueAt(soundIndex,value);
  }
  return s;
}
```

■

Use it like this:

```
> Sound sq440 = Sound.createSquareWave(440,4000);
> sq440.play();
> Sound sq880 = Sound.createSquareWave(880,8000);
> Sound sq1320 = Sound.createSquareWave(1320,10000);
> sq440.write(FileChooser.getMediaPath("square440.wav"));
> sq440.add(sq880);
> sq440.add(sq1320);
> sq440.play();
> sq440.write(FileChooser.getMediaPath("squareCombined.wav"));
```

You'll find that the waves (in the wave editor of MediaTools) really do look square (Figure 10.9), but the most amazing thing is all the additional spikes in FFT (Figure 10.10). Square waves really do result in a much more complex sound.

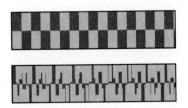

FIGURE 10.9
The 440 Hz square wave (top) and additive combination of square waves (bottom).

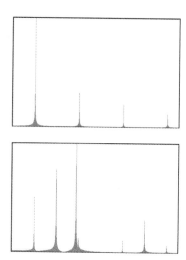

FIGURE 10.10
FFT's of the 440 Hz square wave (top) and additive combination of square waves (bottom).

10.5.6 Triangle Waves

Try triangle waves instead of square waves with this method.

Program 91: Generate Triangle Waves

```
/**
 * Method to create a one second triangle wave sound
 * with the given frequency and maximum amplitude
 * @param freq the desired frequency
 * @param maxAmplitude the maximum amplitude
 * @return the new sound
 */
public static Sound createTriangleWave(int freq,
                                        int maxAmplitude)
{
  Sound s =
    new Sound(FileChooser.getMediaPath("sec1silence.wav"));
  double samplingRate = s.getSamplingRate();
  int value = 0;
  double interval = 1.0 / freq; // length of cycle in seconds
  double samplesPerCycle = interval * samplingRate;
  int samplesPerQuarterCycle =
    (int) (samplesPerCycle / 4);
  int increment =
    (int) (maxAmplitude / samplesPerQuarterCycle);

  // loop through the length of the sound
  for (int soundIndex = 0;
       soundIndex < s.getLength();
       soundIndex++, value = value + increment)
  {
```

```
        // check if the value is equal to the desired max
        if (value >= maxAmplitude ||
            value <= maxAmplitude * -1)
        {
          increment = increment * -1;
          value = value + increment;
        }

        // set the sample value
        s.setSampleValueAt(soundIndex,value);

    }
    return s;
}
```

◼

Since this is a class method it can be invoked using

ClassName.methodName(parameterList).

```
> Sound triangle = Sound.createTriangleWave(440,4000);
> triangle.play();
> triangle.explore();
```

You have seen other class (static) methods. What about `Math.abs(int number)`, `FileChooser.pickAFile()`, and `ColorChooser.pickAColor()`? All of these are class methods which is why you can invoke them using

ClassName.methodName(parameterList).

Class methods are useful for general methods that don't require an object of the class to be created (`Math.abs`) or for methods that create objects of the class, like `createTriangleWave`.

10.6   MODERN MUSIC SYNTHESIS

Additive synthesis is how early music synthesizers worked. Nowadays, additive synthesis isn't too common because the sounds that it generates aren't natural sounding. Synthesizing from recorded sounds is quite common, but it isn't pure synthesis in the sense of creating sounds out of nothing.

The most common synthesis technique today is probably *FM synthesis* or *frequency modulation synthesis*. In FM synthesis, an oscillator (a programmed object that generates a regular series of outputs) controls (modulates) frequencies with other frequencies. The result is a richer sound, less tinny or computer sounding.

Another common technique is *subtractive synthesis*. In subtractive synthesis, out-and-out *noise* is used as the input, and then *filters* are applied to remove unwanted frequencies. The result is, again, a richer sound, though typically not as rich as FM synthesis.

Why would we want to create sounds or music with computers anyway? What's the point when there are lots of great sounds, music, and musicians in the world?

The point is that if you want to tell someone else *how* you got that sound, so that they could replicate the process, or even modify the sound in some way (perhaps making it better), a program is the way to do it. A program succinctly captures and communicates a process—how a sound or piece of music is generated.

10.6.1 MP3

Nowadays, the most common kind of audio file that you have on your computer is probably an MP3 (or perhaps MP4 or one of its related or descendant file types). MP3 files are sound (and video, in some cases) encodings based on the MPEG-3 standard. They are audio files, but compressed in special ways.

One way in which MP3 files are compressed is called *lossless compression*. As we know, there are techniques for storing data that use fewer bits. For example, we know that every sample is typically two bytes wide. What if we didn't store every sample, but instead stored the *difference* from the last sample to the current sample? The difference between samples is usually much smaller than 32,767 to −32,768—it might be +/−1,000. That takes fewer bits to store.

But MP3 also uses *lossy compression*. It actually throws away some of the sound information. For example, if there's a really soft sound immediately after or simultaneous with a really loud sound, you won't be able to hear the soft sound. A digital recording keeps all those frequencies. MP3 throws away the ones you can't actually hear.

WAV files are kind of compressed, but not as much as MP3, and they only use lossless techniques. Some WAV files use MP3 compression which makes them really MP3 files. MP3 files tend to be much smaller than the same sound in a WAV format. AIFF files are similar to WAV files.

10.6.2 MIDI

MIDI is the *Musical Instrument Digital Interface*. It's really a set of agreements between manufacturers of computer music devices (sequencers, synthesizers, drum machines, keyboards, etc.) for how their devices will work together. Using MIDI, you can control various synthesizers and drum machines from different keyboards.

MIDI doesn't really record what something sounds like, instead it encodes how it is played. Literally, MIDI encodes information like "Press the key down on synthesized instrument X at pitch Y" then later "Release the key Y on instrument X." The quality of MIDI sound depends entirely on the synthesizer, the device generating the synthesized instrument.

MIDI files tend to be very small. Instructions like "Play key #42 on track 7" are only some five bytes long. This makes MIDI attractive in comparison with large sound files. MIDI has been particularly popular for karaoke machines.

MIDI has an advantage over MP3 or WAV files in that it can specify a lot of music in very few bytes. But MIDI can't record any *particular* sound. For example, if you want to record a particular person's style of playing an instrument, or record *anyone* singing, you don't want to use MIDI. To capture actual sounds, you need to record the actual samples, so you'll need MP3 or WAV.

Most modern operating systems have pretty good synthesizers built into them. We can actually use them from Java. We have created a class MidiPlayer that has a method playNote that takes as input a note as a number and a duration (how long to play the sound) in milliseconds. The note numbers correspond to keys, not to frequencies. C in the first octave is 1, C# is 2. C in the fourth octave is 60, D is 62, and E is 64. See http://www.harmony-central.com/MIDI/Doc/table2.html for more information on the note numbers. If you don't specify what instrument you want to play the note on it will simulate a piano.

Here's a simple example of playing some MIDI notes from DrJava.

```
> MidiPlayer player = new MidiPlayer();
> player.playNote(62,250); // d quarter note
> player.playNote(60,500); // c half note
```

The 250 and 500 specify the number of milliseconds to play the note. If you want a measure to take one second (1,000 milliseconds), then a quarter note would be 250 milliseconds and a half note would be 500 milliseconds.

We can write a method to play a song. How about writing a method to play part of *Jingle Bells*? Here is a method that plays the first four measures from it. Put this in the MidiPlayer class (before the ending curly brace) and compile it.

Program 92: Playing a Song

```
/**
 * Method to play the first 4 measures of Jingle Bells
 * with each measure taking 1000 milliseconds (1 second)
 * this is 2/4 time
 */
public void playJingleBells4()
{
  // measure 1
  playNote(52,250); // e eighth note
  playNote(60,250); // c eighth note
  playNote(58,250); // b flat eighth note
  playNote(56,250); // a flat eighth note

  // measure 2
  playNote(52,500); // e quarter note
  rest(250);        // rest
  playNote(52,125); // e sixteenth note
  playNote(52,125); // e sixteenth note

  // measure 3
  playNote(52,500); // e eighth note
  playNote(60,250); // c eighth note
```

```
      playNote(58,250); // b flat eighth note
      playNote(56,250); // a flat eighth note

      // measure 4
      playNote(53,1000); // f half note
   }
```

This method only plays the first four measures of *Jingle Bells*. This may not sound like "Jingle Bells" to you since we are using the original version first published in 1,859 by James Pierpont.

To play this using the default piano sounding instrument do the following:

```
> MidiPlayer player = new MidiPlayer();
> player.playJingleBells4();
```

You can change the instrument that you want to use to play the notes using the method setInstrument(int num) where the num is a number from 0 to 127 that maps to an instrument. We have created constants for some of the instrument numbers as you can see at the top of the MidiPlayer class definition. To play the first four measures of *Jingle Bells* on a flute do the following:

```
> MidiPlayer player = new MidiPlayer();
> player.setInstrument(MidiPlayer.FLUTE);
> player.playJingleBells4();
```

10.6.3   Private Methods

Music often repeats. In *Jingle Bells* the first verse is played and then the refrain. Next the second verse is played, and then the refrain is played again. The first verse and second verse are a bit different, but many of the measures in the two verses are the same. If we want to write a method that plays the first two verses of *Jingle Bells* with each verse followed by the refrain, we could put all the measures in it for both verses and the refrains, but then it would be very long (67 measures). Another option is to pull out the measures in the refrain and make a method that just plays the refrain and then call that method from the one that plays *Jingle Bells*.

Does this new method that plays just the refrain need to be public? If we don't think any other class will need access to the new method we can make it private. Private methods can only be invoked from code in the class that they are declared in. You will get an error if you try to invoke a private method in code that is in another class. Private methods are also called *helper methods*.

To declare a method to be private, use the keyword private for the visibility. Remember that to declare a method you must specify:

visibility returnType methodName(parameterList)

The following method is a private method that will play the refrain of *Jingle Bells*.

Program 93: Playing the Refrain

```java
/**
 * Method to play refrain of Jingle Bells
 */
private void playJingleBellsRefrain()
{
  // measure 1
  playNote(60,250); // c eighth note
  playNote(60,250); // c eighth note
  playNote(60,500); // c quarter note

  // measure 2
  playNote(63,250); // e flat eighth note
  playNote(63,250); // e flat eighth note
  playNote(63,500); // e flat quarter note

  // measure 3
  playNote(60,250); // c eighth note
  playNote(60,250); // c eighth note
  playNote(65,375); // f dotted eighth note
  playNote(65,125); // f sixteenth note

  // measure 4
  playNote(64,1000); // e half note

  // measure 5
  playNote(65,250); // f eighth note
  playNote(61,250); // d flat eighth note
  playNote(56,250); // a flat eighth note
  playNote(64,250); // f eighth note

  // measure 6
  playNote(63,250); // e flat eighth note
  playNote(60,250); // c eighth note
  playNote(56,250); // a flat eighth note
  playNote(56,125); // a flat sixteenth note
  playNote(58,125); // b flat sixteenth note

  // measure 7
  playNote(60,250); // c eighth note
  playNote(58,250); // b flat eighth note
  playNote(56,250); // a flat eighth note
  playNote(58,250); // b flat eighth note

  // measure 8
  playNote(60,1000); // c half note

  // measure 9
  playNote(60,250); // c eighth note
  playNote(60,250); // c eighth note
  playNote(60,500); // c quarter note
```

```
// measure 10
playNote(63,250); // e flat eighth note
playNote(63,250); // e flat eighth note
playNote(63,500); // e flat quarter note

// measure 11
playNote(60,250); // c eighth note
playNote(60,250); // c eighth note
playNote(65,250); // f eighth note
playNote(65,250); // f eighth note

// measure 12
playNote(64,1000); // e half note

// measure 13
playNote(53,250); // f eighth note
playNote(61,250); // d flat eighth note
playNote(60,250); // c eighth note
playNote(58,250); // b flat eighth note

// measure 14
playNote(56,250); // a flat eighth note
playNote(63,250); // e flat eighth note
playNote(62,250); // d eighth note
playNote(63,125); // e flat sixteenth note
playNote(63,125); // e flat sixteenth note

// measure 16
playNote(65,250); // f eighth note
playNote(63,250); // e flat eighth note
playNote(61,250); // d flat eighth note
playNote(58,250); // b flat eighth note

// measure 17
playNote(56,500); // a flat quarter note
rest(500); // rest
}
```

■

Assume that we have written the methods that play the two verses as private methods. Here is a method that will play the first two verses of Jingle Bells with each verse followed by the refrain.

Program 94: Playing Jingle Bells

```
/**
 * Method to play Jingle Bells
 */
public void playJingleBells()
{
  // play verse 1
  playJingleBellsV1();
```

```
    // play refrain
    playJingleBellsRefrain();

    // play verse 2
    playJingleBellsV2();

    // play refrain
    playJingleBellsRefrain();
  }
```
■

The advantage to breaking methods into smaller reusable methods is that if there is a mistake in one of the smaller methods it is easier to find and fix. If we had created one very long method with all the measures in it, we probably would have copied and pasted the measures in the refrain. If we had to fix notes in the refrain, we would have to fix them in both copies of it. By pulling out repeated code, we have only one copy of it to fix and check for errors.

10.7   CONCEPTS SUMMARY

In this chapter we introduced class methods, private methods, and building methods from other methods.

10.7.1   Class Methods

Class methods are general methods like `Math.abs(int num)` or methods that create objects like `Sound.createTriangleWave(int freq, int maxAmplitude)`. Class methods do not work on object data! There is no implicit current object passed to a class method so you can't use the keyword `this`.

Class methods are defined with the keyword `static` on the method declaration: *visibility* `static` *returnType methodName(parameterList)*.

public static `Sound createTriangleWave(`**int** `freq,` **int** `maxAmplitude)`

You can invoke a class method using `ClassName.methodName(parameterList)`. To invoke the class method `createTriangleWave` on the class `Sound` and then save a reference to the new `Sound` object in a variable called `triangle` do the following:

```
> Sound triangle = Sound.createTriangleWave(440,4000);
```

If the method doesn't use object data, then it can be a class method. If a method does use object data, then it *should* be an object method.

10.7.2   Private Methods

Private methods can only be invoked from code in the same class that they are declared in. Use private methods to break down long public methods into smaller reusable parts.

To declare a method to be private use the `private` keyword for the visibility. Remember that to declare a method you can use *visibility* [static] *returnType methodName*(*parameterList*). The `static` keyword is optional and is used for declaring class methods.

private void playJingleBellsRefrain()

If you try to access a private method from code outside the class the method is defined in, you will get an error.

```
> MidiPlayer player = new MidiPlayer();
> player.playJingleBellsRefrain();
java.lang.IllegalAccessException: Class
koala.dynamicjava.interpreter.EvaluationVisitor can not access a
member of class MidiPlayer with modifiers "private"
    at sun.reflect.Reflection.ensureMemberAccess(Reflection.java:57)
    at java.lang.reflect.Method.invoke(Method.java:317)
```

10.7.3 Build a Program from Multiple Methods

You can build a program (method) from several methods. If you want to play a whole song like *Jingle Bells*, you can break it into smaller reusable methods.

```
/**
 * Method to play Jingle Bells
 */
public void playJingleBells()
{
  // play verse 1
  playJingleBellsV1();

  // play refrain
  playJingleBellsRefrain();

  // play verse 2
  playJingleBellsV2();

  // play refrain
  playJingleBellsRefrain();
}
```

Long methods are hard to read and understand. Try to break down methods into smaller parts.

PROBLEMS

10.1 What are each of the following:

- MIDI
- MP3
- A class method
- Sound pitch

- A static method

- Private visibility

10.2 When should you make a method `private`? Should you ever change a `private` method to a `public` method? Should you ever change a `public` method to a `private` one?

10.3 When should you make a method `static`? Can `static` methods access object data?

10.4 Write a method to triple the frequency of a sound. Use Program 83 (page 319) as a starting point.

10.5 Write a method to quadruple the frequency of a sound. Use Program 83 (page 319) as a starting point.

10.6 Write a method to play a sound with the frequency changed 10 times. Use Program 87 (page 324) as a starting point.

10.7 Write a method that will play half of one sound, and then the second half of the first sound added to the first half of another sound, and then the last half of the second sound. Use Program 80 (page 314) as a starting point.

10.8 Write a method that will blend three sounds. Start with one sound for 20,000 samples, then blend the first and second sounds for 20,000 samples, then the second and third sounds for 20,000 samples, and then the third sound for 20,000 samples. Use Program 80 (page 314) as a starting point.

10.9 Create a method that will create a pyramid shaped sound wave. Use Program 91 (page 332) as a starting point.

10.10 Rewrite the echo method (Program 81 (page 315)) to generate *two* echoes back, each `delay` samples previous. Hint: Start your index loop at `2*delay + 1`, then access one echo sample at `index-delay` and another at `index - 2*delay`.

10.11 How long is a sound compared to the original when it's been frequency doubled (Program 83 (page 319))?

10.12 How long is a sound compared to the original if you increment the sourceIndex by 3 each time through the loop in Program 83 (page 319)?

10.13 Hip-hop DJ's move turntables so that sections of sound are moved forward and backward quickly. Try combining backward play (Program 78 (page 305)) and frequency shifting (Program 83 (page 319)) to get the same effect. Play a second of a sound quickly forward, then quickly backward, two or three times. (You might have to move faster than just double the speed.)

10.14 Consider changing the `if` block in the frequency shift method (Program 86 (page 323)) to `sourceIndex = sourceIndex - getLength(source)`. What's the difference from just setting the `sourceIndex` to 1? Is this better or worse? Why?

10.15 If you use the shifting method (Program 86 (page 323)) with a factor of 2.0 or 3.0, you'll get the sound repeated or even triplicated. Why? Can you fix it? Write `shiftDur` that takes a number of samples (or even seconds) to play the sound.

10.16 Change the `shift` method in Program 86 (page 323) to `shiftFreq` which takes a frequency instead of a factor, then plays the given sound at the desired frequency.

10.17 Using the sound tools, figure out the characteristic pattern of different instruments. For example, pianos tend to have a pattern the opposite of what we created—the amplitudes *decrease* as we get to higher sine waves. Try creating a variety of patterns and see how they sound and how they look.

10.18 When musicians work with additive synthesis, they will often wrap *envelopes* around the sounds, and even around each added sine wave. An envelope *changes* the amplitude over time: It might start out small, then grow (rapidly or slowly), then hold at a certain value during the sound, and then drop before the sound ends. That kind of pattern is sometimes called the *attack-sustain-decay (ASD) envelope*. Pianos tend to attack quickly then decay quickly. Flutes tend to attack slowly and sustain as long as you want. Try implementing that for the sine and square wave generators.

10.19 Write a method to play a simple song like *Jingle Bells*. The song should have at least one repeating part. Make sure that you create a private method for the repeating part.

10.20 Create a static method of the `Picture` class which will create and return a `Picture` object from a passed file name. Is this better or worse than using a constructor that takes a file name?

TO DIG DEEPER

Good books on computer music will talk a lot about creating sounds from scratch like in this chapter. One of Mark's favorites for understandability is *Computer Music: Synthesis, Composition, and Performance* by Dodge and Jerse [8]. The bible of computer music is Curtis Roads's massive *The Computer Music Tutorial* [24].

One of the most powerful tools for playing with this level of computer music is *CSound*. It's a software music synthesis system, free, and totally cross-platform. The book by Richard Boulanger [5] has everything you need for playing with CSound.

jMusic is a free programming library written for musicians in Java (see `http://jmusic.ci.qut.edu.au/jmtutorial/t1.html`). It allows you to compose music. It can also import and export MIDI and audio files.

Chapter Learning Objectives

The computer science goals for this chapter are:

- To define a class including the fields, constructors, and methods.
- To override an inherited method.
- To start using a debugger.
- To overload constructors.
- To create, initialize, access, and process an array.
- To create accessor and modifier methods.
- To introduce runtime exceptions.
- To create a main method.
- To create Javadoc comments.
- To introduce dynamic binding.

In object-oriented programming the focus is on *objects*. We identify the objects that we will need to accomplish a task. We determine a type for those objects (classify them) and write a class definition for each type. The class definition contains information on the data for each object (the fields), the different ways to initialize the data for each new object (the constructors), and the things objects will need to

343

know how to do (the methods). Up to now we have only written methods, but now we will write entire classes. Each class will have fields, constructors, and methods.

11.1   IDENTIFYING THE OBJECTS AND FIELDS

Say that we want to write a program to track the grades of students. One way to start identifying the classes that we will need is to underline the nouns in the problem description. If we do this we get grade and student. Which of these should be a class, and which should be a field?

To decide whether a noun needs to be a class or a field, determine whether it has more than one piece of data associated with it. A student should have a name and some grades. A student has more than one piece of data associated with it. So student should be a class. Nouns that have other nouns associated with them are classes.

What about name? Well, a name can be represented by a string and it belongs to a student, so it will be a field of a Student class. What about grade? Well, a grade can be represented by a number and it also belongs to a student, so it too will be a field of a Student class. Simple data that can be represented by numbers or strings are usually fields. To determine which class the field belongs to, ask who owns the data, or who should know the data. A student should know her name and her grades.

Making it Work Tip: Class Names should be Singular

Class names should be singular, not plural. We called this the Student class, not the Students class. We can create many Student objects from this Student class. ∎

11.2   DEFINING A CLASS

The computer doesn't know what we mean by a student, so we need to define it for the computer. We need to specify the name of the class, the data that objects of the class will have, how to initialize each object's data when a new object of the class is created, and what methods the object will know how to do. We do this by creating a class definition. A class definition for a Student class looks like this:

```
public class Student
{
}
```

We could also write this as:

```
public class Student {
}
```

This declares a public class called Student. Public classes can be used by all other classes. By convention, class names start with an uppercase letter and the first letter of each additional word is uppercase. Notice the curly braces. They enclose a block of code that is associated with this class. All fields, constructors, and methods should be inside the open '{' and close '}' curly braces for the class. We also indent the code inside the curly braces to make clear that the code is *inside* the class definition. This class must be saved in a file called Student.java.

Debugging Tip: Naming Class Files

Each class that you define is usually saved in a separate file. The name of the file *must* match the name of the class followed by the extension ".java". So a class named Student must be defined in a file Student.java. A class named Turtle must be defined in a file Turtle.java not turtle.java or TurTLE.java. Case is important in Java! ∎

Create a new class in DrJava by clicking on the New button. This will create a blank area in the definitions pane. Type your class definition there. When you are ready, you can save it to a file by clicking on the Save button. Use the directory chooser to pick where to save the file and give it the same name as the class name. When you have saved the file, you will see Student in the file pane (Figure 11.1).

11.2.1 Defining Fields

Next, we want to add the fields that each student object will have. Each student should have a name and some grades. We next need to decide what *type* to use for each of these. A name can be represented by a String object. What type should we use for the grades? Let's say that there will be at most five grades and they can have a decimal point in them. We could name these grade1, grade2, grade3, and so on, but it is easier to store them in an array. Remember that you can declare a variable that will refer to an array object using:

type[] *name*;

or

type name[];

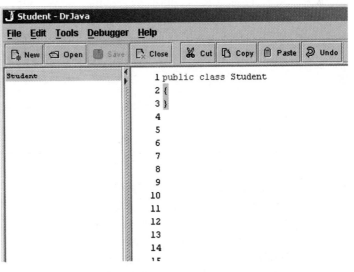

FIGURE 11.1
DrJava with the class definition for Student.

Debugging Tip: Use Square Brackets with Arrays

Be careful not to use curly braces '{}' in place of the square brackets '[]' when you declare an array!

We declare fields by specifying the visibility, type, and name of the field.

visibility type name;

private String name;

We can also specify an initial value for the field as the result of some expression.

visibility type name = expression;

private String name = "Unknown";

The *visibility* for fields is usually private so that an object can control its own data. Would you like objects of other classes to directly access and change a Student object's data? You certainly wouldn't want this for your bank account! Objects are responsible for their data, and to be responsible they need to control who has direct access to their data. So you should nearly always make your fields private.

The *type* is a class name if the field is an object or one of the primitive types (int, double, boolean, etc). Remember that you can declare an array by adding '[]' after the type. You can have arrays of primitives or objects.

The *name* should be appropriate for what the field represents. The convention for field names is to start with a lowercase letter and uppercase the first letter of each additional word.

Fields are *automatically* initialized if no other initialization is specified in the declaration. The default is to initialize object references to null, numbers to 0, and boolean variables to false.

Let's add a field of type String for the name, and a field which is an array of type double for the grades to the Student class.

Program 95: A Student Class

```
public class Student
{

    ///////////// fields /////////////
    private String name;
    private double[] gradeArray;

}
```

We have now defined a class, Student, and when an object of that class is created it will have two fields in it: name and gradeArray. The Student object will also have a reference to the object that defines the class (an object of the class named

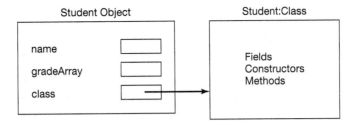

FIGURE 11.2
Showing a student object with a reference to its class.

Class—Figure 11.2). Thus, it will know that it is an object of the class Student. Every object has a reference to the class that created it. When an object is sent a message, it first looks in the class that created it for the method to execute. If it doesn't find it there, it will look in the parent class of the class that created it. If it doesn't find it there, it will look in the grandparent of the class that created it. It will keep looking up the ancestor tree until it finds the method to execute.

11.2.2 Inherited Methods

What would happen if we compile this and create a student object and print it out using System.out.println()?

```
> System.out.println(new Student());
Student@2bd3a
```

Well, it looks like a Student object was created, but what are the strange numbers and letters after the '@'? By default, when you print out an object you just get the class name followed by the unsigned hexadecimal representation of the *hash code* of the object. What does that mean? It is used to tell whether two objects are the same object or different objects, and may be based on the address of the object in memory.

```
> System.out.println(new Student());
Student@3ae941
> System.out.println(new Student());
Student@1e4853f
```

Notice that the hash codes for the two student objects above are different because two distinct Student objects were created.

```
> Student s1 = new Student();
> Student s2 = s1;
> System.out.println(s1);
Student@676437
> System.out.println(s2);
Student@676437
```

Notice that in this case we see the same hash code. Both s1 and s2 refer to the same Student object.

How did the Student objects know to print this out? Every class inherits this ability from the class Object. We didn't specify that the class Student inherits from the class Object, but if you don't specify a parent to inherit from in your class definition, your class **will** inherit from the class Object. When one class inherits from another, it gets *all* the methods and fields from that parent class. So, since the Object class has a toString() method in it that prints out the class name and the hash code, and the class Student inherits from the class Object, all Student objects also know how to do this.

You could have explicitly named the parent class for Student by using the extends keyword on the class definition followed by the name of the parent class. The parent class is the class the child class is inheriting from. So Object is the *parent class* of Student, and Student is a *child class* of Object. A parent class is also called a *superclass* or a *base class*. A child class is also called a *subclass* or a *derived class*.

```
public class Student extends Object
{
}
```

A class is only allowed to have one parent class, and if none is specified the default will be Object.

When you call the method System.out.println and pass it any object, it will call the method toString() on that object. When the toString() method is invoked on a Student object, first the runtime environment will look for that method in the Student class. If that class has a toString() method, it will be executed. Since the Student class doesn't have a toString method, it will next check the parent class of Student which is Object. The Object class does have a toString() method, so it will be executed. This method prints out the name of the class for the object and the hash code.

Because each object keeps a reference to its class, you can get its class using the getClass() method inherited from Object. This returns an object of the class named Class which represents the Student class. Each class also knows its parent class, and you can get that by using the method getSuperclass() (Figure 11.3).

```
> Student student1 = new Student();
> Class studentClass = student1.getClass();
> System.out.println(studentClass);
class Student
> Class parentClass = studentClass.getSuperclass();
> System.out.println(parentClass);
class java.lang.Object
```

11.2.3 Overriding Inherited Methods

To change what happens when we print out a Student object, we should create a method called toString() in our Student class. The method toString() returns a String object with information about the current object. Creating a method with the same *method signature* (method name and parameter list) as a parent method,

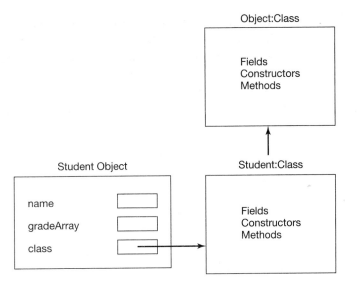

FIGURE 11.3
Showing a student object with a reference to its class and a reference from the class to its parent class.

will result in that method being called *instead of* the method defined in the parent. This is called *overriding* a method. This works because when a method is invoked on an object, the runtime will look for the method starting with the class of the current object. If the method isn't found there, it will next check the parent class of the current class. It will keep looking in the parent class of each class until it finds the method. We know that the method must be somewhere or else the code wouldn't have compiled.

Program 96: Student Class with a Method

```
public class Student
{

    /////////////// fields ///////////////
    private String name;
    private double[] gradeArray;

    /////////// methods ///////////////
    public String toString()
    {
        return "Student object named: " + this.name;
    }
}
```

If you create a student object and print it out you will get:

```
> System.out.println(new Student());
Student object named: null
```

Making it Work Tip: The this Keyword

The keyword this is how you can refer to the current object inside of a method. We want to print out the name of the current object so we use this.name to refer to that. We can leave off the this. and the compiler will add it for us.

11.2.4 Default Field Initialization

When an object is created, *all* of the fields of the object are initialized. Object fields that aren't explicitly initialized by assignment statements in the declaration will be null, number fields will be 0, and boolean fields will be false. In Figure 11.4, we see that the default for name is null since it is an object reference. This will also be the default value for the gradeArray since an array is also an object.

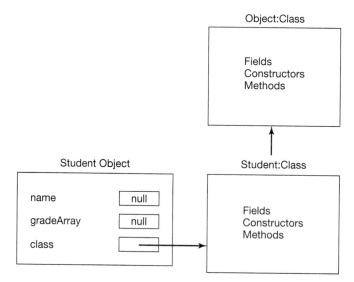

FIGURE 11.4
Showing a student object with the default initialization of the fields.

How do we set the values of the fields so that one student object is different from another? To do this we create *constructors* to initialize the values of the fields.

11.2.5 Declaring Constructors

A constructor is automatically called after a new object is created using the new operator. The constructor sets up the object, which usually means initializing the fields. You might say, "Wait a minute, we didn't define a constructor in the Student class, so how could one have been called?" If the compiler doesn't see *any* constructors it creates one that doesn't take any parameters and doesn't change the value of the fields. A constructor that doesn't take any parameters is called the *no argument constructor*. To create a constructor use:

visibility ClassName(paramList)

Notice that this looks like a method declaration except it doesn't have a return type and the name is the same name as the class. Constructors usually have `public` visibility.

Common Bug: Constructors don't have a Return Type!

If you add a return type to a constructor, the compiler will think that you are creating a method. Constructors do *not* have a return type (not even void)! Constructors *must* use the name of the class for the name before the parameter list.

■

Let's create a constructor for a `Student` object that takes the name to use for that `Student` object as a parameter.

Program 97: Student Class with a Constructor

```
public class Student
{

    /////////// fields ///////////////////
    private String name;
    private double[] gradeArray;

    /////////// constructors ///////////
    public Student(String theName)
    {
        this.name = theName;
    }

    ////////// methods //////////////
    public String toString()
    {
        return "Student object named: " + this.name;
    }
}
```

■

Now when we create a `Student` object, we can initialize the name.

```
> System.out.println(new Student("Amy Clark"));
Student object named: Amy Clark
```

What happens now if we try to use the no argument constructor?

```
> System.out.println(new Student());
java.lang.NoSuchMethodException: Student constructor
```

Notice that we got a compiler error (the error that you get may be somewhat different if you are using Java 5.0) that says that there is no constructor that doesn't take any arguments in the class `Student`. What happened to the no argument constructor? Well, since we now have at least one constructor in the class `Student`, the compiler will no longer add the no argument constructor for us. If we want one, we will need to add it ourselves.

Here we have added a no argument constructor that leaves all the field values alone:

Program 98: Student Class with Multiple Constructors

```java
public class Student
{

    /////////// fields //////////////////
    private String name;
    private double[] gradeArray;

    /////////// constructors //////////////
    public Student() {}

    public Student(String theName)
    {
      this.name = theName;
    }

    /////////// methods //////////////
    public String toString()
    {
      return "Student object named: " + this.name;
    }
}
```

11.2.6   Using a Debugger

How do you figure out what your program is doing (if it runs)? This is the process of *debugging*. Debugging is figuring out what your program is doing, how that differs from what you *want* it to be doing, and how to get it from where it is to where you need it to be.

One of the ways to trace what is happening in your programs is to add print statements using System.out.println(). It is often a good way to start debugging when you aren't certain what is happening. You can print out the value of variables at particular points in a method to see if you are getting what you expect. We could add a System.out.println(this.name) before we set the current object's name to the passed name in the constructor. This should show that it was initialized to null originally.

Computer Science Idea: Learn to Trace Code!

The most important thing that you can do when debugging your programs is to be able to trace your code. Think about your program the way that the computer does. Walk each line and figure out what it does.

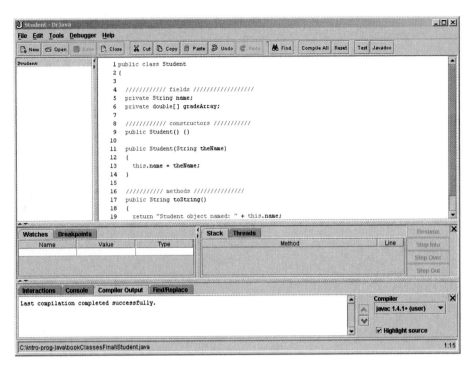

FIGURE 11.5
DrJava with debug mode turned on.

Another way to walk through your code with even more control is to use a *debugger*. A debugger is a tool that helps you walk through your program and see exactly what is happening. Most integrated development environments (IDEs) have a debugger with similar capabilities. A debugger can save you *hours* of frustration, so it is worth spending some time learning to use one!

To use the debugger in DrJava, you need to click on DEBUGGER in the menu and then check the DEBUG MODE checkbox. This will modify the way the DrJava windows look (Figure 11.5).

The debug mode adds some windows for debugging. Don't worry about these for now. The most common thing to do in a debugger is set *breakpoints*. This is a place that you want to stop execution so that you can see what is going on. Let's set a breakpoint in the constructor at the line that assigns the value of the name in the current object. Execution will stop *before* this line is executed.

To set a breakpoint in DrJava you can right-click on a line of code and then click on TOGGLE BREAKPOINT in the popup menu. You can also click on a line of code and then click on DEBUGGER and then on TOGGLE BREAKPOINT ON CURRENT LINE. In DrJava, once you set a breakpoint the line is highlighted in red (Figure 11.6), other IDEs may use another way to show a breakpoint. The key point is that *all* debuggers allow you to set breakpoints.

Now when you execute the following:

```
> System.out.println(new Student("Amy Clark"));
```

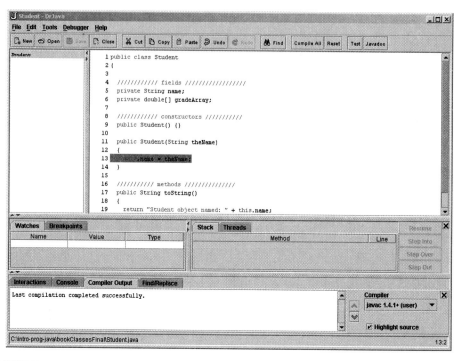

FIGURE 11.6
A breakpoint highlighted in red.

You will notice that the execution will stop and the breakpoint line will be highlighted in blue (Figure 11.7). The STACK tab will show the line number and the method name where we have stopped. We have stopped at line 13 in the class Student. The <init> is the name the debugger gives to constructors.

Now what do we want to do? At this point we can type things in the interactions pane to investigate the values of the variables and fields that are in scope.

```
> this.name
null
> this.gradeArray
null
> theName
"Amy Clark"
```

From these values we see that the fields did get assigned the default values. And, we see that the parameter theName has a value of "Amy Clark". Let's let execution go forward by one step and then stop again. We do this by clicking on the STEP OVER button.

We can check the value of the current object's name using the interactions pane (Figure 11.8).

```
> this.name
"Amy Clark"
```

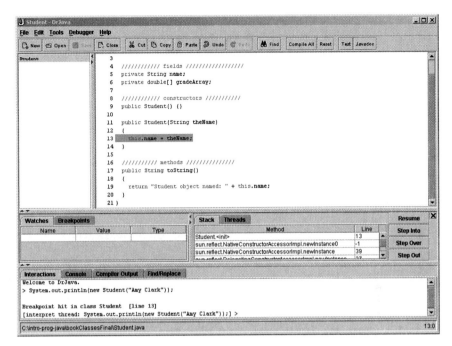

FIGURE 11.7
Execution stops at the breakpoint.

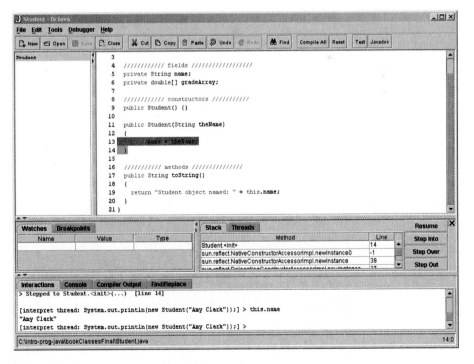

FIGURE 11.8
After clicking on Step Over.

We can let execution continue from here by clicking on the RESUME button. We can also stop debugging at anytime by clicking on the 'X' at the upper right of the debugging windows (to the right of the RESUME button).

11.3   OVERLOADING CONSTRUCTORS

We can overload constructors, just as we overloaded methods. The parameter lists must be different. This can mean that they take a different number of parameters and/or that the types are different. In the above code we have two constructors. One takes no parameters, and one takes a String object, which is the name to use.

Here we have added another constructor that takes the name and an array of grades.

Program 99: Student Class with Three Constructors

```
public class Student
{

    /////////// fields ///////////////////
    private String name;
    private double[] gradeArray;

    /////////// constructors ////////////
    public Student() {}

    public Student(String theName)
    {
      this.name = theName;
    }

    public Student(String theName, double[] theGradeArray)
    {
      this.name = theName;
      this.gradeArray = theGradeArray;
    }

    ////////// methods ///////////////
    public String toString()
    {
      return "Student object named: " + this.name;
    }
}
```

To use this constructor we need to pass in a name as a String object and an array of grades of the type double.

11.4   CREATING AND INITIALIZING AN ARRAY

Remember that we can declare an array using:

type[] *name*;

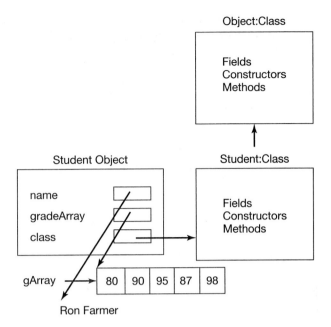

FIGURE 11.9
Showing a student object after a constructor that takes a name and array of grades has executed.

But this doesn't actually create the array object! It only declares a variable that will *refer* to an array object. To create an array use:

new *type*[*numElements*];

or, if you want to initialize the elements of an array when you create it, you can use:

type[] *name* = {*elem1,elem2,elem3,...*};

So to create a Student object and pass in a name and an array of five grades you can use the following (see the result in Figure 11.9):

```
> double[] gArray = {80, 90, 95, 87, 98};
> System.out.println(new Student("Ron Farmer", gArray));
Student object named: Ron Farmer
```

Or you can create the array and separately fill in the grades:

```
> double[] gArray = new double[5];
> gArray[0] = 80;
> gArray[1] = 90;
> gArray[2] = 95;
> gArray[3] = 87;
> gArray[4] = 98;
```

```
> System.out.println(new Student("Ron Farmer", gArray));
Student object named: Ron Farmer
```

It doesn't matter whether you initialize the array when you create it or after you create it using the indices. In this case the values in the array are exactly the same. If you initialize the array when you create it, the array length is set to the number of items between the curly braces.

11.4.1 Calculating the Grade Average

It might be nice to change the toString method to add the average of the grades for this student to the string that it returns. Since this is something that objects of other classes might want to ask a Student object, we should make calculating the average a public method.

This method should first check if there is a grade array yet. If there isn't, it should return 0.0 for the grade point average. What if there are 0 grades? This could cause a divide by zero runtime exception. So we should also return 0.0 for the average if there are no grades in the array.

If there are grades in the grade array, we can sum the grades and divide by the number of grades to get the average. We can loop through the array, using a for loop that starts with an index of 0, and loops while the index is less than the length of the array. We will need to declare a variable to hold the sum. This should also be of type double since the grades are of type double. Each time through the loop we should add the current grade (at the current index value in the array of grades) to the sum. After the loop we can calculate the average as the sum divided by the number of grades, which is also the length of the array. Remember that you can get the length of an array using arrayObj.length.

Program 100: Student Class with Average Calculation

```
public class Student
{

    ////////// fields //////////////////
    private String name;
    private double[] gradeArray;

    ////////// constructors //////////////
    public Student() {}

    public Student(String theName)
    {
        this.name = theName;
    }

    public Student(String theName, double[] theGradeArray)
    {
        this.name = theName;
```

```java
      this.gradeArray = theGradeArray;
    }

    /////////// methods ///////////////
    public double getAverage()
    {
      double average = 0.0;

      if (this.gradeArray != null && this.gradeArray.length > 0)
      {
        double sum = 0.0;
        for (int i = 0; i < this.gradeArray.length; i++)
        {
          sum = sum + this.gradeArray[i];
        }
        average = sum / this.gradeArray.length;
      }
      return average;
    }

    public String toString()
    {
      return "Student object named: " + this.name +
             " Average: " + this.getAverage();
    }
}
```

If we try this out we get:

```
> double[] gArray = {80, 90, 95, 87, 98};
> System.out.println(new Student("Ron Farmer", gArray));
Student object named: Ron Farmer Average: 90.0
> double[] gArray2 = {92,94,97,91,93};
> System.out.println(new Student("Sue Lane",gArray2));
Student object named: Sue Lane Average: 93.4
```

Since we made the method getAverage() public, we can also invoke it directly on a Student object from the interactions pane (which is outside the current class).

```
> double[] gradeArray3 = {55, 85, 73, 92, 81};
> Student student1 = new Student("Bill Simpson",gradeArray3);
> System.out.println(student1.getAverage());
77.2
```

11.4.2 Using Step Into in the Debugger

We can use the debugger again to check that things are working the way that we expect. Click on DEBUGGER and check the DEBUG MODE checkbox. Create a breakpoint at the first line in the constructor that takes a name and a grade array (Figure 11.10). Create another breakpoint in the first line of the toString method. You can set as many breakpoints as you want.

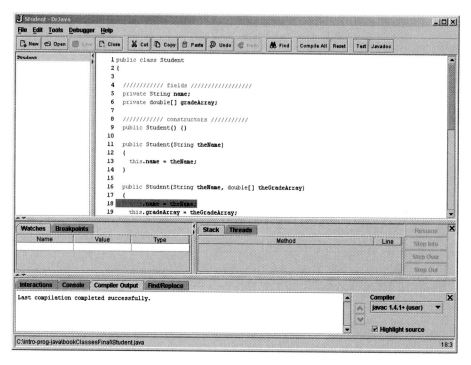

FIGURE 11.10
Breakpoint in the constructor that takes a name and grade array.

Now let's execute this with

```
> double[] gArray = {80, 90, 95, 87, 98};
> System.out.println(new Student("Ron Farmer", gArray));
```

Execution will stop before the execution of the line that assigns the passed name to the current object's name (Figure 11.11). We can see that the current object fields have their default values by typing the following in the interactions pane. We can also check the values of the parameters to the constructor.

```
> this.name
null
> this.gradeArray
null
> theName
"Ron Farmer"
> theGradeArray[0]
80.0
```

We can use the STEP OVER button to execute the current line of code and then stop again after it has executed (Figure 11.12). If we do this, we can check the value of the current object's name again and see that it has been set to the value of the parameter.

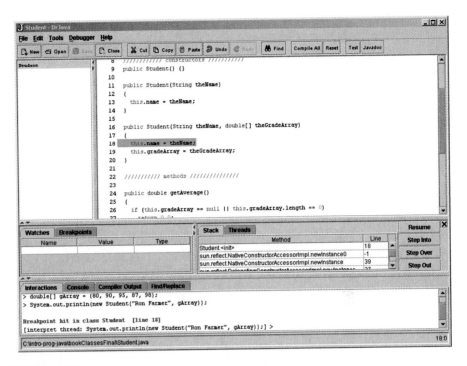

FIGURE 11.11
Execution stopped at the breakpoint.

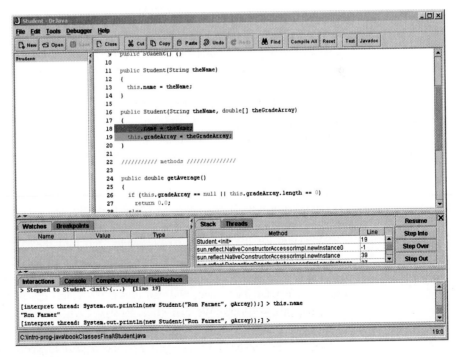

FIGURE 11.12
Execution stopped after step over.

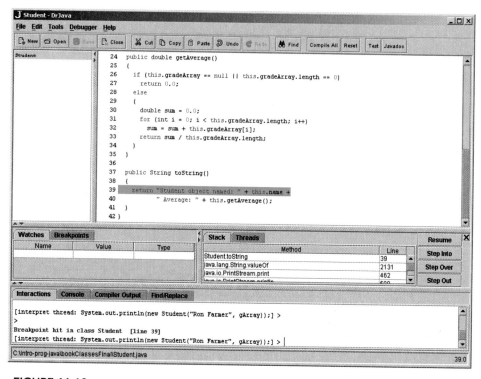

FIGURE 11.13
Execution stopped at the second breakpoint.

We can continue to click on Step Over to execute each line of code and stop again. We can use the interactions pane to print out the values that have been changed. Or at this point we can click on RESUME to let the program continue without stopping until the next breakpoint, or until it finishes.

Execution will stop at the second breakpoint in the method toString (Figure 11.13). We can see from the STACK tab that it is stopped at line 39 in the method toString in the class Student. If, at this point, we want to see what happens when we execute the this.getAverage() method we can use STEP INTO instead of STEP OVER. Using STEP INTO will take us *into* a method which is invoked on the current line. If we use STEP OVER it would just execute the method and stop after it. We wouldn't get to see what happens *inside* the method.

After we use the STEP INTO button to step into the current line of code execution will stop at the first line of the getAverage method (Figure 11.14). We can use the STEP OVER button to execute each line in this method and stop after each to see what happened. We can check the value the of the sum variable each time through the loop. We can click RESUME when we want to continue execution.

If you ever use STEP INTO when you meant to use Step Over, all you have to do is click on STEP OUT. Clicking on STEP OUT will finish execution of the current method and stop at the line following the line that called the current method.

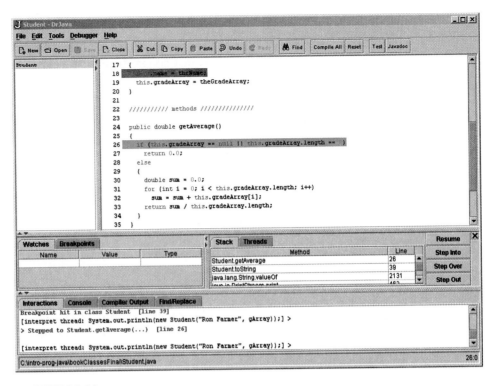

FIGURE 11.14
Execution stopped at the beginning of getAverage.

11.5   CREATING ACCESSORS (GETTERS) AND MODIFIERS (SETTERS)

Now we can create a Student object with a name and an array of grades. How do we access the data in the fields? We can access public fields using dot notation: (*objectRef.fieldName*). We have used this to access the public length field of arrays (gradeArray.length). What happens when we try this with private fields?

```
> System.out.println(student1.name);
java.lang.IllegalAccessException: Class
koala.dynamicjava.interpreter.EvaluationVisitor can not access a
member of class Student with modifiers "private"
    at sun.reflect.Reflection.ensureMemberAccess(Reflection.java:57)
    at java.lang.reflect.Field.doSecurityCheck(Field.java:811)
    at java.lang.reflect.Field.getFieldAccessor(Field.java:758)
    at java.lang.reflect.Field.get(Field.java:228)
```

If we try to use dot notation to access the private field of an object from outside the class it is declared in, we will get a compiler error. Fields that are declared to be private can only be accessed directly inside of the same class definition. This means that objects of other classes won't be able to access this data directly (using *objectRef.fieldName*) in the interactions pane.

11.5.1 Creating Accessors (Getters)

In order to let objects of other classes access the information in private fields, we need to create public methods that access the private fields. Accessors are methods that return private field information. By convention these are declared as:

```
public type getFieldName()
```

The method that will return the value of the name is:

```
public String getName() { return this.name; }
```

Notice that we put the code for the method on the same line as the method declaration. This is okay for short methods and is often used for accessors. We could also have written this as follows:

```
public String getName()
{
    return this.name;
}
```

Should we create a method to return the array of grades? If we return the array, we lose control over it. We could create a method that returns a value from the array for a given index.

```
public double getGrade(int index)
{
    return this.gradeArray[index];
}
```

Computer Science Idea: Protecting Object Data

Objects should protect their data and make sure that it stays in a correct state. One of the ways that objects protect their data is by having private fields and providing public accessors that allow other classes to view the data. But accessors need to be careful that they don't allow objects of other classes to directly modify the data. ∎

11.5.2 Creating Modifiers (Setters)

What if we want to change one of the grades? Since the grade array is `private`, we can't directly modify it outside of the class definition. If we try to change it directly in the interactions pane, we will get an `IllegalAccessException`.

```
> student1.gradeArray[0] = 90;
java.lang.IllegalAccessException: Class
koala.dynamicjava.interpreter.EvaluationVisitor can not access a
member of class Student with modifiers "private"
    at sun.reflect.Reflection.ensureMemberAccess(Reflection.java:57)
    at java.lang.reflect.Field.doSecurityCheck(Field.java:811)
    at java.lang.reflect.Field.getFieldAccessor(Field.java:758)
    at java.lang.reflect.Field.get(Field.java:228)
>
```

But we do need a way to change an incorrect grade. We can do this by asking the object to change the value for a grade. The object can refuse to change the grade and should refuse if the user inputs an invalid value (like -30). Methods that modify fields are called *modifiers* or *mutators*. The Java convention is to declare these as follows:

```
public returnType setFieldName(type param1Name,
                               type param2Name, ...)
```

Here is a method that will try to change the grade stored at a passed index to a passed new grade. If the new grade is less than 0 or the grade array is null, it won't change the grade and will return false. Otherwise it will change the grade and return true. Methods that modify a value can return a boolean to indicate whether the modification was successful or not.

```
public boolean setGrade(int index, double newGrade)
{
  if (newGrade < 0 || this.gradeArray == null)
    return false;
  else
  {
    this.gradeArray[index] = newGrade;
    return true;
  }
}
```

If the no argument constructor or the constructor that just takes the name was used to create a Student object, the grade array will be null. We need some way to set it. One way is to pass in the grade array to use. We can decide to only allow this if the grade array is currently null.

```
public boolean setGradeArray(double[] theArray)
{
  if (this.gradeArray != null)
  {
    return false;
  }
  else
  {
    this.gradeArray = theArray;
    return true;
  }
}
```

You can have more than one return statement in a method as shown above. This method could be written with only one return statement as follows:

```
public boolean setGradeArray(double[] theArray)
{
  boolean result = false;

  // only set the gradeArray if it is null
  if (this.gradeArray == null)
```

```
    {
      this.gradeArray = theArray;
      result = true;
    }
    return result;
  }
```

Which way is better? Both give the same result so the true test is which is easier for another person to understand and change? Beginners often think the first approach is better but the second approach will be easier for another person to understand and change.

Here is a method that will set the student's name only if it is currently null; otherwise it will leave the current name alone. It will return true if the name is changed and false otherwise.

```
public boolean setName(String theName)
{
  boolean result = false;
  if (this.name == null)
  {
    this.name = theName;
    result = true;
  }
  return result;
}
```

Why only change the name if it is null? This is a public method, meaning that objects of other classes can invoke this method. Do we want to let objects of classes other than Student change a student's name once it is initially set? In this case we have chosen not to allow this. One of the advantages of object-oriented programming is that the data and methods are *encapsulated* in the class definition. This means that the data is grouped with the methods that affect it inside of a class. If the data get into an incorrect state, we know that the class isn't doing its job of protecting the data.

11.6 CREATING A **MAIN** METHOD

Up to now we have created objects and tried out new methods in the interactions pane. However, there is a special method called a *main method* that you can use to create objects and invoke methods. A main method must have the following method declaration:

public static void main(String[] args)

The method must be a `public static` method called `main` and must take an array of `String` objects as a parameter. It doesn't matter if you call the array of strings `args` or some other name. The convention is just to use the name `args`. It must be a `public` method so that it can be called by objects of other classes. It must be static because no objects of the class exist when you start execution of the method. The first thing you usually do in a main method is create one or more objects of the class and then invoke a method or methods on the created objects.

Here is a `main` method that you can use to create some students:

```
public static void main (String[] args)
  {
    Student student1 = new Student("Barb Ericson");
    System.out.println(student1);
    double[] gradeArray1 = {90,88,95,96,93};
    Student student2 = new Student("Mark Guzdial",gradeArray1);
    System.out.println(student2);
  }
```

In DrJava you can execute the `main` method of the current class by clicking on TOOLS and then RUN DOCUMENT'S MAIN METHOD. It will show output in the interactions pane and in the console pane.

```
> java Student
Student object named: Barb Ericson Average: 0.0
Student object named: Mark Guzdial Average: 92.4
```

If you are using the command-line tools from Sun you can invoke a `main` method on a class using:

```
java ClassName
```

As you may have noticed, this is what DrJava does when you ask it to run the document's `main` method.

11.7   JAVADOC COMMENTS

We have only used comments to highlight the different parts of a class definition: fields, constructors, and methods. You *should* add Javadoc comments to your class definition. Javadoc is a utility from Sun that allows you to create *HTML* (Hyper-Text Markup Language) documentation from special Javadoc comments in your source code. Comments make it easier to figure out what a class is for and what is happening in it.

You might think that you don't need to comment a class if you are the only one using it, but the point of creating a class is to make reusable pieces. Comments are notes in plain language that will help you *and* others understand and reuse the class. All of the classes that are part of the Java language have Javadoc comments in them. The API documentation was created by running the Javadoc utility on the source files.

11.7.1   Class Comment

You *should* add a comment just before the class definition to explain the class and to give the author's name. Javadoc comments start with '`/**`' and end with '`*/`'. They can take up several lines. Here is an example of a class comment:

```
/**
 * Class that describes a student.  A student has a name and an
 * array of grades.  You can get information about a student
 * such as her/his name and grade average.
```

```
*
* @author Barb Ericson
*/
public class Student
```

Notice that the Javadoc comment is just before the class declaration. It tells something about the purpose of the class. It also should tell who the author or authors are. If there is more than one author you just add another '@author' tag. The '@author' tag is just one of many special tags defined in Javadoc that will pull particular information out of the source code and format it in the HTML documentation.

11.7.2   Method Comments

You should add a comment before each method. This comment should describe the purpose of the method, any parameters to the method, and what is returned from the method (if anything). Here is an example of a method comment:

```
/**
 * Method to set a grade in the grade array
 * @param index the index to set the grade at
 * @param newGrade the new grade to use
 * @return true if success, else false
 */
public boolean setGrade(int index, double newGrade)
{
```

Notice that it has two '@param' tags because it has two parameters. Also notice that it has a '@return' tag since it returns a value. Here is another method comment:

```
/**
 * Method to return the average of the grades for this student
 * @return the average of the grades or 0.0 if no grade array
 * or no grades
 */
public double getAverage()
```

Notice that this one doesn't have any '@param' tags in it. This is because it doesn't have any parameters. It does have the '@return' tag in it because it does return a value.

11.7.3   Constructor Comments

You can add Javadoc comments to constructors as well. They look like method comments. Of course you won't need any '@return' tags since constructors do not return a value.

11.7.4   Generating the Documentation

Once you add Javadoc comments to your class you can generate HTML documentation in DrJava by clicking on the JAVADOC button. This will generate all the HTML documentation for all classes that are in the same directory as all the open files. This is how the API for Java 1.5 (5.0) (http://java.sun.com/

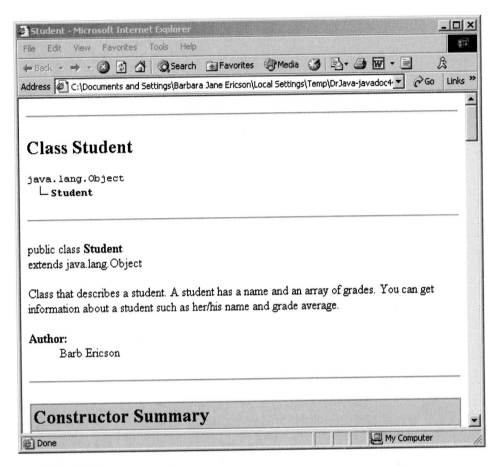

FIGURE 11.15
Showing the HTML documentation generated from Javadoc comments.

j2se/1.5.0/docs/api/) was created. You can see the API for Java 1.4.2 at
`http://java.sun.com/j2se/1.4.2/docs/api/`.

You can also see a preview of the HTML documentation for just the current
class by clicking TOOLS and then on PREVIEW JAVADOC FOR CURRENT DOCUMENT
(Figure 11.15). This can be useful to check what the documentation looks like so
far. It will also show you where you need to add documentation.

If you aren't using DrJava you can create the HTML documentation using the
Javadoc utility that comes with Java. You can open a command prompt and go to
the directory with the Java source in it and then type `javadoc *.java` to create the
documentation for all the source files in the directory. To create the documentation
for just the `Student` class use `javadoc Student.java`.

11.8   CREATING ANOTHER CLASS

What if we want to represent a class period? We might want to keep track of the
teacher's name, the period number, and the students in that period.

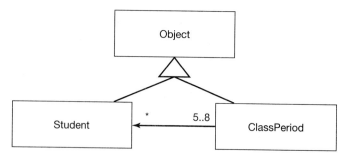

FIGURE 11.16
UML class diagram.

Should we just add this to the class Student? A student is in a class period, but a student *isn't* a class period. It sounds like we need another class which we could name ClassPeriod. The teacher's name can be represented by a String object. We can use the type int to represent the period number. What type would we use for the students in the period? This can be an array of Student objects. If we know the maximum number of students that we can have in a class, we can go ahead and create an array of that size. Say we can only have 35 students at most.

Computer Science Idea: UML Class Diagrams

The standard way to show object-oriented designs is to use a *UML* class diagram. UML means the Unified Modeling Language. A class diagram shows each class in a rectangular box and relationships between classes with lines. A straight line (perhaps with an arrow at one end) shows an association between two classes. A straight line ending with an open triangle indicates inheritance. The open triangle is at the parent class end.

In Figure 11.16 we see that we have two classes in our design so far: Student and ClassPeriod and that both of these inherit from the class Object. There is a line connecting Student and ClassPeriod with an arrow pointing to the Student class. This means that a ClassPeriod object will keep track of the Student objects in it. The '*' at the end of the line near the Student class shows us that a ClassPeriod object can have 0 to many Student objects associated with it. The '5…8' at the ClassPeriod end means that a Student object can have five to eight ClassPeriod objects associated with it. ■

We have enough information to begin the new class declaration:

```
/**
 * ClassPeriod represents a class period which has a teacher,
 * a period number, and an array of students
 */
public class ClassPeriod
{
  //////////////// fields ////////////////////////
  private String teacherName;
  private int periodNumber;
  private Student[] studentArray = new Student[35];

}
```

11.8.1 Adding Constructors

Next we need to add constructors. We might not know anything about this new class period, or we might know only the teacher name, we might know both the teacher name and period number. We will create constructors for each of these cases.

The constructors are declared inside of the open and close curly braces that define the block for the class definition. Be sure to add the constructors before the closing curly brace '}' that ends the class definition.

```
/////////////////// constructors ///////////////////
/**
 * No-argument constructor.  Leaves fields with
 * default values.
 */
public ClassPeriod() {}

/**
 * Constructor that takes just the teacher's name
 * @param name the name for the teacher
 */
public ClassPeriod(String name) {  this.teacherName = name; }

/**
 * Constructor that takes the teacher's name and period number
 * @param name the name for the teacher
 * @param num the number for the class period
 */
public ClassPeriod(String name, int num)
{
  this.teacherName = name;
  this.periodNumber = num;
}
```

11.8.2 Adding Accessors and Modifiers

Since the fields are `private` they can only be directly accessed by code in the current class definition. In order to let code from other classes (declared in other files) be able to ask a `ClassPeriod` for its information we need to provide public methods that return the information. We do this by creating methods called accessors.

Methods should be added *before* the closing curly brace '}' in the block that follows the class declaration.

```
/////////////////////////// methods ///////////////////////////

/**
 * Method to get the teacher's name
 * @return the name of the teacher, or null if none yet
 */
public String getTeacherName() { return teacherName; }
```

```
/**
 * Method to get the period number
 * @return the number for this period
 */
public int getPeriodNumber() { return periodNumber; }
/**
 * Method to get a student based on the index
 * @return the student at this index or null if none at this
 * index
 */
public Student getStudent(int index)
{
    return studentArray[index];
}
```

What if we want to *set* the value of a field? We need to create public methods that allow these values to be set. These are called modifier or mutator methods.

We have to decide when this is allowed. Should another class be able to set the teacher name, or should we only allow it to be set if it is currently null? Does it ever happen that a teacher's name will change during the school year? Sure, a teacher may get married and change her name. Or what if a teacher leaves during the school year due to illness or pregnancy? We should allow the name to be changed.

What about the period number? Does this ever change? Probably not, so let's not allow it to change if it has been set. We will be able to tell if it has been set because the default value for a number field is 0 and class periods start with 1.

Should we allow another class to change the array that `studentArray` refers to? Probably not, but we can change the student in the array at a specified index.

```
/**
 * Method to set the teacher's name
 * @param name the name to use
 */
public void setTeacherName(String name)
{
    this.teacherName = name;
}
/**
 * Method to set the period number (if it hasn't been set)
 * @param num the number to use
 * @return flag to say if set worked
 */
public boolean setPeriodNumber(int num)
{
    if (this.periodNumber == 0)
    {
        this.periodNumber = num;
        return true;
    }
    else
        return false;
}
```

```java
/**
 * Method to set the student at an index
 * @param studentObj the student object to use
 * @param index the index to set the student at
 */
public void setStudent(Student studentObj, int index)
{
  this.studentArray[index] = studentObj;
}
```

11.9 REUSING A CLASS VIA INHERITANCE

Many children have a hard time with the concepts of left and right. Even some adults get these confused. Let's create a new class `ConfusedTurtle` that will turn right when asked to turn left and will turn left when asked to turn right. How can we do this?

In Section 11.2.2 we saw that you can specify the parent class when you declare a class using the `extends` keyword. If you don't specify the parent class the parent class will be `Object`. So to create a class `ConfusedTurtle` that is a child of the `Turtle` class do the following:

```java
public class ConfusedTurtle extends Turtle
{
}
```

Because the class `ConfusedTurtle` inherits from the class `Turtle` it inherits all its fields and methods. We want to override the method `turnLeft()` and have it turn right instead. How can we do this? We could just have it call the method `turnRight()` but we are overriding this method as well. We really want to call the method in the parent class `Turtle`. Java gives us a way to do this using the keyword `super`. Usually the Java Virtual Machine (JVM) will start looking for a method in the class that created the current object. But if we use the keyword `super` to invoke a method, we will start looking for the method in the *parent* class of the class that created the current object.

```java
public class ConfusedTurtle extends Turtle
{
  /**
   * Method to turn right (but a confused
   * turtle will actually turn left)
   */
  public void turnRight()
  {
    super.turnLeft();
  }
```

```
/**
 * Method to turn left (but a confused
 * turtle will actually turn right)
 */
public void turnLeft()
{
  super.turnRight();
}
}
```

If we try to compile this we will get an error. The problem is that we haven't created any constructors yet. The compiler will try to add the no-argument constructor for us. But since `ConfusedTurtle` inherits from `Turtle` it will also add a call to `super()` which is a call to the parent's no-argument constructor. It does this to allow initialization of the inherited fields. But, the `Turtle` class doesn't have a no-argument constructor. Remember that we always passed a `World` object when we created a new `Turtle` object (Section 3.4.2).

If we check the `Turtle` class we don't see a constructor that takes a `World` object. But there is a constructor that takes a `ModelDisplay` object. The `World` class implements the `ModelDisplay` interface so we can call this constructor and pass in a `World` object. We need to add a constructor to the `ConfusedTurtle` class that takes a `ModelDisplay` object. Then, the first thing we will do is call the parent constructor that takes a `ModelDisplay` object. To do this we use `super(modelDisplayObj)`. A call to a superclass (parent) constructor *must* be the first line of code in a constructor. If the compiler doesn't find a call to the parent constructor as the first line of code in a child constructor, it will add a call to the parent's no-argument constructor.

```
public class ConfusedTurtle extends Turtle
{
  /////////////// constructors //////////////////////

  /**
   * A constructor that takes a ModelDisplay object
   * @param modelDisplayObj the thing that does the display
   */
  public ConfusedTurtle(ModelDisplay modelDisplayObj)
  {
    // use parent constructor
    super(modelDisplayObj);
  }

  /////////////// methods //////////////////////////

  /**
   * Method to turn right (but a confused
   * turtle will actually turn left)
   */
  public void turnRight()
  {
    super.turnLeft();
  }
```

```
/**
 * Method to turn left (but a confused
 * turtle will actually turn right)
 */
public void turnLeft()
{
  super.turnRight();
}
}
```

To try this out we can do the following:

```
> World world = new World();
> ConfusedTurtle fred = new ConfusedTurtle(world);
> fred.forward();
> fred.turnLeft();
> fred.forward();
> fred.turnRight();
> fred.forward();
```

Notice that the ConfusedTurtle object still knows how to go forward. The only difference between it and a Turtle object is what happens when it is asked to turn left or right, as shown in Figure 11.17.

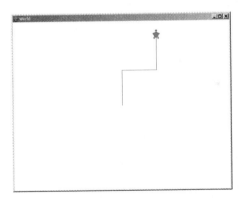

FIGURE 11.17
Result of commands to a confused turtle.

What happens if we also override the turn method in the ConfusedTurtle class to actually turn (360 - the passed degrees)?

```
/**
 * Method to turn by the passed degrees
 * (a confused turtle will turn by 360- the
 * passed degrees)
 */
public void turn(int degrees)
{
  super.turn(360-degrees);
}
```

We can try this out in the interactions pane with the following:

```
> World world = new World();
> ConfusedTurtle fred = new ConfusedTurtle(world);
> fred.turn(90);
> fred.forward();
> fred.turnLeft();
> fred.forward();
> fred.turnRight();
> fred.forward();
```

If we try this out in the interactions pane we will see that the `turn` method is doing the right thing but the `turnLeft()` and `turnRight()` methods are not (Figure 11.18). What happened? We have to remember that the Java Virtual Machine will *always* start looking for a method in the class that created the current object (unless we use `super.method()`).

When we call `turnLeft()` on a `ConfusedTurtle` object it will invoke the method in the `ConfusedTurtle` class (Figure 11.19). In that method we call `super.turnRight()`. This will start looking for the `turnRight()` method in the `Turtle` class but not find such a method. Then it will look in the parent class of `Turtle`, which is `SimpleTurtle`. The `turnRight()` method in `SimpleTurtle` contains `this.turn(90);` (Figure 11.19).

Once again, we will start looking for the `turn` method in the class that created the current object which was the `ConfusedTurtle` class (Figure 11.19). The `turn(int degrees)` method in the `ConfusedTurtle` class contains the line `super.turn(360-degrees);`. This will start looking for the `turn` method in the `Turtle` class and not find it. It will then look in the parent class of the `Turtle` class and find it in `SimpleTurtle`. This will change the heading and redisplay the turtle.

To fix this problem we need to change the `turnRight()` method in the `ConfusedTurtle` class to call `super.turn(-90)` to make it turn left. We will also change the `turnLeft()` method in the `ConfusedTurtle` class to call `super.turn(90)` to make it turn right.

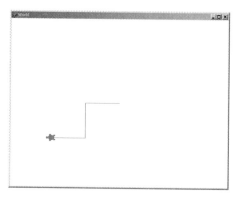

FIGURE 11.18
Result of overriding the `turn` method.

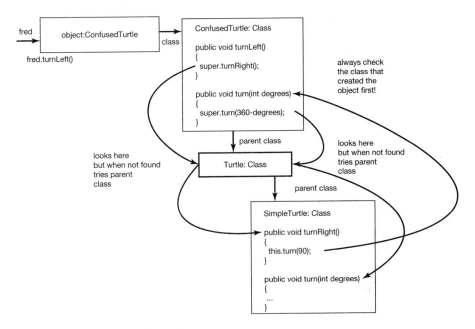

FIGURE 11.19
Diagram of the methods executed by `fred.turnLeft()`.

```
/**
 * Class for a confused turtle.  A confused turtle is like
 * a turtle but it turns right when asked to turn left and left
 * when asked to turn right.
 * @author Barb Ericson
 */
public class ConfusedTurtle extends Turtle
{
  /////////////// constructors /////////////////////////

  /**
   * A constructor that takes a ModelDisplay object
   * @param modelDisplayObj the thing that does the display
   */
  public ConfusedTurtle(ModelDisplay modelDisplayObj)
  {
    // use parent constructor
    super(modelDisplayObj);
  }

  /////////////// methods /////////////////////////////

  /**
   * Method to turn right (but a confused
   * turtle will actually turn left)
   */
  public void turnRight()
```

```
    {
      // turn left instead
      super.turn(-90);
    }

    /**
     * Method to turn left (but a confused
     * turtle will actually turn right)
     */
    public void turnLeft()
    {
      // turn right instead
      super.turn(90);
    }

    /**
     * Method to turn by the passed degrees
     * (a confused turtle will turn by 360- the
     * passed degrees)
     */
    public void turn(int degrees)
    {
      super.turn(360-degrees);
    }
  }
```

Now if we try this out it should work correctly (Figure 11.20).

```
> World world = new World();
> ConfusedTurtle fred = new ConfusedTurtle(world);
> fred.turn(90);
> fred.forward();
> fred.turnLeft();
> fred.forward();
> fred.turnRight();
> fred.forward();
```

11.9.1 Dynamic (Runtime) Binding

Every object in Java keeps a reference to the class that created it. You can say that an object knows what type it is. When a method is invoked on an object, the Java Virtual Machine (JVM) will always start looking for it in the class that created the object, unless you use super.method(), which will start looking for the method in the parent class of the class that contains the currently executing code.

When you declare a variable you can assign an object to it that is of the declared type, *or any child of the declared type*. So we can declare a variable of the type Turtle and use it to reference an object of the class ConfusedTurtle. When we invoke a method on a variable, it will first look for that method in the class that created the object that the variable refers to. If we invoke the method turnLeft() on a variable that was declared to be of type Turtle, but was created by the class ConfusedTurtle the method in ConfusedTurtle will be executed. This is due to

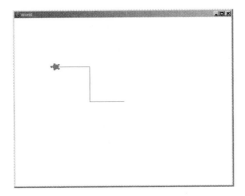

FIGURE 11.20
Result of fixing the methods `turnLeft()` and `turnRight()`.

dynamic or *runtime* binding. The method that is executed depends on the type of the object when the programming is running, not on the declared type of the variable.

When we execute the following in the interactions pane, we will get the same result as before (Figure 11.20).

```
> World world = new World();
> Turtle fred = new ConfusedTurtle(world);
> fred.turn(90);
> fred.forward();
> fred.turnLeft();
> fred.forward();
> fred.turnRight();
> fred.forward();
```

Objects always know what type they really are!

11.10 CONCEPTS SUMMARY

In this chapter we have created classes with fields, constructors, and methods. We have shown how to create, initialize, and access an array. We have shown how to override an inherited method. We have shown how to use a debugger. We have shown how to use Javadoc comments to document a class. We explained how dynamic binding results in methods being invoked based on the class that created the current object.

11.10.1 Declaring a Class

To declare a class you use:

```
public class Student
{
    // all fields, constructors, and methods
}
```

This will declare the class Student, which will be a child of the class Object. You could have also declared this as:

```
public class Student extends Object
{
    // all fields, constructors, and methods
}
```

This is using the extends keyword to explicitly say that this class inherits from the Object class. If no extends keyword is used, the class will automatically inherit from the class Object.

11.10.2 Fields

A field declaration looks very much like a local variable declaration except that it is inside the class definition and it should be preceded by the keyword private.

```
public class Student
{
    private String name;
    private double[] gradeArray;
}
```

Objects *should* protect their data from direct use by objects of other classes by making their data private.

11.10.3 Constructors

To declare a constructor you will usually use the keyword public followed by the class name and then a parameter list.

```
public Student() {}
```

The above constructor doesn't take any parameters and doesn't initialize the fields so they will have their default values. This is called a no-argument constructor. By default, numbers are initialized to 0, object references to null, and boolean fields to false. A no-argument constructor will automatically be added by the compiler, if you don't have any constructors declared in your class. But if you declare any constructors, the no-argument constructor won't be automatically added. In addition, if you don't have a call to a superclass constructor in your constructor, one will be added that calls the superclass no-argument constructor.

A constructor is always called when a new object is created. It is used to initialize the fields in the new object. You can have several constructors as long as the parameter lists are different. In other words, you can overload constructors just as you can overload methods.

Here is a constructor that takes a name for the new Student object:

```
public Student(String theName)
{
    this.name = theName;
}
```

11.10.4   Arrays

To create an array use the new keyword followed by a type and then the size in square brackets:

```
double[] gradeArray = new double[5];
```

You can create arrays of objects too:

```
Student[] studentArray = new Student[20];
```

You can also initialize the contents of the array when you create it by putting values inside of an open and close curly brace and separating the values with commas:

```
double[] gradeArray = {90.5, 23, 99, 87.5, 96};
```

11.10.5   Using a Debugger

Most IDEs have debuggers. A debugger is a tool that helps you see exactly what is happening in a program. The main thing that you do with a debugger is set breakpoints, which are places to stop and see what is happening.

Once you have stopped at a breakpoint you can examine the values of variables and fields. You can use STEP OVER, which executes the current line of code and then stops again. You can use STEP INTO, which will go into any method call on the current line and then stop. You can use STEP OUT to let a current method finish executing and stop again in the method that called the current method. You can use RESUME which will continue executing until another breakpoint or until execution of the program finishes.

11.10.6   Javadoc Comments

You *should* document your code to make it more reusable both by yourself and others. You should include at least a comment before the class definition and before each method.

A class comment should explain the purpose of the class and identify the author. Here is an example of a class comment:

```
/**
 * Class that describes a student.  A student has a name and an
 * array of grades.  You can get information about a student
 * such as her/his name and grade average.
 *
 * @author Barb Ericson
 */
public class Student
```

A method comment should describe the purpose of the method. It can list any preconditions that should be true before the method is called and any postconditions that will be true when the method has finished. It should also explain any parameters to the method and what is returned (if anything) from the method. Here is an example of a method comment:

```
/**
 * Method to get the grade in the grade array
 * at the passed index
 * @param index the index that we want the grade for
 * @return the grade in the grade array at this passed index
 */
public double getGrade(int index)
```

PROBLEMS

11.1   What is the answer to each of the following?

- What is a field?
- What is a constructor?
- What does override mean?
- How do you specify the parent class of the class you are declaring?
- If you don't specify a parent class is there still a parent class?
- How do you overload a constructor?
- What is the difference between override and overload?
- How do you create an array?
- How do you access elements of an array?
- How do you initialize the elements of an array?
- What is a Javadoc comment?
- Can objects of a different class (in a different file) directly access private fields?
- Can objects of a different class (in a different file) directly access public fields?
- What is an accessor method?
- What is a modifier method?
- What does encapsulate mean?
- What does `super.method()` do?
- What does `super()` do?

11.2   Which of these is the correct class definition for a `Teacher` class?

- public CLASS Teacher
- public class Teacher
- public class TEACHER
- public class Teacher []
- public class Teacher extends Object, Person

11.3   Which of these correctly defines a field in a class?

- private INT count;
- public INT count;

- private int count = "HI";
- private int count;

11.4   Which of these correctly defines a constructor in the class `Student`?

- PUBLIC STUDENT ()
- public STUDENT ()
- PUBLIC student()
- public void Student()
- public Student()

11.5   What other methods do all classes inherit from the `Object` class?

11.6   Create a class `CartoonPanel` and create a constructor that takes an array of `Picture` objects and displays them from left to right like a cartoon in a newspaper. You can use the `scale` method to scale the pictures to fit. You can create a new picture to use to display the cartoon on.

11.7   Modify the `Student` class `getAverage()` method to drop the lowest grade when calculating the average. You will need to loop through the array and find the lowest grade.

11.8   What class does `Turtle` inherit from (in your `bookClasses` directory)? What class does `Picture` inherit from? What class does `FileChooser` inherit from? What class does `World` inherit from?

11.9   What methods did the class `Turtle` inherit from its parent class?

11.10   What methods did the class `Picture` inherit from its parent class?

11.11   How many constructors does the `Turtle` class have? How are they different?

11.12   How many constructors does the `Picture` class have? How are they different?

11.13   Add method comments for all the methods in the `Student` class.

11.14   Add another constructor for the `Student` class that takes a name and a number which is the number of grades this student will have. It should create the `gradeArray` based on the passed number of grades.

11.15   Add a `picture` field to the `Student` class and create constructors that take a `Picture` object as well. Also create accessors and modifier methods for the picture field. Add a `show()` method which will show the `Picture` object if it isn't null.

11.16   Write the definition for a class `Car` which has the manufacturer, model, year, and number of doors. An example car has a manufacturer of Toyota, a model of Camry, a year of 2000, and a number of doors of 4. Be sure to code all accessor and modifier methods.

11.17   Write the definition for a class `Book` which has a title, an author, an ISBN number, a price, and the year it was published. Be sure to code all accessor and modifier methods. You can use the information for this book as a test case.

11.18 Write the definition for a class Address which has line1, line2, city, state, and zip code. Be sure to code all accessor and modifier methods. Create an Address object with your address information in it.

11.19 Write the definition for a class CreditCard which has a number, an expiration date, and a name. Be sure to code all accessor and modifier methods.

11.20 Write a main method in the Picture class to create a Picture object and show it.

11.21 Write a main method in the Sound class to create a Sound object and play it.

11.22 Write a method in the Turtle class that takes an array of Picture objects. Use the drop(Picture p) method in Turtle to drop pictures at different locations in a circle.

11.23 What is the output from this:
```
> Object obj = new Student("Susan Dorda");
> System.out.println(obj);
```
Can you explain why we get this result?

11.24 What is the output from this:
```
> Object obj = new ClassPeriod("Mary Engelhardt",3)
> System.out.println(obj);
```
Can you explain why we get this result?

PART 4 TEXT, FILES, NETWORKS, DATABASES, AND MULTIMEDIA

12 Creating and Modifying Text

12.1   TEXT AS UNIMEDIA

12.2   STRINGS: CHARACTER SEQUENCES

12.3   FILES: PLACES TO PUT YOUR STRINGS AND OTHER STUFF

12.4   OTHER USEFUL CLASSES

12.5   NETWORKS: GETTING OUR TEXT FROM THE WEB

12.6   USING TEXT TO SHIFT BETWEEN MEDIA

12.7   CONCEPTS SUMMARY

Chapter Learning Objectives

The media learning goals for this chapter are:

- To generate a form letter.
- To manipulate structured text, such as a delimited string.
- To write programs that read from files and write to files.
- To write programs that directly access and use text information from the Internet.
- To write a program that modifies another program.
- To generate randomly structured text.
- To use text to change encodings of information, e.g., creating visualizations of sounds.

The computer science goals for this chapter are:

- To manipulate strings.
- To read and write files.
- To handle exceptions.
- To use a dynamic array: `ArrayList`.
- To explain interfaces.
- To work with file structures.
- To write programs that manipulate programs, which leads to powerful ideas like interpreters and compilers.
- To use classes in packages that you have to import.
- To iterate with a `while` loop.
- To access the Internet via a program.

12.1 TEXT AS UNIMEDIA

Nicholas Negroponte, founder of the MIT Media Lab, said that what makes computer-based multimedia possible is the fact that the computer is actually *unimedia*. The computer really only understands one thing: zeros and ones. We can use the computer for multimedia because any medium can be encoded in these zeros and ones.

But he might as well have been talking about *text* as the unimedia. We can encode any medium as text, and what's even better than the zeros and ones, we can *read* the text! Later in this chapter, we map sounds to text and then back to sounds. But once we're in text, we don't have to go back to the original medium: We can map sounds to text and then to pictures, and thus create *visualizations* of sounds.

The World Wide Web is primarily text. Visit any Web page, then go to the menu of your Web browser and choose "View the source." What you will see is text. Every Web page is actually text. That text references pictures, sounds, and animations that appear when you view the page, but the page itself is defined as text. The words in that text are in a notation called *HyperText Markup Language (HTML)*.

12.2 STRINGS: CHARACTER SEQUENCES

Text is typically manipulated as *strings*. In Java a string is a sequence of characters. Strings in Java are *not* just arrays of characters as they are in some other languages, like C. Strings are objects of the `String` class.

You use a double quote to indicate the start and end of a string in Java. If you want to write a Java program that creates HTML pages, you will need strings that contain quotes. If you want the string to *include* a double quote, you must use a backslash '\' in front of it.

```
> System.out.println("He said, \"Hi.\"");
He said, "Hi."
```

You can include single quotes in strings.

```
> System.out.println("He won't go out!");
He won't go out!
```

A string contains a sequence of characters. We can think about the characters of the string as being in boxes, each with its own index number. You can get a character from a string using the method `charAt(index)`.

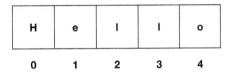

```
> String hello = "Hello";
> System.out.println(hello.charAt(0));
H
> System.out.println(hello.charAt(2));
l
```

You can use a `for` loop to walk through all the characters of a string.

```
> String test = "Hello";
> for (int i = 0; i < test.length(); i++)
    System.out.println(test.charAt(i));
H
e
l
l
o
```

Notice that you *do* need the parentheses after `length()`. It is a method of the `String` class, *not* a public field as it is for an array.

12.2.1   Unicode

Java uses *Unicode* to encode each character. Unicode is an encoding for characters where two bytes are used for each character. Two bytes gives us 65,536 possible combinations. Having that many possible combinations allows us to go beyond a simple Latin alphabet, numbers, and punctuation. We can represent Hiragana, Katakana, and other *glyph* (graphical depictions of characters) systems.

What this should tell you is that there are many more possible characters than can be typed at a standard keyboard. Not only are there special symbols, but there are invisible characters like tabs and backspace. We specify these in Java strings (and in many other languages, such as C) using *backslash escapes*. Backslash escapes are the backslash key \ followed by a character.

- \" allows for a double quote inside of a string.
- \t is the same as typing the tab key.
- \b is the same as typing the backspace key (which is not a particularly useful character to put in a string, but you can). When you print \b, it shows up as a box on most systems—it's not actually printable.
- \n is the same as typing the enter/return key. It is often called the *new-line* character.
- \uXXXX where XXXX is a code made up of 0-9 and A-F (known as a *hexadecimal* number) represents the Unicode character with that code. You can look up the codes at http://www.unicode.org/charts.

Here are some strings with special characters in them. Try out a string with a backspace in it for yourself.

```
> System.out.println("A string with a tab \t in it");
A string with a tab     in it
> System.out.println("A string with a newline character \n in it");
A string with a newline character
 in it
```

12.2.2   String Methods

The String class has many methods for working with String objects. These methods are useful for processing text.

- charAt(int position) returns the character at the given position in the string. The first character is at position 0, just as the first element of an array is at index 0.

  ```
  > String str1 = "Bye";
  > System.out.println(str1.charAt(0));
  B
  ```

- compareTo(Object o) returns a negative number if this object is less than the passed object, 0 if this object is equal to the passed object and a positive number if this object is greater than the passed object.

  ```
  > String str1 = "Bye";
  > String str2 = "Hi";
  > String str3 = new String("Bye");
  > System.out.println(str1.compareTo(str2));
  -6
  > System.out.println(str2.compareTo(str1));
  6
  > System.out.println(str1.compareTo(str3));
  0
  ```

- substring(int n, int m) returns a new string which is a *substring* of the string starting at the *n*th character and preceding up to *but not including* the *m*th character. A substring includes part of the original string.

  ```
  > String str2 = "Do you go to school?";
  > String str3 = str2.substring(3,6);
  > System.out.println(str3);
  you
  ```

- substring(int n) returns a new string which is a substring of the string starting at the *n*th character and including the rest of the characters in the string.

  ```
  > str3 = str2.substring(6);
  > System.out.println(str3);
   go to school?
  ```

- startsWith(String prefix) returns true if the string starts with the given prefix, else it will return false.

  ```
  > String letter = "Mr. Guzdial requests the ";
  > letter = letter + "pleasure of your company ...";
  > System.out.println(letter.startsWith("Mr."));
  true
  > System.out.println(letter.startsWith("Mrs."));
  false
  ```

- endsWith(String suffix) returns true if the string ends with the given suffix, else it will return false.

```
> String filename="barbara.jpg";
> if (filename.endsWith(".jpg"))
    System.out.println("it is a picture");
it is a picture
```

- indexOf(String str) returns the first index of the passed str, if it is found. If str isn't in the current string, it will return −1.

```
> System.out.println(letter);
Mr. Guzdial requests the pleasure of your company ...
> System.out.println(letter.indexOf("Guzdial"));
4
> System.out.println(letter.indexOf("Mark"));
-1
```

- indexOf(String str, int fromIndex) returns the first index of the passed str at or after the passed fromIndex, if it is found. If str isn't in the current string at or after the fromIndex, it will return −1.

```
> String t = "That which is, is.  That which is not, is not.";
> System.out.println(t.indexOf("is",14));
15
```

- lastIndexOf(String str) returns the last index of the passed str, if it is found. If str isn't in the current string, it will return −1.

```
> String s = "It is a nice day, isn't it?";
> System.out.println(s.lastIndexOf("it"));
24
```

- lastIndexOf(String str, int index) returns the last index of the passed str found looking backward starting at index. If str isn't in the current string before the given index, it will return −1.

```
> String s = "It is a nice day, isn't it?";
> System.out.println(s.lastIndexOf("is",17));
3
```

- toUpperCase() returns a new string with all the characters in uppercase.

```
> System.out.println("Hello".toUpperCase());
HELLO
```

- toLowerCase() returns a new string with all the characters in lowercase.

```
> System.out.println("Hello".toLowerCase());
hello
```

- replace(String oldStr, String newStr) returns a new string with the characters in the oldStr replaced with the characters in the newStr for all occurrences of the oldStr. This is new in Java 1.5.

```
> System.out.println(letter);
Mr. Guzdial requests the pleasure of your company ...
> System.out.println(letter.replace("a","!"));
Mr. Guzdi!l requests the ple!sure of your comp!ny ...
```

- `replaceAll(String regex, Sting newStr)` this will return a new string with all the matching substrings specified by the regular expression (`regex`) replaced with the characters in `newStr`. A regular expression can be just a string of characters, or it can also use special characters to indicate that it will match any character, any digit, only uppercase characters, and so on. If you use it with a string of characters, it is the same as the `replace` method.

```
> System.out.println(letter);
Mr. Guzdial requests the pleasure of your company ...
> System.out.println(letter.replaceAll("a","!"));
Mr. Guzdi!l requests the ple!sure of your comp!ny ...
```

To replace all digits (0–9) with a space, do:

```
> String test = "This9 is a test7";
> System.out.println(test.replaceAll("\\d"," "));
This  is a test
```

To remove all non-digits, do:

```
> String input = "7a8c";
> System.out.println(input.replaceAll("\\D",""));
78
```

- `replaceFirst(String regex, Sting newStr)` this will return a new string with the first substring that matches the regular expression specified by `regex` replaced with the characters in `newStr`. A regular expression can be just a string of characters or it can also use special characters to indicate that it will match any character, any digit, only uppercase characters, and so on.

```
> System.out.println(letter);
Mr. Guzdial requests the pleasure of your company ...
> System.out.println(letter.replaceFirst("a","!"));
Mr. Guzdi!l requests the pleasure of your company ...
```

- `split(String regex)` this will return an array of `String` objects. It will split the current string into many strings by breaking it wherever it matches the regular expression specified in `regex`.

```
> System.out.println(letter);
Mr. Guzdial requests the pleasure of your company ...
> String[] strArray = letter.split(" ");
> for (int i = 0; i < strArray.length; i++)
      System.out.println(strArray[i]);
Mr.
Guzdial
requests
the
pleasure
of
your
company
...
```

- `trim()` this will return a new string with all white space (spaces and tabs) removed from the beginning and end of the string.

```
> String strWithSpaces = "    Janet Hund    ";
> System.out.println(strWithSpaces.trim());
Janet Hund
```

These methods can be *cascaded* —one modifying the result of another.

```
> String test ="This is a test of Something."
> System.out.println(test.substring(5).toUpperCase());
IS A TEST OF SOMETHING.
```

12.2.3 Processing Delimited Strings Using Split

Sometimes you get data for an object as a *delimited* string. A delimited string is a string with special characters that separate the string into different parts. If we read student data from a file it may be represented in a file as a delimited string. In the strings below the name is separated from the grades by ':' and the grades are separated from each other with a comma (',').

```
Jane Dorda        :88, 92, 95, 87, 93, 85
Mike Koziatek     :75, 92, 83, 81, 91, 87
Sharquita Edwards:91, 93, 95, 92, 94, 99
```

Let's add another constructor to the `Student` class which takes a delimited string, the delimiter that separates the name from the grades, and the delimiter that separates the grades. It should *parse* (break it up into parts) the delimited string and fill in the `Student` fields. We can use the `split` method of the `String` class to split the string into the name and grades and then split again to split the grades up into an array of strings. We will need to convert the array of strings into an array of doubles. To do this we can use the method `parseDouble(String doubleStr)`, which is a class (`static`) method of the `Double` class.

Making it Work Tip: Converting Strings to Numbers

You often need to convert something from a string to a number. Remember that these are represented differently in the computer. Each of the wrapper classes (Integer, Float, Double, etc.) has a class (`static`) method to do this. Each of these can result in a runtime exception (error) if the string doesn't contain a valid number. To convert a string to an integer, use `Integer.parseInt(intStr)`.

Program 101: Constructor that Takes a Delimited String

```
/**
 * Constructor that takes a delimited string, the
 * name delimiter, and the grade delimiter.  It fills
 * in the fields from the delimited string.
 * @param delimString student information as a
 * delimited string
 * @param nameDelim what delimits the name field
```

```
 * from the grades
 * @param gradeDelim what delimits the grades
 */
public Student(String delimString,
               String nameDelim,
               String gradeDelim)
{
  // split string based on name delimiter
  String[] splitArray = delimString.split(nameDelim);
  this.name = splitArray[0].trim();

  // get the grade string and break it and convert to double
  String grades = splitArray[1];
  String[] gradeStrArray = null;
  if (grades != null)
  {
    gradeStrArray = grades.split(gradeDelim);
    this.gradeArray = new double[gradeStrArray.length];
    for (int i = 0; i < gradeStrArray.length; i++)
      this.gradeArray[i] =
          Double.parseDouble(gradeStrArray[i]);
  }
}
```

You can try this out using the following `main` method:

```
/* Used to test */
public static void main (String[] args)
{
  // test the constructor that takes a delimited string
  Student student3 =
    new Student("Susan Ericson:50,60,70,80,90,100",":",",");
  System.out.println(student3);
}
```

Compile and run `Student` to test the new constructor.

```
> java Student
Student object named: Susan Ericson Average: 75.0
```

12.2.4   Strings Don't Have a Font

Strings don't have a *font* (characteristic look of the letters) or *style* (boldface, italics, underline, and other effects applied to a string) associated with them. Font and style information is added to strings in word-processors and other programs. Typically, these are encoded as *style runs*.

A style run is a separate representation of the font and style information with indices into the string for where the changes should take place. For example, The old *brown* fox **runs** might be encoded as [[bold 0 6][italics 8 12]].

Most software that manages formatted text will encode strings with style runs as an *object*. Objects have data associated with them, perhaps in several parts (like strings and style runs). Objects know how to act upon their data, using *methods* that may be known only to objects of that type. If the same method name is known to multiple objects, it probably does the same thing, but maybe not in the same way.

12.3   FILES: PLACES TO PUT YOUR STRINGS AND OTHER STUFF

Files are large, named collections of bytes on your hard disk. Files typically have a *base name* and a *file suffix*. The file `barbara.jpg` has the base name of "barbara" and a file suffix of "jpg" that tells you that the file is a JPEG picture.

Files are clustered into *directories* (sometimes called *folders*). Directories can contain files as well as other directories. There is a base directory on your computer which is referred to as the *root directory*. On a computer using the Windows operating system, the base directory will be something like `C:\`. A complete description of what directories to visit to get to a particular file from the base directory is called a *path*.

```
> String filename=FileChooser.pickAFile();
> System.out.println(filename);
C:\Documents and Settings\Mark Guzdial\mediasources\640x480.jpg
```

The path that is printed tells us how to go from the root directory to the file `640x480.jpg` in Mark's `mediasources` directory. We start at `C:\`, choose the directory `Documents and Settings`, then the directory `Mark Guzdial`, then the directory `mediasources`.

We call this structure a *tree* (Figure 12.1). We call `C:\` the *root* of the tree. The tree has *branches* where there are sub-directories. Any directory can contain more directories (branches) or files, which are referred to as *leaves*. Except for the root, each *node* of the tree (branch or leaf) has a single *parent* branch node, though a parent can have multiple *children* branches and leaves.

We need to know about directories and files if we're going to manipulate files. If you're dealing with a big Web site, you are going to be working with a lot of files.

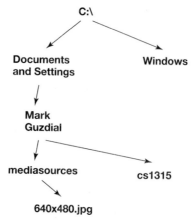

FIGURE 12.1
Diagram of a directory tree.

If you are going to be dealing with video, you will have about 30 files (individual frames) for each second of video. You don't really want to write a line of code to open each frame! You want to write programs that will walk directory structures to process Web or video files.

12.3.1 Reading from Files

To read from a file we need a *class* that knows how to read from a file. In Java the input and output classes are in the package `java.io`. A class that knows how to read from a character-based file is: `FileReader`. The class `FileReader` has a constructor that takes a file name as a string (an object of the `String` class).

However, we won't use this class directly. When you read from a file you are moving data from secondary storage (disk) into memory. Reading from secondary storage is much slower than reading from memory. So it is better to read a block of data from the disk into memory and then read from memory as you need the data than to read a line at a time from the disk. This is called *buffering* the data. We will use a class to do this for us: `BufferedReader`. The class `BufferedReader` has a constructor which will take a `FileReader` as a parameter.

Whenever we are working with files, things can go wrong. The file that we are trying to read from may not exist. The disk could go bad and stop working as we are reading from it. How do we deal with these problems? Java *requires* that the programmer write code to handle some kinds of exceptional events. We use the shorthand *exception* to mean exceptional event.

12.3.2 Handling Exceptions

Execution begins in a `main` method. The `main` method typically creates an object or objects and then calls at least one method. When it calls that other method, the `main` method probably isn't finished—the computer has to *remember* where it was in the `main` method so that it can come back to the exact same spot. A method that is called from the `main` method may call other methods—again, from somewhere in the middle of the method, so the computer has to keep track of where it was in those other methods, too. Each time a new method is called, the reminder of where the *calling* method stopped is added to the top of the *call stack* (Figure 12.2).

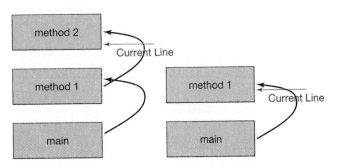

FIGURE 12.2
Showing a call stack before a method returns and after.

The call stack keeps track of all the method calls between the original call to main and the currently executing method. When a method is done executing, it is removed from the top of the call stack, and execution continues from where the calling method paused. So a call stack is like a trail of bread crumbs, in that it shows how you got to the currently executing method.

If we change the getAverage method in the Student class to no longer check whether the gradeArray is null or has a length of zero, we will get a runtime exception if we execute the following main method:

```java
public static void main (String[] args)
  {
    Student student1 = new Student("Barb Ericson");
    System.out.println(student1);
    double[] gradeArray1 = {90,88,95,96,93};
    Student student2 = new Student("Mark Guzdial",gradeArray1);
    System.out.println(student2);
  }
```

This runtime exception will print out the current call stack.

```
> java Student
java.lang.NullPointerException:
  at Student.getAverage(Student.java:109)
  at Student.toString(Student.java:120)
  at java.lang.String.valueOf(String.java:2131)
  at java.io.PrintStream.print(PrintStream.java:462)
  at java.io.PrintStream.println(PrintStream.java:599)
  at Student.main(Student.java:129)
```

Making it Work Tip: Viewing Line Numbers in DrJava

To see the line numbers in DrJava, click on EDIT, then on PREFERENCES, and then on DISPLAY OPTIONS, and check the SHOW ALL LINE NUMBERS checkbox in the PREFERENCES window. Then click on OK.

■

From the call stack we can see that a NullPointerException was encountered at line 109 in the getAverage method of the Student class. The getAverage method was called at line 120 of the method toString in the class String. We can continue following the call stack back to line 129 of the main method of the Student class.

When an exceptional event happens during execution of a method, an object of the class java.lang.Exception, or an object of one of the children classes of java.lang.Exception will be created (Figure 12.3). The runtime environment will look for a method in the call stack that handles this exception. Some exceptions are runtime exceptions such as ArrayIndexOutOfBoundsException. Methods are *not* required to handle runtime exceptions. If no method handles a runtime exception, execution will stop and information about the exception will be printed (including information about the call stack). Other exceptions *must* be handled or the code will not compile. These are called *checked exceptions*. Runtime exceptions are *unchecked*

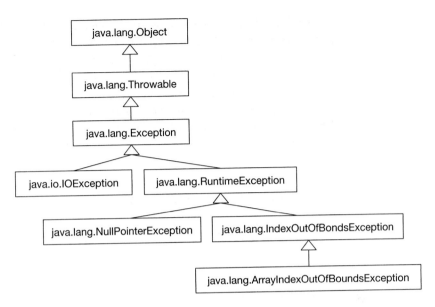

FIGURE 12.3
A depiction of the inheritance tree for some exception classes.

exceptions, meaning that they don't have to be checked for in the code in order for the code to compile.

To handle checked exceptions in Java you can either catch the exception or throw it. We will cover throwing exceptions in the next chapter. To catch an exception you will use *try, catch,* and *finally blocks*. The *try block* is a block of code that the runtime will *try* to execute. The statements in the try block are executed one after another until either you reach the end of the try block or an exception occurs.

If an exception occurs during the execution of a try block, a *catch block* will execute. A catch block will catch objects of the specified Exception class *and* objects of all classes that inherit from the specified class. You can have more than one catch block following a try block. If you do have more than one catch block, be sure to catch the most specific exception before you catch a more general one.

The optional finally block is used to do clean-up no matter what happens in the try and/or catch blocks. It will always execute regardless of whether an exception occurs or not.

```
try {
    // statements that can cause exceptions
} catch (Exception ex) {
    // what to do if an exception happens
} finally {
    // what to do no matter what happens above
}
```

Here is an example class that has a method that will read and print the contents of a file. Notice that since we are using classes from package java.io we need to import the classes.

Debugging Tip: Can't Resolve Class Names

If you get a compiler error that says it can't resolve a class name that you think should be part of the Java language, then you probably forgot to use an import statement and used just the class name. You can either use the full name for the class, which is packagename.ClassName, or you can use an import statement to import just the class (import java.io.BufferedReader), or import all classes in that package (import java.io.*). Import statements tell Java where to look for classes. They *don't* make your program any bigger by including code from other files. The import statements *must* go before the class declaration in the file.

Program 102: Sample Class to Read from a File

```java
import java.io.*;

/**
 * Class that allows you to easily read and print out the
 * contents of a file
 * @author Barb Ericson
 */
public class SimpleReader
{
  /**
   * Method to read a file and print out the contents
   * @param fileName the name of the file to read from
   */
  public void readAndPrintFile(String fileName)
  {
    String line = null;

    // try to do the following
    try {

      // create the buffered reader
      BufferedReader reader =
        new BufferedReader(new FileReader(fileName));

      // Loop while there is more data
      while((line = reader.readLine()) != null)
      {
        // print the current line
        System.out.println(line);
      }

      // close the reader
      reader.close();

    } catch(FileNotFoundException ex) {
      SimpleOutput.showError("Couldn't find " + fileName +
                             " please pick it.");
      fileName = FileChooser.pickAFile();
      readAndPrintFile(fileName);
```

```
    } catch(Exception ex) {
      SimpleOutput.showError("Error reading file " + fileName);
      ex.printStackTrace();
    }
  }

  public static void main(String[] args)
  {
    SimpleReader reader = new SimpleReader();
    reader.readAndPrintFile("test.txt");
  }
}
```

The method readAndPrintFile will loop reading from the BufferedReader a line at a time until the line that is returned from the method readLine is null. If the line isn't null it will be printed out. A null line will mean that we have reached the end of the current file. Once the end of the file is reached, it will close the BufferedReader, which will also close the file.

If the file isn't found, it will inform the user using a class that we developed, SimpleOutput, that makes it easy to show a dialog box to the user. Next it will use FileChooser to try to pick the file name. Then it will invoke the method again with the new file name.

If some other exception occurs during the execution of the try block, an error message will be displayed to the user using SimpleOutput and the call stack will be displayed by the Exception object using the method printStackTrace.

This method does not contain the optional finally clause. Why not? Well, we could move the reader.close() into a finally clause because we always want to close the file even if there is an exception, but the close can also cause an exception. So let's leave it in the try block.

Notice that we catch FileNotFoundException *before* we catch Exception. The class FileNotFoundException is a child of the class Exception, so we can't switch the order or we would never reach the second catch block. Catching Exception first would also catch FileNotFoundException since it is a child of Exception.

Let's add a static method to the Student class that will read student information from a file and create new student objects. We don't know how many Student objects we will be creating. What size array should we use? We could make it hold 35 elements, but that may be way too big or too little. It would be nice to have an array that can grow or shrink as needed to fit the data that we put in it. Java does provide this as part of the *collection classes*. The collection classes are classes that hold collections of objects. These classes are in package java.util.

12.3.3   Working with an ArrayList

A java.util.ArrayList object has an array that can grow or shrink as needed. It stores items in an array, so it preserves the order of elements. It keeps elements in order and allows duplicate elements.

Here are some of the methods of the class `ArrayList`:

- `add(Object o)` will add the passed object (o) to the end of the list (next open position in the array).

- `add(int index, Object o)` will set the object at the given `index` to the passed object (o). If an object is at that index it will be moved to (index + 1). If an object was at (index + 1) it will be moved to (index + 2). So all objects at the passed index or above will change to the location specified by their (current index + 1).

- `get(int index)` will return the object at the passed `index` in the array

- `set(int index, Object o)` will set the value at this `index` in the array to the passed object (o). If an object is at that index it will be moved to (index + 1). If an object was at (index + 1) it will be moved to (index + 2). So, all objects at the index or above will change to the location specified by their (current index + 1).

- `size()` returns the number of elements in the list

- `remove(int index)` removes the object at the passed `index`. Any objects with a current index value greater than this will change to (current index −1).

We had used an array of `Student` objects in the class `ClassPeriod` and we had created an array of size 35. But, what if we have less students than this in the array? Then we are wasting space. But, what if we have more students than this in the class period? Then we will get an `ArrayIndexOutOfBoundsException` if we try to add more than 35 `Student` objects to the array. It would be better to use an `ArrayList` to hold the `Student` objects in the class period.

We can change the field in the `ClassPeriod` class from an array of `Student` objects to a list of `Student` objects:

```java
private List studentList = new ArrayList();
```

You may be thinking, "Why is the type of the `studentList` field given as `List` instead of `ArrayList`?" We do this to make it easy to swap out one class for another. The type `java.util.List` is actually an *interface*. An interface is a special kind of class in Java that only defines public *abstract methods* and/or constants. Abstract methods are methods that don't have a block of code associated with them. The following is the Java 1.4 declaration of the interface `java.lang.Comparable`.

```java
package java.lang;
public interface Comparable
{
    int compareTo(Object o);
}
```

As you can see the method `compareTo` doesn't have a block of code associated with it. Interfaces can only be used to declare public abstract methods and constants. Look up the interface `java.util.List` in the API and see what abstract methods are part of that interface. Notice that an interface can inherit from another interface. What interface does List inherit from? When an interface inherits from another interface it inherits all the methods and constants from the parent interface.

A class that *implements* an interface will override the abstract methods and provide code for them. An object of a class that implements an interface can be declared to be of the interface type. Since the class `ArrayList` implements the `List` interface, an `ArrayList` object can be declared to be of type `List`.

The `String` class implements the `Comparable` interface. You will often implement the `Comparable` interface in classes you create. This allows you to use general sorting programs that only care that the objects that are being sorted are of the type `Comparable`. What does it mean to compare two students and decide whether one is less than, equal to, or greater than the other? You have to decide what it means when you implement the method `compareTo` in the `Student` class. You may compare based on grades or names. The `String` class compares the characters in the two string objects alphabetically.

Why would you want to specify the interface name as the type of a variable? There are several classes in Java that implement the interface `List`. If we change our minds about which actual class to use, and we have only specified the actual class one time (when we create the object) then it makes it easy to swap out the class for another class that implements the same interface.

Making it Work Tip: Use Interface Names Instead of Class Names

If you are declaring a variable for an object of a class that implements an interface, you may want to use the interface name as the type instead of the class name. This will let you use a different class in the future. This is especially true for the collection classes in package `java.util`. Use `List` instead of `ArrayList`, `Set` instead of `HashSet`, and `Map` instead of `HashMap`.

So interfaces make it easy to plug classes together and to swap out one class for another that implements the same interface. Think of this like LEGO™ blocks. All LEGO™ blocks have the same interface and will snap together. You can easily pull off one and replace it with another. Or, you can think of this like your computer's USB interface. The computer doesn't care what type of thing you plug into the USB port. It only cares that the thing understands the USB interface. So you can plug in a digital camera, a key drive, or a mouse.

Computer Science Idea: Decoupling Classes

One of the goals of object-oriented programming is to *decouple* classes. Decoupling means minimizing the number of changes you have to make to class A if you change class B and A refers to B. Interfaces let us decouple classes because one class can refer to an object of another class using the interface name as the type. This allows us to substitute class C for class B if classes B and C implement the same interface, without making many changes to class A.

We also need to change the accessors and modifiers and any other methods that used the `studentArray` to work with the `studentList`. Here are the modified methods in the `ClassPeriod` class.

```
/**
 * Method to get a student based on the index
 * @return the student at this index
 */
public Student getStudent(int index)
{
  return (Student) this.studentList.get(index);
}

/**
 * Method to set the student at an index
 * @param studentObj the student object to use
 * @param index the index to set the student at
 */
public void setStudent(Student studentObj, int index)
{
  this.studentList.add(index,studentObj);
}

/**
 * Method to return the number of students in the period
 * @return the number of students in the period
 */
public int getNumStudents()
{
  int total = 0;
  for (int i = 0; i < this.studentList.size(); i++)
  {
    if (this.studentList.get(i) != null)
      total++;
  }
  return total;
}
```

Notice in the method `getStudent` that we have to cast the object that we get from the passed index in the list back to a `Student` object. Why do we have to do that? All of the collections classes in the package `java.util` such as `List`, `Set`, and `Map` hold objects. Our `Student` class inherits from the `Object` class so all `Student` objects are also considered objects of the `Object` class. When we pull objects back out of a collection class we can continue to treat them as objects of the `Object` class, but often we want to treat them as objects of their original class. But, the compiler doesn't know that the `Object` that we pull out of the collection class is a `Student` object. We have to tell it that it is by casting back to the `Student` class. As of Java 5.0 (1.5) you can use generics to tell the compiler the types of things in collection classes and then you don't need to cast the objects that you get back from collection classes to their original types. We cover generics in the next chapter.

Let's add another constructor to the `ClassPeriod` class that will take the teacher's name, the period number, and the name of a file that has student information in it. We will add a private method that will read the student information from the file and create the `Student` objects.

Program 103: Constructor that Takes a File Name

```
/**
 * Constructor that takes the teacher's name, period number,
 * and a file name that contains the student information
 * @param name the name for the teacher
 * @param num the period number
 * @param fileName the name of the file with the student
 * information
 */
public ClassPeriod(String name, int num, String fileName)
{
  this.teacherName = name;
  this.periodNumber = num;
  loadStudentsFromFile(fileName)
}
```

Now we need to create the `loadStudentsFromFile` method that takes the file name to read from. It will read student information from a file a line at a time and create the `Student` objects. It will call the constructor that takes a delimited string to fill in the fields from the line. It will add the newly created `Student` objects to the list of students.

Program 104: Loading the Student Information from a File

```
/**
 * Method to read student information from a file and create
 * a list of student objects
 * @param fileName the name of the file to read from
 * @param nameDelim the delimter between the name and grades
 * @param gradeDelim the delimiter between the grades
 */
private void loadStudentsFromFile(String fileName)
{
  String nameDelim = ":";
  String gradeDelim = ",";
  String line = null;
  try {

    // open the file for reading
    BufferedReader reader =
      new BufferedReader(new FileReader(fileName));

    // loop reading from the file
    while ((line = reader.readLine()) != null)
    {
      studentList.add(new Student(line,nameDelim,gradeDelim));
    }
  } catch (FileNotFoundException ex) {
    fileName = FileChooser.pickAFile();
    loadStudentsFromFile(fileName);
```

```
      } catch (Exception ex) {
        System.out.println("Exception while reading from file " +
                           fileName);
        ex.printStackTrace();
      }
    }
```

■

Here is a revised `main` method for the `ClassPeriod` class that will test the new constructor that takes a file name to read the student information from.

```
/**
 * Main method
 * @param args the arguments to execution
 */
public static void main(String[] args)
{
  ClassPeriod period =
    new ClassPeriod("Ms. Clark",5,"student.txt");

  // print info about the class period
  System.out.println(period);

  // print info for each student
  for (int i = 0; i < period.studentList.size(); i++)
    System.out.println("Student " + i + " is " +
                        period.getStudent(i));

}
```

Running this `main` method will result in:

```
Class Period 5 taught by Ms. Clark with 3 students
Student 0 is Student object named: Jane Dorda Average: 90.0
Student 1 is Student object named: Mike Koziatek Average: 84.84
Student 2 is Student object named: Sharquita Edwards Average: 94.0
```

12.3.4   Writing to a File

To read from a file we used an object of the `FileReader` class, along with an object of the `BufferedReader` class to handle the buffering of the data in memory from the disk. We will do much the same thing when we write to a file. We will use a `BufferedWriter` which will buffer the data until there is enough to write to the file efficiently. We will use a `FileWriter` to handle the actual writing of the data to a file. The class `BufferedWriter` has a constructor which will take a `FileWriter` as a parameter.

Here's an example of writing a silly file. The method `newLine()` will print a new line that is correct for the operating system that the program is running on. Some programs use the special character `'\n'`, but this isn't correct for all operating systems. It is better to use the `newLine()` method.

Program 105: Sample Class for Writing to a File

```java
import java.io.*;

/**
 * Class that shows how to write to a file
 * @author Barb Ericson
 */
public class SimpleWriter {
  /**
   * Method to write a silly file
   */
  public void writeSillyFile()
  {
    try {
      // try to open the buffered writer
      BufferedWriter writer =
        new BufferedWriter(new FileWriter("silly.txt"));

      // write out the file
      writer.write("Here is some text.");
      writer.newLine();
      writer.write("Here is some more.");
      writer.newLine();
      writer.write("And now we're done.");
      writer.newLine();
      writer.newLine();
      writer.write("THE END");
      writer.close();
    } catch (Exception ex) {
      System.out.println("Error during write of silly.txt");
    }
  }

  public static void main(String[] args)
  {
    SimpleWriter writer = new SimpleWriter();
    writer.writeSillyFile();
  }

}
```

■

Executing the main method of this class will create a file with the following contents:

```
Here is some text.
Here is some more.
And now we're done.

THE END
```

12.3.5   Generating a Form Letter

We have used the split method of the String class to separate a delimited string into parts. We can also write methods that will *assemble* text. One of the classic structured texts that we're all too familiar with is spam or form letters. The really good spam writers (if that's not a contradiction in terms) fill in details that actually do refer to *you* in the message. How do they do that? It's pretty easy—they have a method that takes in the relevant input and plugs it into the right places.

Program 106: A Form Letter Generator

```java
import java.io.*;
/**
 * Class used to generate form letters
 * @author Barbara Ericson
 */
public class FormLetterGenerator
{

  /**
   * Method to generate a form letter
   * @param isMale true if this is for a male
   * @param String lastName the last name for the recipient
   * @param String city the name of the city for the recipient
   * @param eyeColor the eye color of the recipient
   */
  public void writeLetter(String title, String lastName,
                          String city, String eyeColor)
  {
    String fileName = lastName + "Letter.txt";

    // try to open the file and write to it
    try {

      // create the buffered writer to use to write the file
      BufferedWriter writer =
        new BufferedWriter(new FileWriter(fileName));

      // write the beginning of the letter
      writer.write("Dear " + title + " " + lastName + ", ");
      writer.newLine();
      writer.newLine();

      // write the body of the letter
      writer.write("I am writing to remind you of the offer");
      writer.newLine();
      writer.write("that we sent to you last week.  ");
      writer.write("Everyone in");
      writer.newLine();
      writer.write(city +
                   " knows what an exceptional offer this is!");
      writer.newLine();
```

```
        writer.write("(Especially those with lovely eyes of " +
                eyeColor + "!)");
        writer.newLine();
        writer.write("We hope to hear from you soon.");
        writer.newLine();
        writer.newLine();

        // write the ending
        writer.write("Sincerely,");
        writer.newLine();
        writer.write("I. M. Acrook");

        // close the file
        writer.close();
      } catch (Exception ex) {
      System.out.println("Error writing to " + fileName);
      }
    }
  }

  public static void main(String[] args)
  {
    FormLetterGenerator formGenerator =
        new FormLetterGenerator();
    formGenerator.writeLetter("Mr.","Guzdial","Decatur","brown");
  }

}
```

How it Works

This method takes a title, a last name (family name), a city, and an eye color as input. It opens a file with a name created by appending `Letter.txt` to the last name. It writes out a bunch of text, inserting the parameter values into the right places. Then it closes the `BufferedWriter` which will close the file.

When the `main` method is executed, it creates a file with the following contents.

```
Dear Mr. Guzdial,

I am writing to remind you of the offer that we sent to you last
week.  Everyone in Decatur knows what an exceptional offer this
is! (Especially those with lovely eyes of brown!) We hope to hear
from you soon.

Sincerely,
I. M. Acrook
```

12.3.6 Modifying Programs

Now let's start *using* files. Our first program will do something pretty interesting—let's write a program to *change* another program.

Here is the program we will modify:

```java
import java.awt.*;
import java.awt.font.*;
import java.awt.geom.*;

/**
 * Class to create a cartoon out of a picture
 * @author Barb Ericson
 */
public class Cartoon
{

    /////////// fields ////////////////////
    private Picture picture;


    ////////// constructor //////////////
    /**
     * Constructor that takes the picture
     * @param p the picture to use
     */
    public Cartoon(Picture p) { this.picture = p; }

    ////////// methods //////////////////
    /**
     * Method to add a word balloon that contains the message
     * @param message the text to show
     * @param xPos the top left for the word balloon
     * @param yPos the top left for the word balloon
     */
    public void addWordBalloon(String message,int xPos,int yPos)
    {
        // get the Graphics2D
        Graphics g = this.picture.getGraphics();
        Graphics2D g2 = (Graphics2D) g;

        // get the font information for the message
        Font font =  Font("Arial",Font.BOLD,24);
        FontRenderContext frc = g2.getFontRenderContext();
        Rectangle2D bounds = font.getStringBounds(message,frc);
        LineMetrics metrics = font.getLineMetrics(message,frc);
        float lineHeight = metrics.getHeight();
        float ascent = metrics.getAscent();

        // draw the ellipse for the word balloon
        double ellipseWidth = bounds.getWidth() * 1.5;
        double ellipseHeight = bounds.getHeight() * 2.0;
        g2.setColor(Color.WHITE);
```

```
    g2.fill(new Ellipse2D.Double(xPos,yPos,
                                 ellipseWidth,
                                 ellipseHeight));

    // draw the message centered in the ellipse
    float x0 = (float) ((ellipseWidth - bounds.getWidth()) / 2 +
                    xPos);
    float y0 = (float) ((ellipseHeight - lineHeight) / 2 +
                    yPos + ascent);
    g2.setColor(Color.BLACK);
    g2.setFont(font);
    g2.drawString(message,x0,y0);
  }

  public static void main(String[] args)
  {
    Picture picture =
      new Picture(FileChooser.getMediaPath("horse.jpg"));
    Cartoon cartoon = new Cartoon(picture);
    cartoon.addWordBalloon("Just Horsing Around!",42,20);
    picture.explore();
  }

}
```

Common Bug: Failure to Set the Media Path

Remember to set the directory for your media by executing
`FileChooser.setMediaPath("fullDirectoryPath/");` before you use
`FileChooser.getMediaPath("name.jpg");`. Replace `fullDirectoryPath` with the full
path name for the directory (like `c:/intro-prog-java/mediasources/`). Be sure to
include a final '`/`' character in the directory name. If you don't set the media directory
before you try to use it, the file may not be found.

Run the `main` method for this class. It will create a cartoon by adding a word
balloon to a picture. It will display the cartoon. To modify this file we will read the
`Cartoon.java` file, and replace the current word balloon text with different text.

To do this we will first loop reading a line at a time until we either reach the end
of the file or find the text we want to replace. We can look for the text to replace
using the `String` method `indexOf`. If we haven't reached the end of the file or
found the text to replace, we will just add the current line to a list of lines. We can
use an `ArrayList` to hold the list of lines.

If we stopped the first loop because we found the text to be replaced, we will
replace the text and add the modified line to the list of lines. Next we need to loop
till the end of the file adding each additional line to the list of lines.

At this point we have reached the end of the file and we can close the file. Then
we open it again for writing and write all the lines in the list to the file. Finally, we
can close the file.

Program 107: A Program that Changes Another Program

```java
import java.util.*;
import java.io.*;

/**
 * Class to demonstrate using a program to modify another program
 * @author Barb Ericson
 */
public class FileModifier
{
  /**
   * Method to modify the first string in a method to
   * be the passed changed text
   * @param fileName the file name for the class to modify
   * @param textToChange the text to change
   * @param changedText the new text to use for the text to
   * change
   */
  public void modifyFile(String fileName,
                         String textToChange,
                         String changedText)
  {
    List lineList = new ArrayList();
    String line = null;
    int pos = 0;

    // try the following
    try {

      // open the file to read from
      BufferedReader reader =
        new BufferedReader(new FileReader(fileName));

      /* loop while there are more lines in the file
       * and we haven't found the text to change yet
       */
      while((line = reader.readLine()) != null &&
            line.indexOf(textToChange) < 0)
      {
        lineList.add(line);
      }

      /* If we get there we either ran out of lines or we
       * found the text to change
       */
      if (line != null)
      {
        // get the position of the text to change
        pos = line.indexOf(textToChange);
```

```java
      // modify the string
      lineList.add(line.substring(0,pos) +
                    changedText +
                    line.substring(pos +
                              textToChange.length()));


      // loop till the end of the file adding the rest
      while ((line = reader.readLine()) != null)
      {
        lineList.add(line);
      }

    }

    // now close the file
    reader.close();

    // create a writer to write out the file
    BufferedWriter writer =
      new BufferedWriter(new FileWriter(fileName));

    // loop writing out the lines
    for (int i = 0; i < lineList.size(); i++)
    {
      writer.write((String) lineList.get(i));
      writer.newLine();
    }

    // close the writer
    writer.close();
  } catch (FileNotFoundException ex) {
    SimpleOutput.showError("Couldn't find file " + fileName);
    fileName = FileChooser.pickAFile();
    modifyFile(fileName,textToChange,changedText);
  } catch (Exception ex) {
    SimpleOutput.showError("Error during read or write");
    ex.printStackTrace();
  }
}

// Main method to run
public static void main(String[] args)
{
  FileModifier fileMod = new FileModifier();
  String file =
    "C:\\intro-prog-java\\bookClassesFinal\\Cartoon.java";
  fileMod.modifyFile(file,
                    "Just Horsing Around!",
                    "What's up, Wilbur?");
 }
}
```

■

How it Works

This program opens up the file `Cartoon.java`. It loops reading a line at a time from the file until it finds the text to change or reaches the end of the file. If it finds the text to change, it will replace the text with the new text and add that modified string to the list of lines. Then it will loop adding any additional lines in the file to the list of lines. After it has reached the end of the file, it will close the file and then open it up again and write all the lines in the list to the file. It will close the file again when it has finished writing all the lines.

After you execute the `main` method of this class, open `Cartoon.java` to verify that it did change the string. You should compile `Cartoon.java` and then run the `main` method to see the change. Here is what the `main` method will look like after it has been changed (Figure 12.4):

```java
public static void main(String[] args)
{
  Picture picture =
    new Picture(FileChooser.getMediaPath("horse.jpg"));
  Cartoon cartoon = new Cartoon(picture);
  cartoon.addWordBalloon("What's up Wilbur?",42,20);
  picture.explore();
}
```

This is how vector-based drawing programs work. When you change a line in AutoCAD or Flash or Illustrator, you're actually changing the underlying representation of the picture—in a real sense, a little program whose execution results in the

FIGURE 12.4
Original cartoon (left) and after the class has been modified (right).

picture you're working with. When you change the line, you're actually changing the program, which is then re-executed to show you the updated picture. Isn't that slow? Thank God for Moore's Law! Computers are fast enough that we just don't notice.

Being able to manipulate text is particularly important for gathering data on the Internet. Most of the Internet is just text. Go to your favorite Web page, then use the VIEW SOURCE option in the menu. That's the text that defines the page you're seeing in the browser. Later, we'll learn how to download pages directly from the Internet, but for now, let's assume that you've saved (*downloaded*) pages or files from the Internet onto your disk, and then we'll do searches from there.

For example, there are places on the Internet where you can grab sequences of nucleotides associated with things like parasites. Mark found a file that looks like this:

```
>Schisto unique AA825099
gcttagatgtcagattgagcacgatgatcgattgaccgtgagatcgacga
gatgcgcagatcgagatctgcatacagatgatgaccatagtgtacg
>Schisto unique mancons0736
ttctcgctcacactagaagcaagacaatttacactattattattattatt
accattattattattattattactattattattattattactattattta
ctacgtcgcttttttcactccctttattctcaaattgtgtatccttccttt
```

Let's say that we had a subsequence (like "ttgtgta") and we wanted to know which parasite it was part of. The parasite information is between the '>' and the end of the line containing the '>'.

We can loop reading this file a line at a time until we find the sequence. We can append each line to a string and add a new line character '\n' to the string to help determine the end of each line. Once we find the sequence we can look backward in the string for the last '>' character. Then we can look forward from that index to the next new line character ('\n'). The parasite information will be the characters between the two found indices.

Program 108: Finding a Subsequence in Parasite Nucleotide Sequences

```java
import java.io.*;

/**
 * Class that searches a file for a given sequence and reports
 * on the name where that sequence was found
 * @author Barb Ericson
 */
public class SequenceSearcher
{
  /**
   * Method to search for a given sequence and then
   * report on the name
   */
  public String getNameForSequence(String fileName, String seq)
  {
    String info = "";
    String line = null;
    String name = null;
```

```java
  // try the following
  try {

    // read from the file
    BufferedReader reader =
      new BufferedReader(new FileReader(fileName));

    // loop till end of file or find sequence
    while ((line = reader.readLine()) != null &&
          line.indexOf(seq) < 0)
    {
      // add to string with new line character
      info = info + line + "\n";
    }

    // if get here either end of line or we found the sequence
    if (line != null)
    {
      // look backward for the last >
      int firstIndex = info.lastIndexOf('>');

      // look forward from the > for the new line character
      int secondIndex = info.indexOf('\n',firstIndex);

      // get the name between the > and new line
      name = info.substring(firstIndex+1,secondIndex);
    }

  } catch (FileNotFoundException ex) {
    SimpleOutput.showError("Couldn't find file " + fileName);
    fileName = FileChooser.pickAFile();
    getNameForSequence(fileName,seq);
  } catch (Exception ex) {
    SimpleOutput.showError("Error during read or write");
    ex.printStackTrace();
  }

  return name;
}

public static void main(String[] args)
{
  SequenceSearcher searcher = new SequenceSearcher();
  String fileName = FileChooser.getMediaPath("parasites.txt");
  String seq = "ttgtgta";
  String name = searcher.getNameForSequence(fileName,seq);
  if (name == null)
    System.out.println("The sequence " + seq +
                       " wasn't found in " + fileName);
  else
```

```
                System.out.println("The sequence " + seq +
                            " was found in " + name);
    }
}
```

■

How it Works

The method `getNameForSequence` takes a file name to search and the sequence to search for. It will loop through the lines in the file until it finds the sequence to search for. Each line read from the file is appended to the string referred to by the variable `info` along with a new line character (`'\n'`). When the sequence that we are searching for is found we look backward in the `info` string for the last `'>'`. Then we look forward from that index till we find the new line character. The name is the substring between the two found indices.

There are programs that wander the Internet, gathering information from Web pages. For example, Google's news page (`http://news.google.com`) isn't written by reporters. Google has programs that go out and snag headlines out of *other* news sites. How do these programs work? They simply download pages from the Internet and chop out the desired pieces.

For example, let's say that you wanted to write a function that would give you the current temperature by reading it off a local weather page. In Atlanta, a good place to find the current weather is `http://www.ajc.com/weather`—the weather page of the *Atlanta Journal-Constitution*. By viewing source, we can find where the current temperature appears in the page, and what the key features of the text are around it to grab just the temperature. Here's the relevant part of the page that Mark found one day:

```
<td ><img src="/shared-local/weather/images/ps.gif" width="48"
height="48" border="0"><font size=-2><br></font><font size="-1"
face="Arial, Helvetica, sans-serif"><b>Currently</b><br> Partly
sunny<br> <font size="+2">54<b>\&deg;</b></font><font face="Arial,
Helvetica, sans-serif" size="+1">F</font></font></td> </tr>
```

You can see the word `Currently` in there, then the temperature just before the characters `<b>&deg`. We can write a program to chop out those pieces and return the temperature, given that the weather page is saved in a file named `ajc-weather.html`. This program won't *always* work. The page format will change and the key text we're looking for might move or disappear. But as long as the format is the same, this recipe will work.

Program 109: Get the Temperature from a Weather Page

```java
import java.io.*;

/**
 * Class to find the temperature in a web page.
 * @author Barb Ericson
 */
```

```java
public class TempFinder {

  /**
   * Method to find the temperature in the passed
   * file
   * @param fileName the name of the file to look in
   */
  public String getTemp(String fileName)
  {
    String seq = "<b>&deg";
    String temp = null;
    String line = null;

    // try the following
    try {

      // read from the file
      BufferedReader reader =
        new BufferedReader(new FileReader(fileName));

      // loop till end of file or find sequence
      while ((line = reader.readLine()) != null &&
             line.indexOf(seq) < 0)
      {}

      // if there is a current line
      if (line != null)
      {
        // find the temperature
        int degreeIndex = line.indexOf(seq);
        int startIndex = line.lastIndexOf('>',degreeIndex);
        temp = line.substring(startIndex + 1, degreeIndex);
      }

    } catch (FileNotFoundException ex) {
      SimpleOutput.showError("Couldn't find file " + fileName);
      fileName = FileChooser.pickAFile();
      temp = getTemp(fileName);
    } catch (Exception ex) {
      SimpleOutput.showError("Error during read or write");
      ex.printStackTrace();
    }
    return temp;
  }

  public static void main(String[] args)
  {
    TempFinder finder = new TempFinder();
    String file = FileChooser.getMediaPath("ajc-weather.html");
    String temp = finder.getTemp(file);
    if (temp == null)
      System.out.println("Sorry, no temp was found in " + file);
```

```
        else
          System.out.println("The current temperature is " + temp);
      }
}
```

How it Works

This function assumes that the file `ajc-weather.html` is stored in the media folder specified with `setMediaPath`. The method `getTemp` opens the file and reads a line at a time until it reaches the end of the file or finds the sequence. If we find the sequence we save the position where we found it. Then we look backward from there for the index of the last `'>'`. The temperature is between these two indices.

If we run the `main` method of this class we get:

```
> java TempFinder
The current temperature is 54
```

12.4 OTHER USEFUL CLASSES

In every programming language, there's a way of extending the basic functionality of the language. In Java, we do this with classes. Java comes with an extensive library of classes that you can use to do a wide range of things, such as accessing the Internet, generating random numbers, and accessing files in a directory—a useful thing to do when developing Web pages or working with video. These classes are grouped into packages. We have been working with several classes from the `java.io` package. But there are many other useful classes and many more packages.

Let's get a list of the contents of a directory as our first example. The class we'll use is the `java.io.File` class. This is a class that represents a file or directory pathname. There is a `list` method in the `File` class that will list all of the files and directories in a directory. It returns an array of `String` objects.

```
> import java.io.File;
> File dir = new File("C:\\intro-prog-java\\mediasources\\");
> String[] pathArray = dir.list();
> for (int i=0; i < 5; i++) System.out.println(pathArray[i]);
swan.jpg
MattScotland.jpg
twoSwans.jpg
kidsTree.jpg
redDoor.jpg
```

We can use the `list` method to add text to pictures in a directory. We could insert a copyright claim. The method `list` just returns the base filename and suffix. That's enough to make sure that we have pictures and not sounds or something else. But, it doesn't give us complete paths for creating a new `Picture`. To get a complete path, we can append the directory to the name we get from the method `list`.

Program 110: Add Text to All Pictures in a Directory

```java
import java.io.*;

/**
 * Class to work with files in a directory
 */
public class DirectoryWorker {
  /**
   * Method to add a string to every picture in directory
   * @param dir the name of the directory
   * @param text the text of the string to add
   */
  public void addStringToPictures(String dir, String text)
  {
    String name = null;

    // create the object that represents the directory
    File file = new File(dir);

    // Get the array of names in the directory
    String[] nameArray = file.list();

    // loop through the names
    for (int i = 0; i < nameArray.length; i++)
    {
      name = nameArray[i];

      // if this is a picture file
      if (name.indexOf(".jpg") >= 0)
      {
        // create the picture object
        Picture p = new Picture(dir + name);

        // add the text to the picture
        p.drawString(text, 5,
                    p.getHeight() - 50);

        // save the changed picture to a file
        p.write(dir + "titled-" + name);
      }
    }
  }

  public static void main(String[] args)
  {
    DirectoryWorker worker = new DirectoryWorker();
    worker.addStringToPictures(
      "c:\\intro-prog-java\\mediasources\\",
      "Copyright 2005");
  }
}
```

How it Works

The method `addStringToPictures` takes a directory (a path name, as a string) and the text to add as input. It creates a `File` object using the name of the directory and then it gets a list of file and directory names in that directory using the method `list`. It loops through the array of names, and if the current name has ".jpg" in it, it will create a `Picture` object from it and draw a string on the picture. It will then write the changed picture back out adding "titled-" in front of the name. It writes the changed picture to the same directory it read the original picture from.

12.4.1   Another Fun Class: Random

Another fun and useful class is `java.util.Random`. It is in the `java.util` package. It has a method `nextDouble()` that generates random numbers (evenly distributed) between 0 and 1.

```
> import java.util.Random;
> Random randomGen = new Random();
> for (int i = 0; i < 5; i++)
    System.out.println(randomGen.nextDouble());
0.9534889951932188
0.9713266979695472
0.2678907619250269
0.5310776290468512
0.9586483089727932
```

It also has a method `nextInt(int n)` which generates a random number between 0 (inclusive) and n (exclusive). To generate random numbers from 0 to 10 use `nextInt(11)`.

```
> for (int i = 0; i < 5; i++)
    System.out.println(randomGen.nextInt(11));
9
1
4
3
8
>
```

Random numbers can be fun when they're applied to tasks like picking random words from a list. We can generate random sentences by randomly picking nouns, verbs, and phrases from arrays of `Strings`.

Program 111: Randomly Generate Language

```
import java.util.Random;

/**
 * Class to generate sentences
 * @author Barb Ericson
 */
```

```java
public class SentenceGenerator
{
  /////////// fields ////////////
  private String[] nounArray = {"Mark", "Adam", "Angela",
    "Larry", "Jose", "Matt", "Jim"};
  private String[] verbArray = {"runs", "skips", "sings",
    "leaps", "jumps", "climbs", "argues", "giggles"};
  private String[] phraseArray = {"in a tree", "over a log",
    "very loudly", "around the bush",
    "while reading the newspaper",
    "very badly", "while skipping",
    "instead of grading"};
  private Random randGen = new Random();

  ////////////// methods /////////////////////////////////////////
  /**
    * Method to generate a random sentence
    * @return a random sentence
    */
  public String generateRandomSentence()
  {
    String sentence =
      nounArray[randGen.nextInt(nounArray.length)] + " " +
      verbArray[randGen.nextInt(verbArray.length)] + " " +
      phraseArray[randGen.nextInt(phraseArray.length)] + ".";

    return sentence;
  }

  public static void main(String[] args)
  {
    SentenceGenerator sentenceGen = new SentenceGenerator();
    for (int i = 0; i < 5; i++)
      System.out.println(sentenceGen.generateRandomSentence());
  }
}
```

```
> java SentenceGenerator
Jose runs around the bush.
Mark jumps while reading the newspaper.
Matt jumps very badly.
Angela skips very loudly.
Angela jumps while reading the newspaper.
```

How it Works

This class has arrays of nouns, verbs, and phrases. The method generateRandom-Sentence uses a random number generator (Random) to randomly pick a noun, verb, and a phrase and it returns the created sentence.

The basic process here is common in simulation programs. What we have here is a structure defined in the program: a definition of what counts as a noun, a verb, and a phrase, and a rule about how to put them together. A sentence is a noun, then a verb, and finally a phrase. The sentence gets filled in with random choices. The interesting question is how much can be simulated with a structure and randomness. Could we simulate intelligence like this? And what's the difference between a *simulation* of intelligence and a really thinking computer?

Imagine a program that reads input from the user, then generates a random sentence. Maybe there are a few *rules* in the program that searches for keywords and responds to those keywords, like:

```
if (input.indexOf("mother") >= 0)
  System.out.println("Tell me more about your mother...");
```

Joseph Weizenbaum wrote a program like this many years ago, called *Doctor* (later known as Eliza). His program would act like a Rogerian psychotherapist, echoing back whatever you said, with some randomness in it, but searching for keywords to seem like it was really "listening." It was meant as a joke, not a real effort to create a simulation of intelligence. To Weizenbaum's dismay, people took it seriously! They really started treating it like a therapist. Weizenbaum changed his research direction from *artificial intelligence* to concern over the ethical use of technology, and how easily people can be fooled by technology.

12.5   NETWORKS: GETTING OUR TEXT FROM THE WEB

A *network* is formed whenever distinct computers communicate. Rarely does the communication take place with voltages over wires, the way that a computer encodes zeros and ones internally. It's too hard to maintain those voltages over distances. Instead, zeros and ones are encoded in some other way. For example, a *modem* (literally *modulator–demodulator*) maps zeros and ones to different audio frequencies. When we hear these different tones, it sounds like a bunch of buzzing bees to us, but to modems, it's pure binary.

Like onions and ogres, networks have layers. At the bottom level is the physical substrate. How are the signals being passed? Higher levels define how data is encoded. What makes up a zero? What makes up a one? Do we send a bit at a time? A *packet* of bytes at a time? A packet of bytes is like a letter in an envelope in that it contains data and a header that gives the information needed to get the data from the source to the destination.

Higher-level layers define the *protocol* for communication. A protocol is a set of rules that guide how an activity is performed. How does my computer tell your computer that it wants to talk, and what it wants to talk about? How do we address your computer at all? By treating these as distinct layers, we can easily swap out one part without changing the others. For example, most people with a direct connection to a network use a wired connection to an *Ethernet* network, but Ethernet is actually a mid-level protocol that works over wireless networks, too.

Humans have protocols, too. If Mark walks up to you, holds out his hand, and says, "Hi, my name is Mark," you will most certainly hold out your hand and say something like "Hi, my name is Gene" (assuming that your name is Gene—if it wasn't, that would be pretty funny). There's an unwritten protocol for humans about how to greet one another. Computer protocols are about the same things, but they're written down to communicate the process exactly. What gets said isn't too different. One computer may send the message 'HELO' to another to start a conversation (We don't know why the protocol writers couldn't spare the extra 'L' to spell it right), and a computer may send 'BYE' to end the conversation. (We even sometimes call the start of a computer protocol the "*handshake*.") It's all about establishing a connection and making sure that both sides understand what's going on.

The *Internet* is a network of networks. If you have a device in your home so that your computers can talk to one another (e.g., a *router*), then you have a network. With just that, you can probably copy files between computers and print. When you connect your network to the wider Internet (through an *Internet Service Provider* (*ISP*)), your network becomes part of the Internet.

The Internet is based on a set of agreements about a whole bunch of things:

- *How computers will be addressed*: Currently, each computer on the Internet has a 32-bit number associated with it—four byte values, that are usually written like this separated by periods "101.132.64.15." These are called *IP addresses* (for Internet Protocol addresses).

  There is a system of *domain names* by which people can refer to specific computers without knowing their IP addresses. For example, when you access `http://www.cnn.com`, you are actually accessing `http://64.236.24.20`. (Go ahead and try it! It works.) There is a network of *domain name servers* that keep track of names like "www.cnn.com" and map them to addresses like "64.236.24.20." You can be connected to the Internet and still not be able to get to your favorite Web sites if your domain name server is broken—but you might be able to get to it if you type in the IP address directly!

- *How computers will communicate*: Data will be placed in *packets* which have a well-defined structure, including the sender's IP address, the receiver's IP address, and a number of bytes per packet.

- *How packets are routed around the Internet*: The Internet was designed in the time of the Cold War. It was designed to withstand a nuclear attack. If a section of the Internet is destroyed (or damaged, or blocked as a form of censorship), the packet routing mechanism of the Internet will simply find a route around the damage.

But the topmost layers of the network define what the data being passed around *means*. One of the first applications placed on top of the Internet was electronic mail. Over the years, the mail protocols have evolved to standards today like *POP* (Post Office Protocol) and *SMTP* (Simple Mail Transfer Protocol). Another old and important protocol is *FTP* (File Transfer Protocol).

These protocols aren't super-complicated. When the communication ends, one computer will probably say 'BYE' or 'QUIT' to another. When one computer tells another computer to accept a file via FTP, it literally says "STO filename" (again, early computer developers didn't want to spare the two more bytes to say "STORE").

The *World Wide Web* is yet another set of agreements, developed mostly by Tim Berners-Lee. The Web is based on top of the Internet, simply adding more protocols on top of the existing ones.

- *How to refer to things on the Web*: Resources on the Web are referenced using *URLs*, *Uniform Resource Locators*. A URL specifies the protocol to use to address the resource, the domain name of the *server* that can provide the resource, and the *path* to the resource on that server. For example, a URL like `http://www.cc.gatech.edu/index.html` says "Use the HTTP protocol to talk to the computer at www.cc.gatech.edu and ask it for the resource index.html."

  Not every file on every computer attached to the Internet is accessible via a URL! There are some preconditions before a file is accessible via a URL. First, an Internet-accessible computer has to be running a piece of software that understands a protocol that Web browsers understand, typically HTTP or FTP. We call a computer that is running such a piece of software a *server*. A browser that accesses a server is called a *client*. Second, a server typically has a *server directory* which is accessible via that server. Only files in that directory, or subdirectories within that directory, are available.

- *How to serve documents*: The most common protocol on the Web is *HTTP*, *HyperText Transfer Protocol*. It defines how resources are served on the Web. HTTP is really simple—your browser literally says to a server things like "GET index.html" (just those letters!).

- *How those documents will be formatted*: Documents on the Web are formatted using *HTML, HyperText Markup Language*.

You'll notice the term *HyperText* showing up frequently in reference to the Web. HyperText is literally non-linear text. It's a term invented by Ted Nelson to describe the kind of reading that we all do commonly on the Web but that didn't exist before computers: Read a little on one page, then click a link and read a little over there, then click BACK and continue reading where you left off. The basic idea of HyperText dates back to Vannevar Bush, who was one of President Franklin Roosevelt's science advisors. He wanted to create a device for capturing flows of thought, which he called a *Memex*. But not until computers came along would this be possible. Tim Berners-Lee invented the Web and its protocols as a way of supporting rapid publication of research findings with connections between documents. The Web is certainly *not* the penultimate HyperText system. Systems like the ones that Ted Nelson worked on wouldn't allow "dead links" (links that are no longer accessible). But for all its warts, the Web *works*.

A browser (like Internet Explorer, Netscape Navigator, Mozilla, Opera, and so on) understands a lot about the Internet. It usually knows several protocols, such as HTTP, FTP, *gopher* (an early HyperText protocol), and *mailto* (SMTP). It knows HTML, how to format it, and how to grab resources referenced within the HTML, like JPEG pictures. For all of that, though, it's possible to access the Internet without nearly that much overhead. Mail clients (e.g., Outlook and Eudora) know some of these protocols without knowing all of them.

Java, like other modern languages, provides classes to support access to the Internet without all the overhead of a browser. Basically, you can write little programs that are clients. Java's class `java.net.URL` allows you to open URLs and read them as if they were files. It has a method `openStream` which returns an object of the class `java.io.InputStream` which can be used to read from the URL.

We have been using `FileReader` to read from files. The class `FileReader` is a child of the more general class `InputStreamReader` which is a child of the class `Reader` (Figure 12.5). We can create an object of the class `InputStreamReader` using the `InputStream` object. The class `InputStreamReader` is also a child of the class `Reader`. Finally, we can create a `BufferedReader` object by passing it a `InputStreamReader` object. The class `BufferedReader` has a constructor which takes a `Reader` object. Since `FileReader` and `InputStreamReader` both inherit at some point from the `Reader` class they can both be used to create a `BufferedReader` object. This is because when a variable gives a class name as a type *any* class that inherits from the given type can be used instead. An object of a child class or even a grandchild class *is an object* of the inherited class so this substitution is allowed.

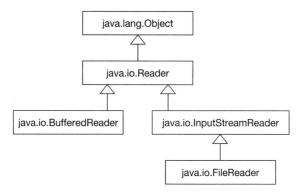

FIGURE 12.5
A depiction of the inheritance tree for some of the Reader Classes.

Using these classes, we can create another method to read the temperature directly from the Internet in the class `TempFinder`. The Web site has changed since when we originally saved a page from it in `ajc-weather.html`. Now we will look for `'&ordm'` and we will read from `http://www.ajc.com/`.

Program 112: Get the Temperature from a Live Weather Page

```
import java.io.*;
import java.net.URL;

/**
 * Class to find the temperature in a web page.
 * @author Barb Ericson
 */
```

```java
public class TempFinder {

  /**
   * Method to find the temperature in the passed
   * file
   * @param fileName the name of the file to look in
   */
  public String getTemp(String fileName)
  {
    String seq = "<b>&deg";
    String temp = null;
    String line = null;

    // try the following
    try {

      // read from the file
      BufferedReader reader =
        new BufferedReader(new FileReader(fileName));

      // loop till end of file or find sequence
      while ((line = reader.readLine()) != null &&
             line.indexOf(seq) < 0)
      {}

      // if there is a current line
      if (line != null)
      {
        // find the temperature
        int degreeIndex = line.indexOf(seq);
        int startIndex = line.lastIndexOf('>',degreeIndex);
        temp = line.substring(startIndex + 1, degreeIndex);
      }

    } catch (FileNotFoundException ex) {
      SimpleOutput.showError("Couldn't find file " + fileName);
      fileName = FileChooser.pickAFile();
      temp = getTemp(fileName);
    } catch (Exception ex) {
      SimpleOutput.showError("Error during read or write");
      ex.printStackTrace();
    }
    return temp;
  }

  /**
   * Method to get the temperature from a network
   * @param urlStr the url as a string
   * @return the temperature as a string
   */
  public String getTempFromNetwork(String urlStr)
  {
```

```java
String temp = null;
String line = null;
String seq = "&ordm";

try {

  // create a url
  URL url = new URL(urlStr);

  // open a buffered reader on the url
  InputStream inStr = url.openStream();
  BufferedReader reader =
    new BufferedReader(new InputStreamReader(inStr));

  // loop till end of file or find sequence
  while ((line = reader.readLine()) != null &&
         line.indexOf(seq) < 0)
  {}

  // if there is a current line
  if (line != null)
  {
    // find the temperature
    int degreeIndex = line.indexOf(seq);
    int startIndex = line.lastIndexOf('>',degreeIndex);
    temp = line.substring(startIndex + 1, degreeIndex);
  }

} catch (FileNotFoundException ex) {
  SimpleOutput.showError("Couldn't connect to " + urlStr);
} catch (Exception ex) {
  SimpleOutput.showError("Error during read or write");
  ex.printStackTrace();
}
return temp;
}

public static void main(String[] args)
{
  TempFinder finder = new TempFinder();
  String file = FileChooser.getMediaPath("ajc-weather.html");
  String temp = finder.getTemp(file);
  if (temp == null)
    System.out.println("Sorry, no temp was found in " + file);
  else
    System.out.println("The current temperature is " + temp);
  String urlString = "http://www.ajc.com/";
  temp = finder.getTempFromNetwork(urlString);
  if (temp == null)
    System.out.println("Sorry, no temp was found at " +
                       urlString);
```

```
        else
          System.out.println("The current temp " +
                             "from the network is " + temp);
     }
}
```

To run this `main` method, simply click on TOOLS, then RUN DOCUMENT'S MAIN METHOD. The output will look something like this:

```
> java TempFinder
The current temperature is 54
The current temp from the network is 82
```

How it Works

This method `getTempFromNetwork` is nearly identical to the last one, except that we're reading the string `weather` from the AJC website *live*. We use the class `URL` to gain the ability to read the Web page as an input stream (a stream of bits). We use `InputStreamReader` to convert the bits into characters. And we use `BufferedReader` to buffer the characters as we read them for more efficient reading. Notice that each object has a specific role to play, and we create several objects to work together to accomplish the task.

One way to make Web pages interactive is to write programs that actually generate HTML. For example, when you type a phrase into a text area then click the SEARCH button, you are actually causing a program to execute on the server which executes your search and then *generates* the HTML (Web page) that you see in response. Java has increasingly been used to generate Web pages.

12.6   USING TEXT TO SHIFT BETWEEN MEDIA

As we said at the beginning of this chapter, we can think about text as the *unimedia*. We can map from sound to text and back again, and the same with pictures. And more interestingly, we can go from sound to text...to pictures!

Why would we want to do any of this? Why should we care about transforming media in this way? For the same reasons that we care about digitizing media at all. Digital media transformed into text can be more easily transmitted from place to place, checked for errors, and even corrected for errors. It turns out that very often when you are attaching binary files to an e-mail message, your binary file is actually converted to text first! In general, *choosing a new representation allows you to do new things*.

Mapping sound to text is easy. Sound is just a series of samples (numbers). We can easily write these out to a file. Let's add a method to do this to the `Sound` class. We will need to convert the number to a string. We can use the method `valueOf` on the `String` class to do this. This is a class (`static`) method so it can be invoked using `String.valueOf`.

Program 113: Write a Sound to a File as Text Numbers

```java
/**
 * Method to write out the values in the sound to a file
 * as text
 * @param fileName the name of the file to write to
 */
public void writeSamplesAsText(String fileName)
{
  int value = 0;

  // try the following
  try {

    // try to open the buffered writer
    BufferedWriter writer =
      new BufferedWriter(new FileWriter(fileName));

    // loop through the samples
    for (int i = 0; i < this.getLength(); i++)
    {
      // get the int value
      value = this.getSampleValueAt(i);

      // write it as a string (text)
      writer.write(String.valueOf(value));

      // add the new line
      writer.newLine();
    }

    // close the writer
    writer.close();
  } catch (Exception ex) {
    SimpleOutput.showError("Error during write");
    ex.printStackTrace();
  }
}
```

To run this we can use the following main method in the Sound class.

```java
public static void main(String[] args)
{
  Sound s = new Sound(FileChooser.getMediaPath("her.wav"));
  s.writeSamplesAsText(FileChooser.getMediaPath("her.txt"));
}
```

After we have compiled the Sound class we can run it using:

```
> java Sound
```

How it Works

We're taking the file name to write to as a parameter. We open the file for writing and then we loop though each sample, converting it to a string and writing the string to a file. We use the `newLine` method of `BufferedReader` to add a new line after we write each sample value as a string.

What can we do with sound values written as text? We can manipulate it as a series of numbers, such as with Excel (Figure 12.6)! We can open Excel and open the file. We can tell it the delimiters are spaces and it will read the numbers into Column A. Once we have the data in Excel we can do modifications, such as multiplying each sample by 2.0.

We can even graph the numbers, and see the same kind of sound graph as we've seen in MediaTools (Figure 12.7). Select the column of numbers and then click on INSERT and CHART. You can just click on the FINISH button to use the defaults. (You might get an error, though—Excel doesn't like to graph more than 32,000 points, and even at 22,000 samples per second, that's not a lot of samples.)

How do we convert a series of numbers back into a sound? Say that you do some modification to the numbers in Excel, and now you want to hear the result. How do you do it? The mechanics in Excel are easy: Simply copy the column you want into a new worksheet, save it as text, then get the pathname of the text file to use in Java.

The program itself is a little more complicated. When going from sound to text, we knew that we could use `getSampleValueAt(i)` to write out all the samples. But how do we know how many lines are in the file? We don't really know until we have read them all in. We have to watch out for two problems: (a) having more lines in the file than we can fit into the sound that we're using to read into, and (b) running out of lines before we reach the end of the sound.

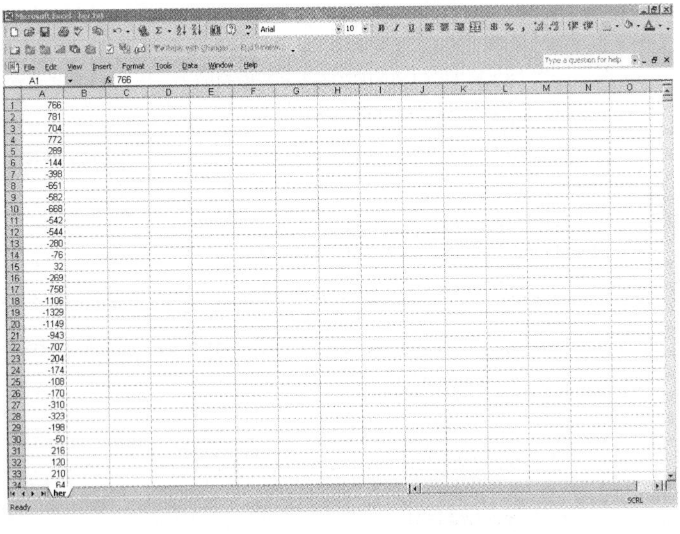

FIGURE 12.6
Sound-as-text file read into Excel.

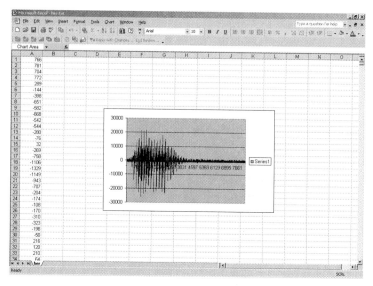

FIGURE 12.7
Sound-as-text file graphed in Excel.

So, for our text-to-sound example, we want to keep reading samples from the file and storing them into the sound *as long as* we have numbers in the file *and as long as* there is still room in the sound. We use the method `Integer.parseInt` to convert the string number into an integer number.

```
> System.out.println("1234" + 5);
12345
> System.out.println(Integer.parseInt("1234") + 5);
1239
```

Does the new method that we are writing work with a current Sound object? No, it creates a Sound object so it can be a class (`static`) method.

Program 114: Convert a File of Text Numbers into a Sound

```
/**
 * Method to create a sound from a text file
 * @param fileName the name of the file to read from
 * @return the created sound object
 */
public static Sound createSoundFromTextFile(String fileName)
{
  String line = null;
  int value = 0;

  // create the sound to read into
  Sound s =
    new Sound(FileChooser.getMediaPath("sec3silence.wav"));
```

```
// try the following
try {

  // create the buffered reader
  BufferedReader reader =
    new BufferedReader(new FileReader(fileName));

  // loop reading the values
  int index = 0;
  while ((line = reader.readLine()) != null &&
         index < s.getLength())
  {
    value = Integer.parseInt(line);
    s.setSampleValueAt(index++, value);
  }

  // close the reader
  reader.close();
} catch (FileNotFoundException ex) {
  SimpleOutput.showError("Couldn't find file " + fileName);
  fileName = FileChooser.pickAFile();
  s = createSoundFromTextFile(fileName);
} catch (Exception ex) {
  SimpleOutput.showError("Error during read or write");
  ex.printStackTrace();
}
return s;
}
```

How it Works

The method `createSoundFromTextFile` takes a filename as input that contains the samples as text. We open up a silent three-second sound to hold the sound. Next we create a `BufferedReader` to read the file. We loop reading the file until *either* the end of the file is reached or the index is equal to the length of the sound. In the body of the loop we convert the string to an integer and then set the sample value at the current index. We increment the current index. When we are done we return the created Sound object.

But we don't *have* to map from sounds to text and back to sounds. We could map a sound to a picture instead! The below program takes a sound and maps each sample to a pixel. All we have to do is to define our mapping, how we want to represent the samples. We chose a very simple one: If the sample is greater than 1,000, the pixel is red; less than −1,000 is blue, everything else is green (Figure 12.8).

We also have to deal with the case where we run out of samples before we run out of pixels. We can add this to the continuation test of a for loop using 'and' (&&).

Program 115: Creating a Picture from a Sound

```
/**
 * Method to turn a sound into a picture
 * @return a created picture
 */
```

```java
public Picture createPicture()
{
  int value = 0;
  Pixel pixel = null;

  // create a picture to write to
  Picture p =
    new Picture(FileChooser.getMediaPath("640x480.jpg"));

  // loop through the pixels
  Pixel[] pixelArray = p.getPixels();

  // loop through the pixels
  for (int i = 0; i < pixelArray.length &&
                  i < this.getLength(); i++)
  {

    // get this pixel
    pixel = pixelArray[i];

    // set the color based on the sample value
    value = this.getSampleValueAt(i);
    if (value > 1000)
      pixel.setColor(Color.RED);
    else if (value < -1000)
      pixel.setColor(Color.BLUE);
    else
      pixel.setColor(Color.GREEN);
  }
  return p;
}
```

FIGURE 12.8
A visualization of the sound "her.wav".

How it Works

In createPicture(), we open up a 640x480 blank picture. We loop while i is less than the number of pixels in the picture and also less than the samples in the current sound. Each time through the loop we get a sample value at i and figure out a mapping to a color, then set the pixel value to that color. Then we increment i. We return the created Picture object at the end of the method.

Think about how WinAmp does its visualizations, or how Excel or MediaTools graph, or how this program does its visualization. Each is just deciding a different way of mapping from samples to colors and space. It's just a mapping. It's all just bits.

Computer Science Idea: It's All Just Bits
Sound, pictures, and text are all just "bits." They're just information. We can map from one to the other as we wish. We merely have to define our representation. ∎

A really smart mathematician, Kurt Gödel, used the notion of encodings to come up with one of the most brilliant proofs of the twentieth century. He proved the *Incompleteness Theorem*, in which he proved that any powerful mathematical system *cannot* prove all mathematical truths. He figured out a mapping from mathematical statements of truth to numbers. This was long before we had ASCII, which maps numbers to characters. Once the mathematical statements were numbers, he was able to show that there are numbers representing true statements that could not be derived from the mathematical system. In this way, he showed that no system of logic can prove all true statements. By changing his encoding, he gained new capabilities, and thus was able to prove something that no one knew before.

12.7   CONCEPTS SUMMARY

In this chapter we have learned about handling exceptions, reading and writing files, reading from the Internet, using import statements, using while loops, manipulating String objects, and using ArrayList objects (dynamic arrays).

12.7.1   Exceptions

An exception occurs when something goes wrong. Exception handling shouldn't be used to handle normal execution of a program, but it is used to handle exceptional events. For example if you try to read from a file and the file doesn't exist, you will get a FileNotFoundException. If you try to write to a file and the disk is full, you will get an IOException. If you try to invoke a method on a object reference that is null, you will get a NullPointerException. Each of these exceptions inherits from java.lang.Exception, and each is an object. Every exception knows how to print the call stack (using the method printStackTrace()) which is helpful in figuring out where the exception occurred and how it got there.

There are two kinds of exceptions: checked and unchecked. The programmer must do something to handle checked exceptions. You can either catch exceptions or throw them. The programmer is not required to handle unchecked exceptions such as `NullPointerException` or `ArrayIndexOutOfBoundsException`.

To catch an exception use:

```
try {
    // statements that can cause exceptions
} catch (Exception ex) {
    // what to do if an exception happens
} finally {
    // what to do no matter what happens above
}
```

The `finally` block is optional. If a `finally` block is present it will be executed both if an exception occurs and if an exception does not occur.

You can have more than one `catch` block. All `Exception` objects inherit from `java.lang.Exception`. When you catch an `Exception` object you will also catch all objects that inherit from the type you specified.

12.7.2   Reading and Writing Files

The classes that handle reading and writing files are in the package `java.io`. Each class in the package is responsible for one task and the classes can be combined in different ways to solve different problems. Classes that work with character data are `Reader` and `Writer` classes. Classes that work with binary data are `Stream` classes. A stream is a series of bits.

To read files we created a `BufferedReader` using a `FileReader` to buffer the data from the disk after it is read from the file. We used the `readLine()` method of `BufferedReader` to loop reading from the file until the returned `String` was null. Reading from a file can cause checked exceptions so we enclosed the code in a `try` block and added `catch` blocks to catch the exceptions.

To write files we created a `BufferedWriter` using a `FileWriter` to buffer the data in before writing it to the file. We used the `write` method to write `String` objects to the file and we used the `newLine()` method to force a new line in the file. Writing to a file can cause checked exceptions so we enclosed the code in a `try` block and added `catch` blocks to catch the exceptions.

We also used the `File` class to get a list of the files in a directory.

12.7.3   Reading from the Internet

To create a program that reads directly from the Internet we used the URL class from the java.net package. We created a URL object from a string representation of a URL. Then we used the `openStream()` method on the URL object to get back a `java.io.InputStream` object which knows how to read from a stream of bytes. We used the `InputStream` object to create a `java.io.InputStreamReader` object which knows how to turn the bytes into characters. We created a `java.io.BufferedReader` object from the `InputStreamReader` to handle the buffering of the data in memory. Then we were able to use the readLine() method of BufferedReader to read from the network.

12.7.4 Import Statements

Whenever we use classes from a package other than java.lang we have to specify either the full name of the class or use an import statement before the class declaration. The full name of a class is the package name followed by a '.' and then the class name. The full name of the BufferedReader class is java.io.Buffered-Reader. If we want to refer to this in our code as just BufferedReader we need an import statement before the class declaration. We can import this as:

import java.io.BufferedReader;

which imports just that class. Or we can use:

import java.io.*;

which allows us to use all the classes in that package. It doesn't include any code, it just tells the compiler where to look for the class. If you are using more than one class from a package, this second way is easier.

12.7.5 While Loops

Even though for loops and while loops are the same as far as the computer is concerned, people use them in different ways. Use a for loop when you know how many times the loop will execute and a while loop when you want to loop as long as a boolean test is true. We used a while loop to read lines from a file until the line read was null, which indicates that we have reached the end of the file.

```
// Loop while there is more data
while((line = reader.readLine()) != null)
{
    // print the current line
    System.out.println(line);
}
```

Methods Summary

String methods   Strings are sequences of characters. The first character is at index 0. You can get the length of a string using the method length(). Here are the other methods we covered:

stringObj.charAt(int position)	Returns the character at the given position in the string. The first character is at position 0, just as the first element of an array is at index 0.
substring(int n,int m)	Returns a new string which is a *substring* of the string starting at the nth character and preceding up to *but not including* the mth character. A substring includes part of the original string.

substring(int n)	Returns a new string which is a substring of the string starting at the *n*th character and including the rest of the characters in the string.
startsWith(String prefix)	Returns true if the string starts with the given prefix, else it will return false.
endsWith(String suffix)	Returns true if the string ends with the given suffix, else it will return false.
indexOf(String str)	Returns the first index of the passed str, if it is found. If str isn't in the current string it will return −1.
indexOf(String str, int fromIndex)	Returns the first index of the passed str at or after the passed fromIndex, if it is found. If str isn't in the current string at or after the fromIndex, it will return −1.
lastIndexOf(String str)	Returns the last index of the passed str, if it is found. If str isn't in the current string it will return −1.
lastIndexOf(String str, int index)	Returns the last index of the passed str found looking backwards starting at index. If str isn't in the current string before the given index it will return −1.
toUpperCase()	Returns a new string with all the characters in uppercase.
toLowerCase()	Returns a new string with all the characters in lowercase.
replace(String oldStr, String newStr)	Returns a new string with the character in the oldStr string replaced with the character in the newStr string for all occurrences of the oldStr string. This is new in Java 1.5.
replaceAll(String regex, String newStr)	Returns a new string with all the matching substrings specified by the regular expression (regex) replaced with the characters in new-Str. A regular expression can be just a string of characters or it can also use special characters to indicate that it will match any character, any digit, only uppercase characters, etc.
replaceFirst(String regex, String newStr)	Returns a new string with the first substring that matches the regular expression specified by regex replaced with the characters in new-Str. A regular expression can be just a string of characters or it can also use special characters to indicate that it will match any character, any digit, only uppercase characters, etc.

split(String regex)	Returns an array of String objects. It will split the current string into many by breaking it into new strings whenever it matches the regular expression specified in regex.
trim()	Returns a new string with all white space (spaces and tabs) removed from the beginning and end of the string.

ArrayList Methods

An ArrayList is a dynamic array (an array that can grow or shrink as needed). It is in the package java.util. It implements the java.util.List interface and thus an object of the class ArrayList can be referred to by a variable declared as type List. The methods that we covered are:

add(Object o)	Adds the passed object to the end of the list (next open position in the array).
add(int index, Object o)	Adds the passed object to the list at the given index. If another object is at that index it will be moved to (index + 1). If an object was at (index + 1) it will be moved to (index + 2). So, all objects at the passed index or above will change to the location specified by their (current index + 1).
get(int index)	Returns the object at this index in the list
set(int index, Object o)	Sets the value at this index in the list to the passed object. If an object is at that index it will be moved to (index + 1). If an object was at (index + 1) it will be moved to (index + 2). So, all objects at the index or above will change to the location specified by their (current index + 1).
size()	Returns the number of elements in the list
remove(int index)	Removes the object at the passed index. Any objects with a current index value greater than this will change to (current index −1).

File Methods

We have only covered one method of the java.io.File class. The method list() returns an array of String objects which are the names of all the items in the directory represented by the File object.

Random Methods

We have covered two methods of the java.util.Random class. The method nextDouble() will return a double between 0 and 1.0 inclusive. The method nextInt(int num) will return an integer between 0 (inclusive) and num exclusive.

PROBLEMS

12.1 Go to a page with a lot of text in it, like `http://www.cnn.com` and use your browser's menu to SAVE the file as something like `mypage.html`. Edit the file using an editor like Window's Notepad. Find some text in the page that you can see when you view the page, like a headline or article text. *Change it!* Instead of "protestors" rioting, make it "College students" or even "kindergarteners." Now OPEN that file in your browser. You've just rewritten the news!

12.2 Fill in the letter of the definition next to the appropriate phrase below. *(Yes, you will have one unused definition.)*

___ `Domain Name Server` ___ `Web Server` ___ `HTTP` ___ `HTML`
___ `Client` ___ `IP Address` ___ `FTP` ___ `URL`

(a) A computer that matches names like *www.cnn.com* to their addresses on the Internet.

(b) A protocol used to move files between computers, e.g., from your personal computer to a larger computer that acts as a Web server.

(c) A string that explains how (what protocol) and on what machine (domain name) and where on that machine (path) a particular file can be found on the Internet.

(d) A computer that offers files through HTTP.

(e) The protocol on which most of the Web is built, a very simple form aimed at rapid transmission of small bits of information.

(f) What a browser is (like Internet Explorer) when contacting a server like *yahoo.com*

(g) The tags that go into Web pages to identify parts of the page and how they should be formatted.

(h) A protocol that is used for transmitting e-mail between computers.

(i) The numeric identifier of a computer on the Internet—four numbers between 0 and 255, like *120.32.189.12*

12.3 Write short essay responses to these questions.

(a) Give one example of a task for which you *would not* write a program, and give another example of a task for which you *would* write a program.

(b) What's the difference between an array, a matrix, and a tree? Give an example where we have used each to represent some data of interest to us.

(c) Why is a tree a better representation for files on a disk than an array? Why do you have many directories on your disk, and not just one gigantic one?

(d) What are some advantages that Vector-Based graphics have over Bitmap Graphical representations (like JPEG, BMP, GIF)?

12.4   For each of the below, see if you can figure out the representation in terms of bits and bytes.

     (a) Internet addresses are four numbers, each between 0 and 255. How many bits are in an Internet address?

     (b) In the programming language Basic, lines can be numbered, each one between 0 and 65,535. How many bits are needed to represent a line number?

     (c) Each pixel's color has three components: Red, green, and blue, each of which can be between 0 and 255. How many bits are needed to represent a pixel's color?

     (d) A string in some languages can only be up to 1,024 characters. How many bits are needed to represent the length of a string?

12.5   Respond to the below Internet-related questions:

     (a) What's a Domain Name Server? What does it do?

     (b) What are FTP, SMTP, and HTTP? What are they each used for?

     (c) What is HyperText?

     (d) What's the difference between a client and a server?

     (e) How does knowing how to manipulate text help you in gathering and creating information on the Internet?

     (f) What is the Internet?

     (g) What is an ISP? Can you give an example of one?

12.6   You've seen code to mirror pictures in Program 19 (page 135), and you've seen code to mirror sounds in Program 79 (page 306). It should be pretty easy to use the same algorithm to mirror *text*. Write a function to take a string, then return the mirrored string with the front mirrored to the back.

12.7   Write a method in the `Picture` class to convert a `Picture` object into a `Sound` object using the average of the color values. Map all values from 0 to 84 to the maximum negative sound value, map all values from 85 to 169 to 0 and all values above 170 to the maximum positive value.

12.8   Read a file of text and modify each character, such as change 'a' to 'b' and 'b' to 'c' and so on. Write a class, `Encoder`, that encodes the text and another class, `Decoder`, to decode the text.

12.9   Modify the `Student` class to implement the `java.lang.Comparable` interface. This means that you will need to provide the method `compareTo(Object o)` which should return 0 if the current student object is equal to the passed object, a negative number if the current student object is less than the passed object, and a positive number if the current student object is greater than the passed number. You can use the `compareTo` method of the `String` class to compare the student's names.

12.10   Write a program to read a list of words from a file and then output a new file with the letters scrambled using `Random`.

12.11 Write a program to ask the user for a word to check the spelling of and then use a dictionary on the Internet to check the spelling. Tell the user whether the word is spelled correctly or not. You can use the class `SimpleInput` to get the word from the user and the class `SimpleOutput` to tell the user whether the word is spelled correctly or not. Both `SimpleInput` and `SimpleOutput` are classes that come with the book.

12.12 Modify the `Student` class to use an `ArrayList` instead of an array to hold the grades. Change the method `getAverage` to walk through the `ArrayList`.

12.13 Read the nouns, verbs, and phrases for the `SentenceGenerator` class from files. Use an `ArrayList` instead of an array for each of these.

12.14 Extend the form letter recipe to take an input of a pet's name and type, and reference the pet in the form letter. `"Your pet "+petType+","+petName+" will love our offer!"` might generate `"Your pet poodle, Fifi, will love our offer!"`.

12.15 Imagine that you have a list of all the genders (as single characters) of the students in your class, in order of their last name. The list will look something like "MFFMMMFFMFMMFFFM" where "M" is Male and "F" is Female. Write a function (below) `percentageGenders(string)` to accept a string that represents the genders. You are to count all of the "M"'s and "F"'s in the string, and print out the ratio (as a decimal) of the each gender. For example, if the input string were "MFFF," then the function should print something like "There are 0.25 Males, 0.75 Females." (Hint: Better multiply something by 1.0 to make sure that you get floats not integers.)

12.16 You worked late into the night on an assignment and didn't realize that you wrote a huge section of your term paper with your fingers on the wrong home keys!

Where you mean to type: "This is an unruly mob." You actually typed: "Ty8s 8s ah 7hr7o6 j9b."

Basically you swapped: 7 for U, 8 for I, 9 for O, 0 for P, U for J, I for K, O for L, H for N, and J for M. (Those were the only keystrokes that you got wrong—you caught yourself before you got much further.) You also never touched the shift key, so it's all lowercase letters that you care about.

Knowing Java as you do, you decide to write a quick program to fix your text. Write a method `fixItUp` that takes a string as input and returns a string with the characters put the way that they ought to have been.

12.17 The government has data for baby names from 1879 up to the previous year at `http://www.ssa.gov/OACT/babynames/`. Get the top 1,000 names for the year you were born and save it to a file. Write a method that will find the popularity of a passed name for that year for a given gender (some names are used for both boys and girls).

12.18 You can get historical weather data from `http://www.ndbc.noaa.gov/Maps/northeast_hist.shtml`. Use this site to get data for a location and write methods to find the hottest and coldest date for that location.

12.19 In sleep research a patient is hooked up to electrodes and data is recorded for the eight hours or so that the patient sleeps. This results in a large file of numbers. One way that researchers work with this data is to map it to sounds and then listen for repetitions. Find a file of large numbers on the Internet and see if you can map it to sound sample values in such a way that you can hear repetition.

12.20 Write a simple Eliza program. You can use the class `SimpleInput` to ask questions and the class `SimpleOutput` to show responses. Both `SimpleInput` and `SimpleOutput` are classes that come with the book.

12.21 Write a class `GraphicsInterpreter` that reads in a file of graphics *commands*. The class `GraphicsInterpreter` should have a method `interpret` that takes a filename as input (a `String`), reads the graphics commands from the file, and then returns a `Picture` with the graphics commands executed on it. The method `interpretCommands` starts out by creating a 640x480 blank picture, then draws on that, and returns it.

There are two kinds of commands:

- "line 10 20 300 400" should draw a line from (10,20) to (300,400). You can assume that those are single spaces between the coordinates.

- "circle 100 200 10" draws a circle whose upper-left hand corner is (100,200) with a diameter for 10.

An input graphics command might look like:

```
circle 20 20 100
circle 300 20 100
line 210 120 210 320
line 210 320 310 320
line 20 350 400 350
```

The `main` method for `GraphicsInterpreter` might look like this:

```java
public static void main(String[] args)
{
  GraphicsInterpreter interpreter =
    new GraphicsInterpreter();
  String fileName =
    FileChooser.getMediaPath("graphics-commands.txt");
  Picture p = interpreter.interpretCommands(fileName);
  p.show();
}
```

CHAPTER

13 Making Text for the Web

13.1 HTML: THE NOTATION OF THE WEB

13.2 WRITING PROGRAMS TO GENERATE HTML

13.3 DATABASES: A PLACE TO STORE OUR TEXT

13.4 RELATIONAL DATABASES

13.5 CONCEPTS SUMMARY

Chapter Learning Objectives

The media learning goals for this chapter are:

- To gain some basic skill with HTML.
- To automatically generate HTML for input data, like an index page for a directory of images.
- To use databases to generate Web content.

The computer science goals for this chapter are:

- To use another number base, hexadecimal, for specifying RGB colors.
- To create and use helper methods.
- To allow a method to throw an exception.
- To introduce the "unnamed" package.
- To introduce Map, which maps keys to values.
- To introduce generics for typing collections.
- To introduce using an Iterator to process the elements of a collection.
- To explain what SQL is and what it has to do with relational databases.

13.1 HTML: THE NOTATION OF THE WEB

The World Wide Web is mostly text, and most of that text is in the specification language *HTML* (HyperText Markup Language). HTML is based on *SGML* (Standard General Markup Language), which is a way of adding additional text to one's text to identify logical parts of the document: "This is the title," "This is a heading," and "This is just a plain ole paragraph." Originally, HTML (like SGML) was supposed to identify *just* the logical parts of a document—how it *looked* was up to the browser. Documents were *expected* to look different from one browser to another. But as the Web has evolved, two separate goals developed: Being able to specify *lots* of logical parts (e.g., including prices, part numbers, stocker ticker codes, temperatures, etc.), and being able to control formatting.

For the first goal, *XML* (eXtensible Markup Language) evolved that allows you to define new tags like <partnumber>7834JK</partnumber>. For the second goal, things like *cascading style sheets* were developed, which give you control over the way the page is displayed. Yet another markup language, *XHTML*, was developed, which is HTML in terms of XML.

For most of this chapter, we'll be introducing XHTML, but we're not going to distinguish it from original HTML. We'll just talk about it as HTML.

We're not going to have a complete tutorial for HTML here. There are many of these available, in both print and on the Web, and many are high-quality. Enter "HTML tutorial" into your favorite search engine and take your pick. Instead, we'll talk here about some general notions of HTML, and mention the tags that you should really know.

A markup language means that additional text is inserted into the original text to identify the parts. In HTML, the inserted text, called *tags*, are delimited with angle brackets—less-than and greater-than signs. For example, <p> starts a paragraph, and </p> ends a paragraph.

Web pages have several parts, and the parts nest within each other. The first is a *DOCTYPE* right at the top of the page that announces the *kind* of page this is—whether the browser should try to interpret it as HTML, XHTML, CSS, or what. Following the doctype comes a heading (<head>...</head>) and a body (<body>...</body>). The heading can contain information like the title *nested* within it—the ending of the title comes *before* the ending of the head. The body can have many pieces nested within it, such as images and paragraphs. All of the body and heading nests within <html>...</html> tags. Figure 13.1 shows a simple web page's source, and Figure 13.2 shows how the page appeared in Internet Explorer. Try this yourself! Type it in a simple text editor and save it with a html file suffix, and then open it in a Web browser. The only difference between this file and any Web page is that this file lives on your disk. If it were on a Web server, it would be a Web page.

Common Bug: Browsers are Forgiving, but Usually Wrong

Browsers are very forgiving. If you forget the DOCTYPE or make mistakes in the HTML, it will literally guess at what you meant and then try to show it. Murphy's Law, though, says that it will probably guess *wrong*. If you want your Web page to look just the way you want, get the HTML right.

Here are some of the tags that you should know:

- The <body> tag can take parameters to set the background, text, and link colors. These colors can be simple color names like "red" or "green," or they can be specific RGB colors.

  You specify colors in *hexadecimal*. Hexadecimal is another number system. Decimal is base 10. Hexadecimal is base 16. The decimal numbers 1 to 20

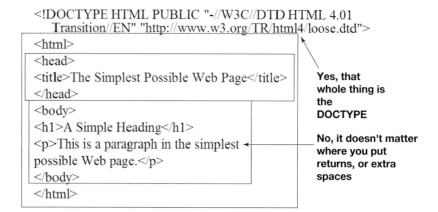

FIGURE 13.1
Simple HTML page source.

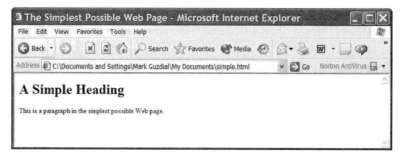

FIGURE 13.2
Simple HTML page open in Internet Explorer.

translate to hexadecimal 1, 2, 3, 4, 5, 6, 7, 8, 9, A, B, C, D, E, F, 10, 11, 12, 13, and 14. Think of hexadecimal "14" as 16 plus 4, which is 20.

The advantage of hexadecimal is that each digit corresponds to 4 bits. Two hexadecimal digits correspond to a byte. Thus, the three bytes of RGB colors are six hexadecimal digits, in RGB order. Hexadecimal FF0000 is red—255 (FF) for red, 0 for green, and 0 for blue. 0000FF is blue. 000000 is black, and FFFFFF is white.

- Headings are specified using tags `<h1>...</h1>` through `<h6>...</h6>`. Smaller numbers are more prominent.

- There are lots of tags for different kinds of styles: Emphasis `<em>...</em>`, italics `<i>...</i>`, boldface `<b>...</b>`, bigger `<big>...</big>` and smaller `<small>...</small>` fonts, typewriter font `<tt>...</tt>`, pre-formatted text `<pre>...</pre>`, block quotes `<blockquote>...</blockquote>`, and subscripts `<sub>...</sub>` and superscripts `<sup>...</sup>` (Figure 13.3). You can also control things like font and color using the `<font>...</font>` tags.

- You can force a new line using `<br />`.

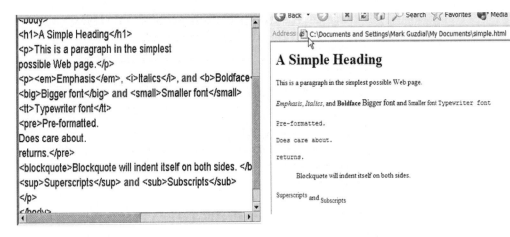

FIGURE 13.3
HTML styles.

```
<!DOCTYPE HTML PUBLIC "-
    //W3C//DTD HTML 4.01
    Transition//EN"
    "http://www.w3.org/TR/html4/loose.dtd
    ">
<html>
<head>
<title>The Simplest Possible Web
    Page</title>
</head>
<body>
<h1>A Simple Heading</h1>
<p>This is a paragraph in the simplest
    <br /> possible Web page.</p>
<image src="mediasources/flower1.jpg" />
</body>
</html>
```

FIGURE 13.4
Inserting an image into an HTML page.

- Use the `<image src="image.jpg"/>` tag to insert images (Figure 13.4). The `image` tag takes where to get the image information from as the `src=` parameter. The source can be specified in one of several ways.

  - If it's just a filename (like `"flower1.jpg"`), then it's assumed to be an image in the same directory as the HTML file referencing it.

  - If it's a path, it's assumed to be a path *from the same directory as the HTML page* to that image. So if we had an HTML page in `"My Documents"` that referenced an image in my `mediasources` directory, we might have a reference to `"mediasources/flower1.jpg"`. You can use UNIX (or DOS) conventions here, e.g., `".."` references the parent directory, so `"../images/flower1.jpg"` would say to go to the parent directory, then down to `images` to grab image `flower1.jpg`.

– It can also be a complete URL—you can reference images on other servers entirely!

You can also manipulate the width and height of images with options to the image tag, e.g., `<image height="100" src="flower.jpg">` to limit the height to 100 pixels and to adjust the width so that the picture keeps its height to width ratio. Using the optional `alt`, you can specify the text to be displayed if the image can't be displayed, e.g., for audio or Braille browsers.

- You use the *link or anchor tag* `<a href="someplace.html">from text</a>` to create links from the current text (source anchor) to somewhere else (destination anchor). In this example, `someplace.html` is the *destination* anchor for the link—it's where you go when you click on the *link*. The source anchor for the link is the "from text". The source anchor can be text or an image. As seen in Figure 13.5, the destination anchor can also be a complete URL.

Notice, too, in the Figure 13.5 that line breaks in the source file don't show up in the browser. We can even have line breaks in the middle of a link tag, and they don't impact the actual display of the link. The breaks that *matter* (that show up in the browser) are generated by tags like `<br />` and `<p>`.

- You can create bullet lists (*unordered lists*) and numbered lists (*ordered lists*) using the `<ul>...</ul>` and `<ol>...</ol>` tags, respectively. Individual items are specified using the tags `<li>...</li>`.

- Tables are created using `<table>...</table>` tags. Tables are constructed out of table rows using `<tr>...</tr>` tags, and each row can have several table data items identified with `<td>...</td>` tags (Figure 13.6). Table rows nest within tables, and table data items nest within table rows.

There is *lots* more to HTML, such as frames (having subwindows within one's HTML page window), divisions (`<div />`), horizontal rules (`<hr />`), applets, and

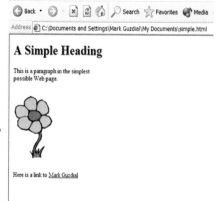

FIGURE 13.5
An HTML page with a link in it.

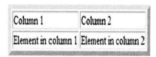

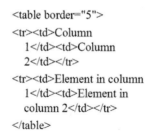

```
<table border="5">
<tr><td>Column
   1</td><td>Column
   2</td></tr>
<tr><td>Element in column
   1</td><td>Element in
   column 2</td></tr>
</table>
```

FIGURE 13.6
Inserting a table into an HTML page.

more. We have only covered the most critical tags for understanding the rest of this chapter. You can search the Web for HTML tutorials.

13.2   WRITING PROGRAMS TO GENERATE HTML

HTML is *not* a programming language. HTML can't specify loops, conditionals, variables, data types, or anything else we've learned about specifying process. HTML is used to describe structure, not process.

That said, we can easily write programs to generate HTML. Remember that to have quotes inside of a `String` object in Java we need to use '\"'.

Program 116: Generating a Simple HTML Page

```java
import java.io.*;

/**
 * Class used to write web (HTML) pages
 * @author Barb Ericson
 */
public class WebPageWriter {

  /**
   * Method to write an example web (HTML) page
   */
  public void writeExamplePage(String fileName)
  {
    // try the following
    try {

      // open a file for writing
      BufferedWriter writer =
        new BufferedWriter(new FileWriter(fileName));
```

```
        // start the html page
        writer.write("<!DOCTYPE HTML PUBLIC \"-//W3C//DTD " +
                     "HTML 4.01 Transition//EN\" " +
                     "\"http://www.w3.org/TR/html4/loose.dtd\">");
        writer.newLine();
        writer.write("<html>");
        writer.newLine();

        // write out the header
        writer.write("<head><title>A simple web page" +
                     "</title></head>");
        writer.newLine();

        // write out the body
        writer.write("<body>");
        writer.newLine();
        writer.write("<h1>A Simple Heading</h1>");
        writer.newLine();
        writer.write("<p>Some simple text</p>");
        writer.newLine();
        writer.write("</body>");
        writer.newLine();

        // end the page
        writer.write("</html>");

        // close the writer
        writer.close();
      } catch (Exception ex) {
        ex.printStackTrace();
      }

  }

  public static void main(String[] args)
  {
    WebPageWriter writer = new WebPageWriter();
    writer.writeExamplePage("simple.html");
  }
}
```

That works, but it's really boring. Why would you write a program to write a file that you can easily create with a text editor? You write programs in order to have reusable parts, communicate process, and allow for tailoring. Let's write a method that creates a homepage.

Program 117: Initial Homepage Creator

```
/**
 * Method that will write out a homepage for a person
 * with the passed name
```

```java
 * @param name the name of the person that this homepage
 * is for
 * @param interests a list of the person's interests
 */
public void writeHomepage(String name, String interests)
{
  // try the following
  try {

    // open a file for writing
    BufferedWriter writer =
      new BufferedWriter(new FileWriter(name + ".html"));

    // start the html page
    writer.write("<!DOCTYPE HTML PUBLIC \"-//W3C//DTD " +
                 "HTML 4.01 Transition//EN\"");
    writer.newLine();
    writer.write("\"http://www.w3.org/TR/html4/loose.dtd\">");
    writer.newLine();
    writer.write("<html>");
    writer.newLine();

    // write out the header
    writer.write("<head><title>" + name +
                 "'s Homepage</title></head>");
    writer.newLine();

    // write out the body
    writer.write("<body>");
    writer.newLine();
    writer.write("<h1>Welcome to " + name +
                 "'s Homepage</h1>");
    writer.newLine();
    writer.write("<p>I am interested in " +
                 interests + "</p>");
    writer.newLine();
    writer.write("</body>");
    writer.newLine();

    // end the page
    writer.write("</html>");

    // close the writer
    writer.close();

  } catch (Exception ex) {
    ex.printStackTrace();
  }
}
```

We can modify the main to test this as well:

```
public static void main(String[] args)
{
  WebPageWriter writer = new WebPageWriter();
  writer.writeExamplePage("simple.html");
  writer.writeHomepage("Mark", "reading");
}
```

By executing the main we get:

```
<!DOCTYPE HTML PUBLIC "-//W3C//DTD HTML 4.01 Transition//EN"
"http://www.w3.org/TR/html4/loose.dtd">
<html>
<head><title>Mark's Homepage</title></head>
<body>
<h1>Welcome to Mark's Homepage</h1>
<p>I am interested in reading</p>
</body>
</html>
```

Debugging Tip: Write the HTML, First

Programs to generate HTML can get confusing. Before you get started trying to write a method, write the HTML. Make up a sample of what you want the HTML to look like. Make sure that it works in your browser. Then write the method that generates that kind of HTML.

Modifying this program is painful, though. There is so much detail in the HTML, and all that quoting is confusing. We're better off creating *helper methods* to break up the program into pieces that are easier to manipulate. This is an example of using *procedural abstraction*. In procedural abstraction we try to break a task down into subtasks. We can create a method for each subtask. This makes the top level method easier to read and understand.

If we break writing things to the HTML page into smaller methods, we have the problem of what to do with exceptions. Each time we write to a file we could get an IOException. We could add a try and catch block to every small method but that would make them bigger and would mean repeating a fair amount of code. Another approach is to let the small methods *throw* the IOException and only catch them and handle them in the larger method that calls the smaller methods.

To allow a method to throw an exception, all we have to do is add the throws ExceptionClass to the method declaration after the parameter list. This is the keyword throws followed by the class name of the exception that it is throwing.

Here's another version of the method that creates helper (private) methods to do most of the work. Each private method can throw an IOException. This means that the method that calls this method either has to also throw this exception or must catch it.

Program 118: Improved Homepage Creator

```java
/**
 * Method to write the doctype and html tags
 * @param writer the writer to use
 * @throws IOException
 */
private void writeStart(BufferedWriter writer) throws
  IOException
{
  // write the document type
  writer.write("<!DOCTYPE HTML PUBLIC \"-//W3C//DTD " +
               "HTML 4.01 Transition//EN\"");
  writer.newLine();
  writer.write("\"http://www.w3.org/TR/html4/loose.dtd\">");
  writer.newLine();

  // start the html page
  writer.write("<html>");
  writer.newLine();
}

/**
 * Method to write the title out
 * @param writer the writer to use
 * @param title the title to use
 * @throws IOException
 */
private void writeHead(BufferedWriter writer, String title)
  throws IOException
{
  writer.write("<head><title>" + title + "</title></head>");
  writer.newLine();
}

/**
 * Method to write the body of the page
 * @param writer the writer to use
 * @param body the body to write
 * @throws IOException
 */
private void writeBody(BufferedWriter writer, String body)
  throws IOException
{
  writer.write("<body>" + body + "</body>");
  writer.newLine();
}
```

```java
/**
 * Method to finish the html page
 * @param writer the writer to use
 * @throws IOException
 */
private void writeEnd(BufferedWriter writer)
  throws IOException
{
  writer.write("</html>");
}

/**
 * Method for writing a homepage for the passed
 * name
 * @param name the person's name
 * @param interests a list of the person's interests
 */
public void writeHomepageV2(String name, String interests)
{

  // try the following
  try {

    // open a file for writing
    BufferedWriter writer =
      new BufferedWriter(new FileWriter(name + ".html"));

    // write the start
    writeStart(writer);

    // write the header
    writeHead(writer,name + "'s Homepage");

    // write the body
    writeBody(writer,"<h1>Welcome to " + name +
              "'s Homepage</h1>" +
              "<p> I am interested in " + interests);

    // end the page
    writeEnd(writer);

    // close the writer
    writer.close();

  } catch (Exception ex) {
    ex.printStackTrace();
  }
}
```

Notice that we now have helper methods that are easy to reuse. We can use the new helper methods to write out different pages.

> **Debugging Tip: Don't Forget to Close the File!**
>
> Be sure to close the `BufferedWriter` when you are done writing. The strings are actually buffered in memory and are not written to the file until there is enough in the buffer to efficiently write to the disk, or until you close the `BufferedWriter`.

13.2.1 Creating a Web Page from a Directory

We can grab content for our Web pages from anywhere we want. Here is a recipe that can pull information out of a directory provided as input and generate an index page of those images (Figure 13.7). We're not going to show the code for the `writeStart()` and other helper methods here—we'll just focus on the part we care about. And that is how we should think about it—just the part we care about, and we write `writeStart()` once and then forget about it!

Up to now we have been using the `newLine()` method of the `BufferedWriter` class to force a new line. But if we are writing lots of text out together, we may want to add a special character to force a new line to our `String`. The problem is that the special character is different on different operating systems. The best way to handle this is to use the `System` class to find out the right special characters to use for the current operating system. We can do this by using

```
String endOfLine = System.getProperty("line.separator");
```

The method `getProperty` will return the value of the specified property on the current system. You can use this method to get other information about the current system, such as the directory separator and the version of Java being run.

Here is a method that you can add to the `WegPageWriter` class to generate a Web page with thumbnails of the images in a directory, as seen in Figure 13.7.

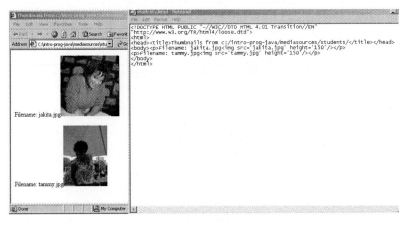

FIGURE 13.7
Creating an image thumbnail page.

Program 119: Generate an Image Thumbnails Page

```java
/**
 * Method to create a page with thumbnails of all the images
 * in a directory
 * @param directory the directory to create the page for
 */
public void createImagePage(String directory)
{
  String name = null;
  String body = "";
  String endOfLine = System.getProperty("line.separator");

  // try the following
  try {

    // create the File object
    File dir = new File(directory);

    // get the full path name of the directory
    String pathName = directory + dir.getName() + ".html";
    BufferedWriter writer =
      new BufferedWriter(new FileWriter(pathName));

    // write the start
    writeStart(writer);

    // write the head
    writeHead(writer,"Thumbnails from " + directory);

    // get the array of items in the directory
    String[] items = dir.list();

    // loop through the array
    for (int i = 0; i < items.length; i++)
    {
      name = items[i];
      if (name.indexOf(".jpg") >= 0)
      {
        body = body + "<p>Filename: " + name +
          "<img src='" + name + "' height='150'/></p>" +
          endOfLine;
      }
    }

    // write the body
    writeBody(writer,body);

    // write the end
    writeEnd(writer);
```

```
      // close the writer
      writer.close();

   } catch (Exception ex) {
      ex.printStackTrace();
   }
}
```

■

We can modify the `main` method of `WebPageWriter` to test this method. We can *comment out* the other tests that we did in the `main` method. Commenting code out means that it won't be executed but it is still around if we want to use it again.

```
public static void main(String[] args)
{
   WebPageWriter writer = new WebPageWriter();
//    writer.writeExamplePage("simple.html");
//    writer.writeHomepage("Mark", "reading");
//    writer.writeHomepageV2("Barb", "horseback riding");
   String dir = "c:/intro-prog-java/mediasources/students/";
   writer.createImagePage(dir);
}
```

Executing this main will result in the creation of the Web page shown in Figure 13.7.

13.2.2   Creating a Web Page from other Web Pages

We can pull information off of the Web to create new Web content. That's how sites like *Google News*[1] work. Here's a version of our homepage creator that gathers the temperature live (designed especially for Atlanta).

Program 120: Generate Homepage with Temperature Information

```
/**
 * Method for writing a homepage for the passed
 * name that displays the current weather
 * @param name the person's name
 * @param interests a list of the person's interests
 */
public void writeHomepageV3(String name,
                           String interests)
{
   // get the current temperature
   TempFinder tempFinder = new TempFinder();
   String urlString = "http://www.ajc.com/";
   String currTemp = tempFinder.getTempFromNetwork(urlString);

   // try the following
   try {
```

[1] http://news.google.com

```
            // open a file for writing
            BufferedWriter writer =
             new BufferedWriter(new FileWriter(name + ".html"));

            // write the start
            writeStart(writer);

            // write the header
            writeHead(writer,name + "'s Homepage");

            // write the body
            writeBody(writer,"<h1>Welcome to " + name +
                    "'s Homepage</h1>" +
                    "<p> I am interested in " + interests +
                    ".</p><p>Right now it is " + currTemp +
                    " degrees.</p>");

            // end the page
            writeEnd(writer);

            // close the writer
            writer.close();

        } catch (Exception ex) {
          ex.printStackTrace();
        }
    }
}
```

This method can be tested by the following main method:

```
public static void main(String[] args)
{
  WebPageWriter writer = new WebPageWriter();
  writer.writeHomepageV3("Letisha","flying planes");
}
```

Debugging Tip: Make Sure that You Have an Internet Connection!
If you try to execute the main method and you don't have an Internet connection, an exception will occur. Make sure that your connection is working before you try this!

Notice that we can reuse classes that we wrote, too. We just used an object of the class TempFinder in the method writeHomepageWithWeather. This is one of the great things about object-oriented programming: creating classes that you can reuse. We didn't need to import anything to use this class. We didn't have to use an import statement because the classes are in the same package. If you don't have a package statement in your code as the first executable line in the file, then your class is automatically put in the "unnamed" package. Since we didn't have a package statement in either TempFinder or in WebPageWriter, they are both in the "unnamed" package.

13.2.3 Adding Randomness to a Homepage

Remember the random sentence generator? We can add that, too.

Program 121: Homepage Generator with a Random Sentence

```
/**
 * Method for writing a homepage for the passed
 * name that displays the current weather and a
 * random sentence
 * @param name the person's name
 * @param interests a list of the person's interests
 */
public void writeHomepageV4(String name,
                                  String interests)
{
  // get the current temperature
  TempFinder tempFinder = new TempFinder();
  String urlString = "http://www.ajc.com/";
  String currTemp = tempFinder.getTempFromNetwork(urlString);

  // get the random sentence
  SentenceGenerator sentenceGen = new SentenceGenerator();
  String sentence = sentenceGen.generateRandomSentence();

  // try the following
  try {

      // open a file for writing
      BufferedWriter writer =
       new BufferedWriter(new FileWriter(name + ".html"));

      // write the start
      writeStart(writer);

      // write the header
      writeHead(writer,name + "'s Homepage");

      // write the body
      writeBody(writer,"<h1>Welcome to " + name +
              "'s Homepage</h1>" +
              "<p> I am interested in " + interests +
              ".</p><p>Right now it is " + currTemp +
              " degrees.</p>" +
              "<p>The random thought for the day is:  " +
              sentence + "</p>");

      // end the page
      writeEnd(writer);

      // close the writer
      writer.close();
```

```
    } catch (Exception ex) {
      ex.printStackTrace();
    }
  }
}
```

We can test this method with the following `main` method:

```
public static void main(String[] args)
{
  WebPageWriter writer = new WebPageWriter();
  writer.writeHomepageV4("Matthew","playing video games");
}
```

How it Works

Let's walk through the whole large example.

- Execution will start in the `main` method, which first creates an object of the class `WebPageWriter`, and then invokes the method `writeHomepageV4`.

- The method `writeHomepageV4` starts executing with the `name` parameter referring to "`Matthew`" and the `interests` parameter referring to "`playing video games`".

- An object of the class `TempFinder` is created and `getTempFromNetwork` is used to get the current temperature from `http://www.ajc.com/`.

- An object of the class `SentenceGenerator` is created and a random sentence is generated by the method `generateRandomSentence()`.

- Execution continues in the `try` block. We try to create a `BufferedWriter` object using a `FileWriter` object with a file name of the passed name followed by ".html".

- We invoke the method `writeStart` to write out the beginning of the HTML file.

- We invoke the method `writeHead` to write out the head of the HTML file.

- We invoke the method `writeBody` to write out the body of the HTML file. This includes the passed name, interests, current temperature, and the random sentence.

- We invoke the method `writeEnd` which writes out the end of the HTML file.

- We close the `BufferedWriter` which finishes writing out the buffered data and closes the file.

- If an exception occurs during the execution of code in the `try` block, execution will jump to the `catch` block. The stack trace (call stack) will be printed.

Where do you think large Web sites get all their information? There are *so* many pages in those Web sites. Where do they get it all? Where do they store it all?

13.3   DATABASES: A PLACE TO STORE OUR TEXT

Large Web sites use *databases* to store their text and other information. Sites like ebay.com, amazon.com, and CNN.com have large databases with lots of information in them. The pages at these sites aren't generated by somebody typing in information. Instead, programs walk over the database gathering all the information and generating HTML pages. They might do this on a timed basis, to keep updating the page. (See the "last generated" information at CNN.com or Google News.)

Why do they use databases rather than simple text files? There are four reasons:

- Databases are fast. Databases store *indices* that keep track of where key information (like last name or ID number) is in a file, so that you can find "Guzdial" right away. Files are indexed on filename, but not on the content *in* the file.

- Databases are standardized. You can access Microsoft Access, Informix, Oracle, Sybase, MySQL databases from any number of tools or languages.

- Database access can be *distributed*. Multiple people can be putting information into a database and pulling information out of a database, from different computers across a network.

- Databases store *relations*. Databases store names for the *fields* of data. When databases know which fields are important (e.g., which ones you're going to search on most often), the database can be indexed on those fields.

A database stores data based on keys. Keys are unique identifiers for a row in a table of information.

13.3.1   Key and Value Maps

In Java you can use a `java.util.Map` to store key and value pairs. Both the keys and the values *must* be objects. Maps can't have duplicate keys. Each key will map to only one value. However, you can have duplicate values.

Have you ever seen a bunch of post office boxes at your post office? Each of these is like a map in that you can take something out of the box if you have the key. You can also put something into the box if you have the key.

Map is actually an interface. Several classes implement this interface (HashMap, TreeMap, Hashtable, ...). We will use the class `java.util.HashMap` to create a map from a husband's name to his wife's name.

```
> import java.util.*;
> Map wifeMap = new HashMap();
> wifeMap.put("Fred","Wilma");
> wifeMap.put("Barney","Betty");
> System.out.println("Fred's wife is " + wifeMap.get("Fred"));
Fred's wife is Wilma
> System.out.println("Barney's wife is " + wifeMap.get("Barney"));
Barney's wife is Betty
```

Notice that we can refer to a `HashMap` object with an object reference of type `Map`. Since the class `HashMap` implements the `Map` interface we can use just the interface name as the type. This allows us to easily change this to another class that implements the `Map` interface in the future without changing many lines of code. If in the future we want to keep the keys in sorted order, we could use a `TreeMap` instead.

You can put any object in a map as the key and any object in a map as a value. You can even create a map that has another map as the value. Here we have created a map of categories with two categories to start with: "friends" and "family". Each of these keys maps to another map with a name as the key and a phone number as a value.

```
> import java.util.*;
> Map categoryMap = new HashMap();
> Map friendsMap = new HashMap();
> Map familyMap = new HashMap();
> categoryMap.put("friends",friendsMap);
> categoryMap.put("family",familyMap);
> friendsMap.put("Suz","555 213-2392");
> friendsMap.put("Shayna","555 421-3938");
> familyMap.put("Mom","555 321-3928");
> familyMap.put("Dad","555 321-3927");
```

What if you want to store phone numbers on your computer? And what if you want a way to quickly look up the phone number for a given name. A map makes it very easy to look up a value given a key. We can use a map of a name to a phone number. Let's create a class `PhoneBook` which will have a field that is a map of names to phone numbers. We will want to keep the names and phone numbers around, so we will read them from a file. That way we can edit the file to add or remove names and phone numbers.

13.3.2 Downcasting

Maps hold key and value pairs where both the key and value are objects. But, what if we actually use a `String` object for the key and value? This is allowed because the `String` class inherits from the `Object` class so *it is a type of* object. But what if we want to use it as a `String` object again when we get it back from a map?

```
> import java.util.*;
> Map testMap = new HashMap();
> testMap.put("theKey","theValue");
> String value = testMap.get("theKey");
Error: Bad types in assignment
```

Why do we get an error? The value *is* an object of the `String` class. Yes, but the compiler doesn't know that. All the compiler knows is that the map holds objects, not strings. We need to tell it to convert the type to `String` using a cast. You may remember casting as the way that we told the compiler that we were aware that putting a double value into an integer value could lose data.

```
> int floor = 1.0 / 3;
Error: Bad types in assignment
> int floor = (int) 1.0 / 3;
> System.out.println(floor);
0
```

We need to do the same thing when we convert a type from a more general type to a more specific type. This is also called *downcasting*. It tells the compiler to use the specified type for the object. Of course, you could get a runtime exception, if the object isn't really of the type that you are trying to cast it into.

```
> Integer intObj = (Integer) testMap.get("theKey");
java.lang.ClassCastException: intObj
```

Here is the class that represents a phone book. Notice that the method getPhone-Number does use a downcast to change the object (the phone number) returned from the Map to type String.

Program 122: Phone Book Class

```java
import java.util.*;
import java.io.*;

/**
 * A class that represents a phone book.  This phone
 * book maps names to phone numbers. This will
 * read the phone book information from a file.
 */
public class PhoneBook
{
  ///////////////////// fields /////////////////////////

  private String fileName;
  private Map phoneMap = new HashMap();

  ///////////////////// constructors /////////////////////

  /**
   * Constructor that takes a file name and reads
   * in the names and phone numbers from a file
   * @param file the name of the file to read
   */
  public PhoneBook(String file)
  {
    this.fileName = file;

    // read the map information in from the file
    readInfoFromFile();
  }
```

```
//////////////// methods ////////////////////

/**
 * Get the phone number for the passed name
 * @param name the name to look up in the map
 * @return the phone number if found, else null
 */
public String getPhoneNumber(String name)
{
  String phoneNumber = (String) phoneMap.get(name);
  return phoneNumber;
}

/**
 * Method to read the phone information from a
 * file and use it to fill the map
 */
public void readInfoFromFile()
{
  String line = null;
  String[] phoneArray = null;

  try {

    // create the reader
    BufferedReader reader =
      new BufferedReader(new FileReader(fileName));

    // loop reading from the file
    while ((line = reader.readLine()) != null)
    {
      if (line.indexOf(":") >= 0)
      {
        phoneArray = line.split(":");
        phoneMap.put(phoneArray[0].trim(),
                     phoneArray[1].trim());
      }
    }

    // close the reader
    reader.close();

  } catch (FileNotFoundException ex) {
    SimpleOutput.showError("Couldn't find file " + fileName);
  } catch (Exception ex) {
    ex.printStackTrace();
  }

}
```

```java
/* main for testing */
public static void main(String[] args)
{
    PhoneBook phoneBook = new PhoneBook("barbsPhoneBook.txt");
    System.out.println(phoneBook.getPhoneNumber("Shayna"));
    System.out.println(phoneBook.getPhoneNumber("Dentist"));
}

}
```

13.3.3 Generics

Java version 5.0 (also known as 1.5) added generics. You can use generics to specify the type of objects used in collections and this eliminates the need to downcast when you get objects back from a collection. To use generics you simply add type information when you declare a variable that refers to a collection object and when you create a collection object. To declare a field that is a map with `String` objects used as both the keys and the values use:

```java
private Map<String,String> phoneMap =
    new HashMap<String,String>();
```

Doing this eliminates the need to cast the value returned from the collection to a string when you assign it to a variable that refers to an object of the `String` class.

```java
String phoneNumber = phoneMap.get(name);
```

Here is the PhoneBook class changed to use generics.

Program 123: Java 5.0 Version of the Phone Book

```java
import java.util.*;
import java.io.*;

/**
 * A class that represents a phone book.  This phone
 * book maps names to phone numbers. This will
 * read the phone book information from a file.
 */
public class PhoneBook
{
    ///////////////////// fields /////////////////////////////

    private String fileName;
    private Map<String,String> phoneMap =
        new HashMap<String,String>();

    ///////////////////// constructors //////////////////////

    /**
     * Constructor that takes a file name and reads
     * in the names and phone numbers from a file
```

```java
 * @param file the name of the file to read
 */
public PhoneBook(String file)
{
  this.fileName = file;

  // read the map information in from the file
  readInfoFromFile();
}

///////////////////// methods /////////////////////////

/**
 * Get the phone number for the passed name
 * @param name the name to look up in the map
 * @return the phone number if found, else null
 */
public String getPhoneNumber(String name)
{
  String phoneNumber = phoneMap.get(name);
  return phoneNumber;
}

/**
 * Method to read the phone information from a
 * file and use it to fill the map
 */
public void readInfoFromFile()
{
  String line = null;
  String[] phoneArray = null;

  try {

    // create the reader
    BufferedReader reader =
      new BufferedReader(new FileReader(fileName));

    // loop reading from the file
    while ((line = reader.readLine()) != null)
    {
      if (line.indexOf(":") >= 0)
      {
        phoneArray = line.split(":");
        phoneMap.put(phoneArray[0].trim(),
                     phoneArray[1].trim());
      }
    }

    // close the reader
    reader.close();
```

```
    } catch (FileNotFoundException ex) {
      SimpleOutput.showError("Couldn't find file " + fileName);
    } catch (Exception ex) {
      ex.printStackTrace();
    }

  }
  /* main for testing */
  public static void main(String[] args)
  {
    PhoneBook phoneBook = new PhoneBook("barbsPhoneBook.txt");
    System.out.println(phoneBook.getPhoneNumber("Shayna"));
    System.out.println(phoneBook.getPhoneNumber("Dentist"));
  }

}
```

■

What if we want to print out all of the names and phone numbers in the phone book? How can we loop through a Map? You can get a set of all of the keys in a map using the method keySet(). This returns an object of a class that implements the java.util.Set interface. A set is something that holds non-duplicate items. It may not preserve the order of the items in the set. Contrast this with the List interface, which does preserve the order of the items in the list, and does allow duplicate items in the list.

If you are using Java 5.0 (1.5) or above, you can loop through the items in a set using a for-each loop. Here is a method that will print out all the data in the phone book.

Program 124: The Method printBook with a for-each Loop

```
public void printBook()
{
  // get the set of keys
  Set<String> keySet = phoneMap.keySet();

  // loop through the keys
  for (String key : keySet)
  {
    System.out.println("Name: " + key +
                       ", Phone number: " +
                       phoneMap.get(key));
  }
}
```

■

Another way to loop through a collection is to use another interface: java.util. Iterator. Classes that implement this interface will let you walk through the elements of a collection one at a time using the method next() and you can check if there are more items to process using the method hasNext(). You will need to downcast the object returned from the `Iterator` if you want to treat it as anything other than an object.

Here is the 1.4 version of the method `printBook`:

Program 125: The Method printBook with an Iterator

```java
/**
 * Method to print out the contents of the phone book
 */
public void printBook()
{
  // get the set of keys
  Set keySet = phoneMap.keySet();
  String key = null;

  // loop through the keys
  Iterator iterator = keySet.iterator();
  while (iterator.hasNext())
  {
    key = (String) iterator.next();
    System.out.println("Name: " + key +
                  ", Phone number: " +
                  phoneMap.get(key));
  }
}
```

13.4   RELATIONAL DATABASES

Most modern databases are `relational` databases. In relational databases, information is stored in tables (Figure 13.8). Columns in a relational table are named, and rows of data are assumed to be related.

Complex relationships are stored across multiple tables. Let's say that you have a bunch of pictures of people, and you want to keep track of which people are in which pictures—there can be more than one person in a given picture. You might record a

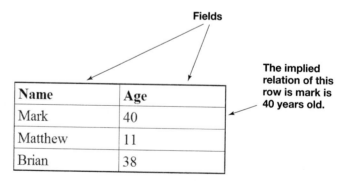

Fields

The implied relation of this row is mark is 40 years old.

Name	Age
Mark	40
Matthew	11
Brian	38

FIGURE 13.8
An example relational table.

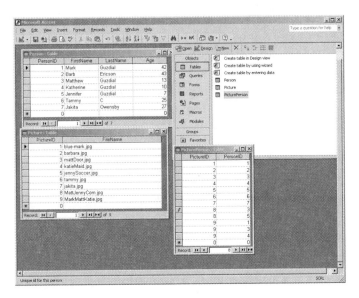

FIGURE 13.9
Representing more complex relationships across multiple tables.

structure like that in a collection of tables: Person, Picture, and PicturePerson. The table Person would store information about a person. The table Picture would store information about a picture. And the table PicturePerson would hold the relationships between the picture and the person or people in it (Figure 13.9).

How would you use tables like in Figure 13.9 to find a picture that has Tammy in it? You start up by looking up the person identifier (PersonID) in the Person table (6), then find a picture which has that person identifier associated with it (6) in the PicturePerson table, then use the picture identifier (PictureID) to look up the picture name in the Picture table, to get the result of tammy.jpg. How about figuring out who's in that picture? You can look up the picture identifier in the Picture table, then find the person identifiers that are related to that picture identifier in the PicturePerson table, and then look up the people's names in the Person table.

We call this use of multiple tables to answer a *query* (a request for information from a database) a *join*. Database joins work best if the tables are kept simple, where there is only a single relation per row.

13.4.1 SQL

How do you communicate what you are looking for to a database? You typically use *SQL* (*Structured Query Language*) to manipulate and query databases. There are actually several languages that are part of the SQL database language family, but we're not going to make distinctions here. SQL is a large and complex programming language, and we're not going to even attempt to go over all of it. But we are going to touch on enough of it to give you a sense of what SQL is like and how it's used.

SQL can be used with many different databases, including Microsoft Access. There are also freely available databases like *MySQL* that use SQL and can be controlled from Java. If you want to play with the examples we'll be doing here, you can either use Microsoft Access or MySQL.

If you want to use MySQL you will need to install it from `http://www.mysql.com`. You will also need to download the *driver* that allows Java programs to talk to the MySQL database.

13.4.2   Getting Started: Drivers and Connections

To manipulate a relational database from Java, you need to work with objects in the `java.sql` package. The first thing you need to do is load the driver class. The driver is the object that knows how to handle requests to that particular database. You load a database driver by using the following:

```
Class.forName("driverName");
```

This uses a class (`static`) method on the class `Class` that loads a class based on its name. The `driverName` is the full name (the package name followed by `'.'` then the class name) of the driver class. To connect to an Access database you can use the `sun.jdbc.odbc.JdbcOdbcDriver` class. To connect to a MySQL database, you can use the `com.mysql.jdbc.Driver` class.

Anytime you want to communicate with the database you will need to create a `Connection` object. A connection specifies the database that you want to communicate with and optionally ensures that you protect the database by using a login and password.

```
Connection connection =
    DriverManager.getConnection(url,"login","password");
```

There is also a version of the `getConnection` method that only takes the URL. This is a class (`static`) method on the `DriverManager` class. To connect to an Access database we use a *JDBC* to *ODBC* bridge. JDBC refers to the classes in the `java.sql` package that work with databases. ODBC stands for Open DataBase Connectivity and was developed by Microsoft. The JDBC to ODBC bridge translates JDBC operations into ODBC operations. In order to use this we need to create an ODBC data source.

On a Windows machine open the control panel and open the ODBC Data Source Administrator window (Figure 13.10). Make sure that the USER DSN tab is showing and then click on ADD to add a new data source.

This will display a window titled "Create New Data Source" (Figure 13.11). Click on MICROSOFT ACCESS DRIVER and then on FINISH to create a data source to a Microsoft Access database.

This will let you map an ODBC name to a Microsoft Access file. Use this window (Figure 13.12) to create a `person` data source that maps to the `person.mdb` database in the bookClasses directory.

Many databases limit the number of connections that there can be to the database at the same time. However, many different programs can be connected to a database

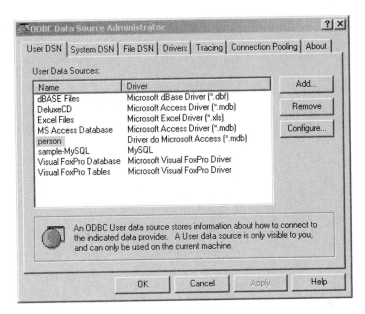

FIGURE 13.10
ODBC data source administrator window.

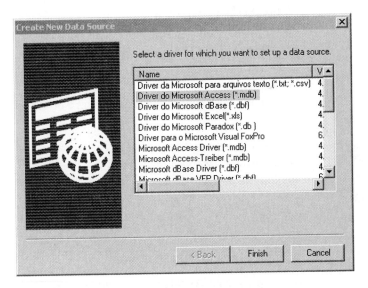

FIGURE 13.11
Create new data source window.

at the same time. So when you use a connection in your program, you need to close it when you are finished with it, to let other programs use it. It is best to create a connection each time you need to communicate with a database and then close it after each communication. Most database drivers *pool* (keep track of) connections so that when you create one, the driver takes one from the pool of free connections

FIGURE 13.12
An ODBC data source for the Microsoft Access person database.

and when you close a connection, the driver releases it to the free pool. To close a connection use:

```
connection.close();
```

All of the methods that work with databases can cause an SQLException. You will need to either throw exceptions or catch them. To catch the exceptions, put the code that can cause exceptions in a try block and catch the exceptions in catch blocks.

Here is a class that shows how to load a driver and create and close a Connection object.

Program 126: Database Manager Class

```java
import java.sql.*;

/**
 * Class that handles the connection with the database
 */
public class DatabaseManager
{
    /////////////// fields //////////////////////////////

    private String driverName;
    private String urlStr;

    ///////////   constructors //////////////////////////

    /**
     * Constructor that takes the driver name and url
     * @param driver the class that communicates with the
```

```
 * database
 * @param url the url of the database as a string
 */
public DatabaseManager(String driver, String url)
{
  this.driverName = driver;
  this.urlStr = url;

  // try the following
  try {

    // load the driver class
    Class.forName(driver);

  } catch (ClassNotFoundException ex) {
    SimpleOutput.showError("Can't find the driver class " +
                           driver + ", check the classpath");
  }
}

/////////////// methods ///////////////////////////

/**
 * Method for testing the connection
 */
public void testConnection()
{
  // try the following
  try {

    // open the connection to the database
    Connection connection =
      DriverManager.getConnection(this.urlStr);

    // tell the user the connection was opened
    System.out.println("Connection established");

    // close the connection
    connection.close();

    // tell the user the connection was closed
    System.out.println("The connection was closed");

  } catch (SQLException ex) {
    SimpleOutput.showError("Trouble with the " +
                           "database connection");
    ex.printStackTrace();
  }
}
```

```
/* main for testing */
public static void main(String[] args)
{
  // create the database manager for an Access database
  DatabaseManager dbManager =
    new DatabaseManager("sun.jdbc.odbc.JdbcOdbcDriver",
                        "jdbc:odbc:person");

  // create the database manager for a MySQL database
  // new DatabaseManager("com.mysql.jdbc.Driver",
  //                     "jdbc:mysql://localhost:3306/person");

  // test a query
  dbManager.testQuery("Select FirstName, Age From " +
                      "Person Where Age > 40", 2);
}

}
```

13.4.3 Querying the Database

Think about selecting data in a database as literally selecting, as you would in a word-processor or spreadsheet, the rows that you want in the table. Some examples of selection commands in SQL are:

```
Select * From Person
Select FirstName, Age From Person
Select * from Person Where Age > 40
Select LastName, Age From Person Where Age > 40
```

The general syntax for a simple query is: `Select fieldList From Table`.

The field list is a comma-separated list of field (column) names. You can ask for just one field. You can also use `'*'` for the field name to get all of the fields (columns) in the table. You can also add a condition to the query using the keyword "Where" as shown above.

To send a query to a database we need to create a `Statement`. We use the `Connection` method `createStatement` to do this:

```
Statement statement = connection.createStatement();
```

There can only be one statement open at a time on a connection. So we have to use this and close it before we can open another on the same connection.

To execute a query use:

```
ResultSet rs = statement.executeQuery(queryStr);
```

The returned `ResultSet` is like a temporary table that holds the result of the query. To process it we need to walk through each row that is returned and get the data from each column. When it is returned the *cursor* (a pointer to the current row) is positioned *before* the first row. This may sound strange but it allows you to use a `while` loop and loop while the `next` method returns true, which means that there is a next row. The next method also changes the cursor to point to the next row. It is possible that there are *no* rows in the result set.

To process the column data in the result set we use the getXXX(int index) methods where the XXX stands for the type of data that we want to get. The index stands for the column number which starts with 1 (not 0). Or you can use getXXX(String colName) where colName is the name of the column.

Common Bug: Result Sets Column Numbers Start with 1

Most of the items that we have been working with in Java start with the first item at index 0. However, the result set column numbers start with 1. This means that if you are looping through the columns, it is better to start your index variable at 1 and loop while it is less than or equal to the desired number of times you want to loop.

After you process a result set, you must close it and then close the statement. Remember that all of the methods that work with a database can cause a SQLException so all the code needs to be in a try block. Here is an example method that executes a passed query and prints the data from the result set.

Program 127: Method to Display the Results of a Database Query

```java
/**
 * Method to test a query and print the results
 * @param query the query to execute
 * @param numCols the number of columns in the result
 */
public void testQuery(String query, int numCols)
{

  // try the following
  try {

  // open the connection to the database
  Connection connection =
    DriverManager.getConnection(this.urlStr);

  // create a statement
  Statement statement = connection.createStatement();

  // execute the query
  ResultSet rs = statement.executeQuery(query);

  // print out the results
  while (rs.next())
  {
    for (int i = 1; i <= numCols; i++)
    {
      System.out.print(rs.getString(i) + ", ");
    }
    System.out.println();
  }
```

```
        // close the result set
        rs.close();

        // close the statement
        statement.close();

        // close the connection
        connection.close();

      } catch (SQLException ex) {
        SimpleOutput.showError("Trouble with the database " +
                               urlStr);
        ex.printStackTrace();
      }
    }
```

This method can be executed by the following `main` method.

```
/* main for testing */
public static void main(String[] args)
{
  // create the database manager for an Access database
  DatabaseManager dbManager =
    new DatabaseManager("sun.jdbc.odbc.JdbcOdbcDriver",
                        "jdbc:odbc:person");

  // create the database manager for a MySQL database
  // new DatabaseManager("com.mysql.jdbc.Driver",
  //                     "jdbc:mysql://localhost:3306/person");

  // test a query
  dbManager.testQuery("Select FirstName, Age From Person", 2);
}
```

Executing this main will result in the following:

```
Mark, 42,
Barb, 43,
Matthew, 13,
Tammy, 25,
Katherine, 10,
Jennifer, 7,
Jakita, 27,
```

We can narrow the selection by adding a condition to the query.

Program 128: Trying a Query

```
/* main for testing */
public static void main(String[] args)
```

```
{
  // create the database manager for an Access database
  DatabaseManager dbManager =
    new DatabaseManager("sun.jdbc.odbc.JdbcOdbcDriver",
                        "jdbc:odbc:person");

  // create the database manager for a MySQL database
  // new DatabaseManager("com.mysql.jdbc.Driver",
  //                     "jdbc:mysql://localhost:3306/person");

  // test a query
  dbManager.testQuery("Select FirstName, Age From " +
                      "Person Where Age > 40", 2);
}
```

Executing this main will result in:

```
Mark, 42,
Barb, 43,
```

We can now think about doing a join using a conditional select. We want to select the pictures that have Jennifer in them. So, we want the names of the pictures that have a `PictureID` that matches a `PictureID` in the `PicturePerson` table that has her `PersonID` associated with it. You can use the keyword "And" to combine conditionals in SQL. You also need to enclose strings in SQL in quotes. The easiest way to do this in Java is to enclose the strings in single quotes because Java strings use double quotes to signal the beginning and ending of a Java string.

```
public static void main(String[] args)
{
  // create the database manager for an Access database
  DatabaseManager dbManager =
    new DatabaseManager("sun.jdbc.odbc.JdbcOdbcDriver",
                        "jdbc:odbc:person");

  // create the database manager for a MySQL database
  // new DatabaseManager("com.mysql.jdbc.Driver",
  //                     "jdbc:mysql://localhost:3306/person");

  // test a query
  dbManager.testQuery("Select per.FirstName, " +
                      "pict.FileName From " +
                      "Picture as pict, Person as per, " +
                      "PicturePerson as pictPer " +
                      "Where per.FirstName = " +
                      "'Jennifer' And " +
                      "pictPer.PersonID = per.PersonID And " +
                      "pict.PictureID = pictPer.PictureID", 2);
}
```

Notice that you can give the table name an *alias* (another name that you can use to refer to it). Also notice that you need to qualify the field name with the table name when you are pulling data from more than one table. You do this by adding the table name or table alias then `'.'` then the field (column) name.

Running this main will result in the following output:

```
Jennifer, jennySoccer.jpg,
Jennifer, MattJennyCorn.jpg,
```

13.4.4   Using a Database to Build Web Pages

Now let's get back to our `WebPageWriter` class. We can store information in our database, retrieve it, then put it in our Web page—just like Amazon, CNN, and eBay.

Program 129: Building a Web Page with Database Content

```java
/**
 * Method for writing a homepage for the passed
 * first name that displays her/his interests and age
 * @param name the person's first name
 * @param interests a list of the person's interests
 */
public void writeHomepageV5(String name,
                                  String interests)
{
  // Get a DatabaseManager object
  DatabaseManager dbManager =
    new DatabaseManager("sun.jdbc.odbc.JdbcOdbcDriver",
                        "jdbc:odbc:person");

  // get this person's age
  String age =
    dbManager.getStringForQuery(
      "Select Age From Person " +
      "Where FirstName='" + name + "'");

  // try the following
  try {

    // open a file for writing
    BufferedWriter writer =
      new BufferedWriter(new FileWriter(name + ".html"));

    // write the start
    writeStart(writer);

    // write the header
    writeHead(writer,name + "'s Homepage");

    // write the body
    writeBody(writer,"<h1>Welcome to " + name +
              "'s Homepage</h1>" +
              "<p> I am interested in " + interests +
              ".</p><p>I am " + age + " years old</p>");
```

```
        // end the page
        writeEnd(writer);

        // close the writer
        writer.close();

    } catch (Exception ex) {
        ex.printStackTrace();
    }
}
```

■

You can run this with the following main:

```
public static void main(String[] args)
{
    WebPageWriter writer = new WebPageWriter();
    writer.writeHomepageV5("Matthew","playing video games");
}
```

Now we can think about how a large Web site like CNN.com works. Reporters enter stories into a database distributed all over the world. Editors (also distributed, or all in one place) retrieve stories from the database, update them, then store them back. On a regular basis (perhaps more often when a hot story emerges) the Web page generation program runs, gathers up the stories, and generates the HTML. POOF! You have a large Web site! Databases are really critical to how large Web-sites run.

Most Java-generated HTML pages are actually generated by *servlets*. These are Java programs that run on a Web server and dynamically create HTML pages, often based on user input. Many of these servlets are automatically created from *JavaServer Pages* (JSP). These are HTML pages that have Java mixed in or that have special tags that work with Java classes to generate content for the pages.

13.5 CONCEPTS SUMMARY

In this chapter we introduced HTML, and writing programs to generate HTML. We broke a long method into several smaller helper methods. We showed how a method can throw an exception. We talked about the "unnamed" package. We introduced another of the collection classes: HashMap. We introduced generics which allow us to add types to collection classes. We introduced using an Iterator to loop through a collection. We also used JDBC and SQL to query a relational database.

13.5.1 HTML

HTML is the HyperText Markup Language. It consists of tags that you add to text to control how it is displayed in a browser. HTML tags often come in pairs of opening and closing tags like <title>...</title>. Tags that do not have a opening and closing tag look a bit different: <img src='file' height='100' />.

13.5.2 Helper Methods

When a method gets long and hard to read, it is best to break it up into several smaller methods. These are often called helper methods because they help another method accomplish a task. Helper methods are often declared with a visibility of `private`, but they don't have to be. If a helper method is something that another class would like to have access to, it can be `public`. Breaking a method up into smaller methods is also called procedural abstraction.

13.5.3 Throwing an Exception

A method can throw an exception instead of catching it by adding `throws ExceptionName` after the parameter list in the method declaration. Here is an example:

```java
private void writeBody(BufferedWriter writer, String body)
    throws IOException
```

Then, if the exception occurs during the execution of the method, the runtime will look to see whether the method that called the method that throws the exception handles it.

13.5.4 The "Unnamed" Package

All classes that you create will be put into a package. If you don't include a package statement in your file as the first line of executable code in the file, then your class is put in the "unnamed" package and can use other classes that are also in that package. A package statement looks like:

```java
package edu.gatech.intro;

public class Student
```

13.5.5 HashMap

A HashMap is a class that implements the `Map` interface. It is one of the collection classes. It is in the package `java.util`. It allows you to store an object (called the value) which can be retrieved by using another object (the key). There cannot be duplicate keys in a map, and each key maps to one value. You can put values into the map for a key using the method `put(Object key, Object value)`. You can get a value out of the map for a key using the method `get(Object key)`.

13.5.6 Generics

You can use generics to provide type information for collection classes. To do so, just specify the type of the collection class when you create it and also in variables that refer to it. This eliminates the need to downcast an object that you get from a collection back to the original class.

```java
private Map<String,String> phoneMap =
    new HashMap<String,String>();
```

13.5.7 Iterators

If you are using Java 5.0 (1.5) you can use the `for-each` loop to walk through the elements in a collection. You can also use an `Iterator` from package `java.util`. `Iterator` is an interface that provides methods for checking if there are still items in the collection to process (`hasNext()`) and for getting the next item (`next()`). If you assign the item from the collection to an object reference of a type other than `Object`, you will need to downcast (cast to a subclass).

```
// loop through the keys
Iterator iterator = keySet.iterator();
while (iterator.hasNext())
{
  key = (String) iterator.next();
```

13.5.8 JDBC and SQL

JDBC is another name for the classes in the `java.sql` package that let Java programs communicate with databases. We used classes in this package to create a connection to a database (`Connection`), create an object that handles executing SQL (`Statement`), and retrieve the results from a SQL query (`ResultSet`).

SQL (Structured Query Language) is a standard language for manipulating and querying databases. We used it to select data that we wanted from a relational database. It can also be used for creating databases and tables, and for removing or updating data in the tables.

PROBLEMS

13.1 What is meant by each of the following?

- HTML
- XML
- XHTML
- Map
- Set
- List
- Relational Database
- Helper Method
- Database Driver
- Connection
- SQL
- ODBC

13.2 What is the hexadecimal color code for a color with a red value of 255, a green value of 255, and a blue value of 51? What is the hexadecimal color code for a color with a red value of 204, a green value of 0, and a blue value of 204? What is the hexadecimal color code for a color with a red value of 255, a green value of 204, and a blue value of 204? Use a hexadecimal color code to specify the background color for a homepage generated by one of the methods in the class WebPageWriter.

13.3 Using a text editor, write an HTML page that has a table in it. Use a browser to check that it is working. Then add the HTML for the table to the body of a homepage generated with the class WebPageWriter.

13.4 Add a new method like createImagePage in the class WebPageWriter that will create a table where the first row has four columns of pictures. The second row would have the picture file names.

13.5 Add a method to the class WebPageWriter that will print out the file names for all files ending with ".wav" in a passed directory. You can add a link to the sound files name which will play the sound when the user clicks on the link. Just use the link (anchor) tag: <a href="soundFile.wav">soundFile. wav</a>.

13.6 Write a class that will find the most important headline from someplace like cnn.com and use that class to add a headline to the homepage generated by the method writeHomepage in the class WebPageWriter.

13.7 Create a method writeNewsPage in the class WebPageWriter that will create a page of the information you find important from at least three Web sites.

13.8 If you are using Java 5.0 (1.5) or above rewrite the method createStudents in the Student class to use generics with ArrayList and List.

13.9 Modify the PhoneBook class to use a TreeMap instead of a HashMap. Does anything change when you execute the method printBook?

13.10 Create a class PictureBook that is like the class PhoneBook except that it maps a person's name to his or her picture.

13.11 Add a method getName(String phoneNumber) to the PhoneBook class. Can you think of a fast way to look up the name when you are given the phone number?

13.12 Create a main method for the class DatabaseManager that prints out the name and age of all the people who are under 30 in the database.

13.13 Create a main method for the class DatabaseManager that prints out the last name, and age of all the people who are under 30 in the database.

13.14 Create a main method for the class DatabaseManager that prints out the first name, last name, and age of all the people who are under 30 in the database who's first name starts with the letter 'T'.

13.15 Create a main method for the class DatabaseManager that prints out the first name, last name, and age of all the people who are over 30 in the database or who's last name is "Guzdial".

13.16 Add a method getListForQuery(String query) to the DatabaseManager class that will return a List of all the columns in the first row returned in the result set for the passed query. You can find out how many columns have been returned by getting a `ResultSetMetaData` object from the `ResultSet` object using the method `getMetaData()` method. You can then ask the `ResultSetMetaData` object for the number of columns by using the method `getColumnCount()`.

13.17 Add a method `writeHomepageV6` which is like method `writeHomepageV5` except that it also shows all the pictures associated with this person on their generated homepage.

13.18 Your father calls you. "My tech-support people are saying that the company Web site is down because the database is broken. What does the database have to do with our company Web site?" You explain to him how databases can be integral to running large Web sites. Explain both (a) how the Web site comes to be authored through the database and (b) how the HTML is actually created.

13.19 You have a new computer that seems to connect to the Internet, but when you try to go to `http://www.cnn.com` you get a "Server Not Found" error. You call tech support, and they tell you to try to go to `http://64.236.24.20`. That works. Now both you and the tech know what's wrong with your computer's settings. What isn't working properly, since you can get to a site via the Internet but can't get the domain name `www.cnn.com` recognized?

13.20 Add something to your HTML homepage generator that will make random, relevant comments about the weather depending on the temperature.

- If it's going to be less than 32, you want to insert either "Watch out for ice!" or "Is it going to snow?"
- If it's going to be between 32 and 50, you want to insert either "I can't wait for winter to be over!" or "Come on, Spring!"
- If it's over 50 but less than 80, you want to insert either "It's getting warmer!" or "Light jacket weather."
- If it's over 80, you want to insert either "FINALLY! Summer!" or "Time to go swimming!"

TO DIG DEEPER

To learn more about HTML and XHTML, see `http://www.w3.org/MarkUp/`. To learn more about SQL, see `http://www.sqlcourse.com`. To learn more about working with databases in Java, see `http://java.sun.com/docs/books/tutorial/jdbc/`. For information on using servlets and JavaServer Pages (JSP), see `http://www.moreservlets.com/`.

5 MOVIES

Chapter 14   Encoding, Manipulating, and Creating
Movies

483

14 Encoding, Manipulating, and Creating Movies

Chapter Learning Objectives

The media learning goals for this chapter are:

- To create frame-based animations with simple geometric shapes, text, and images.
- To do special effects like fade-out and chromakey in movies.

The computer science goals for this chapter are:

- To explain why movies take so much space to store.
- To add parameters to methods to make them more reusable.
- To reuse earlier methods to make movies.

Movies (video) are actually very simple to manipulate. They are a series of pictures (*frames*). You need to be concerned with the *frame rate* (the number of frames per second), but it's mostly just things you've seen before. We're going to use the term *movies* to refer generically to *animations* (motion generated entirely by graphical drawings) and *video* (motion generated by some kind of photographic process).

What makes movies work is a feature of our visual system called *persistence of vision*. We do not see every change that happens in the world. For example, you don't typically see your eyes blink, even though they do it quite often (typically 20 times a minute). Our eyes retain an image for a short period of time.

If we see one *related* picture after another fast enough, our eye retains the image and our brain sees continuous motion. If the pictures aren't related, our brain reports a *montage*, a collection of disparate (though perhaps thematically connected) images. We refer to this 16 *frames per second (fps)* as the lower bound for the sensation of motion.

Early silent pictures were 16 fps. Motion pictures standardized on 24 fps to make sound smoother. (Ever wonder why silent pictures often look fast and jerky? Think about what happens when you scale up a picture or sound—that's exactly what happens if you play a 16 fps movie at 24 fps.) Digital video (e.g., video cameras) capture at 30 fps. How high is useful? There are some U.S. Air Force experiments suggesting that pilots can recognize a blurb of light in the shape of an aircraft (and figure out what kind it is) in 1/200 of a second! Video game players say that they can discern a difference between 30 fps video and 60 fps video.

Movies are challenging to work with because of the amount and speed of data involved. *Real-time processing* of video (e.g., doing some modification to each frame as it comes in or goes out) is hard because whatever processing you do has to fit into 1/30 of a second! Let's do the math for how many bytes are needed to record video:

- One second of 640×480 frame size images at 30 fps means $30(frames) * 640 * 480(pixels) = 9,216,000$ pixels.

- At 24-bit color (one byte for each of R, G, and B), that's 27,648,000 bytes, or 27 megabytes *per second*.

- For a 90-minute feature film, that's $90 * 60 * 27,648,000 = 149,299,200,000$ bytes — 149 gigabytes.

Digital movies are almost always stored in a compressed format. A DVD only stores 6.47 gigabytes, so even on a DVD the movie is compressed. Movie format standards like *MPEG*, *QuickTime*, and *AVI* are all compressed movie formats. They don't record every frame — they record *key frames* and then record differences between one frame and the next. The *JMV* format is slightly different — it's a file of JPEG images, so every frame is there, but every frame is compressed.

An MPEG movie is really just an MPEG image sequence merged with an MPEG (like MP3) audio file. We're going to follow that lead and *not* deal with sound here. The tools described in the next section *can* create movies with sound, but the real trick of processing movies is handling all those images. That's what we're going to focus on here.

14.1   GENERATING FRAME-BASED ANIMATIONS

To make movies, we're going to create a series of JPEG frames and display them. We have included a class `FrameSequencer` which will help you generate the frames. The class `FrameSequencer` also creates an object of the class `MoviePlayer` to display the frames. The MediaTools application on the CD can reassemble JPEG frames into a JMV movie. You can also use tools such as Apple's QuickTime Pro (http://www.apple.com/quicktime) or ImageMagick (http://www.image-magick.org/), which can also create QuickTime, MPEG, or AVI movies from individual frames (and go in reverse — burst a movie into a bunch of frames).

We'll place all of our frames in a single directory, and number them so that the tools know how to reassemble them into a movie in the right order. We'll literally name our files `frame0001.jpg`, `frame0002.jpg`, and so on with leading zeros, so that the files are in order when placed in alphabetical order.

Here's our first movie-generating program, which simply moves a red rectangle down diagonally (Figure 14.1). We have created a new class `MovieMaker` to hold the methods that make movies.

Program 130: Simple Motion of a Rectangle

```java
import java.awt.*;

/**
 * Class to create frames for a movie
 * @author Barb Ericson
 */
public class MovieMaker {

  /**
   * Method to make a movie that has a rectangle moving
   * around
   * @param directory the directory to put the movie
   * frames
   */
  public void makeRectangleMovie(String directory)
  {
    int framesPerSec = 30;
    Picture p = null;
    Graphics g = null;
    FrameSequencer frameSequencer =
      new FrameSequencer(directory);

    // loop through the first second
    for (int i = 0; i < framesPerSec; i++)
    {
      // draw a filled rectangle
      p = new Picture(640,480);
      g = p.getGraphics();
      g.setColor(Color.RED);
      g.fillRect(i * 10, i * 5, 50,50);

      // add frame to sequencer
      frameSequencer.addFrame(p);
    }

    // replay the movie
    frameSequencer.show();
    frameSequencer.replay(framesPerSec);
  }

  // main for testing
  public static void main(String[] args)
  {
    MovieMaker movieMaker = new MovieMaker();
    String dir = "c:/intro-prog-java/movies/rectangle/";
    movieMaker.makeRectangleMovie(dir);
  }

}
```

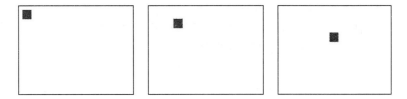

FIGURE 14.1
A few frames from the first movie: Moving a rectangle.

You can change the directory that will hold the created movie frames from what is specified as the `dir` variable in the `main method`. Compile and run the `main` method for the class `MovieMaker`. You should see the rectangle move as shown in (Figure 14.1).

Debugging Tip: Out of Memory Error

Working with the number of pictures you have in a movie can cause Java to run out of memory and you can get an *out of memory error* (`java.lang.OutOfMemoryError`). When the Java Virtual Machine starts it sets aside some memory to work in and it has a limit of how much total it can use. You can change this by adding some arguments for the Java Virtual Machine when you start it. In DrJava you do this by clicking on EDIT, then PREFERENCES, which will display the PREFERENCES WINDOW. Click on MISCELLANEOUS under CATEGORIES on the left, and then enter –Xmx512m –Xms128m to set the maximum amount of memory to 512 megabytes and the starting memory to 128 megabytes. Then click on OK. It may ask if you really are sure that you want to do this, and you should say OK. Click on RESET to have the new settings affect the INTERACTIONS PANE.

You can actually set the maximum to more RAM memory than you have. It will save some of the items in memory to disk and bring them back in when they are needed. This is called *virtual memory*.

You can also do this using the command-line tools from Sun:

```
java –Xmx512m –Xms128m MovieMaker
```

The key part of this recipe is the `g.fillRect(i * 10, i * 5, 50,50);`. Each time through the loop we create a new `Picture` object and then draw the rectangle at a new position in the `Picture` based on the value of the loop index. When we add the `Picture` object to the `FrameSequencer` object, it will write out the frame to the directory. It will also display the current frame using a `MoviePlayer` object.

Here are the first five values in the call to the `fillRect` method:

```
g.fillRect(0,0,50,50);   // i is 0
g.fillRect(10,5,50,50);  // i is 1
g.fillRect(20,10,50,50); // i is 2
g.fillRect(30,15,50,50); // i is 3
g.fillRect(40,20,50,50); // i is 4
```

While `setPixel()` gets upset if you try to set a pixel outside of the bounds of the picture, the graphics methods of the `Graphics` class `drawString` and `fillRect` don't generate errors. They'll simply *clip* the image for the picture, so you can create simple code to make animations and not worry about going out of bounds. This makes creating a tickertape movie fairly simple.

You can add the following method to the `MovieMaker` class to generate a movie with the text appearing on the right side of the picture and moving across to the left.

Program 131: Generate a Tickertape Movie

```
/**
 * Method to create a tickertape movie
 * @param directory the directory to write to
 * @param message the string to display
 */
public void makeTickerTapeMovie(String directory,
                                String message)
{
  int framesPerSec = 30;
  Picture p = null;
  Graphics g = null;
  FrameSequencer frameSequencer =
    new FrameSequencer(directory);
  Font font = new Font("Arial",Font.BOLD,24);

  // loop for 2 seconds of animation
  for (int i = 0; i < framesPerSec * 2; i++)
  {
    // draw the string
    p = new Picture(300,100);
    g = p.getGraphics();
    g.setColor(Color.BLACK);
    g.setFont(font);
    g.drawString(message,300 - (i * 10), 50);

    // add frame to sequencer
    frameSequencer.addFrame(p);
  }

  // replay the movie
  frameSequencer.show();
  frameSequencer.replay(framesPerSec);
}
```

■

You can test this with the following main. You can change the directory that will hold the created movie frames from what is specified as the `dir` variable in the `main` method. The result of running this `main` method is shown in Figure 14.2.

```
public static void main(String[] args)
{
  MovieMaker movieMaker = new MovieMaker();
  String dir = "c:/intro-prog-java/movies/tickertape/";
  movieMaker.makeTickerTapeMovie(dir,"Buy more widgets");
}
```

Buy mo	**Buy more widgets**	dgets

FIGURE 14.2
Frames from the tickertape method.

Can we move more than one thing at once? Sure! Our drawing code just gets a little more complicated. Here's a recipe that uses *sine* and *cosine* to create circular motion to match our linear motion of Program 130 (page 486) (Figure 14.3). You can add this method to the class `MovieMaker`.

Program 132: Move Two Objects at Once

```
/**
 * Method to make a movie that has a two rectangles moving
 * around
 * @param directory the directory to put the movie
 * frames
 */
public void makeTwoRectangleMovie(String directory)
{
  int framesPerSec = 30;
  Picture p = null;
  Graphics g = null;
  FrameSequencer frameSequencer =
    new FrameSequencer(directory);

  // loop through the first second
  for (int i = 0; i < framesPerSec; i++)
  {
    // draw a filled rectangle
    p = new Picture(640,480);
    g = p.getGraphics();
    g.setColor(Color.RED);
    g.fillRect(i * 10, i * 5, 50,50);
    g.setColor(Color.BLUE);
    g.fillRect(100 + (int) (10 * Math.sin(i)),
               4 * i + (int) (10 * Math.cos(i)),
               50,50);

    // add frame to sequencer
    frameSequencer.addFrame(p);
  }

  // replay the movie
  frameSequencer.show();
  frameSequencer.replay(framesPerSec);
}
```

FIGURE 14.3
Moving two rectangles at once.

You can test this with the following main. You can change the directory that will hold the created movie frames from what is specified as the `dir` variable in the `main` method. The result of executing the following `main` method is shown in Figure 14.3.

```java
public static void main(String[] args)
{
  MovieMaker movieMaker = new MovieMaker();
  String dir = "c:/intro-prog-java/movies/rectangle2/";
  movieMaker.makeTwoRectangleMovie(dir);
}
```

We don't have to create our animations out of things that we can draw, like rectangles. We can copy `Picture` objects to different locations. This kind of code runs pretty slowly.

The recipe below moves Mark's head around on the screen. This method took over a minute to complete on a fast computer. You can add this method to the `MovieMaker` class.

Program 133: Move Mark's Head

```java
/**
 * Method to move Mark's head around
 */
public void moveMarksHead(String directory)
{
  // load the picture of Mark
  String fName = FileChooser.getMediaPath("blue-Mark.jpg");
  Picture markP = new Picture(fName);

  // declare other variables
  Picture target = null;
  FrameSequencer frameSequencer =
    new FrameSequencer(directory);
  int framesPerSec = 30;

  // loop creating the frames
  for (int i = 0; i < framesPerSec; i++)
  {
    target = new Picture(640,480);
    target.copy(markP,281,164,382,301,i * 10, i * 5);
    frameSequencer.addFrame(target);
  }
```

```
    // replay the movie
    frameSequencer.show();
    frameSequencer.replay(framesPerSec);
}
```

■

You can test this with the following main. You can change the directory that will hold the created movie frames from what is specified as the `dir` variable in the `main` method. The result of executing the following `main` method is shown in Figure 14.4.

```
public static void main(String[] args)
  {
    MovieMaker movieMaker = new MovieMaker();
    String dir = "c:/intro-prog-java/movies/mark/";
    movieMaker.moveMarksHead(dir);
  }
```

FIGURE 14.4
Frames from moving Mark's head around.

We can use image manipulations that we created in Chapters 4–7, over multiple frames, to create quite interesting movies. Remember the sunset generating program Program 8 (page 109) in class `Picture`? First let's add another method that takes the amount to reduce the blue and green by in the picture.

Program 134: Make Sunset with a Parameter

```
/**
 * Method to simulate a sunset by decreasing the green
 * and blue
 * @param the amount to multiply the original values by
 */
public void makeSunset(double reduction)
  {
    Pixel[] pixelArray = this.getPixels();
    Pixel pixel = null;
    int value = 0;
    int i = 0;
```

```
// loop through all the pixels
while (i < pixelArray.length)
{
  // get the current pixel
  pixel = pixelArray[i];

  // change the blue value
  value = pixel.getBlue();
  pixel.setBlue((int) (value * reduction));

  // change the green value
  value = pixel.getGreen();
  pixel.setGreen((int) (value * reduction));

  // increment the index
  i++;
}
}
```

Now let's create a new method in the class `MovieMaker` to make the sunset happen across many frames (Figure 14.5). To do this we will create a picture of a beach one time and then repeatedly call the method `makeSunset` to keep reducing the blue and green color.

FIGURE 14.5
Frames from the make-sunset movie.

Program 135: Make a Slow Sunset Movie

```
/**
 * Method to slowly create a sunset
 * @param directory the directory to write to
 */
public void makeSunsetMovie(String directory)
{
  // load the picture of the beach
  String fName = FileChooser.getMediaPath("beach-smaller.jpg");
  Picture beachP = new Picture(fName);

  // declare other variables
  Picture target = null;
  FrameSequencer frameSequencer =
    new FrameSequencer(directory);
```

```
    int framesPerSec = 30;
    frameSequencer.show();

    // loop creating the frames
    for (int i = 0; i < framesPerSec; i++)
    {
      beachP.makeSunset(0.95);
      frameSequencer.addFrame(beachP);
    }

    // replay the movie
    frameSequencer.replay(framesPerSec);
  }
```

■

You can test this method with the following `main` method:

```
public static void main(String[] args)
  {
    MovieMaker movieMaker = new MovieMaker();
    String dir = "c:/intro-prog-java/movies/sunset/";
    movieMaker.makeSunsetMovie(dir);
  }
```

The `swapBackground` recipe (Program 43 (page 198)) that we made a while ago can also be used to good effect for generating movies. We can pass in the frame number as the threshold. The effect is a slow fade into the background image (Figure 14.6). Add the following method to the `MovieMaker` class.

FIGURE 14.6
Frames from the slow-fade-out movie.

Program 136: Fade Out Slowly

```
/**
  * Method to create a movie that fades out the person from
  * one background to another.
  * @param directory the directory to write to
  */
public void makeFadeOutMovie(String directory)
{
  // load the pictures
  String kidF = FileChooser.getMediaPath("kid-in-frame.jpg");
```

```
Picture kidP = null;
String wallF = FileChooser.getMediaPath("bgframe.jpg");
Picture wallP = new Picture(wallF);
String beachF = FileChooser.getMediaPath("beach.jpg");
Picture beachP = new Picture(beachF);

// declare other variables
FrameSequencer frameSequencer =
  new FrameSequencer(directory);
int framesPerSec = 30;

// loop creating the frames
for (int i = 0; i < framesPerSec * 2; i++)
{
  kidP = new Picture(kidF);
  kidP.swapBackground(wallP,beachP,i);
  frameSequencer.addFrame(kidP);
}

// replay the movie
frameSequencer.show();
frameSequencer.replay(framesPerSec);
}
```

You can test this method with the following `main` method:

```
public static void main(String[] args)
{
  MovieMaker movieMaker = new MovieMaker();
  String dir = "c:/intro-prog-java/movies/fade/";
  movieMaker.makeFadeOutMovie(dir);
}
```

14.2   WORKING WITH VIDEO FRAMES

As we said earlier, dealing with real video, in real-time, is very hard. We're going to cheat by saving the video as a sequence of JPEG images, manipulate the JPEG images, then convert back into a movie.

To manipulate movies that already exist, we have to break them into frames. The MediaTools application can do that for you (Figure 14.7) as can tools like Apple's QuickTime Pro. The MENU button in the MediaTools application lets you save any *MPEG* movie as a series of JPEG frame pictures.

14.2.1   Video-Manipulating Examples

On your CD is a brief movie of our daughter Katie dancing around. Let's create a movie of Mommy (Barb) watching her daughter—we'll simply composite Barb's head onto the frames of Katie dancing (Figure 14.8).

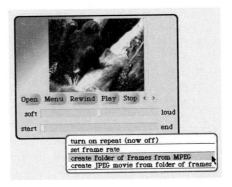

FIGURE 14.7
Movie tools in MediaTools.

FIGURE 14.8
Frames from the Mommy watching Katie movie.

Program 137: Make Movie of Mommy Watching Katie

```
/**
 * Method to make a movie of Barb's head moving
 * and Katie dancing
 * @param dir the directory to read from and write to
 */
public void makeMommyWatchingMovie(String dir)
{
  String barbF = FileChooser.getMediaPath("barbaraS.jpg");
  String katieDir =
  FileChooser.getMediaPath("kid-in-bg-seq/");
  Picture barbP = new Picture(barbF);
  FrameSequencer frameSequencer = new FrameSequencer(dir);
  Picture currP = null;

  // get the array of files in the directory
  File dirObj = new File(katieDir);
  String[] fileArray = dirObj.list();

  // loop through the array of files
  for (int i = 0; i < fileArray.length; i++)
  {
    if (fileArray[i].indexOf(".jpg") >= 0)
    {
      currP = new Picture(katieDir + fileArray[i]);
      currP.copy(barbP,22,9,93,97,i * 3, i * 3);
```

```
            frameSequencer.addFrame(currP);
        }
    }

    // replay the movie
    frameSequencer.show();
    frameSequencer.replay(30);
}
```

You can test this method with the following `main` method:

```
public static void main(String[] args)
{
    MovieMaker movieMaker = new MovieMaker();
    String dir = "c:/intro-prog-java/movies/mommy/";
    movieMaker.makeMommyWatchingMovie(dir);
}
```

We can certainly do more sophisticated image processing than simple composing or sunsets. For example, we can do *chromakey* on movies frames. In fact, that's how many computer-generated effects in real movies are made. To try this out, Mark took a simple video of our three children (Matthew, Katie, and Jenny) crawling in front of a blue screen (Figure 14.9). Mark didn't do the lighting right, so the background turned out to be closer to black instead of blue. That turned out to be a critical error. The result was that the chromakey also modified Matthew's and Katie's pants and Jenny's eyes so that you can see the moon right through them (Figure 14.10). Black is another color that one should *not* use for the background when doing chromakey.

FIGURE 14.9
Frames from the original movie of the kids crawling in front of a blue screen.

FIGURE 14.10
Frames from the kids on the moon movie.

So far we have methods in the `Picture` class that do chromakey with blue and red backgrounds. Let's create another chromakey method that takes the `Color` to compare to and a distance to that color to use.

Computer Science Idea: Use Parameters to Make Methods Reusable

Notice that we are adding new methods that are like our old methods in that they have the same functionality, but they take more parameters. Adding parameters to a method will often make it easier to reuse. Remember that you can have many methods with the same name as long as the parameter list is different. You can even have one method call another with the same name as long as the parameter list is correct. ∎

Program 138: New Chromakey Method

```
/**
 * Method to do chromakey using the passed background
 * color and the distance to the color
 * @param newBg the new background image to use to replace
 * @param color the background color to compare to
 * @param dist the distance that limits the chromakey
 * it will happen if the distance is less than or equal
 * to this value
 */
public void chromakey(Picture newBg, Color color, double dist)
{
  Pixel currPixel = null;
  Pixel newPixel = null;

  // loop through the columns
  for (int x=0; x<getWidth(); x++)
  {

    // loop through the rows
    for (int y=0; y<getHeight(); y++)
    {

      // get the current pixel
      currPixel = this.getPixel(x,y);

      /* if the color at the current pixel is mostly blue
       * (blue value is greater than red and green combined),
       * then use the new background color
       */
      double currDist = currPixel.colorDistance(color);
      if (currDist <= dist)
      {
        newPixel = newBg.getPixel(x,y);
        currPixel.setColor(newPixel.getColor());
      }
    }
  }
}
```
∎

We can use the new chromakey method in the Picture class to create a movie that looks like the kids are crawling on the surface of the moon.

Program 139: Using Chromakey to Put Kids on the Moon

```java
/**
 * Method to make a movie of the kids crawling on the moon
 * @param dir the directory to write the frames to
 */
public void makeKidsOnMoonMovie(String dir)
{
  String kidsDir = FileChooser.getMediaPath("kids-blue/");
  String moonF = FileChooser.getMediaPath("moon-surface.jpg");
  Picture moonP = new Picture(moonF);
  FrameSequencer frameSequencer = new FrameSequencer(dir);
  Picture currP = null;

  // get the array of files in the directory
  File dirObj = new File(kidsDir);
  String[] fileArray = dirObj.list();

  // loop through the array of files
  for (int i = 0; i < fileArray.length; i++)
  {
    if (fileArray[i].indexOf(".jpg") >= 0)
    {
      currP = new Picture(kidsDir + fileArray[i]);
      currP.chromakey(moonP,Color.black,100.0);
      frameSequencer.addFrame(currP);
    }
  }

  // replay the movie
  frameSequencer.show();
  frameSequencer.replay(30);
}
```

You can test this method with the following main method:

```java
public static void main(String[] args)
{
  MovieMaker movieMaker = new MovieMaker();
  String dir = "c:/intro-prog-java/movies/moon/";
  movieMaker.makeKidsOnMoonMovie(dir);
}
```

Mark took a video of fish underwater. Water filters out red and yellow light, so the video looks too blue (Figure 14.11). Let's increase the red and green in the video (yellow is a mixture of red and green light). We had a method that multiplied the red color at each pixel by 1.3. Let's create a new method in the Picture class that will multiply the red and green values by passed multipliers. This way the same method

FIGURE 14.11
Some frames from the original too blue movie.

can be used to increase or decrease the red and green values. Let's call this new method changeRedAndGreen.

Program 140: General Change Red and Green Values

```
/**
 * Method to change the red and green values in the
 * current picture
 * @param redMult the amount to multiply the red by
 * @param greenMult the amount to multiply the green by
 */
public void changeRedAndGreen(double redMult,
                              double greenMult)
{
  Pixel[] pixelArray = this.getPixels();
  Pixel pixel = null;
  int value = 0;
  int index = 0;

  // loop through all the pixels
  while (index < pixelArray.length)
  {
    // get the current pixel
    pixel = pixelArray[index];

    // change the red value
    value = pixel.getRed();
    pixel.setRed((int) (value * redMult));

    // change the green value
    value = pixel.getGreen();
    pixel.setGreen((int) (value * greenMult));

    // increment the index
    index++;
  }
}
```

Now let's create a new method in the class MovieMaker that will increase the red and green in each frame of the movie.

Program 141: Change the Color in the Movie of Fish

```java
/**
 * Method to change the red and green values in the frames
 * @param dir the directory to write the frames to
 */
public void makeFishMovie(String dir)
{
  String movieDir = FileChooser.getMediaPath("fish/");
  FrameSequencer frameSequencer = new FrameSequencer(dir);
  Picture currP = null;

  // get the array of files in the directory
  File dirObj = new File(movieDir);
  String[] fileArray = dirObj.list();

  // loop through the array of files
  for (int i = 0; i < fileArray.length; i++)
  {
    if (fileArray[i].indexOf(".jpg") >= 0)
    {
      currP = new Picture(movieDir + fileArray[i]);
      currP.changeRedAndGreen(2.0,1.5);
      frameSequencer.addFrame(currP);
    }
  }

  // play the movie
  frameSequencer.play(16);
}
```

The result of executing the following main method is shown in Figure 14.12.

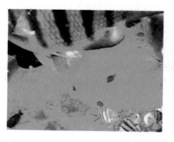 

FIGURE 14.12
Some frames from the color corrected movie.

```java
public static void main(String[] args)
  {
    MovieMaker movieMaker = new MovieMaker();
```

```
    String dir = "c:/intro-prog-java/movies/fish/";
    movieMaker.makeFishMovie(dir);
}
```

14.3 CONCEPTS SUMMARY

In this chapter we explained how movies are stored and why they take up so much space. We created frame-based animations with simple geometric shapes, text, and images. We did special effects on movie frames, such as fading out and chromakey.

We created new versions of methods that take more parameters to make the methods more reusable. We also reused methods that we had created to work on Picture objects. When we program we try to create reusable parts. These reusable parts can be methods and/or classes.

PROBLEMS

14.1 What are each of the following:

- Clipping

- Frames per second

- Frame-based animation

- Persistence of vision

- AVI

- JVM

14.2 How many frames would you need for a two-hour movie with a picture size of 1,024 width by 728 height and 60 frames per second? How much disk space would this movie need?

14.3 Build an animation of at least 3 seconds (48 frames at 16 frames per second or 90 frames at 30 frames per second). Have at least three things in motion during the sequence. You must use at least one JPEG image and one drawn item (like a rectangle or oval or line). For at least one of the things in motion, change the direction that it is moving during the animation.

14.4 Create a movie that has the frames slowly becoming sepia-toned.

14.5 Create a movie that has the frames slowly becoming posterized.

14.6 Create a movie that has a JPEG image rotating in it.

14.7 Create a movie that takes an image and slowly creates the negative of the image.

14.8 Create a new movie that has the kids crawling on the beach.

14.9 Create a new movie like the makeSunsetMovie method that turns the beach black after the blue and green are reduced by a passed amount.

14.10 The site http://abcnews.go.com is a popular news site. Let's make a movie of it. Write a function that will input a directory as a string then:

- Visit `http://abcnews.go.com` and pick out the top three news stories headlines. (Hint: The anchors for the news story headlines all have `<a href="/wire/` before them. Find that tag, then search for the beginning of the anchor `<a`, then you can find the anchor text, which is the headline.)

- Create a tickertape movie on the 640×480 canvas of all three news stories. Have one come across at y=100, another at y=200, and the third at y=300. Generate 100 frames, and don't have the tickertapes move more than 5 pixels per frame. (In 100 frames, you won't make it all the way across the screen—that's fine.) Store the frames to files in the passed directory.

14.11 Change the movie of the kid fading out. Instead of fading in the beach, fade in the original blank wall. The effect should be of the kid disappearing.

14.12 Remember the blending of pictures in Program 28 (page 156)? Try blending one picture into another as a movie, slowly increasing the percentage of the second (incoming) image while decreasing the percentage of the original (outgoing) image.

14.13 Create a movie of a turtle (`turtle.jpg`) crawling across the beach (`beach.jpg`).

14.14 Create a movie of the robot (`robot.jpg`) moving across the moon (`moon-surface.jpg`).

14.15 Create a movie with a filled oval moving up diagonally from the bottom left to the top right of the picture.

14.16 Create a movie with a filled rectangle moving diagonally from the top right of the picture to the bottom left.

14.17 Create a movie with text in a tickertape moving up from the bottom of the picture to the top.

14.18 Create a movie that changes the edge detection amount over time.

14.19 Create a movie that has the text in a tickertape moving diagonally from top left to bottom right.

14.20 Create a movie with the turtle moving across the frames of a movie of a blowhole in directory `mediasources/blowhole`.

14.21 Create a movie that has two filled rectangles that move by a random amount in x and y (< 5 pixels) each time. Make sure that they don't go outside the picture.

PART 6

TOPICS IN COMPUTER SCIENCE

15 Speed

15.1 FOCUSING ON COMPUTER SCIENCE

15.2 WHAT MAKES PROGRAMS FAST?

15.3 WHAT MAKES A COMPUTER FAST?

15.4 CONCEPTS SUMMARY

Chapter Learning Objectives

- To choose between compiled and interpreted programming languages, based on an understanding of machine language and how computers work.
- To know the categories of algorithms based on their complexity, and to avoid intractable algorithms.
- To consider processor choice based on an understanding of clock rates.
- To make decisions about computer storage options when aiming for optimizing speed.

15.1 FOCUSING ON COMPUTER SCIENCE

At this point, you probably have a lot of questions about what you've been doing in this book.

- "Why is Photoshop so much faster on large pictures than the programs I'm writing in Java?"
- "How fast can we get our programs to go?"
- "Does it always take this long to write programs? Can you write smaller programs to do the same things? Can you write programs more easily than this?"
- "What does programming look like in other programming languages?"

The answers to most of these questions are known or studied in *computer science*. This part of the book is an introduction to some of those topics as a signpost to get you started in exploring computer science further.

15.2 WHAT MAKES PROGRAMS FAST?

Where does the speed go? You buy a really fast computer, and a photo editor like iMovie or Photoshop seems really fast on it. Colors change as quickly as you change the slider. But larger pictures don't seem to process as quickly in Java as in Photoshop. Why?

15.2.1   What Computers Really Understand

In reality, computers do not understand Java, C, Visual Basic, Python, or any other language. The basic computer only understands one kind of language—*machine language*. Machine language instructions are just values in the bytes in memory, and they tell the computer to do very low-level activities. In a real sense, the computer doesn't even "understand" machine language. The computer is just a machine with lots of switches that make data flow this way or that. Machine language is just a bunch of switch settings that make other switches in the computer change. We *interpret* those data switchings to be addition, subtraction, loading data, and storing data.

Each kind of computer has its own machine language. Apple computers and computers that run Windows can't run one another's programs, not because of any philosophical or marketing differences, but because each kind of computer has its own *processor* (core of the computer that actually executes the machine language). They *literally* don't understand one another. That's why an .exe program from Windows won't run on a Macintosh, and a Macintosh application won't run on a Windows computer. Those executable files are (almost always) machine language programs.

Machine language looks like a bunch of numbers—it's not particularly user-friendly. *Assembler language* is a set of words (or near-words) that corresponds one-to-one with machine language. Assembler instructions tell the computer to do things like store numbers into particular memory locations or into special locations (variables or registers) in the computer, test numbers for equality or comparison, or add numbers together or subtract them.

An assembler program (and the corresponding machine language generated by an *assembler*) to add two numbers together and store them somewhere might look like this:

```
LOAD #10,R0      ; Load special variable R0 with 10
LOAD #12,R1      ; Load special variable R1 with 12
SUM R0,R1        ; Add special variables R0 and R1
STOR R1,#45      ; Store the result into memory location #45

01 00 10
01 01 12
02 00 01
03 01 45
```

An assembler program that might make a decision could look like this:

```
LOAD R1,#65536   ; Get a character from keyboard
TEST R1,#13      ; Is it an ASCII 13 (Enter)?
JUMPTRUE #32768  ; If true, go to another part of the program
CALL #16384      ; If false, call func. to process the new line

05 01 255 255
10 01 13
20 127 255
122 63 255
```

Input and output devices are often just memory locations to the computer. Maybe when you store a 255 to location 65,542, suddenly the red component of the pixel at (101, 345) is set to maximum intensity. Maybe each time that the computer reads from memory location 897,784, it's a new sample just read from the microphone. In this way, these simple loads and stores handle multimedia, too.

Machine language is executed very quickly. The computer on which this chapter is being typed has a 900 megahertz (Mhz) processor. What that means *exactly* is hard to define, but roughly, it means that this computer processes 900 *million* machine language instructions *per second*. A 2-gigahertz (Ghz) processor handles 2 *billion* instructions per second. A 12-byte machine language program that corresponds to something like a = b + c executes on this mid-range computer in something like 12/900,000,000 of a second.

15.2.2 Compilers and Interpreters

Applications like Adobe Photoshop and Microsoft Word are typically *compiled.* That means that they were written in a computer language like C or C++ and then *translated* into machine language using a program called a *compiler.* Those programs then execute at the speed of that base processor.

However, programming languages like Python, Scheme, Squeak, Director, and Flash are actually (in most cases) *interpreted.* Java can be interpreted, too, but in a subtly different way that is explained later (Section 15.2.3). Interpreted programs execute at a slower speed. It's the difference between *translating* and then doing instructions versus simply doing the instructions.

A detailed example might help. Consider this exercise from an earlier chapter:

> Write a class `GraphicsInterpreter` that reads in a file of graphics *commands*. `GraphicsInterpreter` should know a method `interpret-Commands` that takes a filename as input (a `String`), reads the graphics commands from the file, and then returns a `Picture` with the graphics command executed on it. The method `interpretCommands` starts out by creating a 640 × 480 blank picture, then draws on that, and returns it.
>
> There are two kinds of commands:
>
> - "line 10 20 300 400" should draw a line from (10, 20) to (300, 400). You can assume that those are single spaces between the coordinates.
> - "circle 100 200 10" draws a circle where the enclosing rectangle has an upper-left-hand corner at (100, 200) and a diameter of 10.
>
> An input graphics command might look like:
>
> ```
> circle 20 20 100
> circle 300 20 100
> line 210 120 210 320
> line 210 320 310 320
> line 20 350 400 350
> ```

Here's a solution to the exercise. The implementation here reads a file, a line-at-a-time into a string. It's checked to see if it starts with "circle" or "line." Using

split, it gets chopped into pieces, then each of the little strings (the numbers for
the coordinates) is converted to an integer using Integer.parseInt().

Program 142: Interpret Graphics Commands in a File

```java
import java.io.*;
import java.awt.Color;
import java.awt.Graphics;
import java.awt.Graphics2D;

/**
 * Class that reads in a file of graphics instructions, and
 * executes them, showing the result. Default picture size
 * is 640x480.
 *
 * Format of the file is a bunch of lines of the form:
 * Command X Y <parameters>
 * Commands are:
 * "line" with parameters of start and end X and Y and
 * "circle" with the upper-left corner of the enclosing
 * rectangle and the diameter of the circle
 *
 * For example:
 * line 10 10 50 70
 * circle 10 20 30
 *
 * Which draws a line from (10,10) to (50,70) and a
 * circle at (10,20) with a diameter of 30.
 *
 * @author Barb Ericson
 * @author Mark Guzdial
 */
public class GraphicsInterpreter
{
  /**
   * Method to interpret the commands in the given file
   */
  public Picture interpretCommands(String fileName)
  {
    String line = null;

    Picture frame = new Picture(640,480);
    String [] params = null;
    int x1, y1, x2, y2, diameter;
    Graphics g = frame.getGraphics();
    g.setColor(Color.black);

    // try the following
    try {

      // read from the file
      BufferedReader reader =
        new BufferedReader(new FileReader(fileName));
```

```java
            // loop till end of file
            while ((line = reader.readLine()) != null)
            {
              // what command is this?
              if (line.startsWith("line"))
              {
                // Get the parameters for drawing the line
                params = line.split(" ");
                // params[0] should be "line"
                x1 = Integer.parseInt(params[1]);
                y1 = Integer.parseInt(params[2]);
                x2 = Integer.parseInt(params[3]);
                y2 = Integer.parseInt(params[4]);

                // Now, draw the line in
                g.drawLine(x1,y1,x2,y2);
              }
              else if (line.startsWith("circle"))
              {
                // Get the parameters for drawing the circle
                params = line.split(" ");
                // params[0] should be "circle"
                x1 = Integer.parseInt(params[1]);
                y1 = Integer.parseInt(params[2]);
                diameter = Integer.parseInt(params[3]);

                // Now, draw the circle in
                g.drawOval(x1,y1,diameter,diameter);
              }
              else {
                System.out.println("Uh-oh! Invalid command! "+line);
                return frame;}
            }

        } catch (FileNotFoundException ex) {
          System.out.println("Couldn't find file " + fileName);
          fileName = FileChooser.pickAFile();
          interpretCommands(fileName);
        } catch (Exception ex) {
          System.out.println("Error during read or write");
          ex.printStackTrace();
        }

          return frame;
      }

      public static void main(String[] args)
      {
        GraphicsInterpreter interpreter = new GraphicsInterpreter();
        String fileName =
          FileChooser.getMediaPath("graphics-commands.txt");
```

```
      Picture p = interpreter.interpretCommands(fileName);
      p.show();
   }
}
```

This solution works—see Figure 15.1 which results from executing this program with the `graphics-commands.txt` file containing:

```
circle 20 20 100
circle 300 20 100
line 210 120 210 320
line 210 320 310 320
line 20 350 400 350
```

How it Works

The graphics commands are assumed to be in the file whose filename is passed to the `interpretCommands` method. We open a blank 640 x 480 frame for drawing on, then get the graphics context for drawing on. For each string `line` in the input file, we check to see if it starts with "line" or "circle." If it's a "line", we chop out the starting x and y coordinates and the ending x and y coordinates by using `split` on the string. Then we draw the line. If the command is a "circle," we get the two coordinates and the diameter, and draw the circle as an oval whose height and width are both the diameter. At the end, we return the resulting `Picture` object.

What we've just done is implement a new language for graphics. We have even created an *interpreter* that reads the instructions for our new language and creates the picture that goes along with it. In principle, this is just what Postscript, PDF, Flash, and AutoCAD are doing. Their file formats specify pictures in just the way that our graphics language does. When they draw (*render*) the image to the screen, they are *interpreting* the commands in that file.

While we probably can't tell from such a small example, this is a relatively slow language. Consider the program below. Imagine that we compiled it and ran it—would it run faster than reading the list of commands and interpreting them? Both this program and the list in Figure 15.1 generate the exact same picture.

Program 143: Main with Drawing Commands

```
import java.awt.*;
public class GeneratedDrawing{
 public static void main(String args[]){
   Picture frame = new Picture(640,480);
   Graphics g = frame.getGraphics();
   g.setColor(Color.black);
   g.drawOval(20,20,100,100);
   g.drawOval(300,20,100,100);
   g.drawLine(210,120,210,320);
   g.drawLine(210,320,310,320);
```

```
    g.drawLine(20,350,400,350);
    frame.show();
    } // end main()
} // end class
```

■

FIGURE 15.1
Results of running the GraphicsInterpreter.

In general, we'd probably guess (correctly) that the direct instructions above will run faster than reading the list and interpreting it. Here's an analogy that might help. Mark took French in college, but he says that he is really bad at it. Let's say that someone gave Mark a list of instructions in French. He could meticulously look up each word and figure out the instructions, and do them. What if he was asked to do the instructions again? He would have to look up each word again. What if they asked him to do it 10 times? He would do 10 lookups of all the words.

Now, let's imagine that he wrote down the English (his native language) translation of the French instructions. He can repeat doing the list of instructions as often as you like very quickly. It takes him no time to look up any words (though it probably depends on what he is being asked to do—brain surgery is *out*). In general, figuring out the language takes some time that is just overhead—just *doing* the instructions (or drawing the graphics) will always be faster.

Here's an idea: Could we *generate* the preceding program? Could we write a program that takes as input the graphics language we invented, then writes a Java program that draws the same pictures? This turns out not to be that hard. This would be a *compiler* for the graphics language.

Program 144: Compiler for New Graphics Language

```
import java.io.*;

/**
 * Class that reads in a file of graphics instructions, and
 * then generates a NEW Java Program that
```

```
 * does the same thing as the instructions. The default picture
 * size is 640x480.
 *
 * Format of the file is a bunch of lines of the form:
 * Command X Y <parameters>
 *
 * Commands are:
 * "line" with parameters of start and end X and Y and
 * "circle" with the upper-left corner of the enclosing
 * rectangle and the diameter of the circle
 *
 * For example:
 * line 10 10 50 70
 * circle 10 20 30
 *
 * Which draws a line from (10,10) to (50,70) and a
 * circle at (10,20) with a diameter of 30.
 *
 * @author Barb Ericson
 * @author Mark Guzdial
 */
public class GraphicsCompiler {

  /** Method to write out the prologue for the new program:
   * All the imports, the class definition, main, etc.
   * @param file BufferedWriter to write the prologue to
   **/
  public void writePrologue(BufferedWriter file) {
    try {
      // Write out the prologue lines
      file.write("import java.awt.*;");
      file.newLine();
      file.write("public class GeneratedDrawing{");
      file.newLine();
      file.write(" public static void main(String args[]){");
      file.newLine();
      file.write("  Picture frame = new Picture(640,480);");
      file.newLine();
      file.write("  Graphics g = frame.getGraphics();");
      file.newLine();
      file.write("  g.setColor(Color.black);");
      file.newLine();}
    catch (Exception ex) {
      System.out.println("Error during write of prologue");
    }

  }

  /** Method to write out the epilogue for the new program:
   * Show the picture. Close the main and the class.
   * @param file BufferedWriter to write the epilogue to
   **/
```

```java
public void writeEpilogue(BufferedWriter file){
  try {
    // Write out the epilogue lines
    file.write("  frame.show();"); file.newLine();
    file.write("  } // end main()"); file.newLine();
    file.write("} // end class"); file.newLine();}
  catch (Exception ex) {
    System.out.println("Error during write of epilogue");
  }
}

/**
 * Method to compile the commands in the given file
 * @param fileName the file to read from
 */
public void compileCommands(String fileName)
{
  String line = null;

  String [] params = null;
  int x1, y1, x2, y2, diameter;

  // try the following
  try {

    // read from the file
    BufferedReader reader =
      new BufferedReader(new FileReader(fileName));

    BufferedWriter writer =
      new BufferedWriter(new FileWriter(
    FileChooser.getMediaPath("GeneratedDrawing.java")));

    writePrologue(writer);
    // loop till end of file
    while ((line = reader.readLine()) != null)
    {
      // what command is this?
      if (line.startsWith("line"))
      {
        // Get the parameters for drawing the line
        params = line.split(" ");
        // params[0] should be "line"
        x1 = Integer.parseInt(params[1]);
        y1 = Integer.parseInt(params[2]);
        x2 = Integer.parseInt(params[3]);
        y2 = Integer.parseInt(params[4]);

        // Now, write the line that will LATER
        // draw the line
        writer.write("  g.drawLine("+x1+","+y1+",
                           "+x2+","+y2+");");
```

```java
        writer.newLine();
      }
      else if (line.startsWith("circle"))
      {
        // Get the parameters for drawing the circle
        params = line.split(" ");
        // params[0] should be "circle"
        x1 = Integer.parseInt(params[1]);
        y1 = Integer.parseInt(params[2]);
        diameter = Integer.parseInt(params[3]);

        // Now, draw the circle in
        writer.write("  g.drawOval("+x1+","+y1+",
                    "+diameter+","+
                    diameter+");");
        writer.newLine();
      }
      else {
        System.out.println("Uh-oh! Invalid command! "+line);
        return;}

    }
    writeEpilogue(writer);
    writer.close();

  } catch (FileNotFoundException ex) {
    System.out.println("Couldn't find file " + fileName);
    fileName = FileChooser.pickAFile();
    compileCommands(fileName);
  } catch (Exception ex) {
    System.out.println("Error during read or write");
    ex.printStackTrace();
  }

}

public static void main(String[] args)
{
  GraphicsCompiler compiler = new GraphicsCompiler();
  String fileName =
    FileChooser.getMediaPath("graphics-commands.txt");
  compiler.compileCommands(fileName);
}
}
```

■

How it Works

The compiler accepts the *same* input as the interpreter (a filename to a file that contains our graphics commands), but instead of opening a Picture to write to, we open a file named "GeneratedDrawing.java" in the current mediasources directory. We write to the file the start of a class and a main method using the writePrologue method—the public class GeneratedDrawing, and so on. We also write out the code to create a Picture and a graphics context. Note that we're not really *making* the Picture here—we're simply writing out the Java commands that will make the Picture. The commands will be executed *later* when the class GeneratedDrawing is compiled and its main method is executed. Then, just like the interpreter, we figure out which graphics command it is ("line" or "circle") and we figure out the coordinates from the input string. Then we write out to the code file "GeneratedDrawing.java" the commands to do the drawing. Notice that we're reading the commands when executing the class GraphicsCompiler, and the result is that we're writing the class GeneratedDrawing that will be compiled and executed *later*. At the end of the method compileCommands, we write out commands to show the frame. Finally we close the file.

Now the compiler has a bunch of overhead, too. We still have to do the looking up of what the graphics commands mean. If we only have a small graphics program to run, and we only need it once, we might as well just run the interpreter. But what if we needed to run the picture 10 times, or a 100 times? Then we pay the overhead of compiling the program *once*, and the next nine or 99 times, we run it as fast as we possibly can. That will almost certainly be faster than doing the interpretation overhead 100 times.

This is what compilers are all about. Applications like Photoshop and Word are written in languages like C or C++ and then are *compiled* to *equivalent* machine language programs. The machine language program does the same thing that the C language says to do, just as the graphics programs created from our compiler do the same things as our graphics language says to do. But the machine language program runs *much* faster than we could interpret the C or C++.

Computer Science Idea: Compilers are Actually Programs

Compilers are one of the most magical things in computer science. Look again at the list of graphics commands that generated Figure 15.1. That's a program. Now look again at the Java program that GraphicsCompiler generated. Those are two *completely* different programs, but they *do* the same thing. A compiler writes an entirely new program in one language, given input in a different language. It's a program that writes programs. ∎

15.2.3 The Special Case of Java

Originally, Java programs were designed to be *interpreted*. Java programs didn't originally compile to machine language for whatever computer they were being run on. Java programs compiled to a machine language for a *make-believe processor*—a *virtual machine*. The *Java Virtual Machine* (JVM) doesn't really exist as a physical processor. It's a definition of a processor. What good is that? It turns out that since machine language is *very* simple, building a machine language *interpreter* is pretty easy. It's just like our GraphicsInterpreter except that it reads in the bytes of a machine language program for a JVM, then just does what they say.

The result is that a JVM interpreter can be very easily made to run on just about any processor. That means that a program in Java is compiled *once* and then runs *everywhere*. Devices as small as wristwatches can run the same Java programs that run on large computers, because a JVM interpreter can run even on processors that live on one's wristwatch. There's also an economic argument for virtual machines. Imagine that you're writing software for a programmable toaster oven. If the manufacturer decides to change the processor in the toaster oven, you have to recompile your traditional C or C++ programs to run on the new processor. But if both the old and new processor have JVM interpreters, then your Java programs will run on both without change or recompilation. Thus, a virtual machine can mean that you're less bound to a given processor, and the manufacturer has more flexibility to buy the least-expensive processor available.

On most computers today, Java *does* execute as machine language. Java *can* be compiled to machine language. But even when Java is compiled to JVM machine language, modern JVM interpreters are actually JVM *compilers*. When you tell Java on a Windows or Macintosh computer today "Go run this JVM machine language program," what it actually does is pause a moment, compile the JVM to native machine language, then run the native machine language. Computers are so fast today that you don't really notice the pause while it's compiling.

That's the first part of the answer to the question "Why is Photoshop faster than Java for large programs?" Photoshop is running in native machine code, while our Java programs are running on a JVM interpreter—which, even if it does compile to native machine language first, is still slightly slower than straight machine language.

Then why have an interpreter at all? There are many good reasons. Here are two:

- Do you like the Interactions Pane? Did you even once ever type in some example code just to *try* it? That kind of interactive, exploratory, trying-things-out programming is available with interpreters. Compilers don't let you easily try things out line-by-line and print out results. Interpreters are good for learners.

- Once a program is compiled to Java machine language, it can be used *any-where* from huge computers to programmable toaster ovens—as is! That's a big savings for software developers. They only ship one program, and it runs on anything.

- Virtual machines are safer than running machine language. A program running in machine language might do all kinds of non-secure things. A virtual machine can carefully keep track of the programs that it is interpreting to make sure that they only do safe things, like use only valid indices in arrays.

15.2.4   How Fast Can We Really Go?

The raw power of compiled vs. interpreted programs is only part of the answer of why Photoshop is faster. The deeper part, and one which can actually make interpreted programs *faster* than compiled programs, is in the design of the *algorithms*. There's a temptation to think, "Oh, it's okay if it's slow now. Wait 18 months, we'll get double the processor speed, and then it will be fine." There are some algorithms that are *so* slow, they will never end in your lifetime, and others that can't be written at all. Rewriting the algorithm to be *smarter* about what we ask the computer to do can make a dramatic impact on performance.

An *algorithm* is a description of behavior for solving a problem. A program (classes and methods in Java) are executable interpretations of algorithms. The same algorithm can be implemented in many different languages. There is always more than one algorithm to solve the same problem. Some computer scientists study algorithms and come up with ways to compare and decide which ones are better than others.

We've seen several algorithms that appear in different ways but are really doing the same things:

- Sampling to scale up or down a picture or to lower or raise the frequency of a sound.
- Blending to merge two pictures or two sounds.
- Mirroring of sounds and pictures.

All of these process data in the same way. It's just the data that changes—pixels for pictures, samples for sounds. We say that these are the same algorithms.

We can compare algorithms based on several criteria. One is how much *space* the algorithm needs to run. How much memory does the algorithm require? That can become a significant issue for media computation because so much memory is required to hold all that data. Think about how bad (unusable in normal situations) an algorithm would be that needed to hold *all* the frames of a movie in a list in memory at the same time.

The most common criterion used to compare algorithms is *time*. How much time does the algorithm take? We don't literally mean clock time, but how many steps does the algorithm require. Computer scientists use *Big-Oh notation*, or $O()$ to refer to the magnitude of the running time of an algorithm. The idea of Big-Oh is to express how much slower the program gets as the input data get larger. If the data get twice as large, an $O(n)$ algorithm would take twice as long to run, but an $O(n^2)$ algorithm would take *four* times longer to run. Big-Oh notation tries to ignore differences between languages, even between compiled versus interpreted, and focus on the number of *steps* to be executed.

Think about our basic picture and sound processing examples like `increaseRed` or `increaseVolume`. Some of the complexity of these programs are hidden in provided methods like `getPixels()` and `getSamples()`. In general, though, we refer to these as being $O(n)$. The amount of time that the program takes to run is proportional linearly to the input data. If the picture or sound doubled in size, we'd expect the program to take twice as long to run.

When we figure out Big-Oh, we typically clump the body of the loop into one step. We think about those functions as processing each sample or pixel once, so the real time spent in those programs is the main loop, and it doesn't really matter how many statements are in that loop.

Unless there is another loop in that loop body, that is. Loops are multiplicative in terms of time. Nested loops multiply the amount of time that is needed to run the body. Think about this simple example:

```
> int count = 0;
> for (int x=0; x<5; x++)
      for (int y=0; y<3; y++)
         {count = count + 1;
          System.out.println("Ran "+count+" times: x="+x+" y="+y);}
```

When we run it, we see that it actually executes 15 times—five for the x's, three for the y's, and $5*3 = 15$.

```
Ran 1 times: x=0 y=0
Ran 2 times: x=0 y=1
Ran 3 times: x=0 y=2
Ran 4 times: x=1 y=0
Ran 5 times: x=1 y=1
Ran 6 times: x=1 y=2
Ran 7 times: x=2 y=0
Ran 8 times: x=2 y=1
Ran 9 times: x=2 y=2
Ran 10 times: x=3 y=0
Ran 11 times: x=3 y=1
Ran 12 times: x=3 y=2
Ran 13 times: x=4 y=0
Ran 14 times: x=4 y=1
Ran 15 times: x=4 y=2
```

How about movie code? Since it takes so long to process, is it actually a more complex algorithm? No, not really. Movie code is just processing each pixel once, so it's still $O(n)$. It's just that the n is really, REALLY big!

Not all algorithms are $O(n)$. There is a group of algorithms that are called *sorting algorithms* that are used to order data in alphabetical or numerical order. The simplest of these algorithms (like the *bubble sort* or *insertion sort*) has complexity $O(n^2)$. If a list has 100 elements, it'll take on the order of 10,000 steps to sort the 100 elements with that kind of sort. However, there are smarter algorithms (like the *quicksort*) that have complexity $O(nlogn)$. That same list of 100 elements would only take 460 steps to process. Those kinds of differences start to have huge real clock-time differences when you're talking about processing 10,000 customers to put them in order for reports...

15.2.5   Making Searching Faster

Consider how you might look up a word in the dictionary. One way is to check the first page, then the next page, then the next page, and so on. That's called a *linear search*, and it's $O(n)$. It's not very efficient. The *best case* (fastest the algorithm could possibly be) is that the problem is solved in one step—the word is on the first page. The *worst case* is n steps where n is the number of pages—the word could be on the last page. The *average case* is $n/2$ steps—the word is halfway through.

We can implement this algorithm as a linear search of an array of strings.

Program 145: Linear Search of an Array

```java
/**
 * Class that demonstrates search algorithms
 * @author Mark Guzdial
 * @author Barb Ericson
 **/
public class Searcher
{

  /**
   * Implement a linear search through the list
   **/
  public static String linearFind(String target, String[] list)
  {
    for (int index=0; index < list.length; index++)
    {
      if (target.compareTo(list[index]) == 0)
      {return("Found it!"); }
    }
    return("Not found");
  }

  /** main for testing linearFind */
  public static void main(String[] args)
  {
    String[] searchMe = {"apple","bear","cat","dog","elephant"};
    System.out.println(linearFind("apple",searchMe));
    System.out.println(linearFind("cat",searchMe));
    System.out.println(linearFind("giraffe",searchMe));
  }
}
```

When we run this, we get what we would expect:

```
> java Searcher
Found it!
Found it!
Not found
```

But let's use the fact that dictionaries are already in sorted order. We can be smarter about how we search for a word, and do it in $O(logn)$ time ($logn = x$ where $2^x = n$). Split the dictionary in the middle. Is the word before or after the page you're looking at? If after, look from the middle to the end (e.g., again split the book, but from the middle to end). If before, look from start to middle (split halfway between start and middle). Keep repeating until you find the word or it couldn't possibly be there. This is a more efficient algorithm. In the best case, it's in the first place you look. In the average and worst case, it's *logn* steps—keep dividing the *n* pages in half, and you'll have at most *logn* splits.

Here's a simple (i.e., not the best possible, but illustrative) implementation of this kind of a search, called a *binary search.* Add it to the Searcher class. Then modify the main method as shown below.

Program 146: Simple Binary Search

```java
/**
 * Method to use a binary search to find a target string in a
 * sorted array of strings
 */
public static String binaryFind(String target, String[] list)
{
  int start = 0;
  int end = list.length - 1;
  int checkpoint = 0;

  while (start <= end)
  { // While there are more to search
    // find the middle
    checkpoint = (int)((start+end)/2.0);
    if (target.compareTo(list[checkpoint]) == 0)
    {
      return "Found it!";
    }
    else if (target.compareTo(list[checkpoint]) > 0)
    {
      start=checkpoint + 1;
    }
    else if (target.compareTo(list[checkpoint]) < 0)
    {
      end=checkpoint - 1;
    }
  }
  return "Not found";
}

/**
 * Main for testing binaryFind
 */
public static void main(String[] args)
{
  String[] searchMe = {"apple","bear","cat","dog","elephant"};
  System.out.println(binaryFind("apple",searchMe));
  System.out.println(binaryFind("cat",searchMe));
  System.out.println(binaryFind("giraffe",searchMe));
}
}
```

How it Works

We start with the low-end marker start at the beginning of the list, and end for the last index of the list (length of the list minus one). As long as there is *something* between start and end, we continue to search. We compute checkpoint as halfway between start and end. We then check to see if we found it. If so, we're done and we return. If not, we figure out if we have to move start up to checkpoint or end down to checkpoint and we continue searching. If we ever get through the whole loop, we didn't take the "Found it!" return, so we return that we didn't find it.

To test this, we stuck in a line after assigning checkpoint:

```
System.out.println("Checking at: "+
    checkpoint+" start="+start+" end="+end);
```

Here's the same main running. With this additional statement, we can see how the code narrows in on "apple" then "bear" and then never finds "giraffe."

```
Welcome to DrJava.
> java SearchMethods
Checking at: 2 start=0 end=4
Checking at: 0 start=0 end=1
Found it!
Checking at: 2 start=0 end=4
Found it!
Checking at: 2 start=0 end=4
Checking at: 3 start=3 end=4
Checking at: 4 start=4 end=4
Not found
```

15.2.6 Algorithms that Never Finish or Can't Be Written

Here's a thought experiment: Imagine that you want to write a program that will generate hit songs for you. Your program will recombine bits of sounds that are some of the best riffs you've ever heard on various instruments—some 60 of them. You want to generate every combination of these 60 bits (some in, some out; some earlier in the song, some later). You want to find the combination that is less than 2 minutes 30 seconds (for optimal radio play time) and has the right amount of high and low volume combinations (and you've got a checkSound() function to do that).

How many combinations are there? Let's ignore order for right now. Let's say that you've got three sounds: a, b, and c. Your possible songs are a, b, c, bc, ac, ab, and abc. Try it with two sounds or four sounds, and you'll see that the pattern is the same that we saw earlier with bits: For n things, every combination of include-or-exclude is 2^n. (If we ignore the fact that there is an empty song, it's $2^n - 1$.)

Therefore, our 60 sounds will result in 2^{60} combinations to run through our length and sound checks. That's 1,152,921,504,606,846,976 combinations. Let's imagine that we can do the checks in only a single instruction (unbelievable, of course, but we're pretending). On a 1.5-gigahertz computer, we can handle that many combinations in 768,614,336 seconds. Spell that out: That's 12,810,238 minutes, which is 213,504 hours, which is 8,896 days. That's 24 *YEARS* to run that program. Now, since Moore's Law doubles process rates every 18 months, we can soon run that program in much less time. Only *12 YEARS!*. If we cared about order, too (e.g., abc vs. cba vs. bac), the number of combinations has 63 zeroes in it.

Finding the absolute optimal combination of just about anything is always time expensive. $O(2^n)$ like this is not an uncommon running time for these kinds of algorithms. But there are other problems that seem like they should be doable in reasonable time, but aren't.

One of these is the famous *Traveling Salesman Problem*. Imagine that you're a salesperson, and you're responsible for a bunch of different clients—let's say 30, half the size of the optimization problem. To be efficient, you want to find the shortest path on the map that will let you visit each client exactly once, and not more than once.

The best-known algorithm that gives an optimal solution for the Traveling Salesman Problem is $O(n!)$. That's *n factorial*. To calculate the factorial of a number n you multiply n by $(n - 1)$ then by $(n - 2)$ all the way down to 1. The factorial of 5 is $5 * 4 * 3 * 2 * 1 = 120$.

There are algorithms that take less time to run and give a good path but that path isn't guaranteed to be the shortest. For 30 cities, the number of steps to execute a $O(n!)$ algorithm that finds the shortest path is 30! or 265,252,859,812,191,058, 636,308,480,000,000. Go ahead and run that on a 1.5-gigahertz processor—it won't get done in your lifetime.

The really aggravating part is that the Traveling Salesman Problem isn't some made-up, toy problem. There really are people who have to plan shortest routes in the world. There are similar problems that are basically the same algorithmically, like planning the route of a robot on a factory floor. This is a big, hard problem.

Computer scientists classify problems into three piles:

- Many problems (like sorting) can be solved with an algorithm whose running time has a complexity that's a polynomial, like $O(n^2)$. We call these *class P* (P for Polynomial) problems.

- Other problems, like optimization, have known algorithms (solutions to those problems) but the solutions are so hard and big that we know we just can't solve them in a reasonable amount of time even for reasonable amounts of data. We call these problems *intractable*.

- Still other problems, like Traveling Salesman, *seem* intractable, but maybe there's a solution in class P that we just haven't found yet. We call these *class NP*.

One of the biggest unsolved problems in theoretical computer science is either proving that class NP and class P are completely distinct (i.e., we'll never solve Traveling Salesman optimally in polynomial time), or that class NP is within class P.

You might wonder, "How can we prove *anything* about algorithms?" There are so many different languages, and different ways of writing the same algorithm. How can we positively *prove* something is doable or not doable? We can, it turns out. In fact, Alan Turing proved that there are even algorithms that *can't be written!*

The most famous algorithm that can't be written is the solution to the *Halting Problem*. We've already written programs that can read other programs and write out other programs. We can imagine a program that can read one program and tell us things about it (e.g., how many `print` statements are in it). Can we write a program that will input another program (e.g., from a file) then tell us if the program will ever *stop*? Think about the input program having some complex `while` loops where it's hard to tell if the expression in the `while` loop is ever `false`. Now imagine a bunch of these, all nested within one another.

Alan Turing proved that such a program can never be written. He used proof by absurdity. He showed that if such a program (call it H) could ever be written, you could try feeding that program to itself as input. Now H takes input, a program, right? What if you modified H (call it H2) so that if H would say "This one halts!" H2 would instead loop forever (e.g., `while (true)`). Turing showed that such a setup would announce that the program would halt only if it loops forever, and would halt only if it announces that it would loop forever.

The really amazing thing is that Turing came up with this proof in 1936—almost ten years before the first computers were ever built! He defined a mathematical concept of a computer called a *Turing machine* that he was able to make such proofs about before physical computers were ever built.

Here's another thought experiment for you: Is human intelligence computable? Our brains are executing some process that enables us to think, right? Can we write down that process as an algorithm? And if a computer executes that algorithm, is it thinking? Is a human reducible to a computer? This is one of the big questions in the field of *artificial intelligence*.

15.2.7 Why Is Photoshop Faster than Our Programs in Java?

We can now answer the question of why Photoshop is faster than our programs in Java. First, Photoshop is compiled, so it runs at raw machine language speeds.

But the other part is that Photoshop has algorithms that are smarter than what we're doing. For example, think about the programs where we searched for colors, like in Chromakey or in making hair red. We know that the background color and the hair color was clumped next to one another. What if, instead of linearly searching all pixels, you just searched from where the color was what you were looking for, until you didn't find that color anymore—you reached the boundary. That would be a smarter search. That's the kind of thing that Photoshop does.

15.3 WHAT MAKES A COMPUTER FAST?

Computers are getting faster all the time—Moore's Law promises us that. But that doesn't help us to compare computers that are all of the same Moore's Law generation. How do you compare advertisements in the paper and figure out which of the computers listed is *really* the fastest?

Simply being fast is only one criterion for picking a computer, of course. There are issues of cost, how much disk space you need, what kind of special features you

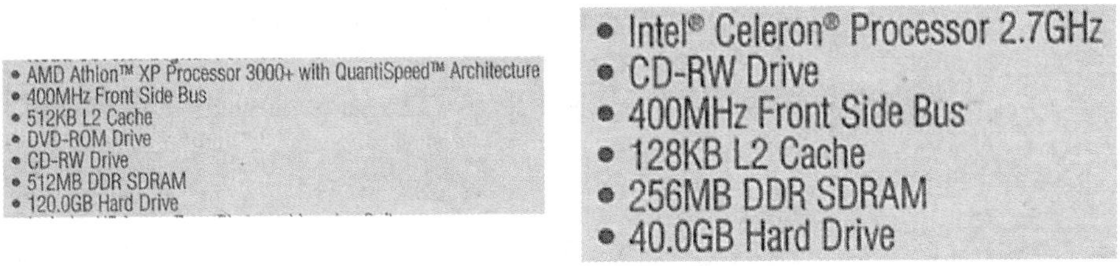

> - AMD Athlon™ XP Processor 3000+ with QuantiSpeed™ Architecture
> - 400MHz Front Side Bus
> - 512KB L2 Cache
> - DVD-ROM Drive
> - CD-RW Drive
> - 512MB DDR SDRAM
> - 120.0GB Hard Drive

> - Intel® Celeron® Processor 2.7GHz
> - CD-RW Drive
> - 400MHz Front Side Bus
> - 128KB L2 Cache
> - 256MB DDR SDRAM
> - 40.0GB Hard Drive

FIGURE 15.2
Sample computer advertisements.

need, and so on. But in this section we'll explicitly deal with what do the various factors in the computer ads (see Figure 15.2 for some examples) mean in terms of computer speed.

15.3.1   Clock Rates and Actual Computation

When computer ads list that they have a "Some-brand Processor 2.8 Ghz" or "Other-brand Processor 3.0 Ghz," what they're talking about is the *clock rate.* The processor is the smarts of your computer—it's the part that makes decisions and does computation. It does all this computing work at a particular *pace.* Imagine a drill sergeant shouting, "Go! Go! Go! Go!" That's what the clock rate is—how fast does the drill sergeant shout "Go!"? A clock rate of 2.8 Ghz means that the clock *pulses* (the drill sergeant shouts "Go!") 2.8 *billion* times per second.

That doesn't mean that the processor actually does something useful with every "Go!" Some computations have several steps to them, so it may take several pulses of the clock to complete a single useful computation. But *in general*, a faster clock rate implies faster computation. Certainly, for the same *kind* of processor, a faster clock rate implies faster computation.

Is there really any difference between 2.8 Ghz and 3.0 Ghz? Or is 1.0 Ghz with processor X about the same as 2.0 Ghz with processor Y? Those are much tougher questions. It's not really that much different than arguing over Dodge versus Ford trucks. Most processors have their advocates and their critics. Some will argue that processor X can do a particular search in very few clock pulses because of how well it's designed, so it's clearly faster even at a slower clock rate. Others will say that Processor Y is still faster overall because its average number of clock pulses per computation is so low—and how common is that particular search that X does so fast, anyway? It's almost like arguing about whose religion is better.

The real answer is to try some realistic work on the computer that you're considering. Does it feel fast enough? Check reviews in computer magazines—they often use realistic tasks (like sorting in Excel and scrolling in Word) to test the speed of computers.

15.3.2   Storage: What Makes a Computer Slow?

The speed of your processor is only one factor in what makes a computer fast or slow. Probably a bigger factor is where the processor goes to get the data that it works with. Where are your pictures when your computer goes to work on them? That's a much more complex question.

You can think about your storage as being in a hierarchy, from the fastest to the slowest.

- Your fastest storage is your *cache memory*. Cache is memory that is physically located on the same silicon chip (or very, very close to that) as your processor. Your processor takes care of putting as much as possible in the cache and leaving it there as long as it's needed. Cache is accessed far faster than anything else on your computer. The more cache memory that you have, the more things the computer can access very quickly. But cache (of course) is also your most expensive storage.

- Your *RAM* storage (whether it's called *SDRAM* or any other kind of RAM) is your computer's main *memory*. RAM (an acronym for *Random Access Memory*) of 256 Mb (megabytes) means 256 *million* bytes of information. It's where your programs reside when they're executing, and it's where your data is that your computer is directly acting upon. Things are in your RAM storage before they're loaded into the cache. RAM is less expensive than cache memory, and is probably your best investment in terms of making your computer faster.

- Your *hard disk* is where you store all your *files*. Your program that you're executing now in RAM started out as an `.exe` (executable) file on your hard disk. All your digital pictures, digital music, word processing files, spreadsheet files, etc., are stored on your hard disk. Your hard disk is your *slowest* storage, but it's also your largest. A hard disk of 40 Gb means that you can store 40 *billion* bytes on it. That's a *lot* of space—and that's pretty small these days!

Movement between levels in the hierarchy means a huge speed difference. Some experts have said that if the speed of access of cache memory is like reaching for a paper clip on your desk, then getting something off the hard disk means traveling to Alpha Centauri—four light-years away from Earth. Obviously, we *do* get things off our disk at reasonable speeds (which really implies that cache memory is phenomenally fast!), but the analogy does emphasize how very different the levels of the hierarchy are in speed. The bottom line is that the more you have of the faster memory, the faster your processor can get the information that you want and the faster your overall processing will be.

You'll see advertisements occasionally mentioning the *system bus*. The system bus is how signals are sent around your computer—from video or network to hard disk, from RAM to the printer. A faster system bus clearly implies a faster overall system, but a faster system bus might not influence (for example) the speed of a Java program. First, even the fastest bus is much slower than the processor—400 million pulses per second versus 4 billion pulses per second. Second, the system bus doesn't usually influence the access to cache or memory, and that's where the majority of the speed is won or lost anyway.

There are things that you can do to make your hard disk as fast as possible for your computation. The speed of the disk isn't that significant for processing time—even the fastest disks are still far slower than the slowest RAM. Leaving enough free space on your disk for *swapping* is important. When your computer doesn't have enough RAM for what you're asking it to do, it stores some of the data that it isn't currently using from RAM on to your hard disk. Moving data to and from your hard disk is a slow process (relatively speaking, compared to RAM access). Having a fast disk with enough free space that the computer doesn't have to search around for *swap space* helps with processing speed.

How about the network? In terms of speed, the network doesn't really help you. The network is magnitudes slower than your hard disk. There are differences in network speeds that do influence your overall experience, but not necessarily the speed of processing on your computer. Wired Ethernet connections tend to be faster than wireless Ethernet connections. Modem connections are slower.

15.3.3 Display

How about the display? Does the speed of your display really impact the speed of your computer? No, not really. Computers are really, *really* fast. The computer can repaint everything on even really large displays faster than you can perceive.

The only place that one might imagine someone arguing that the display speed matters is with really high-end computer gaming. Some computer gamers claim that they can perceive a difference between 50 frames per second and 60 frames per second updates of the screen. If your display was really large and everything had to be repainted with every update, then *maybe* a faster processor would make a difference you could perceive. But most modern computers today update so quickly, you just couldn't tell a difference.

15.4 CONCEPTS SUMMARY

In this chapter we explained compilers and interpreters. We built a small interpreter for a graphics language. We talked about what makes computers fast and slow. We also talked about how to make your programs faster by using different algorithms. We talked about ways to determine and compare the speed of different algorithms.

PROBLEMS

15.1 What are each of the following:

- Interpreter
- Compiler
- Machine language
- Java Virtual Machine (JVM)
- RAM
- Cache
- Class P problems
- Class NP problems

15.2 Find animations of different sorting algorithms on the Web.

15.3 Look up how to do a bubble sort. Write a method to do a bubble sort of an array of names.

15.4 Look up how to do an insertion sort. Write a method to do a insertion sort of an array of names.

15.5 Look up how to do quicksort. Write a method to do quicksort of an array of names.

15.6 How many times will the following code print out the message?

```
String message = "I will be good!";
for (int i = 0; i < 5; i++) {
    for (int j = 0; j < 10; j++) {
        System.out.println(message);
    }
}
```

15.7 How many times will the following code print out the message?

```
String message = "I will be good!";
for (int i = 1; i <= 5; i++) {
    for (int j = 10; j > 0; j--) {
        System.out.println(message);
    }
}
```

15.8 How many times will the following code print out the message?

```
String message = "I will be good!";
for (int i = 1; i <= 5; i++) {
    for (int j = 10; j > 0; j--) {
        for (int k = 0; k < 3; k++) {
            System.out.println(message);
        }
    }
}
```

15.9 What is the Big Oh of the method `clearBlue`?

15.10 What is the Big Oh of the method `lighten`?

15.11 You've now seen some examples of Class P problems (e.g., sorting and searching), intractable problems (optimization of the song elements), and Class NP problems (e.g., Traveling Salesman problem). Search the Web and find at least one more example of each class of problem.

15.12 Try something that takes a while in Java (e.g., chromakey on a large image) so that you can time it on a stopwatch. Now time the same task on several different computers with different amounts of memory and different clock rates (and different amounts of cache, if you can). See what a difference the different factors have in terms of the time it takes to complete the task.

15.13 Trace through the linear and binary search algorithms with a list of 10 items that you make up. Count exactly the number of times through the loop that are executed if the search string is (a) the first item in the list, (b) the last item in the list, (c) the middle item in the list, and (d) not in the list. Are there some situations where linear search is actually *faster* than binary search?

15.14 Don't actually trace it out, but imagine that the list has 1,000,000,000 items in it. Can you use your results from the last exercise to figure out the same loop counts for (a) through (d) for both linear and binary searches if you have a one billion item list?

15.15 Now assume that you're running a 1-*gigahertz* (roughly 1 billion instructions per second) processor, and you can run the whole loop, for either binary or linear search, in five instructions. Exactly how long, in seconds, are each of the results from the last exercise?

15.16 Recall that a linear search is $O(n)$ and a binary search is $O(logn)$. Let's imagine that we have two other search algorithms. The *Bad Search* is $O(n^2)$—on average, it takes n^2 times through the loop to find the element. The *Awful Search* is $O(n!)$. Imagine that we have a 1,000-item list, and the same 1-gHz processor as before, and the loop takes five instructions to run. How long will it take, in seconds, for *Bad Search* and *Awful Search* algorithms to complete an average search? Notice that this is a one *thousand* item list, not a 1-*billion* item list in this example.

15.17 Turing is known for another important finding in computer science, besides the proof that the Halting Problem is unsolvable. He gave us our test for whether a computer has actually achieved *intelligence*. Look up the "Turing Test" on the Web and see if you agree that that test would prove intelligence.

15.18 Define a MoreMath class that has a factorial method that takes an integer and returns the factorial of that integer. Make this method a class method by using the keyword static in the method declaration after the public keyword.

15.19 Create a new linearFind method in the Searcher class that works on any object of the type Comparable and takes a List of Comparable objects.

15.20 Create a new binaryFind method in the Searcher class that works on any object of the type Comparable and takes a List of Comparable objects.

15.21 If there are real problems that have such awful algorithms, and people really need solutions within their lifetimes, how *do* they solve those problems? Sometimes they use *heuristics*—rules that don't lead to a perfect solution, but they lead to a good enough solution. Look up "heuristics" on the Web. Find an example of a heuristic used in chess playing programs.

15.22 Another way around awfully hard algorithms is to use *satisficing* algorithms. There are algorithms that solve the Traveling Salesman problem (i.e., find a route to all the cities) that run in reasonable time—they just don't guarantee the optimal (best possible) solution. Find an algorithm on the Web that does solve the Traveling Salesman problem in reasonable time, but isn't optimal.

TO DIG DEEPER

To learn more about what makes a program work *well*, read *Structure and Interpretation of Computer Programs* [2]. It's not about gigahertz and cache memories; but it's about how you think about your programs to make them work well.

16 JavaScript: A Web Page Programming Language

16.1 JAVASCRIPT SYNTAX

16.2 JAVASCRIPT INSIDE OF WEB PAGES

16.3 USER INTERFACES IN JAVASCRIPT

16.4 MULTIMEDIA IN JAVASCRIPT

16.5 CONCEPTS SUMMARY

Chapter Learning Objectives

- To see variables, iteration, and conditionals in another programming language—and to *recognize* them as understandable.
- To be able to use a little JavaScript in Web pages.
- To be able to handle events in JavaScript.

What do other programming languages look like? That question may be occurring to you now. You might also be champing at the bit to do some programming with things you've heard about, such as Web page programming. In this chapter, we do a little bit of each of these by introducing *JavaScript*, which is a programming language that can be embedded within Web pages to allow control of HTML and pieces of Web pages through programs. JavaScript *isn't* the same language as Java, but they do have many similarities.

16.1 JAVASCRIPT SYNTAX

We call the *look* of a programming language its *syntax*. Java is a fairly traditional programming language in terms of its syntax. It doesn't look much different than C or C++ or other languages. Java was designed to make it easy for C or C++ programmers to learn.

Languages like *Scheme* and *Smalltalk* look much more different. There are several things that you should expect to be different and that you'll need to explore when comparing the syntax (look) of different languages:

- How do you define variables? In many languages, you must *declare* the variables and their *types* (e.g., floating point vs. integer vs. string vs. list) before you can assign them.
- How is each line constructed? In languages like Java and C, each line must end with a semicolon.

- How are *blocks* defined? How do you group statements for loops, conditionals, and function bodies?

- How do you define functions, procedures, methods, classes, and so on?

JavaScript is meant to be a *scripting language.* This means that it's meant to be used easily, by non-professional programmers, to solve relatively simple tasks. No one is going to use JavaScript to write the master calculation program for the IRS, nor something that tracks all the accounts for owners of MasterCards. It's designed to *look* a lot like Java (and C), to make it easier to pick up for people familiar with those kinds of languages.

JavaScript can be used to program the Web *server* or interact with the viewer of the Web page on the *client.* We're going to emphasize the latter. When JavaScript is used on a client machine, it's actually executed by the browser—your browser contains a *JavaScript interpreter.* We call this *client-side JavaScript.*

In JavaScript, variables are supposed to be declared before use, but you don't have to specify their type. The type will be determined based on how you use it. However, JavaScript isn't strict about this—you can simply say a = 12;. But it's more correct to *declare* the variable as something you'll be using by either typing something like var a = 12; or:

```
var a;
...
a = 12;
```

Like Java, JavaScript defines *blocks* using curly braces. You can use any indentation you want, but the block begins with a curly brace and ends with a close curly brace.

```
function test()
{
    document.writeln("This is a test");
}
```

In Javascript you can define *functions* which are like Java methods. The above code defines a function named test that doesn't take any parameters and writes to the HTML document the string This is a test.

We'll find many similarities and differences between Java and JavaScript when we get down to writing individual lines.

- Like Java, JavaScript ends each line with a semicolon (;). You can break up lines so that they are readable to you, as long as each ends with a semicolon.

  ```
  var myvariable = (4 * x) +
                   (5 * y);
  ```

- JavaScript's for is the same as Java's for loop. It is used when you know how many times a loop will be executed. After the keyword for comes a parenthesized list of three expressions separated by semicolons. The first expression is evaluated *before* the for loop begins. The second expression is evaluated at the *end* of the `for` loop to see if we continue looping—if the expression is true, we keep looping. The third expression is what to do before repeating the loop. We'll see a `for` loop later in this chapter.

- In JavaScript, we use `write` and `writeln` instead of Java's `System.out.print` and `System.out.println`, and instead of writing to a Command Area, we'll actually be writing to the HTML page itself!

But in a real sense, these are just details. The basic operation of JavaScript is not unlike Java. Statements are still executed one after the other, there are still variables, loops, and conditionals, and we'll still have functions and methods. All of what you knew before still applies.

JavaScript is *all* about objects. Just about every function is actually a method. There isn't a global `print`, and there's not even a global `write` or `writeln`. Instead, to write into the document, we'll use `document.write()` (or, to end the line with a newline, `document.writeln()`). The `document` here is the HTML document itself.

16.2 JAVASCRIPT INSIDE OF WEB PAGES

JavaScript sits inside of HTML pages—there is no Program Area, nor separate JavaScript files.[1] You use the tags `<script>...</script>` to embed the JavaScript into the HTML. `<script>` tags can go in two places in the HTML document. Inside of the heading (`<head>...</head>`), `<script>` tags usually are used to *define* functions that will be used elsewhere. In the body of the HTML document, `<script>` tags are used to actually execute JavaScript.

Figure 16.1 shows our simple Web page from the HTML chapter (Chapter 13), with an embedded JavaScript function. The function is defined in `<script>` tags in

```
<!DOCTYPE HTML PUBLIC "-//W3C//DTD
    HTML 4.01 Transition//EN"
    "http://www.w3.org/TR/html4/loose.dtd">
<html>
<head>
<title>The Simplest Possible Web Page</title>
<script>
function test()
{
    document.writeln("This is a test");
}
</script>
</head>
<body>
<h1>A Simple Heading</h1>
<p>This is a very simple web page.</p>
<p><image src="mediasources/barbara.jpg" /></p>
<script> test() </script></p>
</body>
</html>
```

FIGURE 16.1
Simple JavaScript function.

[1] It is possible to have JavaScript in separate files, but we're not going to go into how to do that.

```
<script>
function test()
{
    document.writeln("This is a test");
}
</script>
</head>
<body>
<h1>A Simple Heading</h1>
<p>This is a very simple web page.</p>
<p><image src="mediasources/barbara.jpg" />
<script> test() </script></p>
```

Here's a function named "test" with no inputs, that only writes out a string.

Here we execute the function.

FIGURE 16.2
Showing the parts of the simple JavaScript function.

```
<script>
function insertHead()
{
    document.writeln("<h1>This is a test</h1>");
}
</script>
</head>
<body>
<h1>A Simple Heading</h1>
<p>This is a very simple web page.</p>
<p><image src="mediasources/barbara.jpg" />
</p>
<script> insertHead() </script>
</body>
</html>
```

A Simple Heading

This is a very simple web page.

This is a test

FIGURE 16.3
Using JavaScript to insert HTML.

the heading, and then is called down in the body (Figure 16.2). All that this function does is insert the words "This is a test" into the document, at the same place where the function call (`test()`) appears in the document, just below the picture.

JavaScript functions don't have to just insert plain text. They can also insert HTML (Figure 16.3). The HTML, like the text, will be inserted where the JavaScript function is called. The interesting thing about this is that it means that the JavaScript function is called *before* the HTML is formatted. Thus, it's possible to insert headings and other formatting commands into the document.

Of course, it's not too useful to simply insert text into the document that we could have simply typed ourselves. JavaScript, with extensions, can actually do database searches and insert the results into the Web page—that means that you can have Web pages that automatically get updated from a database when the page is served to the user (client). We can show a little bit of that flexibility here. Imagine that you had something you wanted to put into a Web page that's computable, like a list

```
<html>
<head>
<title>The Simplest Possible Web Page</title>
<script>
function countToTen()
{
  document.write("<ul>");
  for (i=1; i<= 10; i++)
  {
      document.write("<li>Item number: "+i+"</li>");
  }
  document.write("</ul>");
}
</script>
</head>
<body>
<h1>A Simple Heading</h1>
<p>This is a very simple web page.</p>
<p><image src="mediasources/barbara.jpg" />
</p>
<script> countToTen() </script>
</body>
</html>
```

A Simple Heading

This is a very simple web page.

- Item number: 1
- Item number: 2
- Item number: 3
- Item number: 4
- Item number: 5
- Item number: 6
- Item number: 7
- Item number: 8
- Item number: 9
- Item number: 10

FIGURE 16.4
Using JavaScript to compute a loop.

```
function countToTen()
{
  document.write("<ul>");
  for (i=1; i<= 10; i++)
  {
    docume  t.write("<li>Item number: "+i+"</li>");
  }
  document.write("</ul>");
}
```

We can write out <ul> and </ul>

Creating an item for each value of i

FIGURE 16.5
Computing a list that counts to ten.

from 1 to 10. Sure you could type it all in, but it's a little tedious. We could ask JavaScript to compute it for us (Figure 16.4).

Let's take apart that function in a little detail (Figure 16.5). The function `countToTen()` starts out by writing the unordered list opening `<ul>`, then each of the list items `<li>`, and then finally the list closing tag `</ul>`.

As we started to explain earlier, `for` loops in JavaScript are the same as Java's `for` loops.

```
for (i=1; i<= 10; i++)
{
        document.write("<li>Item number: " + i + "</li>");
}
```

```
<p>This is a very simple web
    page.</p>
<p><image
    src="mediasources/barbara.jpg"
    />
</p>
<p>This is being served to you on
    <script>document.write(Date());
</script></p>
```

A Simple Heading

This is a very simple web page.

FIGURE 16.6
Inserting the date and time into a Web page.

for loops have three parts, separated by semicolons. The first part is what to do when the loop first starts. Here, it's set the variable i to 1. Next comes how to decide when to stop. Here it's when i becomes greater than 10. Finally, there's what to do each time through the loop. Here it's increment i by one, using a special notation i++ (which means i = i + 1). This notation was invented for the programming language C, and has been adopted by many languages since then.

Most of the operators in JavaScript are the same ones you know from Java: +, -, *, /, <, >, >=, <=, ==, <>, !=, and even ! for logical not. (Like Java, + works in JavaScript to merge two strings together, as well as addition.)

You might be wondering at this point, "Okay, but can we insert anything *useful* with JavaScript?" Sure—anything that you can compute. There are lots of built-in methods that give you all kinds of useful information. You don't even have to write a function—you can just list a script line in the middle of your HTML. In Figure 16.6 you can see a Web page that tells you the time when the page script was being executed.

16.3 USER INTERFACES IN JAVASCRIPT

JavaScript is also really useful for creating Web pages that interact with the user. Here's an example of a JavaScript function that puts up *dialogs*, little windows that interact with the user with prompts and simple buttons (Figure 16.7).

```
function check()
{
  var agree = false;
  agree = confirm("Do you enjoy CS?");
  if (agree)
    notes=prompt("Give me one good thing about CS:");
```

```
    if (! agree)
       notes=prompt("Why don't you like CS?");
    alert("You said:"+notes);
}

<script> check() </script>
</body>
</html>
```

This example uses three kinds of dialogs (exactly the same way that annoying Web pages put these up!):

- A `confirm()` dialog box displays a single line of text and returns `true` or `false`.

- An `alert()` beeps and displays one line with an OK button. There is no return value.

- A `prompt()` asks the user for one line of text, then returns that text.

Now this function runs when you first load the page into your browser. Is that what you really want to happen? The user goes to your page, and suddenly, before any text appears, dialog boxes pop up. It's more natural to have these kinds of boxes pop up when the user clicks on something.

The keys to responding to users are *events*. Events are actions taken by the user that can be caught by your program in JavaScript. We say that an event *triggers* a JavaScript program. Events include the user typing a key, moving the mouse, or clicking the mouse. Example events include:

- onKeyPress is triggered when the user presses a key and releases it.

- onKeyDown and onKeyUp are triggered on either the downstroke or upstroke of pressing a key.

- onClick and onDblClick are triggered on clicking or double clicking on something.

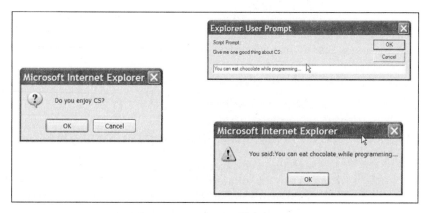

FIGURE 16.7
Example JavaScript dialog windows.

```
<body>
<h1>A Simple Heading</h1>
<p>This is a very simple web page.</p>
<p><image
    src="mediasources/barbara.jpg"
    onClick='alert("You clicked me!")' />
</p>


</body>
```

FIGURE 16.8
Example catching the onClick event.

- onMouseOver, onMouseOut, and onMouseMove are triggered when the mouse is over something, moves off of something, or moves at all when over something.

- onMouseDown and onMouseUp for pressing the mouse key down or back up.

- onChange is triggered when a text field is changed.

There are many more events defined in JavaScript, some of which depend on a specific browser. Netscape Navigator may have some slightly different events than Microsoft Internet Explorer, for example.

To catch one of these events, you assign the event to some JavaScript code in a string. Most of these events can be used with anchor or image tags. onChange can be used with text fields, as we'll see in just a few pages. Figure 16.8 is an example of catching a mouse click event on a picture, then putting up a dialog box in response.

We can use events to do all kinds of different things, including opening a window and going to a new URL in that window. We open windows in JavaScript with the open() function. The open() function takes three inputs: The URL to go to, the name of the window, and optionally, properties of the window to change. Here's an example for opening up a separate window when an image is clicked upon (Figure 16.9).

```
<html> <head> <title>The Simplest Possible Web Page</title>
<script> function goToHawaii()
{
    var win=open('http://www.cc.gatech.edu/~mark.guzdial/hawaii/
              ','Hawaii');


}
</script> </head> <body> <h1>A Simple Heading</h1> <p>This is a
very simple web page.</p>
<p><image src="mediasources/beach.jpg"
onClick="goToHawaii()" /> This page was created on <script>
document.write(Date()); </script></p> </body>

</html>
```

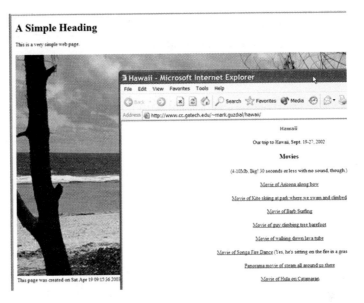

FIGURE 16.9
Opening a JavaScript window.

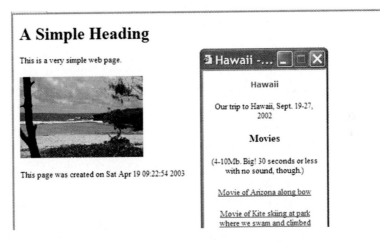

FIGURE 16.10
Changing the new JavaScript window.

Windows are objects in JavaScript. We manipulate their instance variables as *properties*. Here's an example of changing the properties of the window as it opens (Figure 16.10).

```
<head>
<title>The Simplest Possible Web Page</title>
<script>
function goToHawaii()
{
```

```
        var win=open('http://www.cc.gatech.edu/~mark.guzdial/hawaii/
        ','Hawaii', "titlebar=no,width=200");
}
</script>
</head>
```

Windows aren't the only objects in JavaScript with useful properties to change. It turns out that even plain old list items have `style` properties, which in turn have `color` properties. We access these using *dot notation* (Figure 16.11). The current object in JavaScript is called `this`. In this example, list items start in one color, turn another when the mouse comes over them, and another when the mouse leaves.

```
<body> <h1>A Simple Heading</h1> <p>This is a very simple web
page.</p>
<p>Pick any item...</p>
<ul>
<li onmouseover="this.style.color='green'"
onmouseout="this.style.color='black'">Pick me!</li>
<li onmouseover="this.style.color='red'"
onmouseout="this.style.color='yellow'">No, pick me!</li>
<li onmouseover="this.style.color='magenta'"
onmouseout="this.style.color='pink'">No, no -- I'm the one!</li>
</ul>
```

Mostly, when we think about user interfaces, though, we probably think about having *fields* (places where users can type text) and *buttons* (graphical areas where the user can click). To create fields and buttons in HTML (for JavaScript to control and manipulate), we need a *form*. Forms are created with tags `<form>...</form>` (Figure 16.12). Some examples of things we can have in forms include:

- `<input type="text" name="address1">` creates a single-line text field named `address1`.

- `<input type="button" value="Click me">` creates a button that appears on the page as `Click me`.

- `type="textarea"` is for larger text fields with more than one line.

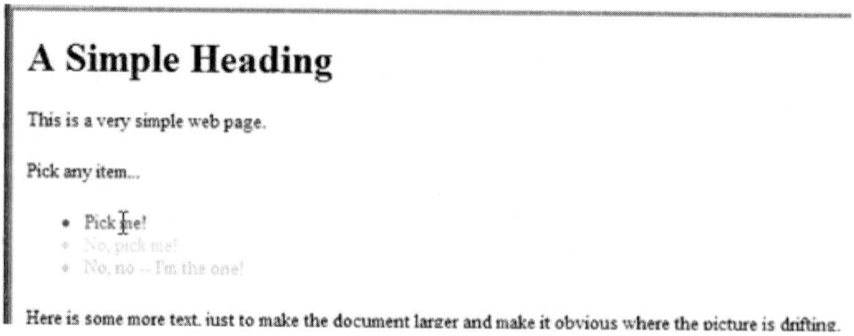

A Simple Heading

This is a very simple web page.

Pick any item...

- Pick me!
- No, pick me!
- No, no -- I'm the one!

Here is some more text, just to make the document larger and make it obvious where the picture is drifting.

FIGURE 16.11
Changing color of list items.

```
<html>
<head>
<title>Simplest Form in HTML</title>

</head>
<body>
<h1>A Simple Heading</h1>
<p>This is a very simple web page.</p>
<form>
<input type="text" name="afield">
<input type="button" value="Click me">
</form>
</body>

</html>
```

A Simple Heading

This is a very simple web page.

[   ] [Click me]

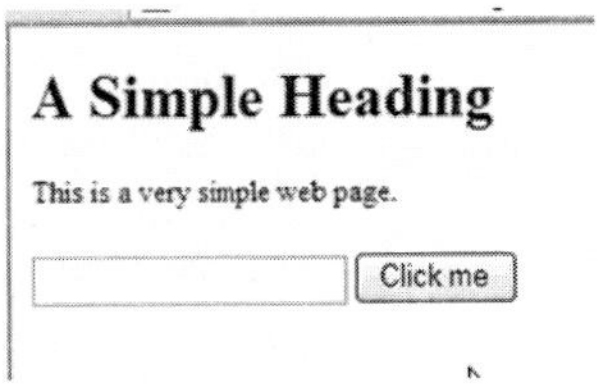

FIGURE 16.12
A simple HTML form.

- `type="radio"` is for radio buttons—those round buttons that usually appear in series where only one in a set can be selected.

Normally, forms are connected to URLs. Form URLs are often *CGI scripts* or *servlets*, little programs (often written in Java!) that will process the form and then respond to the user with a new HTML page. Using JavaScript, we can actually do computation on forms completely from within the HTML page. Figure 16.13 is an inch-to-centimeter converter programmed in JavaScript that uses an HTML form for input. You'll notice several features of JavaScript here—the names of inputs in the form are actually properties of the form. The value of the text area is another property, all of which can be changed.

```
<body>
<h1>Inches/Centimeter
    Converter</h1>
<form>
<p>Centimeters:<input type="text"
    name="cm"
onchange="this.form.inches.value=
    this.value / 2.54"></p>
<p>Inches:<input type="text"
    name="inches"
onchange="this.form.cm.value =
    this.value * 2.54"></p>
</form>
</body>
```

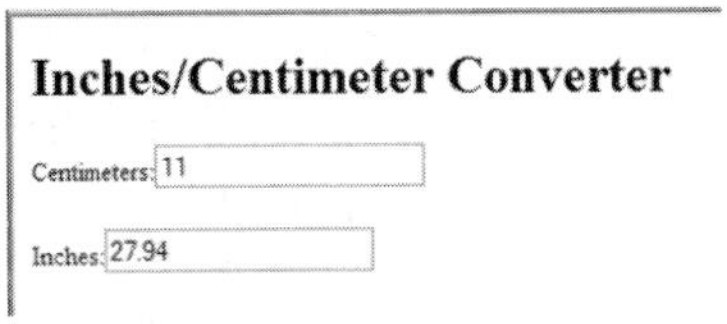

Inches/Centimeter Converter

Centimeters: [11   ]

Inches: [27.94   ]

FIGURE 16.13
Inch/centimeter converter in JavaScript.

16.4   MULTIMEDIA IN JAVASCRIPT

It's possible to do multimedia programming in JavaScript, but not how we've been doing it here. There isn't really a way to manipulate samples or pixels from JavaScript—JavaScript deals with much higher levels of data than that. The most common way to deal with multimedia in JavaScript is through *plugins*. Plugins to the browsers, like Apple QuickTime, RealVideo, and Netscape LiveAudio, can be manipulated from JavaScript.

We can do simple animations in JavaScript. There is a `setInterval()` function that can make a JavaScript function to run at regular intervals—such as when we'd like an animation to update. Divisions (set up with `<div>...</div>` tags) can be controlled with styles (notice the tag at the top) that come from cascading style sheets, and they have positions. Given these two pieces, it's possible to move the picture of Barb slowly over time.

```
<html>
<head>
<title>The Simplest Possible Web Page</title>
<style>
#barb { position: absolute; left:0; top: 0; }
</style>
<script>
function drift()
{
    var object = document.all.barb.style;
    object.pixelTop = object.pixelTop + 5;
    object.pixelLeft = object.pixelLeft + 5;
}
</script>
</head>
<body onLoad="setInterval('drift()',100)">
<h1>A Simple Heading</h1>
<p>This is a very simple web page.</p>
<div id="barb">
<p><image src="mediasources/barbara.jpg"  />
</p>
</div>
<p>Here is some more text, just to make the document larger and
make it obvious where the picture is drifting.
</body>

</html>
```

Okay, this is a pretty contorted example to show a pretty weak animation. JavaScript isn't really designed to do this level of programming. Rather, it's *glue* to make things work together that are already defined at a high level. It doesn't deal well with frames or pixels or samples, but it's great for telling QuickTime to play a movie or to increase the audio in RealAudio.

JavaScript is better than Java for this kind of high-level programming where you're combining things and controlling items on an HTML page. It's very powerful to be able to embed the programming inside the HTML page! But Java is a more full-featured programming language that allows you to do a wide range of things from programming servers to chromakey movies.

16.5 CONCEPTS SUMMARY

JavaScript is a scripting (interpreted) language that is similar to Java that can be used in HTML pages to generate the Web page and to respond to user interaction. You can declare variables, use loops, use conditionals, define and invoke functions in JavaScript. You can respond to user actions by assigning functions to events, like button pushes (onClick). You work with objects in JavaScript, like the document object. You define javascript functions inside of <script>...</script> tags in the header of the HTML page and then invoke these functions in the body of the page.

PROBLEMS

16.1 Write an HTML page that has a button in it. When you click on the button, use JavaScript to change the background color of the button.

16.2 Write an HTML page that has a button in it. When you click on the button, use JavaScript to change some text that tells you the number of times the button was clicked on.

16.3 Write an HTML page that has several radio buttons on it. When a radio button is clicked, update some text on the page to say which radio button is clicked.

16.4 Write an HTML page that has a text field in it. Write some JavaScript to change some text on the page when the string in the text field has been changed. For instance, the user could enter her name in a text field, and the text on the page could change to use her name.

16.5 Write an HTML page that has a button in it. When the cursor is over the button, use JavaScript to change the background color of the button. Change the background color of the button again when the cursor is no longer over the button.

16.6 Write an HTML page that shows a frame from one of the movies. Add a button to the page, and each time the button is clicked show the next frame in the movie.

16.7 Write an HTML page that contains a text field for a phone number and a button. When the button is clicked, check that the text field has only numeric characters (and maybe a dash '-') in it. If not, use an alert dialog to inform the user.

16.8 Write an HTML page that contains a text field for a credit card number and a button. When the button is clicked, check that the text field has only numeric characters in it, and check that the number of characters is 16. If not, use an alert dialog to inform the user.

16.9   Write an HTML page that contains a text field for a name and a button. When the button is clicked, check that the text field has only alphabetic characters (no numbers) in it. If not, use an alert dialog to inform the user.

16.10 Write an HTML page that plays some background music when the page is first loaded. Use a JavaScript function to do this.

16.11 Write an HTML page that has a button, and when you click on the button, some text is displayed in the browser status bar.

16.12 Write an HTML page that has a button, and when you click on the button, display another HTML page in a new browser window.

TO DIG DEEPER

There are a lot of good books on JavaScript. We recommend the books by Danny Goodman, such as *JavaScript and DHTML Cookbook* [12]. There are also many on-line tutorials for learning JavaScript, one of which is at `http://webmonkey.wired.com/webmonkey/programming/javascript/tutorials/tutorial1.html`.

A Quick Reference to Java

A.1   VARIABLES

Variables allow us to associate names with values. In Java you must declare a variable before you use it. To declare a variable you specify a type and a name followed by a semicolon.

```
type name;
```

You can also set the value of the variable when you declare it to the result of an expression.

```
type name = expression;
```

The type can be any of the primitive types (int, boolean, byte, char, double, float, long, short), a class name, or an interface name. The convention is to start variable names with a lowercase letter and uppercase the first letter of each additional word.

```
> int i;
> double totalBill = 32.43 + 20 * 32.43;
> String name = "Mark Guzdial";
> Picture pictureObj;
> List studentList = null;
```

Variable names can be made up of letters, digits, underscores, or currency symbols. They can start with any of these except a digit. Variables can be any word *except* the *reserved words*. The reserved words are:

abstract	assert	boolean	break	byte
case	catch	char	class	const (unused)
continue	default	do	double	else
enum	extends	false	final	finally
float	for	goto (unused)	if	implements
import	instanceof	int	interface	long
native	new	null	package	private
protected	public	return	short	static
strictfp	super	switch	synchronized	this
throw	throws	transient	true	try
void	volatile	while		

Most of the reserved words are also keywords. The only ones that are *not* keywords are `null`, `true`, and `false`. All of the Java reserved words have only lowercase letters.

We can use `System.out.print` or `System.out.println` to print the value of a variable. The second one will also force a new line after the value has printed.

```
> int x = 10
> System.out.println(x);
10
> String name = "Barbara Ericson";
> System.out.println(name);
Barbara Ericson
```

A.2   METHOD DECLARATIONS

Declare a method by specifying the visibility, the return type, the method name, and a parameter list. Method declarations are usually followed by code inside of curly braces which are the statements that will be executed when the method is invoked.

```
visibility returnType name(parameterList)
{
    // statements in the method
}
```

The parameter list is a comma-separated list of the parameters that will be passed to the method. For each parameter, specify a type and a name. Parameters are passed by value, which means that a copy of the value is passed to the method. So primitive variables passed to a method will not be affected by changes in the method after the return from the method, but because the value of an object variable is a reference to the object, a method can change the passed object, and such changes are preserved after the return from the method.

```java
public void changeRedAndGreen(double redMult,
                             double greenMult)
```

The convention is to start a method name with lowercase letters and uppercase the first letter of each additional word. A method can return a value by using the `return` statement. The type of the value being returned must match the specified return type.

```java
/**
 * Method to create a new picture by rotating the current
 * picture by the given degrees
 * @param degrees the number of degrees to rotate by
 * @return the resulting picture
 */
public Picture rotate(int degrees)
{
    // create a new picture object big enough to hold the result
    // no matter what the rotation is
    Picture result = new Picture((int) (Math.ceil(rect.getWidth())),
                                 (int) (Math.ceil(rect.getHeight())));

    // other statements in the method

    return result;
}
```

If a method doesn't return any value, the return type should be `void`.

```java
/**
 * Method to decrease the green in the picture by 30%
 */
public void decreaseGreen()
{
    // method statements
}
```

If you want all other classes to be able to invoke a method, make the visibility of the method `public`. If you only want to use a method in the class it is declared in, then use `private` as the visibility. If you leave off the visibility, then the method can be invoked by all classes in the same package. This is called *package visibility*. You can also use *protected visibility* if you want subclasses to be able to override an inherited method, but be aware that all classes in the same package also have access to the method.

A.3   LOOPS

If you are using Java 5.0 (1.5) you can use a for-each loop. The syntax for a for-each loop is:

```
for (type name : collection)
{
  // statements to execute
}
```

The type is the type of objects in the collection. The name is the local variable name to use. The collection is anything that holds a collection of objects, such as an array, list, or set. The following is an example of using a for-each loop:

```
// loop through all the samples in the array
for (SoundSample sample : sampleArray)
{
    value = sample.getValue();
    sample.setValue(value * 2);
}
```

If you know how many times a loop should repeat, then use a for loop. The syntax for a for loop is:

```
for (initializationArea; continuationTest; changeArea)
{
    // statements in the for loop
}
```

You can declare and initialize local variables in the initialization area. You specify a boolean expression for the continuation test. The loop will continue while the test is true. The change area is where you specify how to change variables after each execution of the loop.

```
// loop through all the pixels
for (int i=0; i < pixelArray.length; i++)
    pixelArray[i].setBlue(0);
```

If you don't know how many times a loop should repeat, then use a while loop. The syntax of a while loop is:

```
while (continuationTest)
{
    // statements in the while loop
}
```

The statements in the curly braces will be executed as long as the continuation test is true. Often you will initialize variables before the while loop begins and change them just before the end of the while loop statements. But you can do this in the continuation test.

```
// Loop while there is more data
while((line = reader.readLine()) != null)
{
    // print the current line
    System.out.println(line);
}
```

A.4 CONDITIONALS

An `if` takes an expression and evaluates it. If it's true, the `if`'s block is executed. If it's false, the `else` block is executed, if one exists. If you have more than two possibilities, you can add `else if` for each additional one.

```
// tint the shadows darker
if (redValue < 60)
{
    redValue = redValue * 0.9;
    greenValue = greenValue * 0.9;
    blueValue = blueValue * 0.9;
}

// tint the midtones a light brown
// by reducing the blue
else if (redValue < 190)
{
    blueValue = blueValue * 0.8;
}

// tint the highlights a light yellow
// by reducing the blue
else
{
    blueValue = blueValue * 0.9;
}
```

A.5 OPERATORS

`+, -, *, /, %`	Addition, subtraction, multiplication, division, and modulus (remainder). Order of precedence is algebraic.
`<, >, ==, !=, <=, >=`	Logical operators less-than, greater-than, equal-to, not-equal-to, less-than-or-equal, greater-than-or-equal.
`&&, ||, !`	Logical conjunctives and, or, and codenot.

A.6   STRING ESCAPES

\t	Tab character
\b	Backspace
\n	New line
\r	Return
\uXXXX	Unicode character, hexadecimal XXXX

A.7   CLASSES

Each class is usually defined in a separate file with the same name as the class name followed by '.java'. The convention is to uppercase the first letter of all words in a class name.

The syntax to declare a class is:

```
visibility class Name
{
    // fields, constructors, and methods
}
```

You can also specify the parent class using the extends keyword. If no parent class is specified, it will be java.lang.Object. A child class inherits public and protected fields and methods.

```
visibility class Name extends ParentName
{
    // fields, constructors, and methods
}
```

A class can also implement several interfaces. The list of interfaces is separated by commas and follows the specification of the parent class if given.

```
visibility class Name extends ParentName
    implements Interface1, Interface2, ...
{
    // fields, constructors, and methods
}
```

Here is an example class declaration. The Student class will inherit from the Object class.

```
public class Student
{
    // fields, constructors, and methods
}
```

A.8   FIELDS

Object fields are the data or state that each object of a class will have. Class (`static`) fields are in the object that defines the class so there is only one and all objects of the class have access to it. Fields are defined inside of a class definition. The convention is to start field names with a lowercase letter and uppercase the first letter of each additional word.

To declare an object field, use:

```
visibility type name;
```

To declare a field and give it a value, use:

```
visibility type name = expression;
```

The visibility for fields is usually `private` so that an object can protect its data from being directly accessed by code in other classes.

To declare a class field, use:

```
visibility static type name;
```

To declare a constant field, use:

```
public static final type name;
```

A.9   CONSTRUCTORS

Constructors are used to initialize the fields in a newly created object. The syntax for a constructor is

```
visibility ClassName(parameterList)
{
    // statements in the constructor
}
```

Constructors are usually defined with `public` visibility. Notice that they do not have a return type. The name on a constructor must match the class name.

A.10   PACKAGES

The Java classes are grouped into packages. You can use any of classes in the package `java.lang`. If you wish to use classes in packages other than `java.lang`, you can use an `import` statement. Import statements go before the class declaration in a file. You can import all the classes in a package using:

```
import name.*;
```

or you can import just a named class using:

```
import name.ClassName;
```

To import all classes in the `java.awt` package use:

```
import java.awt.*;
```

To import just the class `java.awt.Color` use:

import java.awt.Color;

If you don't import the package or the class, you can use the full name, which is the package name followed by '.' and then the class name (`java.awt.Color`).

Here is a table of some of the packages in Java and the interfaces and classes we have used from each of these packages. The interfaces are shown in italics.

java.lang	Basic classes in the language	*Comparable*, Object, String, Math
java.io	Classes for input and output	BufferedReader, BufferedWriter, FileReader, FileWriter, Reader, Writer, File
java.awt	Classes for drawing	*Paint*, Color, Font, Image, Graphics, Graphics2D
java.net	Classes for use with networks	URL
java.sql	Classes for use with databases	*Connection*, *Statement*, *ResultSet*, DriverManager
java.util	Utility and collection classes	*Iterator*, *List*, *Map*, ArrayList, HashMap, TreeMap

Bibliography

1. AAUW, *Tech-savvy: Educating girls in the new computer age*, American Association of University Women Education Foundation, New York, 2000.

2. HAROLD ABELSON, GERALD JAY SUSSMAN, AND JULIE SUSSMAN, *Structure and intepretation of computer programs—2nd edition*, MIT Press, Cambridge, MA, 1996.

3. KEN ABERNETHY AND TOM ALLEN, *Exploring the digital domain: An introduction to computing with multimedia and networking*, PWS Publishing, Boston, 1998.

4. BETH ADELSON AND ELLIOT SOLOWAY, *The role of domain experience in software design*, IEEE Transactions on Software Engineering **SE-11** (1985), no. 11, 1351–1360.

5. RICHARD BOULANGER (ed.), *The csound book: Perspectives in synthesis, sound design, signal processing, and programming*, MIT Press, Cambridge, MA, 2000.

6. AMY BRUCKMAN, *Situated support for learning: Storm's weekend with Rachael*, Journal of the Learning Sciences **9** (2000), no. 3, 329–372.

7. JOHN T. BRUER, *Schools for thought: A science of learning in the classroom*, MIT Press, Cambridge, MA, 1993.

8. CHARLES DODGE AND THOMAS A. JERSE, *Computer music: Synthesis, composition, and performance*, Schirmer Books: London, 1997.

9. MATTHIAS FELLEISEN, ROBERT BRUCE FINDLER, MATTHEW FLATT, AND SHRIRAM KRISHNAMURTHI, *How to design programs: An introduction to programming and computing*, MIT Press, Cambridge, MA, 2001.

10. ANN E. FLEURY, *Encapsulation and reuse as viewed by java students*, Proceedings of the 32nd SIGCSE technical symposium on computer science education (2001), 189–193.

11. JAMES D. FOLEY, ANDRIES VAN DAM, AND STEVEN K. FEINER, *Introduction to computer graphics*, Addison Wesley, Reading, MA, 1993.

12. DANNY GOODMAN, *Javascript & dhtml cookbook*, O'Reilly, Sebastopol, CA, 2003.

13. MARTIN GREENBERGER, *Computers and the world of the future*, Transcribed recordings of lectures held at the Sloan School of Business Administration, April, 1961, MIT Press, Cambridge, MA, 1962.

14. MARK GUZDIAL, *Squeak: Object-oriented design with multimedia applications*, Prentice-Hall, Englewood, NJ, 2001.

15. MARK GUZDIAL AND ANDREA FORTE, *Design process for a non-majors computing course*, SIGCSE '05: Proceedings of the 36th SIGCSE technical symposium on Computer science education, New York, ACM Press, 2005, pp. 361–365.

16. MARK GUZDIAL AND KIM ROSE (eds.), *Squeak, open personal computing for multimedia*, Prentice-Hall, Englewood, NJ, 2001.

17. IDIT HAREL AND SEYMOUR PAPERT, *Software design as a learning environment*, Interactive Learning Environments **1** (1990), no. 1, 1–32.

18. BRIAN HARVEY, *Computer science logo style 2/e vol. 1: Symbolic computing*, MIT Press, Cambridge, MA, 1997.

19. DAN INGALLS, TED KAEHLER, JOHN MALONEY, SCOTT WALLACE, AND ALAN KAY, *Back to the future: The story of Squeak, a practical smalltalk written in itself*, OOPSLA'97 Conference Proceedings, ACM, Atlanta, GA, 1997, pp. 318–326.

20. JANET KOLODNER, *Case based reasoning*, Morgan Kaufmann, San Mateo, CA, 1993.

21. MARGARET LIVINGSTONE, *Vision and art: The biology of seeing*, Harry N. Abrams, New York, 2002.

22. JANE MARGOLIS AND ALLAN FISHER, *Unlocking the clubhouse: Women in computing*, MIT Press, Cambridge, MA, 2002.

23. M. RESNICK, *Turtles, termites, and traffic jams: Explorations in massively parallel microworlds*, MIT Press, Cambridge, MA, 1997.

24. CURTIS ROADS, *The computer music tutorial*, MIT Press, Cambridge, MA, 1996.

Index

Using the Student CD

Included on the CD

- DrJava
- Java (for Windows OS)
- MediaTools
- Squeak
- Sample programs and media files

System Requirements

Below is a list of minimum system requirements to install the software supplied on this CD.

For Windows:

Any Windows system capable of running Java 2 Standard Edition 5.0 (1.5) or 1.4.2 with at least 64 MB RAM:

- Windows XP Professional (with Service Pack 1 or higher)
- Windows XP Home (with Service Pack 1 or higher)
- Windows 2000 Professional (with Service Pack 3 or higher)
- Windows 98, Second Edition
- Windows ME
- Windows Server 2003 (requires 128 MB memory or more)

You will need at least 98 MB available disk space to run Java, and approximately 100 MB more to store MediaTools, Squeak, and the book's sample programs and media files.

For Macintosh:

- To run the 1.4.2 versions of Java and MediaTools: Mac OS X 10.3.4 (Panther) or higher
- To run the 5.0 (also known as "1.5") version of Java and MediaTools: Mac OS X 10.4 (Tiger) or higher

Also required: 100 MB hard disk storage to store MediaTools, Squeak, and the book's sample programs and media files. We recommend 128 MB RAM or more.

Note: Mac OS X 10.4.3 can run Java 5 (1.5), but it must be downloaded from Apple and installed. Mac OS X 10.3 cannot run Java 5, but comes with Java 1.4 installed.

Installation

For detailed instructions on how to install the software on this CD, please refer to the ReadMe file on the CD.